LIKE
HIDDEN
FIRE

LIKE HIDDEN FIRE

The Plot to Bring Down the British Empire

PETER HOPKIRK

KODANSHA INTERNATIONAL
New York • Tokyo • London

Kodansha America, Inc.
114 Fifth Avenue, New York, New York 10011, U.S.A.

Kodansha International Ltd.
17-14 Otowa 1-chome, Bunkyo-ku, Tokyo 112, Japan

Originally published in hardcover in 1994 by Kodansha America, Inc.

First published in Great Britain in 1994
as *On Secret Service East of Constantinople*
by John Murray (Publishers) Ltd.

This is a Kodansha Globe book.

Library of Congress Cataloging-in-Publication Data

Hopkirk, Peter.
[On secret service east of Constantinople]
Like hidden fire: the plot to bring down the British Empire /
Peter Hopkirk.
p.   cm.
Originally published: J. Murray, 1994.
Includes bibliographical references (p.   ) and index.
ISBN 1-56836-127-0
1. Asia—Politics and government.   2. India—Politics and
government—1857–1919.   3. World War, 1914–1918—Asia.   4. World
War, 1914–1918—India.   5. Secret service—Asia—History.
I. Title.
DS35.H64   1994
940.4'86—dc20   94-11184

Manufactured in the United States of America
97 98 99 00 DUNN 10 9 8 7 6 5 4 3 2 1

*To the memory of my mother,
who some fifty years ago read
me John Buchan's* Greenmantle,
*the true story of which I have
told here*

Contents

Illustrations

The author and publishers would like to thank the following for permission to reproduce photographs: Plates 12 and 15, India Office Library; 16 and 18, Dr Hans von Hentig; 21 and 22, Royal Society for Asian Affairs; 23, Air Commodore A. R. D. MacDonell, CB, DFC; 26, Peter Ellis, Esq.

Acknowledgements

My principal debt, as with my previous narratives of imperial rivalry in Central Asia, is to those individuals, on either side, who left first-hand accounts of these turbulent events. For without them this book could never have been written. They include Ambassador Henry Morgenthau, Captain Oskar von Niedermayer, Captain Werner Otto von Hentig, Har Dayal, Raja Mahendra Pratap, Sir Frederick O'Connor, Captain Edward Noel, Major Ranald MacDonell, Captain Reginald Teague-Jones, General Sir Wilfrid Malleson, General Lionel Dunsterville, Sir Percy Sykes, and Morgan Philips Price of the *Manchester Guardian*. All are now dead. Their accounts of the war east of Constantinople are to be found in my bibliography.

Living individuals to whom I owe a considerable debt include Brian Pearce, a Russian scholar and historian, who generously placed at my disposal the material he has gathered, over many years, on the strange affair of the twenty-six Baku commissars and the alleged role of Captain Teague-Jones in their murder. Also Air Commodore A. R. D. MacDonell, CB, DFC, for the portrait of his father, Ranald MacDonell, and for other information on him, and Christian Dewar Durie, for allowing me to read and quote from her grandmother's graphic account of Baku during the Muslim massacres of 1918. Again I am most grateful to Tanya Rose, daughter of M. Philips Price the war correspondent, for information about her father, and to Peter Ellis of Toronto for information about his father, Colonel C. H. Ellis, and for photographs taken by him.

I also have to thank Dr H. W. von Hentig for material, including photographs belonging to his late father, Werner Otto von Hentig, and for most interesting discussions with him about the latter's role in the German mission to Kabul. Mr Paul Bucherer-Dietschi, head of the Stiftung Bibliotheca Afghanica, in Switzerland, kindly clarified important points arising over the mission's leadership. I am most grateful, too, to Angelica Kyang for translating Captain Niedermayer's account of the mission from the German for me, and to Fahad Diba for drawing my attention to material which he came across while compiling the monumental bibliography of Persian history on which he is working.

As a narrative historian, I have found the works of certain specialist historians of this period extremely useful. They include Fritz Fischer, Ulrich Gehrke, Renate Vogel, Frank Weber, Ulrich Trumpener, George Antonius, Firuz Kazem-zadeh, Ronald Suny, William Olson, Bradford Martin, Ludwig Adamec, and Brigadier-General F. J. Moberly, the official British war historian of the Mesopotamian and Persian theatres. Their works are listed in my bibliography.

In view of her interest in Central Asian history and her training as a historian, I am once again fortunate in having Gail Pirkis, formerly of OUP Hong Kong, as my editor. As always, I am much indebted to my wife Kath, herself now the author of a book on Central Asia, for reading every word of my narrative and for making invaluable criticisms and suggestions. She also very kindly prepared the index, as well as the draft maps from which the cartographer, Denys Baker, produced the finished versions – as he has for my previous four books.

NOTE ON NAMES AND SPELLINGS

In the eighty-odd years since these events took place, a number of geographical names and spellings have changed, as they continue to do. For the sake of simplicity, therefore, I have retained those which would have been familiar at the time – hence Constantinople not Istanbul, Tiflis not Tbilisi, Erzerum not Erzurum, Persia not Iran, Mesopotamia not Iraq, Transcaspia not Turkmenistan.

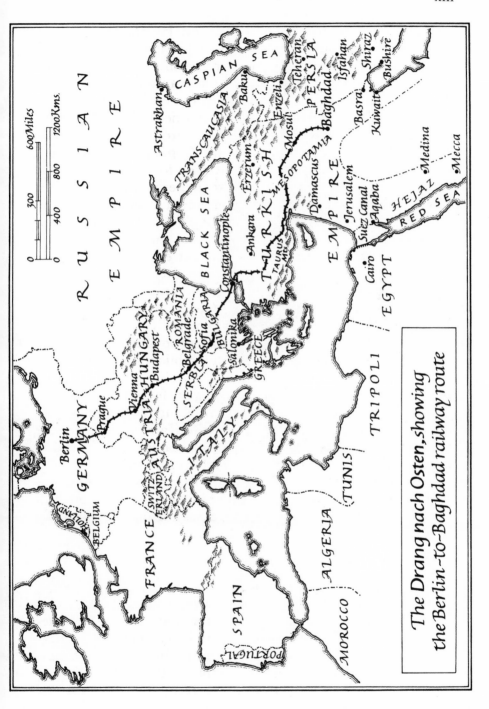

The Drang nach Osten, showing
the Berlin-to-Baghdad railway route

PERSIA, AFGHANISTAN
and
TRANSCASPIA

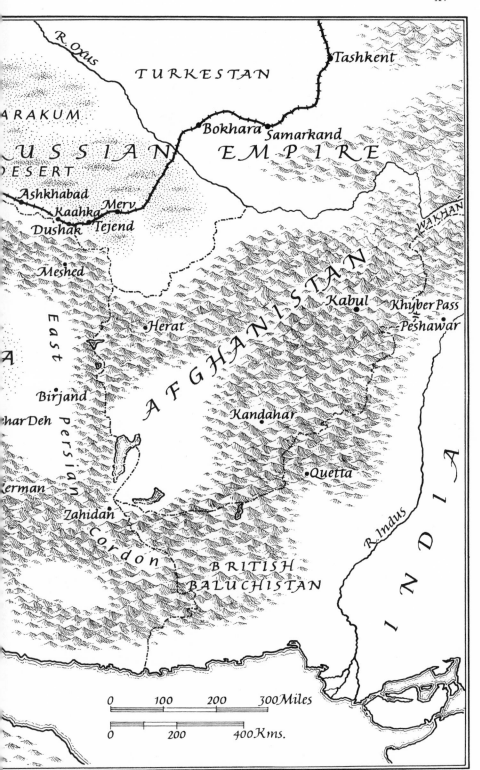

R. Oxus

TURKESTAN

Tashkent

ARAKUM

RUSSIAN

DESERT

Bokhara   Samarkand

EMPIRE

Ashkhabad

Kaahka   Merv

Dushak   Tejend

WAKHAN

Meshed

Kabul   Khyber Pass

East

Herat   Peshawar

A F G H A N I S T A N

A

Birjand

har Deh

Kandahar

Persian

erman

Quetta

Zahidan

Cordon

R. Indus

I N D I A

BRITISH

BALUCHISTAN

0	100	200	300 Miles

0	200	400 Kms.

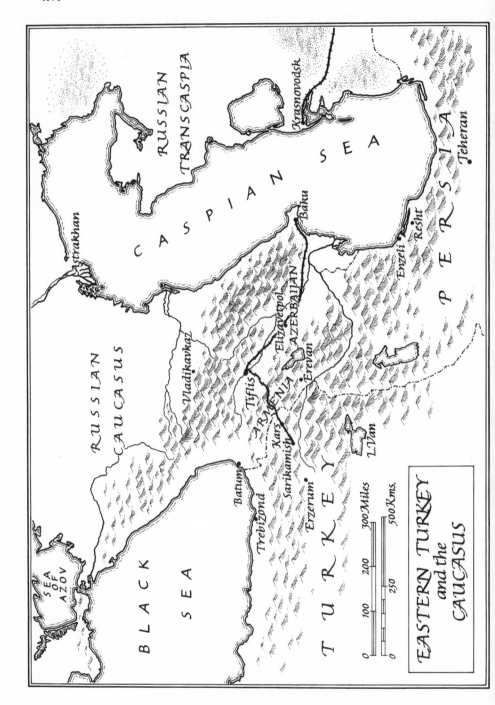

EASTERN TURKEY and the CAUCASUS

Prologue

In the summer of 1914, when Kaiser Wilhelm of Germany realised that he had gravely miscalculated, and that a bloody showdown with Britain was unavoidable, he vowed to unleash against her a Holy War which would destroy her power in the East for ever. 'Our consuls and agents', he ordered, 'must inflame the entire Muslim world against this hateful, lying and unscrupulous nation.' If he had to fight, then here was his chance of bringing down the entire British Empire. He would rally the people of the Ottoman Empire, the Caucasus, Persia and Afghanistan against Britain's far-flung imperial interests. Together they would light the fuse leading towards the greatest, and most vulnerable, of these – India. If India could be wrested from Britain's grasp, then the rest of her ramshackle empire, held together largely by bluster and bluff, would quickly collapse. India itself, Wilhelm's advisers assured him, was a powder keg of disaffection, and needed only the torch of revolution to ignite it. If that were to happen, then India's crown, together with the country's vast wealth, might well pass from his detested British cousin, King George V, to himself.

For years, ever since coming to the throne, Wilhelm had dreamed of making Germany the greatest power on earth, with its armed forces replacing those of Britain as the guardians of the world. This grandiose ambition he had hoped to achieve by means of economic superiority and diplomatic penetration, backed by military and naval muscle, rather than by going to war with his British cousins and rivals. With the aggressive support of Germany's great banking houses, Wilhelm's diplomats and industrialists had plotted and schemed to extend their country's political and commercial interests and influence throughout the world. But it was in the East that they had concentrated their efforts. For in the dying Ottoman Empire they saw their chance, and nothing was spared in securing a place there in the sun for Germany by befriending the then friendless Sultan who had enraged European opinion by his barbaric treatment of his Christian minorities. A weak Turkey dominated by Berlin, Wilhelm decided, would serve as the economic and political base from which an expansionist Germany would spread its power and influence eastwards into Asia. In the event, however, his grandiose schemes had gone disastrously wrong, and had instead plunged Europe into the black abyss of war, dragging with it much of the rest of the world.

This book tells, for the first time, the extraordinary story of how in that war Germany sought to harness the forces of militant Islam to its cause with the help of its ally Turkey. By unleashing a Holy War against them, Wilhelm and his hawkish advisers aimed to drive the British out of India, and the Russians from the Caucasus and Central Asia. It was a bold and adventurous strategy, for there were no precedents for a jihad in modern warfare. Yet, as the German historian Fritz Fischer points out, it was no more than 'the continuation by other means' of the aggressive Eastern policy pursued by Wilhelm since the 1890s. Prussia had once been a tiny, land-locked state whose numerous parts were widely separated from one another by the lands of others. Since then, however, it had come a long way, thanks largely to the genius of Bismarck. Now, Wilhelm was convinced, was Germany's chance to carve out a great new empire in the East.

Masterminded by Berlin, but unleashed from Constantinople, the Holy War was a new and more sinister version of the old Great Game. Fought out between the intelligence services of King, Kaiser, Sultan and Tsar, its battlefield was to stretch from Constantinople in the west to Kabul and Kashgar in the east. It was to spill over into Persia, the Caucasus and Russian Central Asia. It took in the whole of British India and Burma, where Berlin hoped, with the aid of smuggled arms and funds, to foment violent revolutionary uprisings among the restive natives, whether Muslims, Sikhs or Hindus. But the conspiracy's sinuous tentacles stretched far beyond the frontiers of Asia. Berlin's grand design embraced arms dealers in the United States, a remote island rendezvous off Mexico's Pacific coast, and a revolver range in London's busy Tottenham Court Road where assassinations were planned and rehearsed. It would involve schooners loaded with enough arms to launch a second Indian Mutiny, and crates of revolutionary literature smuggled into India behind the innocuous dust-wrappers of the English classics.

However, the main thrust of the Holy War was to be delivered eastwards from Constantinople, across neutral Persia and Afghanistan, and finally down through the passes into India. Berlin's first aim, therefore, was to win the support of the Shah of Persia and the Emir of Afghanistan. If this could be achieved, then their armies, led by German and Turkish officers and spurred on with promises of dazzling loot, could be turned against India. Thus, besides a handful of carefully chosen officers and NCOs, the Holy War need cost virtually nothing. All that it would require would be promises, to be redeemed after the war, and gold, much of which could be plundered from the vaults of British-owned banks in Persia. If, at the same time, India's dissident millions could be persuaded to rise, then the British would find themselves attacked from within and without simultaneously. Meanwhile, the Turks would seek to rally their fellow Muslims in the Caucasus and Central Asia to the banner of the Turco-German Holy War. Greatly encouraged by the reports of their agents on the spot, the strategists in Berlin and Constantinople could visualise the whole of Asia going up in flames, and their British and Russian foes being consumed in the conflagration.

As an infidel, of course, the Kaiser had no authority to summon Muslims to a Holy War. It needed much more than gold, arms and post-war promises to do that. Indeed, only the Ottoman Sultan himself, in his capacity of Caliph of all Islam, had the authority which was required to issue such an awesome order. It was essential, therefore, that Turkey should ally itself with Germany, regardless of the best interests of its

people. Here Wilhelm's far-sighted, if cynical, pre-war culti-
vation of Turkey and its unpopular sovereign paid off hand-
somely. Within three months of the outbreak of war, Turkey
threw in its lot with Germany and Austria-Hungary, and one
week later the Sultan called upon Muslims everywhere to rise
and slay their Christian oppressors 'wherever you may find
them'.

First and foremost this meant, as it was intended to, the
British in India. For there they ruled by far the largest
Muslim empire, in terms of sheer numbers, anywhere on
earth. Indeed, King George V's Muslim subjects greatly outnumbered even those of the Sultan-Caliph himself, and were
many times more than those of Russia and France. The
Kaiser, conveniently enough, had no Muslim colonies or subjects, and had for years been proclaiming himself, to the
intense irritation of the British, Russians and French, the protector of Muslims everywhere. The Sultan's declaration was
to cause considerable alarm among the British in India and in
other regions where Allied subjects lived surrounded by
Muslim populations. Never before in modern times had a
Holy War been declared against a European power, and no
one knew what to expect.

But even for the Germans the Holy War raised one awkward question which had to be addressed lest it undermine the
entire enterprise. What, it would be asked by many Muslims,
was a Christian sovereign doing fomenting and funding a
Holy War aimed at killing those of his own faith? Wilhelm's
advisers, who included a number of eminent German orientalists and scholars, were ready for that one. In mosques and
bazaars throughout the East rumours were circulated that the
German Emperor had been secretly converted to Islam. 'Haji'
Wilhelm Mohammed – as he was now said to call himself –
had even made a pilgrimage, incognito, to Mecca. Muslim
scholars friendly to the cause were able to find mysterious passages in the Koran which purported to show that Wilhelm had
been ordained by God to free the faithful from infidel rule.
Later, word was to be spread that the entire German nation
had followed their emperor's example and converted to Islam
en masse. Finally, false reports of great Turkish and German
victories would be circulated, and these piously attributed to

the righteousness of the Turco-German cause. All this was designed to legitimise Germany's role in the minds of ordinary Muslims.

Meanwhile, in Berlin, small groups of hand-picked German officers were being recruited for the task of setting the East, and ultimately British India, ablaze with the heady message of the Holy War. Liberally supplied with gold, arms and bales of inflammatory literature, they would make their way eastwards from Constantinople, headquarters of this new Great Game, and discreetly enter neutral Persia. There, as they rode across the deserts and mountains towards Afghanistan, they would spread word of the jihad among the tribesmen and villagers along their route and try to win their active support. But it was in the Afghan capital that their most crucial task would lie – that of winning over the powerful Emir to their cause, and persuading him to unleash his tribal armies against India's ill-guarded frontiers. At the same time, in Teheran, similar pressure would be directed against the young Shah to try to draw him and his Muslim subjects into the Holy War. In India itself attempts would be made to coerce leading princes, some of whom were allowed by the British to have their own private armies, into joining the Turco-German cause. Personal letters from Kaiser Wilhelm, promising them almost anything they wanted if they changed sides, were being prepared, sumptuously bound in leather, to be smuggled to them when all was ready.

Such is the story I have to tell. Pieced together from the long-forgotten memoirs of the participants, from diaries, and from the secret intelligence reports of the day, it is moreover a highly topical one in view of what is now going on in this volatile area where the Great Game has never really ceased. To some, fears of a resurgent Russia and Germany may give it an additional significance. But first and foremost it is a tale of courageous and resourceful individuals, of either side, who found themselves caught up in these shadowy events, and I have told it, wherever possible, through their adventures and misadventures.

It was around this colossal conspiracy that John Buchan wove his immortal secret service thriller *Greenmantle*, which in its day outsold even *The Thirty-Nine Steps*. Just as my last

book, *The Great Game*, revealed the real-life world of
Kipling's classic spy story *Kim*, this one unravels the equally
strange events which inspired Buchan's wartime bestseller.
Indeed, as the reader will discover, it contains characters who
might easily have escaped from the pages of *Greenmantle*.
This is not surprising perhaps, for Buchan was himself closely
involved in intelligence work at this time, and had ready access
to secret reports on what the Germans were up to in the East.
As T. E. Lawrence, a friend of Buchan's, observed after the
war: '*Greenmantle* has more than a flavour of truth.'

It is the daring exploits of these individuals which provide
most of the action and excitement in this new and little-known
chapter of the Great Game. However, before we join them on
the shadowy battlefields of Persia, Afghanistan and the
Caucasus, where much of the play takes place, we must first go
briefly back in time to where the story really begins. For
although Kaiser Wilhelm espoused the *Drang nach Osten* –
Germany's drive to the East – with almost messianic fervour,
he was not the first to think of it. The concept dates back to
the middle of the last century, before Wilhelm was even born,
and before Prussia and the other Germanic states had been
welded together by Bismarck to form the monolithic Germany
we know today. It was then that certain far-sighted individuals
– mostly soldiers, political economists and industrialists – first
began to see in the sparsely populated regions of the Sultan's
crumbling empire the answer to their prayers and the solution
to their many problems. So it was that the *Drang nach Osten*
cast its fatal and intoxicating spell over the Teutonic imagination – with cataclysmic consequences, as we shall see.

DRANG NACH OSTEN

'The East is waiting for a man . . .'

Kaiser Wilhelm II

'Where does Germany's future lie? It lies in the East – in Turkey . . . in Mesopotamia . . . in Syria . . .'

Dr Paul Rohrbach,
leading propagandist
for German expansionism

1

A Place in the Sun

Had one been travelling through eastern Turkey in the spring of 1838, one might have been startled to come upon a young Prussian officer perched on a remote hillside carefully sketching an Ottoman fortress. However for Captain Helmuth von Moltke, who was destined to become one of Germany's greatest soldiers, this was no sketching holiday. He was there, on the upper reaches of the Tigris, on strictly professional business. Three years earlier he had been seconded to the Sultan's court as a military adviser, entrusted with the task of helping the Turks to modernise their army along the latest Prussian lines. He had soon found, though, that his advice was being ignored, and had therefore turned his mind to broader considerations. During his many months of travelling through the Sultan's far-flung domains, sketching, surveying and note-taking, the young Moltke had become convinced that the Ottoman Empire was in terminal decline. So corrupt and resistant to reform was it that its eventual collapse was inevitable, leading to a free-for-all among the other powers for the choicest pieces.

Moltke was not the first to have reached this conclusion, for the fate of the Ottoman Empire, the so-called Eastern Question, was already preoccupying European statesmen. But the future Field Marshal, whose military prowess Bismarck would be quick to recognise and harness, was convinced that he had the answer. On his return to Berlin in 1839 from the Sultan's service, he urged his superiors to look closely at Turkey. It was, he argued, ripe for German penetration. It could be linked, both economically and militarily, to Berlin by a railway running through the Balkans, making it the shortest and fastest route to the East, and bypassing the British-controlled sea lanes. In addition, he singled out two areas – the fertile strip between the Tigris and the Euphrates in Mesopotamia, and Palestine – as ideal for his energetic fellow Germans to colonise and transform for future generations. Here, he argued, was Germany's place in the sun. But time was short. Already, he warned, the other European powers were beginning to hover like vultures over the Sultan's disintegrating empire, while his own country was nowhere to be seen.

Moltke was not alone, however, in seeing a future for German emigrants in the moribund Ottoman domains. In 1846, the political economist Friedrich List wrote that the lower reaches of the Danube, the western shores of the Black Sea and the northern half of Turkey 'offer German colonists an abundance of unoccupied and naturally fertile land'. He, like Moltke, called for the building of a railway which would run from Berlin to Baghdad. All this, he argued, could be achieved through 'peaceful penetration', and would be part of a larger, world-wide Teutonic expansion, spearheaded by explorers, doctors, diplomats and businessmen. List's views on Teutonic expansionism were later to earn him the title of 'the first German imperialist'. Another, with somewhat similar views, was Professor Wilhelm Roscher of Leipzig University, who argued that when the Sultan's empire was eventually dismembered the German people should see to it that, as their rightful share of the spoils, they acquired Asiatic Turkey.

The expansionist movement was now gathering pace among intellectuals and academics, with Paul Lagarde, Professor of Oriental Languages at Göttingen, adding his voice to those of Moltke, List and Roscher. Lagarde, the father of the chauvinistic Pan-German movement, contended that it was the historic destiny of the German-speaking peoples to extend their frontiers eastwards. Certain races, he claimed, had become 'degenerate' and 'a burden on history'. They included the Turks, the Jews and the Magyars. They could, though, 'serve as the mortar for a nobler race' – meaning, of course, the Germans. 'Because they know that our life is their death,' he went on, 'they hate and fear us.' Lagarde too saw the Balkans and Asiatic Turkey as ideal for colonisation and economic exploitation.

At that time, of course, such ideas were little more than dreams. For Europe's German-speaking peoples were then still divided, spread through a host of small kingdoms, principalities and independent cities. First this Teutonic jigsaw had to be fitted together to form a unified Germany. It was not until 1871, following successful wars against Denmark, Austria and France, that this was finally achieved – thanks to the vision of Bismarck, and the military genius of Moltke, who by this time commanded the Prussian army. A new nation, largely under Prussian leadership and overflowing with youthful dynamism and ambition, now existed in Europe. It was to prove an uncomfortable bedfellow.

No longer would the call for Germanic expansion be confined to a handful of visionaries and academics. Everyone could now see that if the new nation was to compete with Britain, France, Russia and the other powers it would have to have access to raw materials and overseas markets. Jingoistic societies of all kinds began to spring up, some extolling the superiority of Teutonic culture, others demanding what they saw as Germany's historic rights. Among the foremost was the highly vocal and influential Pan-German League, launched to crusade for the creation of a great new Teutonic empire which would stretch from Berlin to Baghdad and beyond. Its aims were spelt out in a booklet entitled *Germany's Claim to the Turkish Inheritance*, which confidently asserted: 'As soon as events have brought about the dissolution of the Ottoman Empire, no other power will raise any serious objections if Germany claims her share of it.' The new nation's need for *Lebensraum*, or extra living space, it argued, was greater and more urgent than that of the other European powers, most of whom already had overseas territories.

There could be no denying that the Pan-Germanists had a strong case. Britain possessed the largest empire in the world, Russia had Siberia and Central Asia, while France owned large tracts of Africa. Germany, on the other hand, had little by way of colonies, having been such a late starter in the race

for imperial prizes. It had, however, been just in time to join
in the scramble for Africa in the 1880s and 1890s, securing the
Cameroons, South-West Africa and part of East Africa in only
twelve months. But few Germans were willing to emigrate to
these hot and unhealthy spots, to which were added New
Guinea and Samoa. Though their total land mass was several
times that of their homeland, there were never more than
20,000 German settlers living in these African and Pacific
colonies. Indeed, soon fewer than fifty Germans a year were
emigrating there. The vast majority of emigrants headed for
the United States – to the chagrin of the Pan-Germanists, who
saw the nation's lifeblood being drained away for ever as the
emigrants took on American citizenship.

This transatlantic exodus would continue, they pointed out,
until Germany could offer its overflowing population somewhere more salubrious than the steamy jungles of Africa, or
distant corners of the Pacific, in which to build new lives, and
without having to forego their German nationality. For unlike
Britain and France, whose populations remained stagnant or
rose only modestly, that of the dynamic new Germany was
soaring, increasing by half a million per year. From the 1870s
Germany had found itself unable to feed its burgeoning population, and food was having to be imported in ever-increasing
quantities. Nor were its overseas territories of much help here,
all being run at a loss since their acquisition.

It was not surprising, therefore, that more and more
Germans found themselves persuaded by the arguments of
the Pan-German League, and other patriotic bodies, that their
economic future lay in the rich and sparsely populated
Ottoman territories. In industrious German hands, the once
abundant Mesopotamian plain, which had nurtured brilliant
civilisations in the past, could become the bread-basket of a
Greater Germany. To would-be emigrants this area offered
far more attractive prospects than the malarial swamps of
West Africa and the Pacific. There was disagreement, though,
among expansionists over the precise status of such territories,
and how these would be incorporated into a Greater Germany.
The more extreme commentators wanted a genuinely territorial empire, like that of Great Britain, with the Sultan and his
people eventually becoming the Kaiser's subjects, just as the

Indians were Queen Victoria's. More moderate voices argued for a purely economic empire, since this was less likely to result in confrontation with the other European powers, as it could be achieved by stealth, or what was termed 'peaceful penetration'. But on one thing all were agreed. Eventually, even if sovereignty remained nominally in the Sultan's hands, 'Germany's India' could be created amid the ruins of his empire.

Bismarck himself would have no part in these grandiose schemes, however, and gave the expansionists little encouragement or help. He believed that the new Germany that he had created had reached its optimum size, and saw his role as that of consolidating its frontiers and avoiding conflicts with the other major European powers. He regretted the acquisition of Germany's costly colonies in Africa and the Pacific, and at one time even considered offering them to Britain. But this did not mean that he was averse to extending Germany's influence beyond Europe's frontiers, or safeguarding its interests where these appeared to be threatened. So it was, despite his caution and his professed indifference towards the Ottoman Empire, that Germany found itself gradually sucked into the quicksands of Turkey's affairs.

To be just to Bismarck, the approach had come in the first place from the Sultan himself. Abdul Hamid had recently lost his traditional ally and bulwark against Tsarist Russia, Great Britain, and he was now anxiously seeking a replacement. His rift with Britain had followed the anti-European riots of 1882 in Egypt, then officially part of the Ottoman Empire. This had resulted in British troops occupying Egypt, and relations between Constantinople and London, already strained, plunging to a new low. Turkey's relations with its giant neighbour Russia, against whom it had just fought a disastrous war, were even worse. Bismarck's dynamic new Germany, with its formidable military machine and no apparent designs on Abdul Hamid's domains, seemed the most obvious of the European powers to turn to for protection and advice. Even so, as always, Bismarck was wary of risking his good relations with London and St Petersburg. He agreed to send advisers to Constantinople, but only on certain strict conditions. First and foremost, they had to sever all connections with the home government, and be taken into the Sultan's own service. This would enable him, if necessary, to wash his hands of them.

Among those dispatched to Constantinople was a team of Prussian civil servants entrusted with the task of trying to modernise the Ottoman administration along European lines. They were followed by a Prussian military mission commanded by an outstanding officer, General Kolmar von der Goltz. His task, of similarly modernising the Turkish army, was to be made no easier by the Sultan's disconcerting habit of now and again deliberately sabotaging his efforts. For the paranoid Sultan, in perpetual fear of being assassinated or overthrown, was in two minds over the wisdom of having a modern army commanded by European-educated officers. Nonetheless, the general remained in Constantinople for more than a decade, during which time he succeeded, to a considerable degree, in modernising the Sultan's huge but poorly trained and ill-equipped army.

Although the mission was officially in the service of the Ottoman authorities, Berlin too was to benefit from General von der Goltz's presence in Constantinople. Not only was he able to gather detailed intelligence from all parts of the empire, and pass this on to Berlin, but he and his officers also succeeded in securing valuable armaments contracts for German manufacturers. Krupp of Essen thus supplied the Sultan with heavy artillery, Loewe of Berlin with rifles and machine-guns, while Germania of Kiel equipped his navy with the latest torpedoes. Also at this time, a number of German finance houses, led by the formidable Deutsche Bank, began to gain footholds in the Turkish capital, wooing ministers and others in high places with loans at considerably lower rates of interest than those offered by their British and other European rivals. German exporters were quick to follow, their highly trained and motivated salesmen running circles around their more gentlemanly competitors. 'The German export trade', noted *The Times* correspondent in Constantinople, 'owes its success to the stolid, steady perseverance of German industrialists who imitate the methods of the German general staff in neglecting no detail, however trivial, in their plan of campaign.'

Already some far-sighted Germans were beginning to look beyond Turkey's eastern frontiers for new markets, raw materials and other openings. There lay the Shah of Persia's decaying domains, so long the target of Anglo-Russian rivalry, aimed largely at keeping the other side out. Like the Sultan, the Shah now saw in this new and powerful Germany a counterweight to St Petersburg and London. He was therefore only too eager to encourage German interest in his country. He not only asked Bismarck to send him military and civil advisers, but also offered to open up his lands to German settlers. Although wary of getting caught up in the Great Game between Britain and Russia, Bismarck agreed to supply the Shah with a number of retired Prussian officers as advisers, albeit, like those seconded to Turkey, in a strictly private capacity. The Shah also paid a state visit to Germany, and formal diplomatic relations were established between Berlin and Teheran. Some modest arms sales followed, but not much else, for fear of treading on Britain's or Russia's toes in this highly sensitive region.

So long as Bismarck was in charge of Germany's foreign policy, it would remain that way, to the frustration of the expansionists. But then, in the summer of 1888, fate suddenly played into their hands. For in June of that year, Kaiser Wilhelm II succeeded his father as Emperor of Germany. To the exultation of the Pan-Germanists, and others who urged a more adventurous foreign policy, their new sovereign quickly showed himself to be an ardent expansionist. Unlike his cautious Chancellor, the 29-year-old Wilhelm was convinced that his country could find a place in the sun without any risk of alienating the other European powers. The days of Bismarck's pussyfooting were now all but over.

*　　*　　*

It was the young Emperor's misfortune to have been born with a crushed nerve in his neck. Despite the efforts of Europe's best doctors, the result was that his left arm never developed properly, remaining withered and useless, and several inches shorter than his other arm. For a man who wished more than anything else in the world to excel on the battlefield, it was a particularly cruel blow. Wilhelm's disappointment and frustration were to scar him emotionally for life, making him vain, impulsive, bombastic and hypersensitive to slights, whether imagined or otherwise. An awareness that his parents disliked him had made him fiercely ambitious, desperate for admiration and given to theatrical utterances. He was determined to show his family how wrong they were. Had he not been chosen by destiny to rule over a great martial power, this might not have mattered. But these flaws in his character, added to his conviction that he was a leader of genius, were to have tragic consequences for the entire world.

To make matters worse, there were other family complications which put further pressures on him to prove himself. Not only was he Queen Victoria's grandson, but he was also distantly related to Tsar Alexander III of Russia. Wilhelm had a nasty feeling that neither of his fellow sovereigns regarded him at all seriously. Now that he was on the throne, he was determined to win their respect. He would turn Germany from a continental power into a great world power, greater even perhaps than Britain, and himself into someone to be reckoned with. Bismarck, to his cost, was slow to realise what was going on in the young Emperor's mind. As a result he behaved somewhat patronisingly towards him, rarely consulting him on matters of foreign policy, and putting him down firmly whenever he came up with any ideas of his own, dismissing them as silly or even dangerous. Before very long Wilhelm was seething with resentment and humiliation, and determined to rid himself of his obstructive Chancellor so that he alone could shape his country's destiny.

A battle of wills now developed between the two men. The struggle dragged on behind the scenes for eighteen months, before coming to a head in an undignified quarrel in March 1890. During the course of this, the exasperated Bismarck angrily flung his dispatch case on the floor, causing some of the confidential papers to spill out. Snatching up a handful of these, Wilhelm was humiliated to read – as the veteran statesman perhaps intended – that his fellow sovereign and kinsman Tsar Alexander had spoken of him as 'a low type, not to be trusted'. There could be no retrieving the situation now. After dominating European diplomacy for some twenty years, Bismarck was finally brought down by one he had regarded, unwisely, as a pipsqueak. His resignation, which was immediately accepted, left the headstrong young Emperor in sole command of Germany's future. Triumphantly, he told the nation: 'The duties of officer of the watch on the ship of state have fallen to me . . . The waves of opportunity are now beating against our shores. The course remains the same. Full steam ahead!'

The course was to remain anything but the same, as quickly became apparent. Among the first of Bismarck's policies to be jettisoned was that of not getting involved in the Near East, which the Chancellor had so persistently warned against, believing that the hazards of angering Britain and Russia outweighed any possible benefits. But Wilhelm had fallen under the persuasive influence of Count Paul Hatzfeldt, for fourteen years German ambassador to Constantinople, who convinced him that glittering rewards awaited German enterprise in the Sultan's vast virgin territories. With the fortuitous collapse of British influence at the Ottoman court, there was clearly a vacancy for someone else. Now that Bismarck was conveniently out of the way, Hatzfeldt urged his monarch to waste no time in stepping into Britain's still-warm shoes.

Wilhelm required no further encouragement, although he was sensible to the need for caution. Discreet instructions went out to the Wilhelmstrasse, the Foreign Ministry, declaring that from now on Germany would pursue a far more active policy in the East than hitherto. Instead of waiting, like the other European powers, until the Ottoman Empire finally broke up, and then joining in the scramble for the most desirable pieces, Germany would aim to take over Britain's traditional role of propping it up. In the summer of 1894, the Foreign Ministry prepared a highly secret memorandum spelling out the part that Turkey would play in the Emperor's plan for German expansion in the East. From now on it was to be targeted as a market for German goods, a source of valuable raw materials, and an area for long-term investment.

Although, as we have seen, commercial penetration of Turkey by German companies had begun in the 1880s, its scale was modest, since it had never had the enthusiastic support of the Wilhelmstrasse, which was under the thumb of

Bismarck. From now on, however, it would enjoy the patronage and full backing of the Emperor himself. The timing, moreover, could hardly have been better. Since the 1880s, German industry had changed almost beyond recognition. In ten short years, the country had been transformed from an agrarian state into a modern industrial nation. In the early 1880s, German steel output was only 500,000 tons a year. By 1895 it had risen to three million, doubling thereafter every five years until, in 1907, Germany overtook Britain as Europe's foremost steel manufacturer. It was much the same story throughout German industry, especially in the chemical and electrical sectors.

His country's economic miracle could not have come at a more auspicious moment for Wilhelm, for it provided the necessary dynamism, funding and political justification for his expansionist dreams. It could hardly be denied that in order to maintain this spectacular rate of growth, German industry needed access to new overseas markets and sources of raw materials. Its interest in Turkey was therefore quite understandable. In 1895, the British government put forward proposals for the partition of the Ottoman Empire in the event of its collapse, offering Germany a generous share. Berlin, however, showed a surprising lack of interest. The truth was that Wilhelm wanted the lot, and was convinced that by an adroit mixture of commercial penetration and diplomatic seduction he could get it.

Because of the indifference which Bismarck had shown towards the Ottoman Empire, the Germans had an incomplete picture of its economic potential. This had to be remedied forthwith. Accordingly, with the Sultan's agreement, a team of German specialists was dispatched to explore the interior and prepare an inventory of its resources. It was to take them four years, and result in a massive official survey entitled *The Natural Resources of Asia Minor*. At the same time other investigations were being carried out in some of the Sultan's more distant provinces without either his authority or knowledge.

Using archaeology and anthropology as a cover, German travellers and explorers had begun to show an active interest in areas where, until now, few had been sighted. One of the most energetic of these was Max von Oppenheim, an orientalist and ardent believer in his country's destiny in the East. He travelled extensively throughout Mesopotamia and Syria, then Ottoman territories, mapping and taking meticulous notes on everything, from the lie of the land to the number of tents and houses owned by every tribe and village. It was not long before the British guessed that he, and other German scholars, were working for the Kaiser's intelligence services. Indeed, very soon Oppenheim became known to the British as 'the Spy'.

Then, in September 1896, Kaiser Wilhelm played his trump card in a shameless and opportunistic move calculated to outmanoeuvre his European rivals. It came at the very moment when the Sultan had aroused the wrath and indignation of Europe by bloodily crushing Armenian attempts to claim their rights as Ottoman citizens. Misguidedly believing that the Russians and other Christian powers would come to their assistance, the Armenians had staged armed uprisings against the Ottoman authorities in their eastern Turkish homeland. These had resulted, in the summer of 1894 and throughout the following year, in barbaric retribution, during which 50,000 Armenians were slaughtered. In August 1896, in a last desperate attempt to draw attention to their plight and their constitutional demands, armed Armenian nationalists seized the Ottoman Bank in Constantinople. But this simply resulted in further bloodletting in which 5,000 more of their fellow Armenians were killed in the streets of the capital. Only forceful protests by the foreign ambassadors finally halted the slaughter, which was to earn the Sultan the title of 'Abdul the Damned' throughout Europe, and far beyond.

Kaiser Wilhelm, however, saw the Sultan's unpopularity as a godsent opportunity to strengthen his ties with his beleaguered fellow monarch. To show his friendship, on Abdul Hamid's birthday he sent him a signed photograph of himself and his family. On learning of this, liberal opinion in Europe was outraged. Abdul Hamid, needless to say, was overwhelmed by Wilhelm's gesture, and pathetically grateful to find that he had one powerful and sympathetic friend in Europe. He immediately invited the German Emperor to visit

Constantinople as his personal guest, to be followed by a grand tour of any parts of the Ottoman Empire which he might wish to see. This was precisely what Wilhelm had been hoping for. The *Drang nach Osten*, Germany's drive to the East, was about to start with a vengeance.

2

'Deutschland über Allah!'

Kaiser Wilhelm's state visit to the East, which turned out to be more of a triumphal progress, began in Constantinople on October 18, 1898. In the Ottoman capital, the Sultan's only friend was given a lavish and flattering welcome, exceeding anything previously accorded a foreign visitor. A wildly cheering throng greeted him as he rode through the ancient city's cobbled streets, looking regally resplendent in one of the many uniforms which he himself had designed. Nothing was spared for his comfort and enjoyment, with a succession of banquets and ceremonial parades of the Sultan's German-trained troops. Dazzling gifts were exchanged by the two sovereigns, while Wilhelm presented the people of Constantinople with a huge and ornate fountain of his own design, which stands in the Hippodrome to this day.

Certainly all this was an ego trip for the glory-seeking Wilhelm, but it also had longer-term motives. By consolidating, and then exploiting, his new-found friendship with Abdul Hamid, he intended to further his secret ambition of bringing the Sultan's domains under German sway. The linchpin to such dreams was the Baghdad Railway, which would eventually run – or so Wilhelm intended – from Berlin to the Persian Gulf, and from there eastwards perhaps across Persia towards British India. The building of such a rail link, everyone agreed, was an imaginative and sensible idea, since it would provide the shortest and quickest route between Europe and Asia – everyone, that is, except for those responsible for the defence of India, whom the idea filled with horror. Not only would it outflank the Royal Navy and threaten the viability of shipping routes to India and the Far East, but a railway which could carry German exports could also, in time of war, convey troops and artillery. In fact, the first part of the line, running from Berlin through the Balkans to Constantinople, already existed, as did two branch lines stretching into the Turkish interior, one to Ankara and the other to Konia. But what had still to be built was the highly contentious section, which would extend south-eastwards to Baghdad and beyond. It was to try to secure the concession for this that Wilhelm had come to Constantinople.

Although immensely grateful for German support at a time when no one else was willing to grasp his bloodstained hand, the Sultan was far too wily to take Wilhelm's protestations of eternal friendship at face value. Just what, he wondered, was his fellow sovereign up to? Although he could not afford to build the railway himself, his empire being virtually bankrupt, he could see the use to which he could put it in maintaining his authority in his more distant territories. But what was in it for the Germans? Maybe they had designs on his domains. If his own secret service was to be believed, German geologists posing as archaeologists were at that very moment covertly prospecting for oil around Mosul, in northern Mesopotamia. In fact, or so his spies informed him, they had already found it, for an intercepted German report spoke of the region offering 'even greater opportunities for profit than the rich oilfields of the Caucasus'. Although happy to let the Germans build him a railway, and develop the region through which it ran to their mutual benefit, he did not want to be rushed into it. So, when Wilhelm and his retinue left Constantinople for the Holy Land aboard the imperial steam-yacht *Hohenzollern*, it was without the coveted concession, for which he would have to wait a further year.

Despite this, the Kaiser's grand tour of the Sultan's domains, including the Christian sites, proceeded apace, the arrangements having been meticulously planned by Thomas Cook Ltd. The Kaiser's demeanour, however, was to arouse considerable controversy, not to mention scorn from his detractors. On October 29, through a breach cut specially in the walls by his Turkish hosts, Wilhelm rode triumphantly into Jerusalem mounted on a black charger. For the occasion, which received world-wide newspaper coverage, he wore the dazzling white ceremonial uniform of a German field marshal, his helmet surmounted by a huge imperial eagle of burnished gold. On either side of the royal party Turkish mounted police beat back the excited crowds with batons. 'It seemed to me,' wrote one eyewitness, 'that Wilhelm imagined he had taken the city by the sword, instead of arriving there as a tourist. His behaviour was ludicrous beyond description.' Inevitably, so ostentatious and theatrical a display invited much caustic comment, as well as unfavourable comparisons. Even in the Middle Ages, it was pointed out, conquerors had shown fitting humility on entering this city held sacred by three faiths, while Christ had chosen to make his own humble entry astride a donkey.

Finally, ten days later, Wilhelm reached Damascus. There, at the tomb of the great Muslim hero Saladin, he laid a wreath and hung a lamp of solid silver before ordering that a mausoleum of the finest marble be built around it at his expense. Knowing that his words would be spread throughout the East by the highly efficient German propaganda machine, he proclaimed his profound admiration for the chivalrous and saintly warrior who, in the twelfth century, had successfully defended Jerusalem against the English. He also let it be known that he was sickened by the quarrelling that went on among the Christian churches, and that had he not been born a Christian sovereign he would have chosen to be a Muslim one. All this was unashamedly intended to please Muslims everywhere, although many of those present could hardly believe their ears.

But Wilhelm's most audacious bid for the hearts and minds of Muslims was still to come. Emboldened by the seemingly rapturous reception he had been accorded during his tour, he ended his visit by offering what many observers saw as Germany's support for the political aspirations of Muslims living under alien – though not, of course, Turkish – domination. On November 8, at a banquet held in Damascus in his honour, and attended by many Muslim notables, he delivered his now notorious speech. 'His Majesty the Sultan,' he told his awed listeners, 'and the 300 million Muslims scattered

across the globe who revere him as their Caliph, can rest
assured that the German Emperor is, and will at all times
remain, their friend.' Once again, his propaganda experts saw
to it that his words were spread far and wide, while Foreign
Ministry gold ensured his speech fulsome coverage in the
Arabic and Turkish newspapers. At the same time thousands
of brightly coloured postcards bearing his words were run off
and distributed free in the knowledge that many of them
would be mailed to other parts of the Muslim world, including British India and Russian Central Asia.

Until now the British had regarded Wilhelm, with his vain-
glorious posturings, as something of an ass. He was seen as
spoiled but harmless, content with dressing up in ridiculous
uniforms and playing at soldiers. Wilhelm himself was only
too aware of this mortifying image, and resented it deeply.
More than anything else, he wished to be taken seriously by
the rest of the world, especially by the British, whom he
regarded with a mixture of admiration, envy and dislike. By
issuing this rallying call to the world's Muslims, so many of
whom were the subjects of Queen Victoria, as Empress of
India, he was warning the British that they no longer had a
monopoly over the East, and at the same time cocking a snook
at his royal relatives. Clearly Wilhelm was beginning to enjoy
himself.

The cartoonists and satirists had had a field-day lampoon-
ing Wilhelm's extravagant antics during his three weeks as
Abdul the Damned's guest. '*Deutschland über Allah!*' sneered
Punch. However, more sober observers had seen enough to
realise that from now on, without the restraining hand of
Bismarck, Wilhelm would have to be taken far more seriously.
For not only did he command the most powerful army on
earth, but it was also becoming increasingly evident that he
had ambitions to match. To make matters worse, there was
evidence that Wilhelm was increasingly surrounding himself
with sycophants and flatterers only too eager to exploit his
weaknesses for their own ends by fanning the flames of his
personal ambition. They included political adventurers, arms
manufacturers, financiers and hawkish Prussian generals and
admirals – expansionists to a man. There were academics, too,
who produced persuasive historical and economic arguments

for the need for a Greater Germany if the nation was to survive. They were to exert a heady influence in German intellectual circles, not to mention on the Kaiser himself.

One of them, curiously, was an Englishman – Houston Stewart Chamberlain, the son of an admiral. He had lived most of his life in Germany, and had become a passionate champion of the Teutonic cause. 'If Germany does not rule the world,' he warned, 'it will disappear from the map.' Wilhelm was delighted that such views should come from a well-connected Englishman, whose family included a field marshal and a number of generals. He wrote effusively to Chamberlain to thank him. Later, disowned by his family and vilified by the British press, the renegade adopted German citizenship, his views becoming ever more eccentric and extreme. He even argued that Shakespeare, Milton, Dante, Newton and Descartes were really Germans, being originally of Teutonic stock, and forecast that German would eventually replace all other European languages.

But Chamberlain's utterances were mild compared with the bellicose outpourings of militaristic Germans. 'It is proved beyond all shadow of doubt that regular war is the best and noblest form of the struggle for existence,' declared one Pan-German thinker. Another described war as 'a biological necessity of the first importance – the Father of all things,' adding: 'To supplant or be supplanted is the essence of life.' Yet another wrote ominously: 'The hostile arrogance of the other powers absolves us from all our treaty obligations, and forces us, in defending our vital interests, to revive the ancient Prussian policy of conquest.' German artillery on the road to Egypt and India, he declared, 'would be a goal worthy of great sacrifices.' A future German Empire, wrote one professor, 'must stretch from the North Sea to the Persian Gulf, absorbing Holland, Switzerland, the entire Danube basin, the Balkans and Turkey.' The German people, declared another, 'must rise as a master race above the inferior peoples of Europe and the primitive peoples beyond it.'

But it was not only the polemicists and politicians who craved a Greater Germany. The Prussian-dominated military also dreamed of winning glory on the battlefield, as their fathers had against Denmark, Austria and France during the

creation of Germany's European empire under Bismarck.
'How often, while riding in cavalry charges on manoeuvres,'
wrote Kaiser Wilhelm, 'have I heard a comrade galloping
beside me cry out: "*If only this were the real thing!*" ' Such militaristic and expansionist yearnings were also beginning to
strike a chord with the German public, which was particularly
resentful of Britain's domination of world affairs, and not
averse to seeing her cut down to size. 'It is fortunate',
observed Count von Bülow, the Foreign Minister, in a note to
his sovereign, 'that nobody in Britain realises how anti-British
German public opinion is.'

Foremost among the hawks surrounding Wilhelm was
Admiral Alfred von Tirpitz, a keen expansionist and
Germany's Minister for Naval Affairs. Not long before
Wilhelm's departure for Constantinople and the Holy Land,
Tirpitz had convinced him that, in addition to the powerful
army which Bismarck had bequeathed him, he must command
an equally formidable fleet if he was to stand up to Britain,
then the world's greatest sea power. With the backing of such a
super-fleet, he would be in a strong position to browbeat or
bully Britain into conceding to Germany a place in the sun, or
simply to take it by force. The fleet would thus serve as the
instrument needed to secure Germany's breakthrough from
European power to world power. From now on *Weltpolitik* was
to become the driving force behind German foreign policy as
well as Wilhelm's personal ambitions. The word was to mean
different things to different people. To most Germans, at that
time anyway, it simply signified achieving equality with the
other leading powers. But to the hawks it already had only one
meaning. And that was world domination – if necessary
through war.

Naturally there was enthusiastic backing for Tirpitz's fleet-
building plan from the country's steel and armament moguls,
who stood to make fortunes from such a vast construction
programme. What resistance there was came from members of
the Reichstag, though within three years Tirpitz had persuaded them to pay for no fewer than thirty-eight new battleships.
To complete these would obviously take a number of years.
But by the time the last of them was finished, Tirpitz
promised Wilhelm, Germany would have the most formidable

and technically advanced fleet in the world. In the meantime, however, there would be a 'danger period' during which the partly built fleet would not be strong enough to face the might of the Royal Navy should the British decide on a pre-emptive strike, as they had against the Danes a century earlier. To try to reduce the risk of this, by allaying British fears, von Bülow was instructed to keep relations with London as cordial as possible. Given Wilhelm's gift for rubbing people up the wrong way, this was no easy task. For not only had he angered the British with his declamation in Damascus, but also the Russians and the French, both of whom had large Muslim empires.

And that was not all. Even before this he had begun to ruffle Britain's imperial feathers. In January 1896, stung by what he judged to be a personal slight by Lord Salisbury the previous summer, he had sought vengeance by publicly siding with the Boers against Britain. Seen in London as impudent meddling in Britain's colonial affairs, this aroused strong anti-German feeling. The following year he challenged British naval supremacy in the Far East by setting up a formidable naval base on the North China coast. Using the murder of two German missionaries in the interior as an excuse for punitive action, he had sent marines to wrest Tsingtao from a weakly protesting Peking and then swiftly transformed it into a naval stronghold. 'Hundreds of German traders will revel in the knowledge that the German Empire has at last secured a firm footing in Asia,' he told von Bülow, adding that 'hundreds of thousands of Chinese will quiver when they feel the iron fist of Germany heavy on their necks, while the whole German nation will be delighted that its government has done a manly act.' Altogether less delighted, however, were British naval strategists, and those responsible for Britain's Far Eastern interests, not to mention St Petersburg, where the Tsar and his ministers were becoming similarly concerned about the headstrong Wilhelm. Clearly, von Bülow's task of trying to allay British and others' suspicions of what he was up to was going to be an uphill struggle.

Apart from Tirpitz's rapidly growing fleet, the other principal instrument of German expansion was the Berlin-to-Baghdad railway, the concession for the final stretch of which

Wilhelm had by now obtained from his friend Sultan Abdul Hamid. Originally German engineers and military strategists had wanted this to take a more northerly route, via what is now Ankara, the Turkish capital. Not only was this the easiest route in terms of terrain, but it also kept the railway well out of range of British naval guns. However, the Russians had objected strongly, arguing that it would directly threaten their strategic and commercial interests in the Caucasus. Consequently, albeit grudgingly, the Germans agreed to move the route further south, a far more costly undertaking in view of the additional tunnelling involved. This, in turn, led to problems over raising the necessary capital, though these are outside the scope of our narrative. Despite long delays, however, the Germans kept doggedly at it, and in the end the last of many obstacles had been overcome, and the new railway began its remorseless advance eastwards.

By the autumn of 1904, the first 200-kilometre stretch had been completed, and on the Sultan's birthday of that year it was ceremoniously opened to traffic. But by far the most difficult, not to say expensive, sector still lay ahead. This involved dynamiting a labyrinth of tunnels, at a cost of £50,000 a mile, through the 10,000-foot-high mountains of south-eastern Turkey. Nor was that the planners' only headache, for in the meantime a further problem had arisen – that of where the railway was going to terminate. Although known as the Baghdad Railway, its purpose was not simply to carry German exports to this sleepy, fly-blown city in the middle of nowhere. It was intended to do far more than that. Its aim, both commercial and strategic, was to provide a short-cut to India and the East by bypassing the Suez Canal, which could be closed to German shipping in the event of war. It therefore needed a port, from where the rail-borne freight could be moved on by sea, at least until the rail network could be extended across Persia.

The Germans' original intention had been to extend the railway southwards from Baghdad to the head of the Persian Gulf, and build a new port there. The most obvious site for such a terminus was on the shores of the small desert sheikhdom of Kuwait. However, the spectre of an expansionist Germany gaining a strategic foothold anywhere on the Gulf was the stuff of nightmares to those responsible for the defence of India, who had long regarded the waterway as a British lake. On hearing of the proposal, Lord Curzon, the Viceroy, had moved swiftly to block it. Although nominally part of the Ottoman Empire, Kuwait's precise status was at that time somewhat nebulous. For many years Constantinople had shown little interest in this remote and impoverished desert backwater, and Curzon now chose to ignore any claims that the Sultan might have over it.

Already, in an assurance to the House of Lords, the British government had warned that the acquisition by another power of a base of any kind would be viewed as 'a very grave menace' to British interests, which would be resisted by all possible means. Clearly a German-owned port at the head of this vital waterway, directly linked by rail to Berlin, was the thin end of a very dangerous wedge. Amid great secrecy, Curzon dispatched to Kuwait the British Political Resident in the Gulf, Colonel Malcolm Meade. Ostensibly on a shooting trip – the classic British cover for so many Great Game missions – he crossed to the mainland under cover of darkness by dhow. For he was aware that in the harbour at that moment was a visiting Turkish warship. Without the Turks discovering, however, he called on the Emir of Kuwait, with whom he concluded a secret treaty designed to scotch the German plan. Under the terms of this, Britain promised to guarantee the Emir's frontiers and protect his throne, while he pledged himself and his descendants not to cede any lands to any other power, or receive emissaries from one. This effectively gave control of Kuwait's foreign policy to Britain. When, not long afterwards, a Turco-German mission arrived to discuss with the Emir the siting of the new rail terminus, they found him unexpectedly resistant. It did not take them very long to realise that they had been outmanoeuvred by the perfidious British.

In fact, provided the railway advanced no further than Baghdad, or at most the port of Basra on the lower reaches of the Tigris and Euphrates, the British government was willing to countenance it. But there was no shortage of strategists and others who viewed even this with horror, being convinced that Germany was hell-bent on supplanting Britain in the region –

as indeed many of those close to the Kaiser were. By now feelings over the railway were beginning to run high in both
Britain and Germany, resulting in a flood of articles and pamphlets by polemicists and armchair strategists on either side.
Meanwhile, undeterred by the reverse it had suffered over the
choice of terminus, Berlin was proceeding relentlessly with its
penetration of the region. For a start, it greatly extended its
network of consuls, not to mention its intelligence officers,
throughout the East. Until then, the German Foreign
Ministry had been desperately short of experts on the area,
having no possessions of its own there. The fetid, mud-built
towns around the Persian Gulf now began to witness the
arrival of a determined new breed of expatriate. Highly efficient and able, if somewhat humourless, these dedicated individuals were to serve their Kaiser well when Germany's hour
of destiny arrived.

But German penetration of the region was not confined to
diplomats, intelligence officers and railway engineers. At the
same time a small import-export firm, Robert Wonckhaus,
which had begun a few years earlier with one man and a suitcase, started to expand its operations throughout the Gulf
ports. Backed by what the British suspected were German
Foreign Ministry funds, between 1899 and 1906 Wonckhaus
opened offices in Bahrain, Bushire, Basra, Mohammera and
Bandar Abbas. Also in 1906 a German shipping line,
Hamburg-Amerika, inaugurated a regular passenger and
freight service between Germany and the Gulf. Not only did
this directly challenge Britain's long-standing monopoly over
traffic with Europe but, aided by German government subsidies – or so it was claimed – it deliberately set out to undercut
its rivals' passenger and freight charges. Moreover, encouraged by Wonckhaus, now its agent, it began to serve ports
hitherto neglected by the British. For a year or two it ran at a
loss, but soon was in profit. A number of German banks also
extended their operations into the region, again offering better
terms than their principal rival, the British-owned Imperial
Bank of Persia. At the same time German prospectors began
to compete for concessions to explore for oil and other miner-
als, especially along the intended route of the Baghdad
Railway. Last but not least came highly motivated and trained

salesmen, intent on replacing all other European goods in the bazaars of the region with German ones.

Such activities, whether diplomatic or purely commercial, were of course fully within the rights of these enterprising and energetic newcomers. But seen alongside Germany's massive fleet-building programme and ambitious railway plans, this penetration of the Gulf region was to cause growing alarm in London and Delhi. In the spring of 1904 it was therefore decided to dispatch a young political officer of exceptional ability to monitor German activities in the Gulf, and wherever possible to block them. The best way of keeping intruders out, it was reasoned, was by strengthening Britain's ties with the local Arab and Persian rulers. But in a region torn by inter-tribal rivalries and jealousies it required very special talents to achieve this.

The man chosen for the task was Major Percy Cox, an Indian Army officer who had been transferred to the Indian government's élite political service on account of his flair for languages and tribal politics. 'Cox', wrote his biographer years later, 'was near his prime of life, tall and spare, blond and blue-eyed. He moved lithely, and he shot straight. He could manage a difficult horse and a fast camel.' Major, later Colonel, Cox 'said little, listened to everything, and missed nothing.' Gradually he gained the confidence of the tribesmen and the friendship of their leaders, making him a formidable adversary to those bent on dislodging the British from their primacy in the Gulf.

Meanwhile, at home, relations between Britain and Germany were becoming increasingly strained. The principal reason for this was British concern over the Kaiser's new super-fleet and the use to which he intended to put it. 'The German Navy – who is it aimed at?' the *Daily Mail* demanded to know. The British government, too, wanted to know. In January 1907, in a secret memorandum, a Foreign Office mandarin wrote: 'Either Germany is definitely aiming at a general political hegemony and maritime ascendancy, threat-ening the independence of her neighbours and ultimately the existence of England. Or, free from any such clear-cut ambi-tion and thinking for the present merely of using her legiti-mate position and influence as one of the leading powers, she is seeking to promote her foreign commerce, spread the benefits of German culture, extend the scope of her national energies and create fresh German interests all over the world wherever and whenever a peaceful opportunity offers . . . ' Either way, the writer argued, Germany's new *Weltpolitik* represented 'a menace to the rest of the world'.

At the same time, British naval strategists observed with concern that the Kaiser's new battle-fleet was of such limited range that it was effectively a North Sea force, thus making it a direct and unambiguous threat to the United Kingdom. Intelligence sources suggested, moreover, that Tirpitz's programme, carried out amid great secrecy, was in fact proceeding at a much faster pace and on a much bigger scale than hitherto realised. The result was, despite considerable parliamentary resistance, that Britain too began to expand and modernise its navy, the vessels on either side growing bigger and bigger and carrying ever more powerful guns. So began the first arms race of modern times, with other powers such as France, the United States, Japan, Austria and Italy joining in. There were those, even in Germany, who had foreseen the danger of unleashing such a race with Britain. In February 1907, one of Tirpitz's closest advisers had warned of the possible consequences of stepping up the output of Germany's naval shipyards to four dreadnoughts a year. 'The stigma of having caused a fruitless arms race will be impressed on us,' he wrote, 'and the German Empire will encounter even greater animosities than at present when our reputation as a troublemaker is bad enough.' But an even worse consequence, he added, would be if Britain were to match this increased pace of building and thus 'completely obliterate' Germany's hopes of challenging her on the high seas.

By now many people in Britain were beginning to realise that sooner or later an armed showdown with Germany was inevitable. To add to their fears, a spate of novels and other imaginative works began to appear in both Britain and Germany purporting to show what the other side was plotting. The first and most famous of these was *The Riddle of the Sands*, by Erskine Childers, published in 1904. Still widely admired today, it tells how the yachtsman-hero stumbles on a German plan for an invasion of England using a secretly assembled armada of lighters, and so manages to foil it. Kaiser Wilhelm himself plays an overseeing role in the plot. The book enjoyed enormous success, selling several hundred thousand copies in its first year alone. Indeed, so great was its impact that the First Lord of the Admiralty ordered his staff to investigate the feasibility of such an invasion.

Two years later, commissioned by Lord Northcliffe, founder of the *Daily Mail*, and serialised in his newspaper, there appeared William Le Queux's scaremongering novel *The Invasion of 1910*. This effectively took over where Childers left off, describing a successful German invasion of Britain, with all its imagined horrors. Translated into a number of languages, including German, the book sold two million copies worldwide, and greatly boosted the circulation of the *Daily Mail*. A German counter-novel, called *Seestern*, about a secret British plot for a pre-emptive strike against the Kaiser's new battle-fleet, was one of several along such lines which appeared at this time. Also in Germany many people, especially among the military, were beginning to speak openly of *Der Tag* – The Day of Reckoning with Britain – and even drinking toasts to it. In Britain, all this gave rise to a growing invasion mania and spy fever, with wild stories of German waiters and others being infiltrated into the southern counties to serve as a fifth column for *Der Tag*. Such scaremongering, in fact, was not entirely without foundation, for as early as 1897 Kaiser Wilhelm had ordered his staff to explore the feasibility of such an invasion.

The British were not alone in fearing the Kaiser's militaristic and expansionist dreams. The Russians, too, were becoming increasingly perturbed by the *Drang nach Osten*, and the threat it posed to their own regional interests. They not only feared Berlin's growing influence in Constantinople, which commanded their sole exit from the Black Sea and which they had long coveted for themselves, but were also worried lest Wilhelm had designs on their own, mineral-rich Caucasian territories. For they had not forgotten, any more than the British had, his mischievous rallying call to the world's Muslims, many of whom lived in the Caucasus and in Russian Central Asia. It was not without good reason that they had insisted on the Baghdad Railway being re-routed further south, away from their own frontiers with eastern Turkey.

The Tsar's anxiety was understandable, for the Russians had only just begun to recover from a catastrophic war they had fought with the Japanese on their Far Eastern frontier, and had no stomach for any further trials of strength. As it was, popular disillusionment over the army's poor showing, together with economic hardship, had led to widespread social and political unrest at home. Tsar Nicholas needed all the troops he possessed to contain the rising tide of revolution which was threatening his very throne. He was anxious, moreover, to end his country's long-standing rivalry with Britain for dominance in Asia, and the ominous rise of Germany in the East now made this need more pressing. Britain, too, which had received a mauling at the hands of the Boers in South Africa, and worldwide condemnation for its invasion of Tibet, was equally keen to bury the hatchet with St Petersburg. In 1907 the two countries signed a treaty – the Anglo-Russian Convention – which settled their ancient differences, and finally brought the Great Game to an end. Although suspicions of Russian intentions still lingered on in Delhi, in Britain the Russian bogy had been supplanted by the German one.

Under the terms of the new accord, the areas of earlier Anglo-Russian rivalry – Persia, Afghanistan and Tibet – were divided into spheres of political and economic influence. Persia, whose sovereignty and independence both parties pledged themselves to respect, was split three ways. The north was apportioned to Russia, the south to Britain, while the central portion running between them was declared a neutral zone. With regard to Tibet, both powers undertook to refrain from any interference in its internal affairs, and to deal with it only through China, the suzerain power. Finally, Afghanistan was deemed to lie within Britain's sphere of influence. It went without saying that Britain would not interfere in Russian Central Asia, nor Russia in British India.

Germany, needless to say, not being a party to the agreement, was in no way bound by it. Indeed, German penetration of Persia, which the accord had largely been designed to prevent, continued as before. If anything, the Anglo-Russian Convention smoothed the path of the *Drang nach Osten*. For the humiliating discovery that they had been 'shared out' between Britain and Russia, without even being consulted, was to provoke intense hostility towards the two powers among Persians from all walks of life. Naturally, the Germans were not slow to exploit this to the full. A similar resentment was felt in Afghanistan, which also had not been consulted. This, too, the Germans would in due course endeavour to turn to their advantage.

Despite this, in the summer of 1907 Kaiser Wilhelm had distinct feelings of unease. Not only had Britain and Russia now patched up their old differences, but three years earlier the British and their other ancient foes, the French, had done likewise, while in 1893 the French and the Russians had signed a similar alliance. This mutual abandonment of old antagonisms and rivalries in the face of a resurgent Germany was to become known as the Triple Entente – not to be confused with the Triple Alliance, which was a secret defensive agreement signed in Bismarck's day between Germany, Austria-Hungary and Italy. Wilhelm now suddenly began to feel encircled by those he had hoped to keep at loggerheads with one another while he pursued his expansionist dreams. There could be no ignoring the rising tide of hostility towards Germany, however, particularly in Britain. Having no wish to risk a war with the latter before his plans were in place and his super-fleet built, Wilhelm now desperately tried to defuse the situation.

In November 1907 he paid a goodwill visit to Britain, during which he hoped to allay British anxieties and suspicions about his territorial ambitions, particularly over the Berlin-to-Baghdad railway and Tirpitz's new super-fleet. Dressed in the uniform of an honorary British admiral, and accompanied by an entourage of Foreign Ministry and other officials, and a contingent of helmeted Prussian guardsmen, he spent a week attending state and other functions and holding discussions with senior British ministers. He stayed at Windsor, where he enjoyed a cordial reception from his British royal cousins, including King Edward VII, who was known to dislike him. He left for home fully convinced that he had calmed British fears and restored good relations between the two powers. But although his visit was hailed as a success by both governments, British suspicions persisted. For it was clear that not even in the interests of peace, and despite British pressure on him to slow the pace of *Weltpolitik*, was Wilhelm prepared to alter course. Moreover, he left behind him a political time-bomb which was to blow sky-high any improvement in relations which his visit might have brought about.

During his stay in Britain, Wilhelm had held forth at considerable length to a British friend, a regular army colonel, Edward Stuart-Wortley, about relations between their two countries. Months later, Colonel Stuart-Wortley decided to present the Kaiser's views in the form of an interview for the *Daily Telegraph*. But first he wrote to Wilhelm, enclosing a copy of the article, and seeking his permission to use it. Wilhelm was delighted with the interview and flattered at the prospect, rarely enjoyed by sovereigns, of seeing himself in print. The article, which was given considerable prominence by the newspaper, appeared on October 28, 1908, and caused a sensation. The German Emperor began by declaring that he was most anxious to be on good terms with Britain. But he warned that he was losing patience with continual misrepresentations by the British press and other critics. He felt that his 'repeated offers of friendship' were being spurned, while he regarded criticism and misinterpretation of his motives as 'a personal insult'. As for the new fleet he was building, he told the Colonel, the day might well come when the British would be grateful for it in view of Japan's growing might in the Far East. 'You English are mad, mad as March hares,' he went on. 'What on earth has come over you that you harbour such suspicions against us, suspicions so unworthy of a great nation?' His task of trying to restore good relations with Great Britain was made more difficult, he added, by the fact that 'the majority' of Germans – though not, of course, himself – disliked the British.

The result was uproar. What Wilhelm had evidently intended as a plea for better future understanding between the two powers had backfired badly on him. And it was not merely the British whom he had managed to upset. At some point in the interview he had trodden on just about everyone's toes, including the French, the Russians and the Japanese. There was fury in Germany, too, where the right wing accused him of being pro-British, and the left of meddling in things that were no concern of his. Von Bülow, who should have vetted the interview, merely explained to the Reichstag that the sovereign had meant well and would not try his hand at personal diplomacy again. In Britain Wilhelm's efforts were greeted largely with ridicule, for it was no secret that most Germans disliked their North Sea neighbours. With regard to his claim that one day the Royal Navy might be glad of an ally in the Far East, *The Times* pointed out that few of his warships had the coaling capacity to carry them far beyond the North Sea, let alone to the Indian Ocean or the Pacific. Meanwhile, both the British and the Germans continued to build battleships, and relations between the two powers continued to deteriorate.

But the *Daily Telegraph* débâcle was not the only set-back to Wilhelm's plans just then. He had also run into unexpected complications in Turkey and Persia, both of which were so crucial to the success of his *Drang nach Osten*. In 1905, Turkish troops had suddenly crossed the Persian frontier and occupied a number of villages to which the Sultan laid claim. After turning in vain to Britain and Russia for help, the Shah asked the Germans to prevail upon their Turkish ally to withdraw. This placed Wilhelm in an embarrassing position, for he had no wish to fall out with the Sultan, whom he had gone to such pains and expense to cultivate, yet he also needed the Shah's goodwill for the fulfilment of his Eastern dreams. As newcomers to the region, the Germans had not foreseen the pitfalls of trying to befriend, simultaneously, these two ancient foes. Half-hearted attempts by the German ambassador to Constantinople to persuade the Turks to withdraw were rebuffed by the Sultan himself, who demanded to know whose side Germany was on. A stalemate followed, although it was clear to all that Turkey was in the wrong, for no one wished to get involved. Meanwhile the Turks continued moving troops into the disputed region, taking advantage of a revolution which had broken out in Teheran.

Despite all this, Wilhelm managed to cling on to his friendship with both the Sultan and the beleaguered Shah, if only because neither had anyone else to turn to. But then, in July 1908, a seemingly terminal blow befell Wilhelm's plans to take over the Ottoman Empire by stealth. Sick of the Sultan's despotic rule, a group of democratically inspired revolutionaries calling themselves the Young Turks, supported by sympathisers within the army, forced Abdul Hamid to surrender his autocratic powers to an elected, Western-style parliament. Turks, Arabs and Armenians embraced in the street. The millennium had arrived, or so it appeared. Democracy had overnight replaced centuries of oriental despotism. Nonetheless, if only to reassure the European powers, the Sultan was allowed to retain his throne, though not for long. When the following year, with the support of reactionary elements, he attempted to seize power again, he was forcibly deposed and sent into ignominious exile. Mohammed V, his mild and easy-going younger brother, was placed on the Ottoman throne as his compliant successor. So compliant, in fact, was he to prove that he was nicknamed *irade makina*, or rubber stamp, by the Young Turks.

Until then, as Abdul Hamid's principal comforter and ally, Germany had enjoyed primacy over the other European powers in the Ottoman capital. Now, suddenly, it found itself out in the cold, for the Young Turks had no time for the autocratic German Emperor and his like. Indeed, Wilhelm's standing in Constantinople took a further knock when, in October 1908, his Austro-Hungarian friends annexed two Turkish provinces in the Balkans, Bosnia and Herzegovina, and he remained silent. So it was that the Germans found themselves back where they had started, a decade earlier, when Wilhelm first grasped Abdul Hamid's bloodstained hand. To the other European ambassadors in Constantinople it appeared that the Germans were now finished, and that the British, Turkey's friend of an earlier era, would replace them as the guiding power in the Ottoman capital. For it was to the British model that most Young Turks turned as the ideal for their new parliamentary democracy.

But the British threw away this opportunity of stepping into the shoes of the Germans and becoming patrons to Turkey's new but inexperienced rulers. They viewed the Young Turks with some suspicion, seeing them as unprincipled demagogues, under the thumb of Jewish intellectuals and other foreigners. It was to prove a costly mistake. Instead of seizing their chance, they held back, waiting until things had become clearer. Not so the Germans. From their great embassy overlooking the Bosphorus they moved stealthily and purposefully. Aware that the Young Turks were split between genuine idealists and a ruthless clique bent on grabbing power for themselves, they cultivated the latter, whom they saw as Turkey's eventual leaders. They did not have long to wait for their reward.

On January 23, 1913, an armed mob led by three men known to be close to the German ambassador marched on the Sublime Porte, the complex of government offices where the Turkish Cabinet was holding a meeting. Having first cut the telegraph wires, so that help could not be summoned, they forced their way in, shooting dead the War Minister and two army officers who tried to block their way. Then, at gunpoint, they demanded the immediate resignation of the Grand Vizier, or Prime Minister, and the rest of the democratically elected government. Having achieved this, they announced that they now ruled Turkey and its empire in the name of the army and the people. Sultan Mohammed, already only a figurehead, was allowed to remain on the throne to add a spurious legitimacy to the new regime.

The British ambassador immediately telegraphed the Foreign Office informing them of the *coup d'état* and warning that the junta had a 'distinctly German character'. For it was no secret that the young officer, Major Enver, who had led the raid on the Grand Vizier's office, had not only been trained in Germany but had also been Turkey's military attaché there. He was known to be passionately pro-German, as too were most of his fellow conspirators, and also a close friend of the German ambassador, Baron Konrad von Wangenheim, who was in turn an intimate of Kaiser Wilhelm's. It subsequently transpired that the conspirators had informed the ambassador of their nefarious intentions ten days earlier, and that he had made no attempt either to dissuade them or to warn the authorities. Indeed, there were those who believed that Wangenheim himself was behind the plot, and not merely privy to it.

Kaiser Wilhelm was naturally overjoyed at seeing German influence thus restored at Constantinople, since this was crucial to his expansionist dreams. To the British, however, it was very bad news – 'deplorable', one Foreign Office mandarin called it. But whether they liked it or not, for the next six years Enver and his companions would control Turkey's destiny. This would have far-reaching consequences, not just for the Turks, but for the whole world. For it was soon to become evident that Enver, the most ambitious of the new Turkish leaders, harboured dreams that extended far beyond his country's frontiers.

Until then there had only been one would-be Napoleon whose territorial ambitions threatened Britain's interests in the East, and that was Wilhelm. Now, all of a sudden, there were two. What, some asked, if these two wild men, known to share a dislike of Britain, were to join forces to realise their dreams? After all, something like it had very nearly happened once before. That was a hundred years earlier, when Napoleon Bonaparte and Tsar Alexander of Russia had toyed with the idea of marching their armies across Persia and Afghanistan, and together attacking British India, the richest of all imperial prizes. In the event the two men had fallen out, and the threat had promptly collapsed.

For anyone to entertain such ideas in the twentieth century might appear far-fetched – though not, however, to those responsible for the defence of India, who were ever on the look-out for fresh dangers, sometimes to the point of paranoia. While the Russian threat might have receded, there were now others who appeared to have like designs on India. The two most obvious of these, of course, were Wilhelm and Enver. But they were not alone in causing India's defence chiefs to lose sleep. For some time now the authorities had become increasingly aware of a threat of a different kind – a shadowy foe, whose malign hand was directed against the Raj from within.

3

'Like Some Hidden Fire'

In the summer of 1911, the head of the Indian Secret Service, Sir Charles Cleveland, warned the government that his men had uncovered a mysterious and dangerous conspiracy aimed at overthrowing British rule in India. 'Like some hidden fire', he told a gathering of defence chiefs in Simla, this seditious movement was spreading across the country. If extinguished in one place, it immediately flared up in another. The conspirators, he said, were not the usual agitators and hotheads, who were well known to the authorities and carefully watched. These men were highly intelligent and well organised. While maintaining absolute secrecy, they carried out assassinations, bombings and armed robberies – to obtain funds – the length and breadth of India. It all appeared to be part of a skilfully orchestrated overall strategy directed against the British Raj. As to who was behind it, he was unable to say. 'My own impression', he told his audience, 'is that it is directed and controlled by one great intellect – *but whose?*'

As those present were aware, Cleveland's reputation for uncovering native conspiracies, and sending the plotters to the gallows, was legendary. 'His flair', a colleague once observed, 'was amazing. His genius for solving problems was almost uncanny.' Yet this time the Balliol-educated Secret Service chief frankly admitted that he, and the best brains in his organisation, were baffled. Among his listeners that morning was Lieutenant Norman Bray, a young Indian Army intelligence officer, who jotted down Cleveland's words. If the latter's organisation – 'perhaps the most efficient of its kind in the world' – was unable to discover who was behind the conspiracy, he wrote later, then there could only be one explanation. Those directing it must be doing so from outside India's frontiers – beyond the reach of Cleveland's men.

Fears of an enemy within, directed and funded from outside, were nothing new in a country where a handful of Britons controlled the lives and destinies of one-fifth of the entire human race. Ever since the Indian Mutiny, only half a century earlier, Europeans living there had shuddered at the thought of another such bloodbath, this time properly planned and possibly assisted by a hostile foreign power or other agency. After all, there were still men and women living who could remember the bloody horror of the 1857 uprising. The fear of being murdered in one's sleep by one's servants was for many a real one, while for the service chiefs the ultimate nightmare was an armed mutiny in the ranks of the Indian Army, with the disgruntled sepoys turning their weapons against their British officers.

Cleveland's sombre warning came at a time of rapidly worsening violence throughout India, especially in Bengal, most of it directed against the British. In the winter of 1907, two attempts had been made to blow up the official train of Sir Andrew Fraser, the Lieutenant-Governor of Bengal, both of which had failed, although the second left a crater five feet wide on the track. The following year an Indian student had tried to assassinate Fraser with a revolver at close range, though this too had failed due to the weapon misfiring. In November 1909, two bombs were thrown at the open carriage of the Viceroy, Lord Minto, as he and his wife drove through the streets of Ahmedabad, but both fell short. However, two Englishwomen were killed when a bomb was tossed into their carriage in the belief that it contained a British official who had recently survived a parcel-bomb attack.

Following the shooting of a British district magistrate by a Hindu priest, the murder weapon, a modern Browning automatic pistol, was discovered to have been smuggled into the country, together with others, in the false bottom of a suitcase. This suggested that the murder was not an isolated act, but part of something bigger, organised from outside India. Confirmation of this was soon provided by further discoveries, including that of a sophisticated, sixty-page bomb-making manual, likewise smuggled into the country. This not only explained in detail, with diagrams, how to manufacture bombs and explosives, but also how best to use these against individuals, public buildings, banks, police stations, barracks, railways and other key targets. Before long further copies of this work, together with quantities of the chemicals it recommended for explosives-making, began to come to light during police raids. However, it contained no clues as to its author or country of origin.

Although arrests were made, and some of those convicted were hanged, or jailed for long terms, the real brains behind these crimes always managed to avoid capture, giving rise to British fears that they were facing a well-organised conspiracy. For despite the introduction of new emergency laws designed to combat what Sir Charles Cleveland called 'politico-criminal activity', and increasing numbers of arrests, the outrages continued to spread and to multiply. They now included armed raids on trains known to be carrying bullion, and on the homes of wealthy Indians. At the same time arsenals were plundered and weapons seized from isolated police stations. Statues of Queen Victoria and other Raj heroes were tarred or mutilated, and British clubs and churches attacked, while violent riots and other disturbances broke out in a number of major cities. But so far there was no evidence to connect any of this with any foreign power. Nor had the mysterious conspirators succeeded in killing any senior British official, though not for want of trying. Almost all their victims, up to that time, had been Indians – policemen, magistrates, police informers and minor Raj officials.

But then, in the summer of 1909 in the very heart of London, a young Indian assassin had shot dead Sir William Curzon Wyllie, ADC to the Secretary of State for India. At his trial at the Old Bailey, the assassin – a Punjabi called Dhingra – made no attempt to defend himself, merely insisting that his action was morally justified. 'Just as the Germans have no right to occupy your country,' he declared, 'so you have no right to occupy mine.' If an Englishman killed Germans who occupied Britain, Dhingra went on, then he would be hailed as a hero and a patriot. Found guilty, he was sentenced to death and hanged at Pentonville Prison. His last request – that his body should not be touched by a non-Hindu, and that his clothes should be sold to raise money for the anti-British cause – was refused. He was buried within the prison grounds, where his remains lay until returned to India in 1976.

The cold-blooded murder of Curzon Wyllie naturally sent a shockwave through the British Establishment. The assassin's victim was known to be a kindly man, much concerned over the welfare of Indian students in London, and such rank ingratitude seemed utterly incomprehensible. But even now it did not dawn on anyone quite what else might be going on in London under the very noses of the authorities. At the heart of it was India House, officially a hostel for Indian students living in London. Situated at 65 Cromwell Avenue, Highgate, it was a large Victorian house with accommodation for thirty students. In fact, unknown to the authorities, it was the secret headquarters of the Indian revolutionary movement in Britain. Here lectures were given to carefully chosen audiences on topics ranging from revolutionary philosophy and strategy to bomb-making and assassination techniques. In a small outhouse at the back, known as the 'war workshop', Indian chemistry students conducted bomb-making experiments, while elsewhere in the building seditious literature was produced for smuggling into India. This included bomb-making manuals, and pamphlets preaching violence against the British in India, some aimed at inciting sepoy units to mutiny and murder their European officers. In addition, hidden on the premises, was a small arsenal of weapons awaiting dispatch to India by some discreet means.

The evil genius behind these nefarious activities was a 27-year-old Hindu intellectual named Vinayak Savarkar, who was officially the hostel's director. He had come to London in 1906, ostensibly to study law, but in fact to learn the art of bomb-making and revolutionary warfare. At the age of 16, in India, he had solemnly sworn before the awesome Hindu goddess Durga to drive the British out of his homeland. Ever since, he had devoted his life to revolutionary activities, and to recruiting and training others for the task ahead. He would spend long hours in the bomb-making workshop, experimenting and teaching – emerging, one fellow conspirator recalled, 'with the tell-tale yellow stains of picric acid on his hands'. He would also regularly travel down to a pistol range off Tottenham Court Road where he and other young revolutionaries from India House rehearsed the assassinations they planned to carry out, though they were careful not to let the British proprietor realise this.

Savarkar had also written a highly inflammatory account of the Indian Mutiny as seen through Indian eyes. Called *The Indian War of Independence*, this was originally written in the Marathi language and intended for publication and widespread distribution in India. However, the British authorities there got wind of it and somehow managed to obtain part of the text. Its publication, even before it was completed, was banned as seditious, and no printers in India were prepared to take the risk, however sympathetic they might be towards its viewpoint. An English translation was prepared, but British publishers and printers were warned by the Home Office that the book, which called upon Indians to rise once more against their British oppressors, was considered highly seditious.

Finally, after pressure had been put on the French government by the British Foreign Office to prevent it from being produced in Paris, in 1909 a Dutch printer agreed to handle it, the British not discovering until it was too late. Printed with false dust-wrappers, and purporting to be copies of *Pickwick Papers* and other literary classics, the forbidden work was smuggled into India in large quantities. It was very soon to become the bible of political extremists there. Valentine Chirol, Foreign Editor of *The Times*, who managed to obtain an early copy of it, described it as 'a very remarkable history of the Mutiny'. It combined, he observed, 'considerable research with the grossest perversion of facts, and great literary power with the most savage hatred'. Indeed, so inflammatory was it considered by the authorities that the British Museum Library's copy of it was excluded from the catalogue to prevent Indian students in London from reading it. In India the book was to remain banned until the British finally left nearly forty years later. Such notoriety naturally made the work highly sought after, even among Europeans in India, and copies quickly began to change hands at many times the original price, the proceeds going towards the revolutionary cause. As funds swelled, from this and other sources, scholarships were set up for young Indians to come to London to study revolutionary warfare, and named in memory of those who had been hanged by the British.

In view of all this, it may be asked, how was it possible for the authorities in London not to be aware of the evil deeds being plotted against them behind the walls of India House? The principal reason for this failure was the almost total lack of liaison at that time between Sir Charles Cleveland's organisation, based in Simla, and Scotland Yard, then largely unused to the idea of political crime. Indeed, in the summer of 1907, the Under-Secretary of State for India, Sir William Lee-Warner, had complained of the 'utter uselessness' of Scotland Yard in gathering information on the activities of Indian revolutionaries in Britain. The following year, while on a visit to London, the Viceroy's private secretary wrote to warn his chief of the growing hostility of Indian students there towards British rule. As a result, in 1909 it was agreed between the British and Indian governments that a retired Indian Police officer with wide political experience should be employed in London to keep a close if discreet watch on the activities and movements of extremist groups. By this time India House was beginning to come under suspicion, and efforts were made to penetrate what the Press now called 'the House of Secrets', using paid Indian informers. But all this had come too late to save Sir William Curzon Wyllie from the assassin's pistol – handed personally to Dhingra, it later transpired, by Savarkar himself.

Although the police had insufficient evidence to charge him with being an accessory to the shooting, for he had been careful to leave town that day, Savarkar could see that London was rapidly becoming too hot for him. It was only a question of time before the authorities swooped. In early January 1910, therefore, he slipped quietly over to Paris, determined to make it his new revolutionary headquarters, away from the prying eyes of the British authorities. Following his flight, detectives in London and in India had been making up for lost time, however. They had managed to obtain evidence linking him with the smuggling of firearms into India, one of which had been used to kill a British official there. Unknown to Savarkar, a warrant was issued for his arrest in the event of his setting foot again in Britain, while orders were given for extradition proceedings to be commenced against him for trial in India.

In the spring of 1910, despite the urgent warnings of his friends, Savarkar decided to return briefly to London – lured, it has been said, by a female decoy. As he stepped off the boat-train at Victoria Station, he was met and arrested by Scotland Yard officers. Among other charges, he was accused of 'waging war, or abetting the waging of war, against His Majesty the King Emperor of India', and 'conspiring to deprive His Majesty the King of the Sovereignty of British India'. More specifically, he was charged with procuring and distributing arms, inciting people to murder, and delivering seditious speeches. In India, men who had obeyed his bloodthirsty exhortations had been hanged for less than that.

After an order had been obtained from the Bow Street magistrate for his extradition, Savarkar was put aboard a vessel, together with an armed police escort, bound for Bombay. But on reaching Marseilles he managed to squeeze through a porthole while his escort's back was turned and dive into the harbour. He struck out for the shore, where it had been secretly arranged that friends would pick him up in a car. Unfortunately, though, they had lingered too long in a café and were not there to meet him. By this time his escort had caught up with him, and he was dragged back to the ship in handcuffs. Because this occurred on French soil, an international row blew up over the affair, but by then he was safely in Bombay. To hang him, the British authorities knew, would merely make a martyr of him. Instead, the man described by the Governor of Bombay as 'one of the most dangerous men that India has produced' was sentenced to transportation for life to the Andaman Islands, at that time known as Britain's 'Devil's Isle'. So far as the authorities were concerned, Savarkar was safely out of circulation for the rest of his life. However, to the impassioned young revolutionaries he had rallied to the anti-British cause he was to remain a perpetual inspiration. Among them, moreover, there were men only too eager to step into his shoes, and take on the full might of the British Empire. One of these was an Oxford-educated Hindu firebrand named Har Dayal, who had decided to abandon both his scholarship and a brilliant university career rather than accept money from 'the enemy'.

After working at India House, where he came under the heady influence of Savarkar, a year his senior, he had moved briefly to Paris, then a hotbed of revolutionary ideas and activity, where he met exiled Russian revolutionaries willing to pass on to newcomers their painfully acquired experience. But very soon he found himself disagreeing with his co-conspirators over the strategies they should employ against the British in India. The assassination of individuals, he argued, although dramatically spotlighting their cause, could never bring about a nationwide uprising on the scale necessary to crush British rule. Something altogether bigger was called for. 'We must lay the axe to the root of the tree,' he declared, and not merely saw off branches. What was needed was not assassins but a trained army which could be imbued with revolutionary fervour and then infiltrated into India, where secret caches of smuggled arms would be awaiting it. Har Dayal knew, moreover, where such an army might possibly be recruited.

As a result of severe famine in the Punjab between 1905 and 1910, caused by successive monsoon failures, thousands of Sikhs had migrated to Burma, Malaya and China. Some had ventured even further eastwards, settling on the Pacific seaboard of America and Canada. Soon quite large communities of Sikhs and other Indians had established themselves in the San Francisco and Vancouver areas, building their own temples and schools. Many of the men were of fine physique, and a high proportion of them had served in the ranks of the Indian Army. But North America had not turned out to be, for most of them, the promised land they had been led to believe it would be. Their unfamiliar customs made them unpopular with the European majority, with whom they had no common language, while their willingness to work for a mere pittance angered the labour unions. Soon their rapidly swelling numbers began to attract the attention of the immigration service, and they found themselves increasingly isolated and harassed. It was at this moment, in September 1911, that Har Dayal moved to California and set up his revolutionary headquarters among them, safely out of reach of the British authorities.

In India, meanwhile, despite the removal of Savarkar from the scene, the campaign of terrorism continued, with assassinations taking place at the rate of one a fortnight. The victims were mostly Indians, many of them police officers, in British employ. But then on December 23, 1912, the extremists attempted their most ambitious and spectacular attack so far. A bomb was thrown at the Viceroy, Lord Hardinge, as he and his wife rode ceremoniously into Delhi, India's new capital, on the back of an elephant. The explosion was heard six miles away, but the Viceregal couple survived. Lord Hardinge, nonetheless, was seriously injured, his back being badly lacerated by some of the nails, screws and gramophone needles with which the bomb had been packed. The would-be assassin somehow managed to escape, despite the 500 uniformed and 2,500 plain-clothes police officers lining the processional route and mingling with the crowds. The attack caused anger and alarm among Britons both in India and at home, which was reflected in the newspapers. One editorial demanded that for every fresh outrage, twenty-five terrorist suspects should be hanged, while another called for political agitators to be 'flogged in public by the town sweepers'. Only this, it was argued, would bring an end to terrorism.

Although Har Dayal immediately claimed the credit for masterminding the attack, the truth will probably never be known. Nonetheless, the British began to apply every sort of pressure on the American government to have him, and those around him, arrested and extradited. But without any concrete evidence of his personal complicity, and an American public not unsympathetic to the Indians' cause, the prospects of achieving this seemed slender. In the meantime, therefore, a highly experienced former Indian Police officer named William Hopkinson, then working for the Canadian authorities, was discreetly dispatched to San Francisco to investigate Har Dayal's activities. A fluent Hindi speaker, he moved into a hotel, using a false name, close to the revolutionaries' base of operations. His instructions were to keep Sir Charles Cleveland, in Simla, fully informed over what Har Dayal might be planning next, and also to amass enough evidence of his evil doings to convince the US authorities of the disastrous consequences for Anglo-American relations were he allowed to strike again, using them as a safe haven.

It did not take Hopkinson long to discover what was going on. In his first report to Cleveland, in which he described Har Dayal as 'the most dangerous' of the Indian extremists he had yet come across, he warned of the potent influence that this young firebrand was exerting over Indian students at the University of California, where he taught – ostensibly anyway – oriental philosophy. In fact, Hopkinson soon found, he was using his position there to attract the brightest of his students to his cause. At the same time, he and his co-conspirators were actively spreading the revolutionary gospel among the simple, mostly illiterate Sikhs and others forming the now disillusioned immigrant Indian communities along the Pacific coast. Although Hopkinson was not yet aware of it, it was from these sturdy folk that Har Dayal eventually planned to recruit and train his secret army which would drive the British out of India. He named his revolutionary organisation *Ghadr*, meaning Mutiny. Its mouthpiece was a highly seditious newspaper of the same name, which was mailed to sympathisers all over the world. For the movement's activities were not confined to Indians resident in North America. Very soon its tentacles began to stretch across the Pacific to include secret cells in Burma, China, Malaya, Japan and anywhere else where there were expatriate Indian communities. Its membership now ran into many thousands, all sworn to the overthrow of British rule and its replacement with a freely elected republican government.

It was around this time that Har Dayal and his fellow revolutionaries began to realise that help might be at hand from an entirely unexpected quarter. For months now they had been aware of the possibility of a war erupting among the European powers, particularly Britain and Germany. Were this to happen, they now reasoned, Britain's crisis might be their opportunity. Moreover, were they to ally themselves with Germany they might obtain valuable help from Berlin, including arms, money and expert military advice. They were greatly encouraged in this by the publication of a sensational book called *Germany and the Next War*, by General Friedrich von

Bernhardi, a prominent Prussian militarist and propagandist for the Pan-German movement. In this bellicose work the General poured out his country's many grievances, especially those involving Britain, and at the same time called for a war to set these right. Such a conflict, he argued, was not only inevitable but also necessary if Germany was to fulfil its historic destiny.

That was not all he wrote, however. In one chapter, entitled 'World Power or Downfall', he drew attention to the vulnerability of British India, which he saw as a powder keg merely requiring a carefully applied match to explode it. He pointed to the rapidly growing Hindu nationalist movement and to the restlessness of India's Muslim populace. Were the two ever to unite against their European oppressors, he forecast, the subsequent explosion would shake the British Empire to its very foundations. In the event of a war breaking out between Britain and Germany, then almost certainly a violent uprising would follow in India, and very likely in Egypt too.

To Har Dayal and his fellow conspirators this was heady stuff indeed. It showed that the Germans were aware of their movement and its aims, and might well welcome their cooperation, particularly in the event of a war. Har Dayal was determined to make contact with Berlin, and he immediately began to put out cautious feelers to see whether, in the event of Anglo-German hostilities, they might expect Berlin's help. Seemingly, this was done through German diplomats in the United States. The response the Indians got, although equally cautious, was distinctly encouraging. So much so, in fact, that at a meeting of the revolutionaries held in San Francisco on December 31, 1913, the German consul sat on the platform with Har Dayal and the other principal conspirators as a 'special guest'. In his address, Har Dayal is said to have warned those present that very soon Germany would be at war with Britain, and that they should be preparing to sail for India 'for the coming revolution'. He also read extracts from General Bernhardi's book.

The German press, too, had now begun to show an interest in India. On March 6, 1914, the *Berlin Tageblatt* carried a well-informed news report headlined ENGLAND'S INDIAN TROUBLES. This disclosed that there was an organised conspiracy afoot to overthrow British rule from outside the country. The plotters, it told its readers, were mostly based in California, from where they were smuggling arms and explosives into India. This was too much even for the United States authorities who, two weeks later, arrested Har Dayal. The move may have been hastened by the disclosure, during the trial in India of one of Har Dayal's associates, that a proposal had been found, written on the headed paper of the University of California, calling for 'a general massacre of Europeans'.

In a statement issued to the San Francisco newspapers, Har Dayal freely admitted that his life was dedicated to the overthrow of British rule in India, but he denied that he preached assassination or anarchy. He blamed 'the despicable pro-British subservience of the United States' for his arrest, accusing the US authorities of 'licking the boots of England'. After two days in custody, he was released on $1,000 bail, which he promptly skipped, having first handed over the day-to-day running of the *Ghadr* movement to a trusted lieutenant. To explain his disappearance to the American authorities and newspapers, his followers insisted that he had been abducted by British agents. A month later, however, he surfaced in Switzerland, from where he continued to issue directives to his fellow conspirators in California and elsewhere, while keeping his whereabouts secret from all but his closest associates, fearing actual abduction. There he remained, eagerly awaiting the outbreak of what he hoped would be an all-out war between Great Britain and Germany. He did not have to wait long.

The sombre chain of events which led to it hardly needs retelling here. On June 28, 1914, Archduke Franz Ferdinand, heir to the Austro-Hungarian throne, and his wife were shot down by a Serbian student. Urged on by Germany, the Austrians declared war on Serbia, although there was no evidence of any official complicity in the assassination. Next day the Russians, who supported the Serbs, began to mobilize their troops along their frontiers with Germany and Austria-Hungary. The Germans quickly followed suit, and that same day the British government ordered the Royal Navy to sea in readiness for a conflict which now seemed inevitable. Too late,

Kaiser Wilhelm realised with dismay that he had miscalculated. He had staked all on Britain remaining neutral, which would have allowed his armies to crush France before directing their full might against an ill-prepared Russia. One desperate, last-minute attempt by Germany to buy Britain's neutrality was rejected out of hand by the Foreign Secretary, Sir Edward Grey, and within a week Wilhelm found himself at war with Britain, France, Russia and Belgium, and shortly afterwards with Japan.

His bitterness knew no bounds. First and foremost his anger was directed against 'that hated, lying and unscrupulous nation of shopkeepers', the British, and more personally against 'that filthy cur, Grey'. The 'Mad Dog of Europe', as the editorials now called Wilhelm, accused Britain of deliberately plotting with her allies to bring about Germany's downfall. 'So the famous encirclement of Germany', he declared, 'has now finally become an accomplished fact, despite every effort by our politicians to prevent it. The net has been suddenly cast over our head, and England sneeringly reaps the brilliant success of the anti-German world policy which she has persistently pursued and against which we have shown ourselves helpless . . . ' Enraged at seeing his imperial designs thus thwarted, Wilhelm now issued his celebrated order to all German agents and diplomats in the East to unleash the wrath 'of the entire Mohammedan world' against his British cousins.

4

Kaiser Wilhelm's Holy War

There was no shortage of enthusiasts in Berlin for the Kaiser's grand scheme to raise the tribes and peoples of the East against Germany's foes. Foremost among these hawks was Max von Oppenheim, the distinguished oriental scholar, whose idea it almost certainly was in the first place. Some years before the war, while working under diplomatic cover in Cairo, he had prepared for his chiefs in the Foreign Ministry a secret memorandum showing how, in the event of war, militant Islam might be harnessed to the German war machine with what he described as 'incalculable effects'. There is evidence to suggest that it was this which now caught Wilhelm's imagination. Certainly, on the outbreak of war, Oppenheim was summoned immediately to Berlin and told to prepare a plan of precisely how such a campaign of terror might be launched against the Allies, particularly against Britain.

Another powerful champion of a Holy War as a crucial part of German strategy was General Helmuth von Moltke, Chief of the General Staff. It was his celebrated uncle, then Captain Helmuth von Moltke, who seventy years before had first focused attention on the immense opportunities awaiting Germany in the East. The General now urged that 'the fanaticism of Islam' be directed against the British and the Russians by fomenting violent uprisings in India and the Caucasus. The feasibility of such a scheme was endorsed by the renowned Swedish explorer Sven Hedin who, antipathetic to the British and Russians, had placed his formidable experience of the East at Wilhelm's disposal.

Other influential figures in the German Establishment who gave the idea their wholehearted backing included the Prussian steel king, August Thyssen, who dearly wished to see India and its priceless raw materials torn from Britain's grasp. In a bellicose memorandum, penned immediately after war was declared, he urged the permanent annexation of territories rich in the natural resources most needed by German industry. They included the ore- and oil-producing regions of the Caucasus, from where, he argued, 'a fatal blow' could be delivered against India across a compliant Persia. Another influential champion of a German-hatched Holy War was the Professor of Turkish History at Berlin University, Ernst Jackh. An ardent expansionist, he enjoyed the ear and confidence of the Kaiser, whom he greatly encouraged to embark on this grandiose adventure, assuring him that throughout the East the natives were ready to respond to his call.

While some among the military hierarchy had doubts about its prospects of success, the Holy War conspiracy enjoyed the full backing of the Wilhelmstrasse, or Foreign Ministry. In overall charge of planning it, with Oppenheim and Jackh as his advisers, was Arthur Zimmermann, Under-Secretary for Foreign Affairs, later to become Wilhelm's Foreign Minister, who had himself served in the East as a young diplomat. Very soon the project was to become known as the Zimmermann Plan. Another crucial figure in the grand design was the German ambassador to Constantinople, Baron Konrad von Wangenheim. His massive embassy, dominating the Bosphorus skyline and looking eastwards towards Persia, Afghanistan and India, was to become the base from which the Holy War would be launched.

'The big thing', he confided to his American counterpart shortly after the outbreak of war, 'is the Muslim world.' Years later the American ambassador, Henry Morgenthau, recalled: 'Sitting in his office, puffing away at a big black German cigar, he unfolded Germany's scheme to arouse the whole fanatical Muslim world against the Christians.' But first, he told Morgenthau, it would be necessary to bring Turkey – then still neutral – into the war on Germany's side, for only the Sultan had the authority, as the Caliph of Islam, to summon a Holy War. Upon Wangenheim therefore, wrote the American, 'depended the success of the Kaiser's conspiracy for world domination.' His mission was to make absolutely certain that Turkey entered the war as Germany's ally. 'Wangenheim', he added, 'believed that should he succeed in accomplishing this task he would reap the reward which for years had represented his final goal – the Chancellorship of the Empire.'

One of the principal attractions of a Holy War was that it was inexpensive in terms of both manpower and money. A few highly motivated agents, aided by friendly and sympathetic tribesmen, could accomplish what would normally have required several infantry divisions. If it was to achieve its aims, however, it would have to be meticulously planned, something that the Germans were past masters at. Again, suitable leaders would have to be recruited and trained for the unusual task they were to undertake. Work on this was begun at once, so confident was Zimmermann that Wangenheim would succeed in dragging Turkey into the war. What he, but few others, knew was that on August 2, 1914, just two days before Britain and Germany went to war, a secret military alliance had been signed between Wangenheim and the pro-German clique, headed by Enver Pasha, within the Turkish Cabinet. It fell short of an undertaking by Turkey to enter the war on Germany's side, but it was more than half-way there.

The Germans, in fact, had no wish to precipitate Turkey into the war just yet, for the campaign in Europe was still only days old and the Kaiser's generals believed they could win the war fairly swiftly, and would only need the Turks if things went badly wrong. Otherwise Turkey's entry into the war could wait until they had completed their European conquests and were ready to further their ambitions in the East. Nor was Enver in any great haste, since he would need three or four months in which to mobilise his forces and prepare his people for a war which promised to be unpopular. For while the Turks greatly feared Russia's designs on their country – particularly Constantinople and the Straits – few if any harboured ill-feelings towards the British or the French who, after all, had shed blood on their behalf during the Crimean War with Russia. Moreover, those who had had dealings with the Germans found them somewhat overbearing. But then, all of a sudden, something occurred which changed all that, and played straight into the hands of Wangenheim and Enver.

At the time two warships were being built in British ship-yards for the Turkish navy. By far the largest and most modern vessels in the Turkish fleet, these had been paid for largely by public subscription following a nationwide appeal. Officials at every level throughout the Ottoman Empire had accepted a cut in salary to help pay for what were to have been the pride of the Turkish navy and – more important – a counterbalance to Russia's Black Sea fleet. Already Turkish crews were on their way to Britain to pick them up, while in Constantinople a special Navy Week had been declared to welcome the new vessels as they steamed through the Straits and up the Bosphorus. Then suddenly Winston Churchill, First Lord of the Admiralty, announced that the two Turkish warships had been commandeered for use by the Royal Navy. Ironically, the announcement was made on the very day that the Germans and Turks signed their secret alliance. Although London as yet had no inkling of this clandestine accord, it would in fact have more than justified Churchill's decision.

When news reached Turkey that the warships were not coming, there was both disappointment and fury. Thousands of schoolchildren who had contributed their pocket-money to the vessels' purchase marched in protest against the British government's action. Although the Turks were offered full compensation, and Britain was subsequently vindicated by the disclosure of the secret alliance, Anglo-Turkish relations plunged to an all-time low. The effect on Turkish public opinion was an unexpected stroke of luck for Enver and the pro-German faction within the Cabinet. Had ordinary Turks learned of the secret treaty with Germany at that moment, they would no doubt have welcomed it. With Turkish indignation thus at its height, Enver and his German co-conspirators proceeded to play their trump card.

One week after Churchill's seizure of the two Turkish warships, two German cruisers – the *Goeben* and the *Breslau* – sought refuge in the Bosphorus following a desperate chase by a far stronger British force. The British, whose warships were anchored just outside Turkish waters, protested to the Turkish government, then still officially neutral. They demanded that either the vessels and their crews should be interned, as required under international law, or that they should be ordered out of neutral waters to face the Royal Navy. The Turks' answer was dumbfounding. The two German cruisers, they announced, had been purchased by the government to replace the two British-built warships that Churchill had expropriated. They were immediately given new Turkish names, while their German crews donned Turkish naval uniforms, including fezzes.

But this was merely the start of a succession of events which were to end with the Turks being dragged reluctantly into the war. With the campaign in Europe no longer going quite as well as the Kaiser's generals had confidently forecast, Berlin felt that it was now time to play the Eastern card. However, there were still powerful members of the Turkish Cabinet who wished their country to remain neutral. Wangenheim and Enver, both of whom were impatient to bring Turkey in on Germany's side, could see that something drastic must be done to force the hand of the moderates, who, if anything, were gaining support.

On October 27, two and a half months after the outbreak of war, the *Goeben* and the *Breslau*, now renamed the *Sultan Selim* and the *Medilli*, sailed into the Black Sea under sealed orders with other warships of the Sultan's navy. They made straight for the great Russian port of Odessa and, without any prior declaration of war, began to bombard it. A number of vessels, including a Russian cruiser, were sunk, and oil tanks set on fire. After shelling neighbouring Russian ports, the Turkish warships, which were commanded by a German admiral in the Sultan's employ, returned to their base on the Bosphorus. Moderate members of the Turkish Cabinet were aghast at what had been done in their name, and four resigned. Enver, who had engineered the whole affair, claimed that the Russians had been the first to fire, although everyone knew this to be untrue. Enver was called upon to apologise to the Russians. But it was already too late, for by now Russia had declared war on Turkey and the ambassador was hurriedly packing his bags. Moreover, as a result of the Cabinet resignations, the pro-German clique had gained total control of the country's destiny, with Enver as its undisputed dictator.

On October 30, the British and French ambassadors asked for their passports and advised their own nationals to leave, war with Turkey now being seen as inevitable. Two days later, after destroying those sensitive papers that they could not take with them, they themselves left Constantinople on a train laid on specially, which would take them home via European powers then still neutral. There were chaotic scenes at Sirkeci railway station, eastern terminus of the Orient Express, as foreign residents tried to leave. For there were ugly rumours, quite unfounded, of massacres of infidels being planned. Ambassador Morgenthau, now in charge of British and French interests, was at the station to help with the evacuation and to see his colleagues off. 'It was a surging mass of excited and frightened people,' he wrote afterwards. 'The police were there in full force, pushing the crowds back. It was an indescribable mixture of soldiers, gendarmes, diplomats, baggage and Turkish functionaries.' Tempers flared, hats were knocked off and clothing torn. He saw the British ambassador, Sir Louis Mallet, 'involved in a set-to with an officious Turk – the Englishman winning first honours easily', and also spotted the French ambassador 'vigorously shaking a Turkish policeman'.

But not all Turks were glad to see the ambassadors go. Far from sharing Enver's blind admiration for all things German, many were filled with foreboding about the future. They included the Grand Vizier himself, who was known to be strongly opposed to Turkey entering the war, especially on the side of Germany. Before leaving for the railway station, Sir Louis Mallet had driven to his office overlooking the Golden Horn to bid him farewell. Nominally the country's most powerful figure after the Sultan, he was now, like his master, little more than a figurehead, kept there by Enver to give his regime a spurious respectability. Weeping unashamedly, he begged Mallet not to abandon him and those still opposed to Enver's schemes. '*Ne me lachez pas!*' he sobbed in despair. But there was no turning back now. Four days later Britain and Turkey were at war.

*   *   *

Three weeks after Turkey joined the ranks of the belligerents, the Holy War against Britain and her allies was formally declared by the Sultan. Whatever his personal feelings, he was given little choice in the matter, for he was a virtual prisoner of Turkey's new wartime rulers. To Enver it marked the beginning of the realisation of his dream of an empire of Turkish-speaking peoples, ruled by himself, stretching from Constantinople to the very frontiers of China. The proclamation was read out at a solemn ceremony in Constantinople by the Shaikh-ul-Islam, the highest religious authority in the land after the Sultan-Caliph himself. This he did before the great mosque of Mehmet the Conqueror, named after the brilliant Ottoman chieftain who had seized the city from its Christian rulers four centuries before. In his summons to Muslims everywhere to join the Holy War, he ordered them to rise as one and smite their infidel oppressors wherever they could be found. The following day the Sultan's incendiary call was read out aloud in every mosque, and printed in every newspaper, throughout the Ottoman Empire.

But it was among the millions of Muslims living under British and Russian rule that Berlin and Constantinople wanted word of the Sultan's *fatwa* spread. For it was there, under the banner of the Holy War, that they planned to foment violent revolutionary uprisings, and persuade Muslim units of the British and Russian armies to refuse to fight against Turkey or its German ally. Thousands of leaflets were therefore run off the presses of Constantinople for smuggling into India and Egypt, the Caucasus and Central Asia, and other Muslim lands. One of these fell into the hands of Ambassador Morgenthau. It was written in Arabic, the universal language of the Koran, so that it could be read and understood by mullahs and imams everywhere, and passed on to their congregations. Its style, Morgenthau noted, was frenzied and its message one of racial and religious hatred. It contained what the American, a lawyer by training, described as 'a detailed plan . . . for the assassination and extermination of all Christians – except for those of German nationality.'

In *Secrets of the Bosphorus*, his vividly written memoir of wartime Constantinople, Morgenthau quotes extensively from the tract. One passage orders Muslims: 'Know ye that the blood of infidels in the Islamic lands may be shed with impunity – except those to whom the Muslim power has promised security and are allied with it.' Another decrees: 'Take them and kill them whenever you find them. He who kills even one unbeliever among those who rule over us, whether he does it secretly or openly, shall be rewarded by God. And let every Muslim, in whatever part of the world he may be, swear a solemn oath to kill at least three or four of the infidels who rule over him, for they are the enemies of God and of the Faith. A Muslim who does this shall be saved from the terrors of the Day of Judgement.' It was clear, Morgenthau observed, 'that a German hand had exercised an editorial supervision'. For it was repeatedly emphasised that only those Christians 'who rule over us' were to be killed, and not those who had 'a covenant' with the Muslim peoples. This call to massacre innocent men, women and children, he reported, was being 'distributed stealthily' throughout the Muslim world, including British India and Egypt.

Such then was 'the big thing' that Wangenheim had spoken of some weeks earlier, and it was apparent to Morgenthau that his German colleague was closely involved in it. When Morgenthau remonstrated with him over 'the dangers of spreading such incendiary literature among a wildly fanatical people', Wangenheim tried to argue that the Holy War was really 'a great peace offensive' intended to bring the war to a swift conclusion. It had been a grave error, he conceded, to allow Britain to be drawn into the war. If uprisings could be fomented in India, Egypt and other British possessions, then the British Empire would be forced to withdraw from the conflict. 'Even if British Mohammedans refused to rise,' wrote Morgenthau, 'Wangenheim believed that the mere threat of such an uprising would induce England to abandon Belgium and France to their fate.' When Morgenthau protested to Enver in person that mobs were already attacking Christian-owned shops and other establishments in the capital, the Turkish dictator insisted that it was 'all a mistake', and that no harm would befall anyone in the capital.

Meanwhile, however, determined efforts were being made elsewhere in the Muslim world to spread the Holy War. 'Missions were dispatched to reinforce the cold appeal of print,' wrote the Arab historian George Antonius. 'Emissaries of all kinds – itinerant preachers, scholars, learned divines, professional agitators and German orientalists – travelled in all directions open to them, while a few succeeded in insinuating themselves into Egypt, the Sudan and other parts of Africa which were under Allied rule.' Their orders were to win over to the Holy War the non-Turkish Muslim peoples, especially the Arabs, of these regions. The story of how this backfired on them, leading to the Arab Revolt against Turkish rule, has been told many times before, most graphically by T. E. Lawrence, but also by Antonius himself in his classic account of those stirring times, *The Arab Awakening*. Here we are only concerned with those who set out from Constantinople to carry the banner of the Holy War eastwards into Persia, Afghanistan, the Caucasus and Central Asia, and finally – or so they hoped – into British India itself.

Although the plan to launch a Holy War was first and foremost Kaiser Wilhelm's, Enver Pasha too had been quick to see its merits as a means of fulfilling his own dreams. It was his suggestion, weeks before Turkey entered the war, that Berlin should send a carefully chosen team of officers to take part in a secret joint Turco-German mission whose objective would be to bring both Persia and Afghanistan into the war. Escorted by hand-picked Turkish troops, the expedition would cross into Persia the moment the Holy War was declared. Such was the Persians' dislike of both the British and the Russians, Enver reasoned, that Teheran might well join the Holy War against them, or at least turn a blind eye to the mission's presence on their neutral soil. On reaching Kabul, the mission's task would be to persuade the Emir of Afghanistan to join the sacred cause and order his troops and wild tribesmen through the passes into British India. So hostile were the Afghans towards the infidel British, Enver's spies in Kabul assured him, that the Emir would require little coercion. At the same time, preceded by Turkish agents, an Ottoman army would invade the Caucasus, rallying Muslims there to the Holy War and driving out the Russians, before advancing into Central Asia to liberate their Turkic cousins there. Just how these various territories would be shared out between Constantinople and Berlin remained to be worked out afterwards.

The Germans had begun to recruit their team for the joint Afghan mission in the autumn of 1914, two months before

Turkey came into the war and the Holy War was proclaimed. Among the first to be chosen was Wilhelm Wassmuss, a pre-war career diplomat in his mid-thirties, with several years' experience of the East. Although officially German consul at Bushire in the Persian Gulf, the British had little doubt that he was really an intelligence officer, there to further Kaiser Wilhelm's expansionist ambitions. A striking-looking man, who spoke fluent Persian and Arabic, he had travelled widely among the tribes of southern Persia, with some of whose chiefs he was on the closest terms. Physically tough, and capable of being ruthless, his credentials for fomenting trouble could hardly have been bettered. Wassmuss was chosen by Zimmermann and Oppenheim to lead the German contingent, and to handle the diplomatic aspects of its dealings with the Afghans.

To be second in command of the party they picked Captain Oskar von Niedermayer, a regular officer, who had travelled widely in Persia, Baluchistan and India, almost certainly on behalf of German military intelligence. Extremely tough, ruthless and resourceful, he was, in the words of one contemporary, 'the kind of man who made the German army almost invincible'. Niedermayer, who thirsted for adventure in remote places, required no second bidding when summoned to Berlin from the Western Front where he was serving as an infantry officer. He was to be in charge of all military aspects of the mission. Together the two men made a formidable combination for the difficult and hazardous task they were to undertake. They were to be Germany's 'Lawrences' – or, as one British officer christened them, 'Angels of Darkness', for their orders were to spread violence and disorder under the banner of the Holy War, and turn the peoples of the East against the British and their allies.

The officers and NCOs chosen to accompany them were mostly those possessing special skills, or men with first-hand experience of the harsh climate and terrain to which they would be exposed in Persia and Afghanistan. Often this had been acquired in the sweltering interior of Germany's African colonies. Berlin at this time having little or no experience of political or irregular warfare, some of the early recruits, especially those who had served in Africa, were to prove highly unsuitable, leading to their replacement. The total number of individuals finally selected for the mission is therefore somewhat uncertain, although from diaries and other captured documents British intelligence officers identified eighty-four names. This does not include the three Indian revolutionaries, sympathetic tribesmen and Persian mercenaries who were subsequently to swell the expedition's ranks. Nor does it include individual German soldiers who joined them after escaping into Persia and Afghanistan from Russian prisoner-of-war camps in Central Asia.

By now it was time for the party to begin to make its way to Constantinople, headquarters of the Holy War. However, such a large body of fit-looking men of military age and soldierly bearing could hardly fail to attract the attention of British spies as they passed through neutral Romania, let alone that of the Romanian authorities. To avoid the risk of the entire mission being interned, it was decided that they should pose as a travelling circus company. The party's baggage and equipment were labelled accordingly, their tall metal wireless aerials, for communicating with Wangenheim in Constantinople, being described on the waybill as 'tent-poles'.

Despite all this subterfuge, though, whispers of what Berlin and Constantinople had in store for British India began to reach the ears of the authorities there. News of the Sultan-Caliph's call for a Holy War, while not entirely unexpected, had already caused considerable alarm in Delhi. As the most populous Muslim country on earth, British India would clearly be the principal target of the Turco-German conspirators. With Afghanistan ticking away like a time-bomb to the north, a campaign of assassination and terrorism in their midst, and India's own troops urgently needed on other fronts, the British felt increasingly vulnerable. The crucial question was how the country's seventy million Muslims would respond to the Sultan's summons. It was not one, moreover, to which anyone had an answer. For not since the great Arab invasions of the seventh century had a Holy War been launched on such a scale, and never before against a modern European power. 'There is no disguising the fact', the Viceroy, Lord Hardinge, wrote to a friend, 'that our position in India is a bit of a gamble at the present moment.'

But there was worse to come. News now reached Delhi that a small armada of vessels carrying Sikh revolutionaries had set sail from San Francisco, and was at that very moment heading across the Pacific towards India.

5

The Great Indian Conspiracy

Ostensibly the Sikhs were emigrants hurrying home on the outbreak of war – which, as subjects of the King-Emperor, they were fully entitled to do. But the real reason for their sudden return was quite different, as Sir Charles Cleveland, now head of wartime intelligence for India, was perfectly aware. And it was certainly not to offer their loyal services to the Crown. The men, Cleveland knew, were members of Har Dayal's secret revolutionary army, which had sworn to drive the British out of India. Once back in their homeland they planned to melt away until the moment was ripe. Then, on a given signal, they would emerge and stage a violent uprising, using smuggled German-supplied arms and taking the British by surprise.

Much of Cleveland's intelligence on their plans had been fed to him by William Hopkinson, the former Indian Police officer sent to California to penetrate the movement's head-quarters there. But this source had abruptly ceased when Hopkinson was shot dead by a Sikh extremist who had discovered what he was up to. Careful scrutiny, however, of intercepted copies of *Ghadr*, the movement's secret newspaper, showed Cleveland what was being planned. 'KILL ALL ENGLISHMEN!' screamed one headline. Another told all, though, declaring: 'WANTED – HEROIC SOLDIERS FOR SPREADING REVOLUTION. SALARY – DEATH. REWARD – MARTYRDOM. BATTLEFIELD – INDIA.'

Clearly the arrival of shiploads of revolutionary Sikhs called for very careful handling by the authorities, lest an already highly charged atmosphere be exacerbated, and the goodwill and loyalty of the majority of other Indians be lost. A new emergency ordinance was therefore rushed through giving the government special wartime powers for dealing with the sudden influx of emigrants returning from overseas. This allowed the authorities to restrict the movements of anyone deemed to represent a threat. At the same time Cleveland issued a secret instruction to immigration officers at all Indian ports. 'Every Indian returning from America or Canada,' he warned, 'whether labourer, artisan or student, must be regarded as a probable active revolutionary, or at any rate as a sympathiser with the revolutionary party.' He also warned them that some *Ghadr* activists were breaking their journey at Singapore and continuing to India by other vessels in the hope of thereby avoiding suspicion.

Not all of the returning Sikhs were from the United States or Canada. Some vessels were stopping off in Shanghai, Hong Kong and elsewhere in the Far East, where they picked up men recruited from the Indian communities there by Har Dayal's agents. By December 1, 1914, according to Cleveland, around 1,000 overseas Sikhs had reached India. This, he forecast, was only the beginning. 'It is impossible to disregard the effect on these ignorant emigrants of the false German news so sedulously circulated throughout the world,' he declared. 'There is therefore every reason to suppose that those who are now returning represent but the advanced guard of a large army.' Events were to prove him right. In all, during the following months, about 8,000 Sikhs returned from overseas to India and made their way to their ancient homeland in the Punjab.

From the start, such was their fervour for the cause, the Sikhs had great difficulty in maintaining secrecy over their intentions. As early as August 7, under the headline HINDUS GO HOME TO FIGHT IN REVOLUTION, one Pacific coast American newspaper had reported that large numbers of Sikhs were about to sail for India from San Francisco 'where, it is said, a vessel has been chartered to aid in a revolution which is expected to break out in India as a result of England being occupied in the European war.' Another report reaching Cleveland, this time from Hawaii, quoted a party of Sikhs passing through there on a vessel bound for India as boasting that plans for an uprising had been completed, and that it would take place in October. Before embarking on their vessels, the Sikhs were divided into small revolutionary units, each with its own leader. They were told: 'Your duty is clear. Go to India and stir up rebellion in every corner of the country. Rob the wealthy and show mercy to the poor. In this way you will win universal sympathy. Arms will be provided for you on your arrival in India. Failing this you must ransack police stations for rifles.' What weapons *Ghadr* agents had managed to obtain in the United States, mainly revolvers, were distributed among the Sikhs, while others were purchased at ports on the way.

Thanks to such early warnings, together with more detailed intelligence gleaned by Hopkinson before his murder, the authorities had been able to make careful preparations for receiving the influx of Sikhs. As each vessel arrived, the passengers found themselves confronted by teams of British immigration officers armed not only with Cleveland's warning, but also with the names and descriptions of many of the *Ghadr* leaders. Every new arrival was interviewed and a decision made as to how dangerous he was considered to be. Those judged to be a serious threat were immediately interned and held in custody pending prosecution. Some 400, in all, of the 8,000 returning Sikhs were thus locked up. Those regarded as rather less dangerous, but still in need of careful surveillance, were ordered to be confined to their villages, headmen and local police being given the task of ensuring that this was observed. Approximately 2,500 were so restricted. The rest were allowed to return to their villages after being cautioned to be of good behaviour, the local authorities being alerted to their presence and being ordered to keep an eye on them.

Nonetheless, despite this elaborate screening process, some of the most dangerous of the revolutionaries managed to escape detection, while some had returned home before it had been set up. They immediately began to make contact with disaffected elements among the Sikh community, as well as with other revolutionaries elsewhere in India. A wave of violence, which was to last for months, now gripped the Punjab.

'There was a constant series of explosions,' wrote Sir Michael O'Dwyer, the Governor, later. 'All over the Punjab police were murdered; loyal citizens, especially Sikhs known to be assisting the authorities, were shot down or killed by bombs.' Armed robberies, often on the homes and businesses of wealthy Hindus, were carried out to raise funds for the revolutionary cause. Secret bomb-making factories were set up, and persistent efforts made to win over Sikh troops serving in the Indian Army – 'not in all cases', O'Dwyer observed, 'without success.'

The revolutionaries' greatest headache was their desperate lack of arms. They had been led to believe that ample supplies of weapons would be awaiting them on arrival. Where these were supposed to come from, no one really seemed to know, although many of the Sikhs believed that the Germans had promised to supply them. Indeed, there is some evidence to suggest that this may have been Berlin's intention, for large quantities of arms and ammunition were found aboard a German vessel due to sail for the East, which the Italian authorities had interned on the outbreak of war. According to Reuters, the *Bayern* was carrying 'half a million revolvers, a hundred thousand rifles, two hundred thousand cases of ammunition and two complete wireless stations', to mention just part of the ship's arsenal. The very high ratio of revolvers to other weapons suggested to British military experts in India that the arms were on their way, not to a conventional force, but to a major revolutionary movement of some kind. If so, India seemed the most likely choice. Others, including the authors of an official government report on the affair, thought that promises that arms would be awaiting the returning Sikhs were merely 'a fabrication to hearten the *Ghadr* partisans' and to rally those who might be wavering.

The truth will almost certainly never be known, but the Sikhs' failure to find the expected arms, and the arrest by the British of many of their leaders, were not the only disappointments the revolutionaries had faced on arrival in India. They had been assured in San Francisco that the whole of India was in a state of frenzied unrest which, under their leadership, could be transformed into a violent uprising. They were the torch which would ignite the mighty conflagration of the

Indian revolution, bringing British rule to a bloody end. But
that was not what they had found. While few, if any, Indians
loved the British, many had prospered greatly in the compara-
tive stability which the European invaders had brought to
their unruly land. The rest, for the most part, were content to
go along with things as they were. Indeed, the revolutionaries
quickly discovered that many of their fellow Sikhs were prepared to inform on them to the British, while some village
headmen did not hesitate to hand them over to the police.
Furthermore, there was no convenient frontier near at hand
across which they could withdraw between operations, nor a
sympathetic government within easy reach which was willing
to give them assistance. However, this did not dampen their
ardour, even though their campaign of violence so far fell a
long way short of the general uprising they had planned to
unleash. They were still determined to wage war to the death
against the might of the British Raj, and create the utopia
which Har Dayal in San Francisco had promised them.

It was around this time, in December 1914, that the *Ghadr*
leaders in the Punjab managed to make contact with Hindu
fellow revolutionaries in Bengal, more than a thousand miles
to the south-east. The Bengalis had a tradition of violent
resistance to the British, and a wealth of experience in terrorist tactics. One of their foremost revolutionaries, Rash Behari
Bose, who was high on the British list of wanted terrorists,
promised the Sikhs Bengali co-operation, and proposed that
they plan a simultaneous uprising. Cleveland soon became
aware of this liaison, reporting tersely that 'the alliance
between Bengal and Punjab anarchy is complete'. However,
his agents and informers had been unable as yet to discover
what the conspirators were up to.

At a secret meeting in Lahore on February 12, the plotters
finalised their master-plan. It was wholly dependent for its
success upon the co-operation of certain disaffected units of
the Indian Army. For some time now *Ghadr* agitators had
been spreading disturbing rumours through the barracks and
lines of Indian regiments. There were tales of German invincibility, whispers that Sikh troops were being made to have
their long hair cut, and that Indian units were being positioned in front of British ones on the Western Front.

Soundings made among certain units stationed at Lahore, Rawalpindi, Peshawar, Meerut and Benares suggested that men there were ready to join the revolutionaries at a given signal. The mutinous troops would murder their British officers and other government officials, seize armouries and magazines, storm jails in which political prisoners were being held, loot treasuries and banks, and join forces with the *Ghadr* leaders in destroying all traces of European rule.

Declarations of independence were prepared. Flags were made consisting of three colours – red for the Hindus, yellow for the Sikhs and green for the Muslims. This was to be the new national flag of a free and united republican India. It was distributed among those chosen to lead the various *Ghadr* groups into action on the day of the uprising. Their battle-cry was to be '*Maro Ferangi Ko*', or 'Kill the English'. The plot, whose tentacles stretched from the Punjab to Dacca, the capital of East Bengal, 'was not fantastic', in the opinion of O'Dwyer. It was to take place at night, and the first move would be to cut all telegraph lines along which warnings could be sent to other garrisons. There still being no sign of the arms and other assistance they had been hoping for from Germany, the conspirators fixed February 21 as the day when Indians would rise against their oppressors, from one end of the country to the other.

* * *

Meanwhile, as the plotters made their final preparations, momentous events had been taking place elsewhere in the world, which had resulted in major setbacks for both the Germans and their Turkish allies. On the Western Front, the initial German thrust, which the Kaiser and his generals expected to bring about the collapse of France, had been halted and pushed back. Instead of then moving triumphantly into Russia, the Germans found themselves stuck fast for the next three years, amid mounting casualties, on a static front where neither side advanced for more than a few miles. Furthermore, in the first two months of the war they had lost two of their Pacific colonies, Samoa and New Guinea, to Australian and New Zealand troops. This was quickly followed by the seizure of Tsingtao, on the China coast, by the

Japanese, and of Togoland, in West Africa, by the British and French. As the war proceeded, what remained of Germany's pre-war colonial empire was wrested from it by the Allies, bit by bit.

During the first few months of the war, the Turks too suffered two severe blows. Both involved the Holy War which the Sultan had proclaimed only shortly before. The first blow, in January 1915, was struck by the Russians. It had long been the dream of Enver Pasha, now Turkey's military supremo, to recover from Tsarist Russia the lost Ottoman provinces in the Caucasus. When he had done that, and liberated the Turkish peoples there, he planned to march eastwards into Tsarist Central Asia and carve out a great new Muslim empire. Nor did his ambitions end there. To the south-east, with its vast Muslim population, sprawled British India. Like his ally Kaiser Wilhelm, he had a hankering for that too. But the first step was to expel the Russians from the Caucasus, and what better time than now when they were being hard-pressed by the Germans on the Eastern Front. Enver, who believed himself to be a great strategist and commander, was determined to lead his troops in person as they embarked on their crusade against the infidel Russians. While dubious of his chances of success, the Germans strongly encouraged Enver, for his grandiose plan promised to divert Russian units to the Caucasus, thus relieving the pressure on themselves on the Eastern Front. Early in January, leaving the conduct of the war in the hands of his senior staff and German advisers, Enver left Constantinople by the Black Sea for Trebizond, and from there travelled overland to Erzerum, headquarters of the Turkish Third Army, which was to be used in the operation.

Eastern Turkey and the Caucasus were by now in the harsh grip of winter, with the temperature plunging to minus thirty degrees on the bare mountainsides and the passes blocked by snow. What tracks there were had entirely disappeared. As the weather worsened, the fighting along the frontier between Turkish and Russian troops had ground to a halt, with honours roughly even. Both sides had now dug in for the long winter ahead, survival against the elements being the troops' principal concern. The Turkish commander, whom Enver himself had appointed, listened in dismay as his chief outlined his ambitious plans. 'The Russian army must be annihilated now,' Enver declared. 'You must go into action at once.' The Turkish general, an able and experienced soldier who had once taught Enver at staff college, tried arguing with him. 'Wait until the worst of the winter is over and the roads are passable again,' he urged. 'Then I will destroy the Russians and liberate the Caucasus. To attempt it now would be suicidal.' Furious at such criticism by a subordinate, Enver ordered the general to be relieved of his command, storming at him: 'Had you not been my teacher, I would have had you shot.' Instead, he was retired, and Enver personally took over command of the Turkish Third Army. This he renamed 'The Army of Islam', to reflect the momentous role he intended it to play in the Holy War and, ultimately, in redrawing the map of Asia.

Enver, who had never commanded a regiment, let alone a corps or army, in his life, had 90,000 troops at his disposal. The Russian commander had only 60,000, but he had a railway on which he could bring up food, ammunition and reinforcements. Many of the Turkish troops were pitifully equipped for winter warfare. Some even came from the hot plains to the south, possessing only light summer uniforms, thin Arab head-dresses and tattered leather sandals. Few had any idea of what they were fighting for, although they were to show extraordinary courage and endurance, and unquestioning obedience, in the grim struggle ahead. The Russians, for their part, wore long coats and felt boots, and great fur hats which, when covered with snow, made them look like giants.

The precise details of Enver's plan of attack are too complex to go into here, for they involved the separate movements of the three army corps making up the Third Army. Ultimately, however, their success depended on a forced march by 25,000 troops along a secret mountain track to the small Russian garrison town of Sarikamish, today a modest ski resort. If Sarikamish fell, Enver reasoned, then the entire Russian front would collapse, and the Muslim tribes of the Caucasus would rise and join forces with their Turkish liberators. After that would follow Transcaspia, Turkestan and, finally, India. Everything, therefore, depended on the coming battle for Sarikamish, now in the grip of the cruel Anatolian winter.

At first it seemed as though Enver's ambitious plans were working. The advance of the Russians towards Erzerum had been halted, and their forces were being driven back on Sarikamish. Behind them their lines of supply, and indeed of retreat, were becoming increasingly threatened by Turkish flanking movements. In fact, so hopeless did the Russian position appear that a general retreat was all but ordered as the only way of saving the entire force from encirclement and annihilation. However, things were also far from well with the Turks as they struggled through blizzards and snow, sometimes five or six feet deep, to win the objectives set them by Enver and his staff, some of whom were Germans. The casualties from the cold were appalling, reducing some units from 1,000 men to 100 or less. Weakened by hunger, and ill-protected against the sub-zero temperatures, the normally hardy and stoical Turks succumbed to frostbite on a horrifying scale. 'They gave themselves up to the sweetest death they knew,' wrote one Turkish officer. 'Curling themselves round the base of a pine tree, they froze to death.' Others were driven insane by pain, hunger and despair before dying. The rest just kept going.

On Christmas Day it still seemed, despite their casualties, as though the Turks might win through as they closed in over the mountains on the small town of Sarikamish. The Russians, for all their superior clothing, had also suffered cruelly from the cold, official figures putting at 7,000 the number of soldiers who had frozen to death. The following day, moreover, the Turks managed to blow up the railway line which had been bringing up reinforcements, food and ammunition to the beleaguered garrison. Russian morale in the town sank even lower when captured documents revealed that 25,000 Turkish troops were at that very moment making their way across a little-known mountain track to attack them, while another large Turkish force was moving into position to cut off their line of retreat. The destruction of their lifeline, the rail link with Kars and Tiflis, appeared to confirm the truth of such fears. By now news of the impending disaster had reached Tiflis, capital and military headquarters of the Caucasus, and panic-stricken crowds were besieging the railway station there in the hope of escaping the coming Turkish massacres.

What the Russians did not then know was that catastrophe
had befallen the Turks. Of the 25,000 men who had set out
along the mountain track, only 10,000 were still alive. The rest
had frozen to death. Nor had the force sent to cut off the
Russian rear fared much better, losing 7,000 men, more than a
third of its strength. There were several reasons for these
appalling losses. First, in addition to his total lack of experience as an army commander, Enver knew nothing of the
treacherous eastern Turkish winter and the grim consequences if ill-protected troops, however stoical or brave, were
sent to fight there. Second, he and his staff were working from
highly unreliable maps, which often made distances appear far
shorter than they really were. In one instance a fifteen-mile
march, expected to take five hours, turned out to be almost
twice as long. In the event it took the Turks, hungry and
exhausted, a nightmarish nineteen hours, and cost several
thousand lives. To enable them to travel fast through the
mountains towards Sarikamish, Enver had ordered that the
troops travel light. 'Our supply base', he declared, 'is in front
of us.' Although there were no trees on the bare, snow-bound
heights which the men could cut down and burn, incredibly
they were provided with no fuel to carry to keep them warm,
or even alive, during the long and bitter nights. According to
Russian reports, if they are to be believed, some Turkish units
were even ordered to leave their greatcoats and haversacks
behind in order to speed their passage. Finally, just as the
Turks set out across the mountains, it began to snow heavily.
Very soon this had turned into a howling blizzard, effectively
sealing the fate of Enver's Army of Islam.

All this time, until the Turks cut the railway, reinforcements had been reaching the Russian garrison at Sarikamish,
where by now the defenders totalled nearly 14,000 men, mainly infantry. They also had more than thirty field-guns,
although the Turks believed them to have none. Moreover,
the route through the mountains, which Enver thought to be
secret, was clearly marked on Russian staff maps, although it
was not considered suitable for large bodies of troops.
However, thanks to the captured Turkish documents, the
Russian commander had been alerted to the enemy's approach
along it. He was also prepared for an attack from the east by

the Turkish force which had been sent to cut off his retreat, and positioned his men and artillery in readiness to face either or both threats. Not knowing of the devastation wrought among the Turkish troops by the cold, the Russians assumed that the attackers would total in all 45,000, not to mention artillery, with others in reserve.

The Turks attacked on the morning of December 29, advancing on Sarikamish, as the Russians had anticipated, from two directions. The weary, hungry Turks had not been expecting artillery, and the thrust from the east was finally thrown back by Cossack cavalry. At the same time those who had survived the terrible journey through the mountains from the north-west tried to fight their way down through the deep snow to the Russian positions around the town. By this time their numbers had dwindled to just 6,000 men, and they were driven back up the treacherous slopes by the now more numerous defenders, who were well-fed, well-clothed and well-rested, unlike their ragged, starving and frozen attackers. That night, on Enver's orders, the Turks tried once more to fight their way into Sarikamish. Showing extraordinary determination and courage, this time they succeeded, though not for long. Fierce hand-to-hand fighting took place in the darkness, and the streets of the small town were soon littered with dead. At one time the Turks managed to occupy a barracks on the far side of the town, but they were finally driven out by heavy shelling at point-blank range. This was the closest that they were to get to taking Sarikamish.

It was clear even to Enver that his plan had failed, although fighting was to continue for several days in the surrounding mountains before finally petering out in the face of appalling conditions. The Turkish losses were horrifying. Out of the 90,000 men originally under Enver's command, only 15,000 survived. The corpses of the rest littered the passes and the snowfields, where they were devoured by the packs of wolves which roam the mountains of eastern Turkey. 'Badly led and ill equipped,' wrote John Buchan in his history of the war, 'the starving Turkish levies had fought like heroes, and their sufferings were among the most terrible of the war.' Leaving his commanders to clear up the mess, Enver himself hastily returned to Constantinople. There he made every possible effort to conceal the truth, and anyone who spoke of it risked execution. On the night of his return to the capital, with the blood of 75,000 of his countrymen still fresh on his hands, he even went to a concert. 'He seemed perfectly happy,' noted one neutral diplomat who was present.

Kemal Ataturk, the future leader of Turkey, then a young colonel, recalled meeting Enver shortly after his return from Sarikamish. He noticed that he looked pale and thin.

'You must be tired,' he said.

'No, not particularly,' Enver replied.

'What happened?'

'We fought, that's all . . . '

'What's the position now?'

'Very good . . . '

Not wishing to embarrass his superior, Ataturk decided not to pursue the subject further.

But the War Minister's loss of an entire army was not the only blow to befall the Turks during the first few months of hostilities. Within a month of his hasty departure from the bloodied snows of the East, Turkey had suffered a second major reverse as another member of its ruling triumvirate tried his hand at higher strategy – this, too, under the banner of the Holy War.

*　　*　　*

At around the same time that Enver had left Constantinople vowing to drive the infidel Russians from the Caucasus, Djemal Pasha, second only to him in the military hierarchy, was embarking on a similarly ambitious plan to expel the infidel British from another ex-Ottoman territory, Egypt. As he left the capital for Damascus, which was to be his headquarters, he swore to those who saw him off: 'I shall not return to Constantinople until I have conquered Egypt.' He was on his way south to take command of the Turkish Fourth Army, then stationed in Syria, which was to be used to liberate the Egyptians from British rule. A man greedy for power, Djemal planned to carve out for himself a private empire in the Middle East, with Egypt at its heart, just as Enver hoped to do in Central Asia. And just as Enver had reasoned that the Muslims in the Caucasus and beyond would rise to the banner of the Holy War on the approach of a Turkish army, Djemal and his advisers believed that the Egyptian masses would turn in fury on the British when liberation seemed near at hand.

Djemal's first objective was the Suez Canal. If he could seize that, not only would the Egyptians almost certainly rise against their oppressors in every town and village in the country, but Britain's short cut to India and the Far East would be lost to her, preventing her from rushing reinforcements to India when the uprising there took place. Although it happened to coincide nicely with Djemal's own ambitions, the Egyptian crusade officially still formed a crucial part of the Turco-German strategy for bringing down the British and Russian empires in the East – just as Enver's Caucasian crusade had. At least that is what Arthur Zimmermann of the German Foreign Ministry in Berlin, who had masterminded with Max von Oppenheim the Holy War strategy, believed. On the question of Egypt, however, there were some dissenting voices. One of them was Baron Wangenheim, the German ambassador in Constantinople.

While glad to see the Suez Canal seized, or at least blocked, Wangenheim had begun to change his mind over the question of Egypt itself. He revealed his devious thoughts to Henry Morgenthau, his American opposite number, to whom he confided more perhaps than was wise. At first Morgenthau had misunderstood what he was suggesting. 'Naturally', the American recalled later, 'I thought that Wangenheim was worried that Turkey would lose, yet he confided to me that his real fear was that their ally would succeed.' The truth was that he did not want Egypt to fall into Turkish hands, since once there it would be extremely difficult to retrieve. He believed that very soon the warring powers would be forced to come to the negotiating table, with the United States presiding, and some pretty ruthless bargaining ensuing. 'Should Turkey conquer Egypt,' he explained to Morgenthau, 'naturally she would insist at the peace table on retaining this great province, and would expect Germany to support her in this claim.' By then, however, Germany would have no interest in promoting the re-establishment of the Ottoman Empire – rather the reverse. Were Egypt still in Britain's hands, Germany would agree to her keeping it in return for Mesopotamia, that vital link in the Berlin-to-Baghdad masterplan. But as things turned out Wangenheim need not have lost any sleep over Egypt.

Djemal launched his attack on the Suez Canal at first light on February 3, 1915. His force consisted of 25,000 troops, including a company of whirling dervishes in tall conical hats who had been added to give the expedition an odour of sanctity, and the men a feeling of invincibility. With the help of 14,000 camels, and travelling by night, the Turks dragged their guns, and their pontoons for the crossing, across 130 miles of desert to reach the canal – a considerable feat, in the view of strategists. Wells were dug secretly in advance by German engineers, and the men carried special 'desert rations' consisting mainly of biscuits and olives. Djemal's plan was swiftly to establish a bridgehead on the canal at Ismailia, using 5,000 of his best troops and, with luck, catching the British off their guard. This would give him time to bring up his remaining 20,000 men who were following close behind. 'I had staked everything upon surprising the English,' he admitted later in his memoirs. Moreover, heartened by reports that Egypt was ripe for revolt against the British, he had also gambled on the hope that 'Egyptian patriots, encouraged by the capture of Ismailia by Turkish troops, would rise en masse, and that Egypt would be freed in an unexpectedly short time by quite a small force.'

In the event, Djemal was right on neither count. The Egyptian masses, although largely anti-British and pro-German, had no wish to substitute harsh Ottoman rule for the more benign hand of Britain. They did not therefore rally to the call to Holy War when word reached them that the Turks had penetrated as far as the Suez Canal. Nor did Djemal catch those defending the waterway off their guard. For some time British intelligence had been aware of Turkish troop concentrations in southern Syria and Palestine, and an attack on Egypt was thought likely. Indeed, it was as a counter-move to such a threat that the British first considered making a landing at Gallipoli with the aim of seizing Constantinople. Even so, Djemal's men succeeded in crossing the desert and getting quite close to the canal before being detected. But they were running late, and it was already light as the party sent to seize the bridgehead began to lower their pontoons into the water.

As a result, wrote Djemal afterwards, 'the operation took place under the eyes of the English'. According to another account it was the cackling of some chickens which the Turks had unwisely brought with them which alerted the British look-outs to what was happening. A third version credits pilots on aerial reconnaissance with first spotting the danger, while John Buchan says that during the night sentries had seen 'shadowy figures' silently hauling pontoons into position just south of Ismailia, and had raised the alarm.

Whatever the truth, the Turks now found themselves pinned down on the canal bank by a murderous fire from the far side of the waterway. Nonetheless, they managed to get six of their pontoons afloat, only to have them riddled with machine-gun bullets and sunk. One, however, did succeed in reaching the far bank, though the dozen or so Turks aboard it were soon killed or captured. By now the main body had begun to reach the canal, and the battle became general along a stretch of several miles. There were a number of British war-ships on the waterway and the guns of these, as well as those of an armoured train, were directed against the Turks. They fought stubbornly and bravely, but with their pontoons sunk there was little they could do except shoot it out across the canal. Watching the battle from a hilltop three miles away, Djemal realised that his gamble had failed. It would clearly be futile to continue the attack, for very soon the British would bring up reinforcements from the 150,000 troops they had sta-tioned in Egypt. Unless he withdrew his force he would risk losing the lot, just as Enver had done a month earlier at Sarikamish. As it was, according to British figures, 2,000 Turks were killed, although Djemal claimed to have lost only 14 officers and 178 other ranks, plus wounded and prisoners. He certainly deserved to have far heavier losses than even the British estimate, and Sir John Maxwell, Commander-in-Chief in Egypt, was widely criticised for allowing the Turks to escape across the desert with all their guns, instead of destroy-ing them as they fled.

Nonetheless, in the space of only five weeks, two grandiose schemes thought up by the German and Turkish Holy War strategists had ended in humiliating disaster for the Turks – even if Djemal was to claim afterwards that his particular venture was merely a reconnaissance in strength for a full-scale invasion of Egypt later. Meanwhile, in India, Sikh and Hindu revolutionaries were about to launch their own Holy War against the British, with or without German help.

*   *   *

The date chosen for the uprising, it may be recalled, was to be February 21, when disaffected native units of the Indian Army would slaughter their British officers, break into their armouries, distribute weapons to the revolutionaries, and together march on Delhi where they would declare India a republic. Before leaving America and Canada for India, the Sikhs had been led by Har Dayal and others to expect arms and funds from Germany. Disappointingly these had failed to materialise. With the incoming mails closely watched by the authorities, they had, moreover, lost contact with their leaders in San Francisco and, more particularly, with Har Dayal, the high priest of their movement. He was now somewhere in Europe, and clearly unable, or unwilling, to risk joining them in India. Realising that they were now on their own, they had joined forces with the veteran Hindu revolutionaries of Bengal in what they saw as the greatest mass rising since the Indian Mutiny, nearly sixty years earlier.

But the course of the insurrection was not destined to run smoothly, and on February 16, with just five days to go, the leaders were faced by a sudden crisis. The risk of their being betrayed to Cleveland's agents, or of the plot somehow being discovered, was a perpetual fear to the conspirators, for they knew that for them this would mean only one thing, the hangman's noose. On February 16 they became convinced that one of their number, a Sikh named Kirpal Singh, was in fact a police spy. The previous day, when he should have been secretly visiting the barracks of the 23rd Indian Cavalry Regiment, briefing sympathisers on their role in the uprising, he was spotted talking earnestly to a stranger at Lahore railway station. They also noticed that he asked questions about aspects of the plot which did not immediately concern him. Their suspicions thus aroused, they decided to watch him closely but allow him to believe that they trusted him. But so certain were they that he was a police informer that Rash

Behari Bose, the seasoned Hindu revolutionary who now headed the joint conspiracy, decided to bring forward the uprising by two days. At all costs, however, the traitor in their midst must not be allowed to discover this. At the same time messengers were hastily sent to all those actively involved in the plan to inform them of the new date, the night of February 19.

Unfortunately for the conspirators, on the very morning of the uprising one of these messengers returned to the secret revolutionary headquarters in Lahore to say that the 23rd Cavalry Regiment was aware of the changed plan and was ready to rise that night. He blurted all this out in Kirpal Singh's hearing before he could be stopped. The Sikh spy managed to evade his watchers and warn a plain-clothes officer who was keeping the house under surveillance. Immediately, all military establishments and civil authorities were alerted throughout the country, and the plotters' headquarters raided. Realising that they had been betrayed, the conspirators decided to kill the traitor in their midst, but they were too late. The police rushed the building and seized seven of the plotters, as well as bombs, bomb-making equipment, weapons, seditious literature and revolutionary flags. The next morning six more of the ringleaders were arrested when they went to the house to try to discover what had gone amiss, and why the disaffected units had not mutinied during the night.

Meanwhile, following the warning flashed across India, the military had reacted swiftly. Indian guards and sentries on all armouries were immediately replaced by armed British ones, while the cantonments and streets of garrison towns were patrolled by British infantry units. This prompt and decisive action, together with the arrest of most of the principal conspirators, strangled the insurrection at birth. Confronted by cold steel, the mutinous sepoys lost their nerve, and the agitators sent to bring them out simply melted away. Given that the well-armed sepoys had failed to respond to the revolutionary call, it was hardly surprising that the 'regiments of peasants' whom the *Ghadr* leaders had expected to flock to join the insurrection also failed to materialise.

Now came the grim reckoning. Over the next two years, nine special tribunals tried 175 of the revolutionaries. Of the

136 convicted, 38 were sentenced to hang, a similar number to transportation for life, and the rest to imprisonment. In the end only 18 of the death sentences were carried out, the remainder being commuted by the Viceroy, Lord Hardinge, to transportation for life. In addition, 18 sepoys found guilty of complicity in the plot were sentenced to death at their court martial, though only 12 were finally executed. But the principal conspirator, Rash Behari Bose, who claimed to have hurled the bomb at Lord Hardinge in 1912, escaped, fleeing first to Benares and then to Japan. There, although the Japanese were supposedly Britain's allies, he was given sanctuary by highly placed individuals in the government whose expansionist dreams in Asia made them anxious to keep in with the Indian revolutionaries. Bose never returned to India, but spent the rest of the war trying, unsuccessfully, to smuggle arms into the country. In the Second World War, his revolutionary fervour undimmed by age, he tried once again to raise an army which would liberate India. He died in Tokyo in 1945, and thus did not live to see, just two years later, the end of British rule.

What neither Bose nor his co-conspirators had realised when they planned their ill-fated uprising was that Berlin had in fact agreed to supply them with arms, and that secret plans were already afoot to make large purchases of arms in the United States for smuggling into India. Indeed, as hopes of an early German victory in Europe faded, Berlin became increasingly keen on fomenting trouble in India, and a joint Indo-German body, known as the Indian Revolutionary Committee, was set up in Berlin to co-ordinate the efforts of Hindu, Muslim and Sikh revolutionaries. However, the surveillance of suspects and the interception of mail by the British Indian authorities made communication between Berlin and India extremely difficult, not to say hazardous. Not realising that help was at hand, and fired by excessive zeal, Bose and his co-conspirators had risen several months too soon, with disastrous consequences for themselves.

Yet although most of the *Ghadr* leaders were now out of circulation, elsewhere in India, particularly in Bengal, there were still plenty of revolutionaries at large who were prepared to bide their time and await the delivery of German arms. Valuable lessons had been learned from the failure of the

Sikhs to set the Punjab ablaze, and already preparations were being made to receive the weapons at secret depots outside British jurisdiction. One such base was set up on the remote Thai-Burmese frontier, where operations could be planned, men could be trained by German instructors, and arms stored. From here, too, mutinous ideas could be infused into the ranks of Indian Army units serving in Burma, then a province of British India. In the spring of 1915, the plotters were greatly heartened when word reached them that the first shipment of German arms had left the United States. By December, it was whispered, everything would be ready.

But that was not all that was going on in this shadowy game. Alarming intelligence had reached the British that German agents were at that very moment making their way across Persia towards Kabul with the aim of persuading the fiery Afghans to join the Holy War and invade India.

6

Enver Pasha's Bombshell

The original plan worked out between Constantinople and Berlin had been for a joint Turco-German mission to Afghanistan. This was to consist of the German contingent chosen by Zimmermann and Oppenheim, and a strong Turkish military escort of perhaps 1,000 troops. The Turks, under German advisers, would take care of any fighting, if the need arose, during the long advance through Persia, though it was hoped that the local tribes would rally to the sacred cause.

Because it purported to be a Holy War mission, operating among highly sensitive Muslim peoples, it was agreed that the Germans should make their presence as inconspicuous as possible. Enver even suggested that they wear Turkish army uniforms and badges of rank, though the Germans firmly rejected this. Their precise role was still somewhat vague at this stage, for the details were to be resolved in Constantinople. Apart from serving as military advisers to the expedition, however, they would play a major diplomatic role when they reached Kabul. To this end they bore with them flattering personal messages and tempting promises from the German Emperor to the Emir of Afghanistan.

King Habibullah – or so Enver's agents in Kabul insisted – would need no second bidding to join the Holy War and order his fanatical tribal warriors down through the passes into British India. Their encouraging reports bore out the views of the pro-German Swedish explorer Sven Hedin that the Afghans were 'burning with desire' to rid neighbouring India of the infidel British. To Wilhelm and Enver the prospects of thus turning the full fury of Islam against their common enemy, at minimum cost in men and money, seemed highly promising.

From the outset, however, the plan had run into unexpected difficulties. Members of the German mission, it will be recalled, had made their way to Constantinople via neutral Romania posing as a travelling circus company. Their baggage, suitably manifested, followed shortly afterwards by rail. Unfortunately, a sharp-eyed Romanian customs officer became suspicious when one of the wireless aerials, described on the waybill as 'tent-poles', began to protrude through its packing to reveal tell-tale white ceramic insulators. Further investigation brought to light a mobile wireless station, rifles, machine-guns and other highly compromising items. By now the Germans were safely in Constantinople, but unable to proceed with the expedition without this vital equipment. Replacements were hurriedly arranged, and this time their safe passage across Romania was ensured by German agents in Bucharest who first greased the right palms. Eventually, after a delay of several weeks, all the equipment reached Constantinople safely.

Meanwhile, as members of the German mission kicked their heels impatiently while awaiting its arrival, strains had begun to develop between them and their Turkish hosts. Much of the blame for this rested with those in Berlin, notably Zimmermann and Oppenheim, who had vetted the recruits and picked the final team. In addition to individuals of exceptional ability and suitability for such a testing mission, they had chosen others who were to prove totally unsuitable. These included a number of NCOs who had previously served in Germany's African colonies. Although tough and courageous, and used to hard living in extreme heat, they were entirely lacking in the political and personal sensitivity that such a joint venture required. Their abrasiveness and overbearing manner began to upset the Turks, not to mention their own colleagues, and very soon Enver was demanding that these individuals be sent home. This was arranged, but not before they had caused serious damage to the mission's prospects, openly bragging in restaurants and elsewhere in Constanti-

nople that they were bound for Afghanistan. Word of their
presence at the Pera Palace Hotel, and of their boasting, was
quick to reach the ears of neutral diplomats in the Ottoman
capital, and via them the British intelligence service, which
managed to maintain close contact with sympathetic individuals like Morgenthau, the American ambassador.

Even after the misfits had departed, however, disagreements with the Turks and also within the Germans' own
ranks continued. By now the mission members were restless,
and finding the long delays and slow progress in mounting the
joint Turco-German expedition extremely frustrating. As was
inevitable among a group of strong-willed individuals not yet
used to working together, frictions arose. To make matters
worse, there was a division within the group between the military and those of other backgrounds. For apart from putting
Wassmuss, the diplomat, in overall command of the mission,
with Niedermayer, the professional soldier, as his number two,
the Foreign Ministry and General Staff in Berlin, who jointly
controlled the operation, had not worked out a proper chain of
command for the rest of the members. A further irritation was
Enver's insistence that overall command of the expedition,
and of all such operations in the East, should be in Turkish
hands. For he was already beginning to worry about Berlin's
long-term aims in the East, and to see that these might conflict
with his own. At the same time, purely by chance, the
Germans discovered that Enver had already secretly dispatched a small diplomatic team to Kabul, in an apparent
attempt to steal a march on them. In fact, it failed to get there,
but the revelation did nothing to improve the Germans'
mood.

That was not the only shadow cast over the expedition.
Enver's bruising defeat at Sarikamish at the hands of the
Russians, and the Suez Canal débâcle, had begun to focus his
mind on the uncomfortable realities facing him, rather than
vague dreams of a Napoleonic march into Central Asia. Of
more urgent concern to him than the Afghanistan expedition,
therefore, was the threat posed to his eastern frontiers by a
Russian troop build-up in northern Persia. Although in flagrant breach of the latter's declared neutrality, the Russians
had long treated the Shah's north-western provinces as, mili-

tarily speaking, belonging to the Tsar. After diplomatic pressure by Constantinople on Teheran had failed to dislodge the Russian troops, a mixed force of Turkish regulars and Kurdish irregulars had crossed into northern Persia and in January 1915 attacked their stronghold at Tabriz. Protests to both Constantinople and St Petersburg by the Shah over this violation of his neutrality were to no avail. Both warring powers were aware that his writ hardly extended beyond the city limits of Teheran, and this cynical disregard of Persia's neutrality was to continue throughout the war.

The Russians, however, were not the only threat to Turkey's eastern frontiers. On the outbreak of war with Turkey, the military authorities in Delhi had hastily dispatched a seaborne task-force to the head of the Persian Gulf to safeguard British interests there, especially the oilfields, so crucial to the Royal Navy. At the same time, as Enver was uncomfortably aware, the British force posed a serious threat to Baghdad, an important garrison town and the regional capital, which lay only 300 miles away up the River Tigris. And as if that were not enough cause for concern, Turkish and German defence experts in Constantinople were expecting at any moment an Allied attack of some kind in the Dardanelles area, possibly coinciding with a Russian landing, from across the Black Sea, on the shores of the Bosphorus. In view of all this, it was perhaps not surprising that Enver's initial enthusiasm for the Afghanistan adventure, with its promise of 1,000 hand-picked Turkish troops, had begun to wane.

Whether or not Wassmuss had somehow got wind of what was about to happen will probably never be known. But it was at around this time, in January 1915, that he made his dramatic decision to hand over command of the German contingent to Niedermayer and embark on a separate venture of his own. Even his biographer Christopher Sykes, writing only twenty years later, failed to explain satisfactorily what caused him to break away from the main party, and who in Berlin authorised this sudden and unexpected change of plan. One possible explanation is that relations between himself and the rest of the party had deteriorated to a point where it was obviously impossible for him to continue as their leader. Another possibility is that he fell out with Niedermayer over their respective roles in the coming operation, which was part diplomatic and part military, something of which the Germans had little or no previous experience. Certainly, as captured diaries suggest, his colleagues found him moody and difficult to get on with, and it seems that they were not particularly sorry to see him go.

Whatever the reason for his departure, Wassmuss informed his colleagues that he planned to make his way into southern Persia, where he knew many of the tribal leaders from pre-war days, and spread the Holy War there, forcing the British to commit much-needed troops to the region to protect their interests in the lower Gulf. After that, it seems, with the tribes behind him he intended to make his way eastwards to Afghanistan, possibly meeting up with Niedermayer and the others there for the final combined attack on India. No two accounts, whether German or British, seem to tally, however, and in the event Wassmuss never reached Afghanistan. But he was to do more than his fair share of damage to British interests in southern Persia, as will be seen.

It was shortly after his announcement – and he may well have seen it coming – that Enver delivered a terminal blow to the whole idea of a Turco-German expedition to Afghanistan. The news was broken to the Germans during the first week of February 1915 when they arrived in Baghdad, the agreed assembly point for the joint expedition. 'I regrettably have to tell you', Niedermayer was informed by Rauf Bey, the senior Turkish officer who was to have accompanied the mission, 'that three days ago I received orders to the effect that the Turkish expedition to Afghanistan has been called off. I have been instructed to transfer all personnel, weapons and equipment to the Turkish supreme command in Mesopotamia for redeployment against the British in the Basra region.'

Niedermayer and his companions were momentarily stunned by Rauf Bey's bombshell, especially after being kept waiting for so long by the Turks. Asked why the expedition had been cancelled, the Turkish officer produced a number of reasons. For a start, he said, they had been unable to establish contact with the Emir of Afghanistan. They therefore had no way of knowing how the 1,000-strong armed force would be received when it arrived at the Afghan frontier. This, Nieder-

mayer noted sourly in his subsequent account of events, was in
puzzling contrast to the highly optimistic reports, a few
months earlier, of Enver's spies in Kabul. They had insisted
that the Emir and his subjects were burning to join Turkey
and Germany in the war against the British in India. Rauf also
placed some of the blame for the expedition's cancellation on
the German mission, claiming that the 'loose tongues' of some
of the wilder members of the group, since sent home, had
compromised the secrecy of the entire operation, thereby
alerting British intelligence to it. He also blamed the Germans
for undermining the originally agreed concept of the expedition by continually insisting on a more independent role in it
for themselves, something which Enver found unacceptable.
Finally, Rauf drew attention to the extreme difficulties and
dangers of crossing Persia, which suggested to Niedermayer
that it had begun to dawn on the Turks that they might be less
welcome there than they had imagined.

Although profoundly disappointed by the Turkish withdrawal from the Afghanistan adventure, Niedermayer and his
companions were determined not to abandon the idea. Their
aim of bringing Afghanistan, and if possible Persia, into the
war remained unchanged. 'So long as Berlin did not change its
mind,' Niedermayer wrote, 'the plan had to continue, even
without Turkish help. Such an enterprise was not without a
good chance of success.' However, since the mission would no
longer enjoy the protection of a powerful armed escort, the
entire venture would have to be planned completely anew. Yet
there were distinct advantages, Niedermayer reasoned, in proceeding alone. The Turks were making themselves increasingly disliked in Persia. Not only had they carried the war against
the Russians on to neutral Persian soil, but it was also becoming clear that Enver himself had territorial ambitions there.
To make matters worse, Turkish troops engaged in hostilities
with the Russians in north-western Persia were behaving with
extreme brutality towards the local population. Indeed, apart
from a mutual dislike of the Russians, and no great love for the
British, the sole thing that the Turks and the Persians had in
common was their religion. And even there they had differences. For while the Turks were Sunni Muslims, the Persians
were Shiahs. 'In view of all this it seemed very likely that an

all-German expedition would invite less suspicion,' observed Niedermayer optimistically.

But it soon became clear that Rauf had orders to prevent the German party from leaving Turkish soil and entering Persia, which Constantinople regarded as its own preserve. The Turks, meanwhile, continued to send troops across the frontier on the pretext of attacking Russian Cossack units in the north of Persia. This frequently led to bloody clashes with local tribesmen, who resented their intrusion, and a further deterioration in Turco-Persian relations. Because this also damaged the hitherto good name of the Germans in the region, Niedermayer tried to dissuade the Turks from making such incursions, though in vain. He now saw that his only course of action was to move his headquarters to the German Legation in Teheran, which would put him well out of reach of Enver and Rauf, and from where he could shape his plans for the Afghan adventure. He would also be able to gauge the mood of the Shah and his people towards joining in a Holy War against the British and the Russians. The problem was, however, how to give his Turkish allies the slip and cross the closely guarded frontier into Persia with his small party.

Here Niedermayer and his men had an unexpected piece of luck, for at this precise moment there arrived in Baghdad the German Minister to the Shah's court, Prince Henry of Reuss, who was returning to Teheran from leave in Germany. He had orders to spare no efforts to bring Persia into the war, and to give every assistance to Niedermayer in pursuing the same course. The German Minister announced that Niedermayer and his party would accompany him to Persia. Coming from so high-ranking a personage, the Turks felt powerless to object to this. Even so, up to the very last moment, they put every sort of obstruction in the Germans' way, commandeering much of their equipment, including their machine-guns, for service against the British in the south, and sabotaging their links with Berlin and Constantinople. Just as they were about to leave Baghdad, one final attempt was made to hold them up when the Turkish governor of the frontier region, a man who made no secret of his anti-German feelings, refused to let them proceed. However, he was reluctantly overruled by Rauf Bey, who was anxious to avoid a major diplomatic confrontation between Berlin and Constantinople. Finally, on April 3, 1915, the Germans were allowed to cross into Persia. 'I cannot say how glad we were to leave this place of tribulation,' Niedermayer later wrote. But while they had succeeded in shaking off Turkish efforts to thwart them, they now found themselves up against the enemy for the first time. Well aware of the Germans' intentions, the British and Russians had already moved agents into position to report on their movements the moment they entered Persia. 'At Kermanshah, just inside the Persian frontier, an extensive British espionage network had started operating,' Niedermayer reported. Its agents had even infiltrated Turkish territory, and one was discovered carrying detailed intelligence on Niedermayer's party supplied by the Italian consul in Baghdad, who was supposedly neutral at that time. Simultaneously, the British Minister in Teheran was protesting vigorously about the presence in neutral Persia of parties of armed Germans, while British agents were seeking to stir up the wrath of the local tribes against them, using the malign reputation of their Turkish allies to blacken their name.

But to a German officer of Niedermayer's stamp, such things were simply a challenge, the very stuff of war and adventure. A man of extreme determination and ambition, he looked forward with relish to pitting his wits and iron will against his British and Russian adversaries on a battlefield already familiar to him through his pre-war travels. Most of his companions were also eager to get to grips at last with the enemy, for they were now a very different bunch of men from the ill-assorted and quarrelsome group which had originally assembled in Constantinople. First, however, they had to prepare themselves for the long and gruelling journey across Persia to the Afghan frontier, nearly 700 miles away to the east over some of the harshest and bleakest desert on earth.

While he and the German Minister proceeded to Teheran, Niedermayer decided to dispatch the rest of the party, with what equipment they had managed to keep from the Turks, some 200 miles to the south, to the old Silk Road caravan town of Isfahan. Here, as far away as possible from the Russians in the north and the British to the south, they would set up the expedition's base. While awaiting Niedermayer's return, they would send agents ahead to smooth their path by bribing and befriending local Persian officials and tribesmen along their intended route. Meanwhile, Niedermayer and the Minister would endeavour to persuade the Shah and his government to join the war on Germany's, if not Turkey's, side, or at least get them to turn a blind eye to the presence, on their soil, of an armed German party bent on reaching Afghanistan.

On the face of it, the Persians had every reason to wish to see both Britain and Russia humiliated, if not defeated, in the present conflict, having themselves suffered extreme humiliation at the hands of these two powers a few years earlier. In the summer of 1907, it may be recalled, the British and the Russians had agreed, without so much as informing or consulting him, to divide the Shah's kingdom into two spheres of influence. The whole of the north, which included most of the country's principal cities, was to lie within Russia's sphere of influence, while the south, which commanded the entrance to the Persian Gulf and the southern overland route to India, went to Britain. In the middle, dividing the two sectors, stretched a neutral zone. It was this agreement, which also involved Afghanistan and Tibet, which effectively brought Anglo-Russian rivalry in Asia – the Great Game years – to an end, by keeping the Russians away from the frontiers of India, and the British away from those of Russian Central Asia. And while Germany was not mentioned in the agreement – the Anglo-Russian Convention – it was a mutual fear of Berlin's ambitions in the East, the *Drang nach Osten*, which had hastened this rapprochement.

Although the agreement professed to respect Persia's independence and boundaries, the discovery that they had been thus shared out between London and St Petersburg, without any consideration for their feelings, incensed ordinary Persians. They saw it as the first step towards the forcible sharing out of their territory between their two giant neighbours, Russia and British India. However, that was not to say that they now held either the Turks or the Germans in any greater esteem. Enver's invasion of Persian territory, and his scarcely concealed ambition of retaining it, had scotched any likelihood of Turco-Persian co-operation in a Holy War against anyone. This left only the Germans with any hope of bringing Persia into the war against the Allies. But even the Germans, so far as Teheran was concerned, did not have totally clean hands. With the signing of the Anglo-Russian Convention, German prestige in Persia had reached an all-time high, since Kaiser Wilhelm was seen by Persians as their protector from the territorial ambitions of the British and Russians. But then, in the summer of 1911, the German Emperor had signed an agreement with Tsar Nicholas II of Russia which formally recognised the latter's 'special interests' in Persia. This was regarded by the Persians as a betrayal, and the Germans thereby forfeited their friendship and trust. However, by being at war with Britain and Russia, Germany had now gone some way towards repairing the damage, giving Niedermayer reason for cautious optimism.

*　　*　　*

While Niedermayer was thus exploring the mood in Teheran, and in Isfahan the rest of the party were preparing for the coming Afghan adventure, elsewhere the war was claiming many lives but little else. On the Western Front a virtual stalemate had been reached, with neither the Allies nor the Germans making any appreciable gains, despite heavy losses on both sides. The British Expeditionary Force found itself facing the horrors of a German gas attack, and desperately short of shells for its artillery. Following a lengthy naval bombardment of the Turkish forts, a joint Allied force had landed on the Gallipoli peninsula, only to find itself, as in France, bogged down and suffering appalling casualties. After much diplomatic horse-trading, with both sides competing for its favours, Italy had joined the Allied cause, though at first only against its neighbour Austria. In southern Mesopotamia fierce fighting had taken place between Turkish and British Indian troops, while in the Bosphorus and Sea of Marmara British submarines had sunk Turkish vessels in full view of Constantinople. In Britain anti-German riots had taken place in Liverpool following the sinking of the liner *Lusitania*, with children and neutral Americans on board, by a German U-boat; and German Zeppelins had crossed the North Sea and dropped bombs on the eastern counties.

In Berlin, meanwhile, Kaiser Wilhelm had lost none of his

zeal for striking at his British cousins where he believed it would hurt them most. He was determined to go ahead with his plan to unleash the Persians and the Afghans in a Holy War against India's ill-guarded frontiers, with or without the Turks. Not only would this force the British to maintain troops there which would otherwise be deployed on other fronts, but were the native population induced to rise simultaneously against their rulers the British might even be forced to evacuate the country. If so, he could see himself in the not so distant future being crowned as Emperor of India.

Among his military hierarchy an even more ambitious scheme was being looked at. Field Marshal von der Goltz, a soldier with long experience in the East gained as an adviser to the Sultan, raised the possibility of actually invading India, using German troops. Citing successful invasions of the past, including those of Alexander the Great and Nadir Shah of Persia, he argued that there was little to prevent a determined and suitably equipped German force from marching in their footsteps. Similar arguments had been advanced by Russian generals during the Great Game years, and elaborate plans had even been worked out for such an invasion, though in the event these had come to nothing. However, the construction of the Berlin-to-Baghdad railway, von der Goltz pointed out, made the scheme more feasible than in the past, for it enabled large bodies of troops to be moved to the head of the Gulf, together with artillery, and for them to be regularly supplied.

As we have seen, this danger had not gone unnoticed by British strategists when the railway was first mooted. The only problem, so far as the Germans were concerned, was that the railway was not yet finished. The most difficult and hazardous part of its construction, which involved tunnelling through the Taurus mountains of southern Turkey, had still to be completed. In the meantime, troops and munitions bound for Baghdad – the probable staging point for any such invasion – had to be carried laboriously over the passes by truck and mule. Von der Goltz urged therefore that the blasting of the tunnels be given maximum priority, with no cost being spared in getting them finished as soon as humanly possible. Ambassador Wangenheim, however, ever scathing about the military, calculated that the missing stretch of the railway could easily take a further three years to complete, by which time the war might well be over. All along he had been critical of the lack of forethought given by Berlin to the Kaiser's grand design, blaming this for most of the problems which had arisen, including the rift with the Turks.

For their part, however, the planners in Berlin had no such doubts, and were already working on other means of bringing about Britain's downfall in the East. In addition to Niedermayer's efforts in Teheran, and those of Wassmuss in the south, they had one further weapon up their sleeve – the enemy within. Shortly before the crushing by the British of the *Ghadr* uprising in February 1915, but too late to be of any assistance to those on the spot, a secret body called the Indian Revolutionary Committee had been established in Berlin by the German Foreign Ministry. Its purpose was to co-ordinate, under strict German supervision, the activities of Hindu, Muslim and Sikh revolutionaries in fomenting anti-British uprisings in India, and also to supply them with arms, ammunition and funds. Its ultimate objective was the overthrow of British rule in India from within. The importance attached by Berlin to its activities, and the twenty-five Indians working there, is shown by the fact that the three-storey building at No. 38 Wielandstrasse was accorded full embassy status.

Arrangements were soon under way for the clandestine purchase of arms for the revolutionaries eagerly awaiting them in India. Their lack of weapons was seen by those on the spot as the principal cause of the failure of the earlier uprising. This time, properly supplied with arms, and given the reduced numbers of British and Indian troops left to maintain law and order, the conspirators were convinced that they could pull it off. Because of the Royal Navy's effective blockade of Germany's ports, clearly the weapons could not be provided by the Kaiser's own arms industry, which anyway was already fully stretched supplying the needs of his armies in the field. It was decided therefore by the Indian Revolutionary Committee and the German Foreign Ministry to acquire them from neutral sources and smuggle them into India aboard vessels flying neutral flags. The most obvious such source was the United States, where arms were readily available, and not too many questions would be asked.

The purchases were made in February 1915 by German and Indian agents working under Captain Franz von Papen, officially military attaché to Berlin's Washington embassy, but in fact the head of the Kaiser's wartime intelligence operations there. Altogether they managed to acquire 30,000 rifles and pistols, and large quantities of ammunition, from three arms dealers in New York, a fourth in Philadelphia and a fifth in California. At the same time two vessels were obtained – the schooner *Annie Larsen*, which was chartered from its American owners, and the oil-tanker *Maverick*, which was purchased outright and repaired and refitted with funds supplied by von Papen. The arms were now moved to the port of San Diego, on the Pacific coast, where the *Annie Larsen* was docked, waiting to take them on board.

The plan was for them next to be conveyed by the schooner to a remote island off the Mexican coast where they would be transferred to the larger, ocean-going *Maverick* for the long voyage across the Pacific to Java. There they would once again be offloaded, and this time transferred to small fishing vessels chartered locally by German consular officials for the final and most hazardous stage of their journey, into the eager hands of those who would shortly be using them. The bulk of this substantial arsenal was destined for the revolutionaries in India, who would pick it up under cover of darkness in remote creeks on the Bengal coastline. Some of the weapons, however, were earmarked for neighbouring Burma, where a simultaneous uprising was being planned. But these arms would first be smuggled into Thailand, where officials could more easily be bribed. From there they would be carried up to the frontier with Burma and stored in secret caches until they were needed. At the same time, in the Philippines, the German consul was negotiating to buy a further 5,000 rifles and 500 pistols, and to charter a motor-schooner to smuggle these too into Thailand. Also on board the vessel would be two German-born weapons instructors, who would help set up secret training camps in remote jungle clearings. Further arms were being purchased in China from former revolutionaries there, for smuggling into Burma and India by little-known overland routes. Such then were Berlin's plans for getting arms and ammunition to the enemy within.

In the German capital, meanwhile, it had been decided by Arthur Zimmermann and his advisers to strengthen the mission which Niedermayer, then still in Teheran, was planning to lead to Kabul. It was felt that following the Turks' withdrawal from the venture the Emir was unlikely to be impressed by a purely German approach. To give the mission more weight, therefore, it was decided to attach to it, ostensibly as its leader, a prominent Indian who could claim to speak for his fellow countrymen, and invite the Emir to help liberate them from British rule. But who was there to play this leading role?

With the legendary Vinayak Savarkar locked away for life in the Andaman Islands for his revolutionary activities, the most obvious candidate was Har Dayal, founder of the *Ghadr* movement, now in Switzerland following his flight from American justice. On the outbreak of war he had immediately gone to Constantinople to offer his services to the Turks, but had quickly fallen out with them over questions of strategy. Finding Wangenheim more sympathetic to his ideas, in January 1915 he agreed to visit Berlin for further discussions there with the German Foreign Ministry and the Indian Revolutionary Committee. But despite his intellectual brilliance, Har Dayal had never made any pretence of being a man of action, regarding himself purely as a revolutionary strategist and visionary. He had no ambition to lead a clandestine mission to Afghanistan. His health, moreover, was poor and would not have stood up to the gruelling journey across Persia's blazing deserts.

However, he knew the very man for the task – a young and charismatic Indian prince, albeit a minor one, named Raja Mahendra Pratap, who did not hide his intense dislike for the British and his wish to see them driven from his homeland. In February he was invited to come to Berlin from his home in neutral Switzerland to discuss the possibilities. But the Raja, who held himself in high esteem, would only agree to come if he was granted a private audience with the German Emperor. Berlin clearly had high hopes of the Indian, for this was duly arranged by Zimmermann, who stood at a respectful distance while the two men discussed strategies for the expulsion of the British from India. Banquets were thrown in his honour, he was hailed in the German newspapers as 'the Prince of India', and he was taken up in an aeroplane to watch the fighting on the snow-covered Russian front. His views on fomenting a mass uprising in India, and on how to win the support of other Indian princes, were eagerly listened to at the highest level. All this attention proved highly gratifying to him, and he informed his hosts that he was willing to become the titular leader of the Kabul mission.

Because of the departure of Wilhelm Wassmuss to the south, Niedermayer was now without a diplomat with the authority or knowledge to negotiate or sign a treaty with the Emir in Kabul. Chosen therefore to accompany 'the Prince of India' was a Persian-speaking career diplomat who before the war had served in Teheran, Constantinople and Peking. He was Werner Otto von Hentig, aged 29, a fine horseman and an experienced Asian traveller. On the outbreak of war Hentig had volunteered for service with a cavalry regiment, and had fought on the Russian front until recalled to the Foreign Ministry for secret intelligence work in the East. He was now put in charge of the diplomatic side of the mission, his main task commencing only when they reached Kabul. To give the mission further credibility in the eyes of the Emir, it was decided to include in it a leading Muslim revolutionary, Mohammed Barakatullah, whose pre-war anti-British activities had obliged him to flee India. When war broke out he had immediately offered his services to Germany, joining the Indian Revolutionary Committee in Berlin. Finally the mission was provided with a small armed escort of former Indian Army soldiers who had deserted and joined the Turco-German cause.

In addition to being supplied with gold, for bribing Persian and Afghan officials and generally smoothing the way, the mission also carried in its baggage a dazzling selection of gifts for the Emir and his officials. These included bejewelled gold watches, gold fountain pens, gold-topped canes, hand-ornamented rifles and pistols, binoculars, cameras, compasses, a cinema projector and – the very latest thing in German inventiveness – a dozen radio alarm clocks. All were designed to appeal to oriental cupidity, and to demonstrate the superiority of German engineering skills. They also carried with them personal letters from both the German Emperor and the Turkish Sultan to the Emir professing undying friendship and exhorting their fellow sovereign to join the Holy War against Britain and Russia. Finally they bore no fewer than twenty-seven letters, signed by the German Chancellor, to the King of Nepal and to those Indian princes suspected of harbouring anti-British sympathies, some of whom had their own small private armies. These letters, sumptuously bound in leather and written in the recipient's own vernacular, urged the princes to throw in their lot with Germany and Turkey and order their troops and subjects to join the coming revolution. From Kabul they were to be smuggled across the frontier into India, and delivered to their final destinations, by secret couriers.

On April 10, when all was ready, the three men left Berlin by train for Constantinople, where they stayed at the luxurious Pera Palace Hotel, whose Ottoman opulence still delights tourists today. While in the Turkish capital they first learned of the Allied landings at Gallipoli on April 25, news which lent a new urgency to their task of forcing the British to keep troops, desperately needed elsewhere, in India. Before leaving for Baghdad and the Persian frontier, they had an audience with the Sultan at his palace on the Bosphorus at which he wished them every success in their hazardous task. They also held last-minute discussions with Enver Pasha, who was becoming increasingly suspicious of Berlin's intentions, and who seconded to them one of his officers, presumably to keep a close eye on them. Finally, at the beginning of May 1915, they set out for Baghdad, travelling much of the way on the new but unfinished railway, and crossing the Taurus mountains and other trackless stretches on horseback. From Baghdad they entered Persia, making for Isfahan, where they were to join forces with Niedermayer's party and together ride eastwards towards the nearest point on the Afghan frontier.

Niedermayer, meanwhile, had left Teheran, convinced of the futility of trying to persuade the Shah and his ministers to join the Holy War while the Turks were still occupying parts of their country. Indeed, so angry had they been at times with their rapacious neighbour that they had even considered declaring for the Allies. The German officer now rejoined his own men in Isfahan, where he found Hentig and the two Indian revolutionaries awaiting him. Differences immediately arose between the two Germans over who was in overall command of the mission. However, these were quickly settled by Berlin. It was ruled that Niedermayer should assume sole military command, with responsibility for getting the mission safely to Kabul, while Hentig was in charge of all diplomatic questions, especially the crucial negotiations with the Afghan ruler.

At long last, on July 1, the mission was ready to depart. For the two Indians it must have been an anxious moment. Apart from the extreme physical hardships and other hazards facing them, they were only too aware that the hangman's noose awaited them were they unfortunate enough to fall into the hands of the British.

THE NEW GREAT GAME

'I have reports from agents everywhere –
pedlars in South Russia, Afghan horse-dealers,
Turcoman merchants, pilgrims on the road to
Mecca, sheikhs in North Africa, sailors on the
Black Sea coasters, sheep-skinned Mongols,
Hindu fakirs, Greek traders in the Gulf, as well
as respectable Consuls who use cyphers. They
tell the same story. The East is waiting for a
revelation. Some star . . . is coming out of the
West. The Germans know, and that is the card
with which they are going to astonish the
world.'

Sir Walter Bullivant, head of the British Secret Service,
briefing Richard Hannay in
Greenmantle, by John Buchan, 1916

7

The German Lawrence

In the spring of 1915, after a hazardous journey southwards, Wilhelm Wassmuss had reached the shores of the Persian Gulf and set about his task of directing the Holy War against the isolated British communities there. Wearing Persian costume, speaking their language fluently and posing as a Muslim convert, he began to stir up the local tribes in a campaign of murder, violence and sabotage aimed at driving the British from the Gulf, or forcing them to divert troops, badly needed elsewhere, to the spot. He knew, from his former days as German consul at Bushire, that these small outposts were only too vulnerable to attack, having for the most part just locally recruited levies to protect them. He was also on excellent terms with many of the tribal leaders, having often stayed in their tents and villages during his pre-war travels into the interior. With the aid, or so the British claimed, of German gold and extravagant promises, Wassmuss now set out to exploit these old friendships.

The tribesmen, in fact, needed little persuasion, for they harboured a deep resentment towards the British for halting their once highly profitable traffic in smuggled arms from the coast to India's North-West Frontier. They wanted nothing more than to see these self-appointed guardians of the Persian Gulf driven out for ever. Explaining his own conversion to Islam, Wassmuss told them that the German Emperor had himself embraced their faith, and ordered all his subjects to do likewise. The Emperor, he added, had even made a secret pilgrimage to Mecca, thereby entitling him to wear the sacred green turban, and to adopt the name of 'Haji' Wilhelm Mohammed. Wassmuss also told the simple and impressionable tribesmen that he was in direct and regular contact with the Emperor by wireless. To add conviction to this spurious claim, he would put on a theatrical performance with a set of earphones, a steel aerial and a magnet, thereby producing sparks in the darkness and – or so he claimed – 'personal messages' from the Kaiser himself to individual tribal leaders, as well as grandiloquent exhortations to them to join Germany and Turkey in the Holy War against the infidel British. Needless to say, Wassmuss had no wireless set, the nearest German one being nearly 300 miles away, at Isfahan, the staging point for Niedermayer's expedition to Afghanistan.

By means of such tactics, however, the former German consul was soon to prove himself an uncomfortable thorn in the flesh of the British, and a growing threat to their presence in the region. His one-man guerrilla campaign, moreover, would later earn for him the grudging sobriquet from the British of the German 'Lawrence'. Yet, only a few weeks earlier, they had all but had him in the bag. It had come about like this. Even before the war the British had been aware of the illegal activities of German agents, in the guise of consuls and businessmen, in the Persian Gulf, though there was little they could do about it. It was no secret to them that Wassmuss was no ordinary consul. Confirmation of these suspicions had come to light in November 1914 on Turkey's entry into the war, when the British task-force sent to the head of the Gulf to secure its vital oilfields dropped anchor off Bahrain, then a British protectorate. A German commercial agent was caught red-handed there compiling a detailed (and extremely accurate) report on the strength and composition of the British force. Since there was no radio station on the island at that time, a fast dhow was standing by to take the agent's report to the nearest German consulate, at Bushire, for onward transmission. At the same time word reached British intelligence that the German consul at Bushire, a Dr Listermann, was urging local tribesmen to attack the British Residency, which occupied an exposed and isolated position some miles outside the town. It was decided, despite his diplomatic immunity, to arrest Listermann forthwith.

The raid on the German consulate, which met with no resistance other than the furious protests of Listermann, yielded a wealth of highly compromising material, including telegrams and other secret documents and instructions. One telegram advised Listermann of the imminent departure southwards of Wassmuss to organise anti-British activities in his area, and also against India. In the meantime Listermann was ordered to incite the tribesmen to attack the British Residency at Bushire, and to arrange the cutting of the overland telegraph line to India (to which he had replied, somewhat feebly, that he lacked the means). These finds, the British insisted, proved conclusively that the Germans were planning to breach Persia's neutrality by conducting hostilities there, thereby invalidating Listermann's diplomatic immunity. It was clear from the seized documents and telegrams that other Germans living in the Gulf were implicated in Berlin's schemes, and orders were immediately issued for the arrest of all those within reach. Listermann, in the meantime, was sent to India for internment.

Normally, since they were legally responsible for the safety and well-being of the foreign communities in their midst, and it was their neutrality which the Germans were planning to breach, the Persian authorities should have taken such action. However, despite British demands that they curb the illegal activities of the German diplomatic community in cities and towns throughout Persia, the Shah's weak and divided government lacked the will for a showdown with Berlin. To make matters worse, the tribes of the Bushire region were extremely hostile towards the authorities in Teheran, while the Swedish-officered, 6,000-strong Gendarmerie, which was supposed to maintain law and order in central and southern Persia, was known to be sympathetic towards the Germans. The British knew, therefore, that they could look for little protection for their isolated consular and other outposts from that quarter. Meanwhile, more and more Germans, accompanied by small armed escorts which were supposedly for their protection against bandits, were entering Persia claiming to be consuls, albeit without any official accreditation from Teheran, which was powerless to stop them. Wassmuss, who was at that very moment making his way southwards from Baghdad to take up a post as German consul at Shiraz, 120 miles inland from Bushire, was one of them. Now that the gloves were off, and his real purpose in coming had been revealed, it was crucial that he be intercepted.

Travelling with two other Germans, Wassmuss had chosen a route which he hoped would steer them well clear of any trouble, although he had no reason to suspect that the British were aware of his coming or of his intentions. For he had no way of knowing about the raid on the consulate, and the disclosure of their plans. Nor was he aware of the arrest of Dr Listermann, from whom he had hoped to receive the latest news when he reached Shushtar, the half-way point. On getting there he had been somewhat surprised to find no messages awaiting him, but had nonetheless pressed on. Then, on March 5, he and his companions were suddenly set upon by a party of horsemen in the pay of the British. Only then did they realise that their movements had been closely monitored by native spies for much of their journey, and that they had walked straight into a British trap.

The man who had ordered the Germans' seizure had, in fact, been known to Wassmuss before the war, when both were serving in Bushire. In 1904, it may be recalled, when German activities in the Gulf first gave rise to alarm in Delhi and London, a young political officer, Major Percy Cox, had been sent there to keep a close eye on the Germans, and try to frustrate their schemes. Of Wassmuss, who arrived in Bushire in 1909, he later wrote: 'In private life he was well liked by ourselves and the British community in general. On the other hand, as a consular colleague, I found him somewhat troublesome and truculent to deal with, inclined to make up for lack of tact . . . by recourse to threat and bluster.' Now, eleven years later, Cox too was back in the Gulf, again matching his wits against Wassmuss, this time as Major-General Sir Percy Cox. Because of his unique knowledge of the tribal politics and personalities of the Gulf, he had been given extraordinary powers and authority, serving simultaneously as British Resident and Chief Political Officer to the expeditionary force occupying Basra. Since Bushire lay some distance from the actual war zone, Cox based himself at Basra, keeping in close touch with the Residency staff by wireless.

When it was learned that Wassmuss had been captured, a British intelligence officer on Cox's staff, Captain Edward Noel, was immediately dispatched to the spot with a small escort to bring the prisoners in. On his way there he received a message from those holding the Germans asking him whether he wanted them clapped in irons, as was the Persian custom. Declining this as barbaric, Noel nonetheless asked that the utmost vigilance be observed in ensuring that the prisoners did not escape. Noel's concern for the niceties of civilised conduct, even in war, was to rebound on him badly. For when he and his escort reached the spot, they learned to their dismay that Wassmuss had got clean away.

Quite how he managed this is uncertain, for there are various versions of the episode. According to one, he pretended to be greatly concerned about his horse, which he insisted was sick, and made repeated visits to where it was tethered. After a time his guards became careless and ceased accompanying him each time on these visits. Choosing his moment, Wassmuss slipped away in the darkness and rode silently off across the desert to the domains of a tribal leader known to him from before the war, who granted him sanctuary. Another version claims that he squeezed under the edge of his tent when his guards were momentarily distracted and fled barefooted. His two companions and the rest of the party, however, were less fortunate, and were delivered into Noel's custody the following morning, together with large quantities of incendiary literature, and also arms and ammunition. Much of the former at least was clearly intended for India, for it called upon the native troops there to mutiny against their officers and join the Holy War. But that was not all that was found in the Germans' baggage. While it was not recognised for what it was at the time, among the secret papers which Wassmuss was forced to abandon was a code-book. Eventually this was to find its way to London, where it was seized upon by those who instantly realised its significance. In their hands, as will be seen in due course, it was to play a part in changing the entire direction, and perhaps even the final outcome, of the war.

The British in Bushire did not have the necessary forces to pursue Wassmuss through potentially hostile territory, and he was allowed to make his way to Shiraz, the capital of Fars province, 100 miles away. Here he set about establishing his base of operations, ostensibly as German consul. Bitterly angry at being caught napping by the British, and at losing both his two colleagues and all his equipment, he vowed to get even with his foes. But first, through the Persian governor-general of Fars, he tried to bring pressure to bear on the British to free his two companions and hand back the party's baggage. Meanwhile, the British were demanding the immediate expulsion of Wassmuss from Shiraz, warning the Persian authorities that unless they, or their Swedish-officered Gendarmerie, put a stop to the illegal activities of Wassmuss and the other German 'consuls', they themselves would be forced to bring in troops to do so. Realising that he had little hope of securing the release of his fellow countrymen or his baggage through diplomatic means, Wassmuss now turned his attention to preaching the Holy War among the tribesmen, and directing their wrath against the British.

Originally he had intended to use Shiraz as a base from which to attack not only Bushire but also India. For it was here that he planned to light the torch of revolt that would blaze its way eastwards across Persia towards the tribal powder kegs on the North-West Frontier and beyond. Tales would be spread of great German and Turkish victories in the West, of the British and Russians on the run everywhere, and of violent uprisings throughout India. These successes would be trumpeted among the tribes as proof of the righteousness of the Turco-German cause, and of the Holy War, whose sole and noble purpose was to free the peoples of the East from British and Russian oppression. However, the unexpected loss of his baggage, including the bales of specially prepared and translated Holy War leaflets, was a serious blow to Wassmuss's operations against India, forcing him instead to concentrate his efforts against the British in southern Persia alone.

Wassmuss's principal allies in this were the warlike Tangistanis, the tribesmen controlling the coastal plain around Bushire, many of whose chiefs and elders he had known before the war. He also had friends among the supposedly neutral but largely pro-German officers of the local Gendarmerie, who could be relied upon to turn a blind eye to his nefarious doings, and ignore the angry protests of the

British. Wassmuss's wooing of the Tangistani leaders was greatly facilitated by a grievance that they had long harboured against the British. Their northern neighbours and rivals, the powerful Bakhtiaris, were paid substantial revenues by the British for not interfering with the flow of oil from the Anglo-Persian oilfields, which lay in their tribal territory. The Tangistanis received nothing, giving rise to intense jealousy, and hostility towards the British.

On his way south through Bakhtiari territory Wassmuss had tried hard to talk the Bakhtiari leaders into joining the Holy War against the British. 'Why share your oil wealth with the rapacious British?' he chided them. 'Help us to drive them from your lands, and *all* the oil will be yours.' When they pointed out that they lacked the means for extracting the oil themselves, Wassmuss assured them that Germany would very happily send experts to do that for them. But his blandishments fell on deaf ears, for the chiefs were aware that the Germans had no tankers in the Gulf and, more important, that the Royal Navy ruled the waterway. Even so, emboldened by this approach, the Bakhtiari chiefs sought to turn it to their advantage by demanding that the British put a higher price on their loyalty by paying them a more generous royalty. The gambit failed, however, for the British were aware how dependent the Bakhtiaris were upon their gold, and also that neither Wassmuss nor anyone else was in a position to offer them a satisfactory alternative.

But among the neighbouring Tangistanis, meanwhile, Wassmuss was in his element, preaching the Holy War and pretending to receive exhortations and flattering messages for them from the German Emperor on his sham wireless set. A photograph of him taken at this time shows a striking-looking figure in Persian robes, with long flaxen locks and moustache, and a Mauser pistol thrust into his sash. In his eyes, which are turned upwards, there is an almost messianic expression. 'O Persians,' he told them, 'now is the time to give yourselves to the Holy Cause. If you shrink from the sacrifice, when the whole of Islam is threatened by the infidel enemy, what will your answer be to the Prophet on the Day of Judgement?' Very soon, he assured them, the Germans and Turks would invade India, and the East would finally be liberated from the infidel yoke. He had come more than 2,000 miles, he said, to help them drive the hated British from their midst. As they had seen with their own eyes, and heard with their own ears, he was in close touch with the German Emperor, who would himself give the signal to unleash the Holy War.

Alarmed by the menace posed by this ruthless and charismatic enemy, and the inability or unwillingness of the Persian authorities to deal with him, Sir Percy Cox decided to take the law into his own hands by putting a price on Wassmuss's head. He offered a reward of £5,000, later tripled, for the German's capture, dead or alive, but preferably the latter. This was a huge sum in those parts, and a considerable temptation to would-be betrayers. Given time the offer of a reward might eventually have worked among the venal tribesmen, but in the event it was not really put to the test. For when it came to the attention of the Foreign Office in London, the mandarins there were horrified, insisting that assassinations and kidnappings, even of dangerous wartime enemies, were thoroughly un-British. There was never much love lost between London and Delhi, between the Foreign Office and the India Office, and a senior official of the former department denounced Cox's move as 'abhorrent and detestable'. Cox was ordered to withdraw the reward at once, while the Viceroy gave instructions for all mention of it to be expunged from the record. Cox was very soon to get his revenge, however. Some six months later, when the presence of Wassmuss became a real menace to Britain's position in southern Persia, he was asked by an anxious London what could be done to remove the threat. With ill-concealed relish Cox signalled back: 'Fear of exciting the abhorrence and detestation of HMG prevents me from offering any further suggestions.'

London, for its part, was doing all in its power publicly to discredit the Holy War and challenge the spiritual authority of those calling it. The Sultan's claim to be the Caliph of all Islam had never been universally accepted. The views of those Muslim theologians who questioned the Sultan's claim were therefore canvassed and widely publicised. At the same time a determined effort was made to divide the Muslim world, and thus undermine the Holy War, by wooing the Arabs to the Allied cause. The principal aim was to persuade the much revered Grand Sherif of Mecca, guardian of the holy places of Islam, to raise the Arabs of the Ottoman Empire in armed rebellion against their Turkish masters. At the very same time Constantinople was putting every sort of pressure on him to join the Holy War against the Allies. The elderly Sherif stalled, assuring the unsuspecting Turks that he would pray earnestly for their cause, while all the time negotiating secretly with the British.

Wassmuss, meanwhile, with a price no longer on his head, had moved his headquarters from Shiraz to a point only twenty miles from Bushire. Here, with its Union Jack proudly symbolising British power in the Gulf, and only 180 hastily imported Indian troops to defend it, stood the isolated and highly vulnerable British Residency. This was to be Wassmuss's target, the first test of the fighting capacity of his Tangistani warriors. Already he had sent out spies to gauge the strength of the Residency's hurriedly erected defences and its general state of preparedness. With luck the Tangistanis would overwhelm the defenders, whom they greatly outnumbered, and so strike a mortal blow against Britain's prestige and presence in the Gulf. Even if the Residency managed to hold out, the British would be forced to land more troops to punish the tribesmen and prevent further attacks on Bushire and other British outposts in southern Persia. News of such landings, suitably exaggerated, could be used by Wassmuss and his colleagues elsewhere in Persia to inflame public opinion to the point where the Shah and his ministers found themselves dragged into the war. This, in turn, would greatly help Niedermayer and Hentig, at that very moment setting out for Afghanistan, in their task of rallying the Emir to the Holy War.

The Tangistani attackers were divided into two groups, each several hundred strong. They were to advance from both east and south simultaneously, catching the Residency's defenders by surprise. But on the morning of July 12, 1915 – three days before Ramadan – word reached the British that a small party of armed Tangistanis had been spotted advancing across the desert from the south. Immediately a patrol led by a British major and a captain was sent out to investigate, only to run into a far larger enemy force than had been expected. In the ensuing clash, the captain was mortally wounded, while the major lost his life in a gallant attempt to rescue him. A number of Indian troops were also killed or wounded by the Tangistanis, who had a German machine-gun with them, before the remainder managed to reach the safety of the British outposts. Emboldened by this easy victory, and screaming Holy War battle-cries, the triumphant Tangistanis charged towards the British forward positions a mile or so into the desert on the landward side of the Residency. Here, in their slit-trenches, the defenders were waiting for them.

Holding their fire until the tribesmen were within easy range, the well-trained sepoys opened up on them with rifles and machine-guns. Never before, in many years of tribal warfare, had the Tangistanis encountered such accurate and murderous fire. They faltered, then fled the field, leaving behind them many dead and dying. But they did not lack courage. Early the following morning, this time under cover of darkness, they attacked again, only to be driven off with heavy casualties once more. When later that morning patrols were sent out they failed to find any sign of the Tangistanis, while the expected attack from the east never materialised. The tribesmen had apparently witnessed, from a safe distance, the fate of their unfortunate fellows, and instead had melted away into the desert.

Wassmuss's reaction to this defeat is not known, but on one thing he was quickly proved right. Fearing another such attack, this time by a far larger and perhaps better armed Tangistani force, the British decided to occupy Bushire forthwith, replacing the Persian administration with their own. They would continue to do so, they warned Teheran, until the Persians agreed to garrison the town themselves, and guarantee the safety of the Residency and its staff. At the same time a small punitive force of Royal Marines and sepoys was dispatched by sea to teach the Tangistanis a lesson they would not quickly forget. Landing near the tribesmen's mud-built capital, some miles down the coast from Bushire, they destroyed the fortress and cut down all the date palms from which the Tangistanis derived much of their food and revenue. Such high-handedness was precisely what Wassmuss had been hoping for from the British, for it could hardly fail to inflame Persian public opinion and put the Shah and his government under intense pressure to declare war on these invaders of their soil.

For a moment it looked as though Wassmuss might succeed, single-handedly, in plunging Persia into the Holy War. As expected, Britain's intervention sparked off a storm of furious protest, which German diplomats in the capital, and the pro-German nationalist press, did their utmost to exploit. But the Shah's feeble government, already rent by disagreement, and fearful of the Russians seizing Teheran, had no wish to become militarily embroiled with the British too. In the end, after angry protests, Teheran agreed to replace the ineffective governor of Bushire, punish the Tangistani chiefs, and pay compensation to the families of the British and Indian dead. In return, the British agreed to restore Bushire to Persian rule, and withdraw their troops, which were badly needed elsewhere.

But if British fears for Bushire had been stilled, and Wassmuss temporarily repulsed, elsewhere in central and southern Persia German influence was rapidly gaining ground. With the connivance of the pro-German Gendarmerie, the Germans and their local sympathisers were becoming masters of more and more of the principal towns. These included Isfahan, now their main base of operations, and Kermanshah, which controlled the supply route into Persia from Baghdad for smuggled arms, gold and Holy War propaganda, not to mention German officers and NCOs. Using Isfahan as a staging point, small groups of armed Germans were fanning out into the interior, preaching the Holy War and spreading tales of great victories won by Germany and Turkey over the Allies.

Some, however, were bent on carrying the Holy War further afield. The largest and most important of these parties, of course, was that of Niedermayer and Hentig, since it was entrusted with the strategically crucial task of persuading the Emir of Afghanistan to invade India. But there were others, given independent roles by Niedermayer, who were clearly intent on stirring up mischief for the British in India. Lieutenants Zugmayer and Griesinger were reported by British agents in Isfahan to have left for Kerman, a town near-

ly 400 miles to the south-east, not far from the Afghan and
Baluchistan frontiers. Officially they were going to take up
consular posts there. Accompanying them was an armed
escort, supposedly to protect them from the bands of brigands
said to roam that region. A week later, shortly before his own
departure for Afghanistan, Niedermayer dispatched to the
south-east two more German officers, eight NCOs, thirty-two
Persian levies, plus a machine-gun and several mule-loads of
ammunition. Meanwhile the ranks of those arriving in Isfahan
from Baghdad were being swelled by officers and men who
had managed to escape from Russian POW camps and make
their way south into Persia.

To India's defence chiefs the prospect of Afghanistan joining the Holy War was the stuff of nightmares. While the
Shah's forces were little more than a joke, those of the Emir
were anything but. If the Afghans threw in their lot with
Germany and Turkey, it could even affect the outcome of the
entire war. In normal times the Indian Army could have coped
easily enough with such a threat – indeed that is what it was
originally for – but such were the demands of other theatres of
war that the country was perilously short of troops. So much
so, in fact, that when Lord Kitchener had asked the Viceroy,
in June of that year, 1915, to release more troops for other
fronts, he had been refused. If Afghanistan were to join the
war on the enemy's side, then the British in India might well
find themselves fighting for their lives. At all costs the
Germans must be prevented from reaching Afghanistan.

The Viceroy, Lord Hardinge, acted swiftly. Urgent instructions were telegraphed to British consuls in eastern Persia.
Lieutenant-Colonel Wolseley Haig at Meshed, in the north-
east, was advised: 'It is considered of the greatest importance
by the Government of India that no German party should be
permitted to enter Afghanistan.' Because Meshed lay in the
Russian zone, he was further instructed to ask the Russians to
use their troops 'to annihilate or capture' any German parties
detected heading towards the Afghan frontier. 'You should at
the same time', he was told, 'spend secret service money liberally in obtaining information about the numbers, movements
and armaments of the German parties.' All such intelligence
should immediately be telegraphed to Delhi, and to any other

British outposts along the route. Claude Ducat, British consul at Kerman, in south-east Persia, towards which Lieutenants Zugmayer and Griesinger were thought to be heading, received similar instructions. As there were no Russian or other Allied troops in this area, he was told to use secret service funds freely to turn the 'leading men' of the town against the Germans, and get them driven out before they could establish a base there. Meanwhile, the consuls were advised, in co-operation with the Russians a cordon sanitaire of Cossack and Indian Army cavalry units was being hastily deployed along Persia's eastern frontier with Afghanistan and Baluchistan to block and destroy any German groups which managed to get that far. This was to be called the East Persian Cordon.

That such a move, on Persian sovereign territory, was a gross and flagrant violation of its neutrality, was not in doubt. But then so was the deployment of armed German groups which the cordon was designed to prevent. If neither the Persian authorities nor the Gendarmerie (which, ironically, was largely funded by the British government) was willing or able to police the country properly, then the British and Russians would have to do it for them in order to protect their own interests. Even so there were some, including Charles Marling, British Minister to the Shah's court, who feared that such a move might finally drive the Persians, who were wobbling badly, into the German camp. He argued that intense pressure on the Shah's ministers, backed by generous payments to certain key individuals, might persuade them to act forcibly against the Germans in their midst. However, the Viceroy ruled that it was now far too late in the day to try this. Were it to fail, or the Germans to offer more generous sweeteners, then the consequences for India could be catastrophic.

There was no guarantee, of course, that the East Persian Cordon would be able to prevent a determined German party from getting through. The British sector of the frontier alone ran for 500 miles north–south through a desolate wilderness of desert and mountain. To seal this off totally was clearly impossible, since it would require literally thousands of troops who could neither be spared nor supplied. The cordon would have to be operated by small, lightly equipped Indian Army patrols, mounted on camels or on foot, and ready to set out at any hour of the day or night the moment intelligence of an enemy sighting was received. The units chosen to form the cordon were the 28th Indian Light Cavalry and the 19th Punjabi Infantry. They were to be deployed in a chain of widely separated outposts running northwards to the oasis town of Birjand, where the British and Russian zones met. However, because of the enormous distances involved, the cruel terrain and climate, and the formidable task of supplying these remote posts with food, water and ammunition, it was clearly going to take some time to get the cordon fully into position and operational. It had to be assumed that in the meantime, were the Germans to learn of the plan, they would almost certainly try to make a dash for it.

Because of this danger, on July 6, a week after Nieder-mayer's departure from Isfahan, the Viceroy wrote to the Emir of Afghanistan, King Habibullah, to warn him of the Germans' intentions, and to remind him delicately of his treaty obligations to Britain. Officially Afghanistan was neu-tral, while under the terms of an agreement with Britain (dat-ing from the Great Game era) its foreign relations were entirely the responsibility of Delhi. Ultimately, short of send-ing troops, Britain had no way of enforcing these terms if the Emir chose to go back on them. Given a free choice, the Viceroy believed, Habibullah was unlikely to do this, for he would immediately forego the large annual subsidy paid him by the British government. However, it was no secret in Delhi that he was surrounded by relatives and court officials who were bitterly antagonistic towards Britain, and therefore pro-German or pro-Turkish to a man. They included the Emir's brother Nasrullah, who was also Prime Minister, and his own eldest son. Were a German mission to succeed in reaching the Afghan capital, armed with dazzling gifts and extravagant promises, then the Emir might find himself facing intense pressure from those around him to join in the Holy War, or risk being overthrown. The Viceroy's letter, therefore, had to be phrased with extreme tact, lest it appear that he was giving the Emir orders, thus playing into the hands of the anti-British faction at the royal court.

'Information has reached me', the Viceroy wrote, 'that a

number of German agents are now in Persia attempting to stir up trouble, contrary to the law of neutrality, and endeavouring to embroil the Persian government in the present war. These German agents . . . are moving in small parties eastwards, with a view, apparently, to entering Afghan territory.' Here the Viceroy included details of what was known of the numbers of the Germans and their allies, and the weapons they carried. He estimated the total strength of the various groups at around 180 men, including Germans, Austrians, Indians, Turks and Persians.

'That armed parties of this kind should move about in a neutral country, attempting to stir up trouble, is a flagrant breach of the law of neutrality,' the Viceroy continued, adding that while the Persian authorities were being prevailed upon to end such anarchy, some of the Germans and their allies might nonetheless invade 'Your Majesty's territories'. If so, the Viceroy ventured to suggest, then the Emir might choose to deal with them 'like any other neutral country with a strong and effective government', adding, in brackets, 'such as is the Government of Afghanistan.' This would involve arresting, disarming and interning the intruders until the end of the war. 'By such action,' the Viceroy concluded, 'Your Majesty would not only be acting in accordance with the principle of neutrality, to which you are so staunchly adhering, but would also prevent these parties from exciting the more ignorant and fanciful of Your Majesty's subjects by false stories and wild promises.'

In subsequent correspondence he kept the Emir regularly informed of the latest intelligence reaching Delhi on the movements and progress of the various German parties. He also notified him of the decision by the British and Russian governments to deploy, just outside his borders, the East Persian Cordon, with the aim of keeping the Germans and their allies out of Afghanistan and British Baluchistan, the nearest point of British India. 'I think it right', he declared, 'to inform Your Majesty at once of these measures, so that you may not be misled by any wild stories which may reach Kabul of Russian and British forces operating in Persia.' These forces, he assured the Emir, would be small, 'and only sufficient for the purpose of supporting the local Persian authorities against these mischievous intruders.' Here he was being more than a little economical with the truth. As we know, there was no question whatsoever of the cordon troops 'supporting' the local authorities, for when it came to curbing the Germans the Persians were nowhere to be seen. However, the Viceroy clearly intended to make the Allied intervention appear legitimate, though it is doubtful whether he fooled the wily and well-informed Emir for a moment.

Meanwhile, from the garrison town of Quetta, the East Persian Cordon was being hurriedly thrown into place, and the troops briefed on their task amid this harsh landscape, with its stinging sandstorms and furnace-like heat. While staff officers were frantically organising supply lines several hundred miles long, a network of paid native informants was being set up by intelligence officers to shadow and report on strangers halting at the rare villages and water-holes leading towards Afghanistan and Baluchistan. But in an area nearly twice the size of Britain, with virtually no roads or telegraph lines, intercepting these shadowy intruders in the deserts and mountains of eastern Persia was a pretty thankless task. Or as one senior British officer put it: 'The exciting game of hunt the slipper had begun – with the odds greatly in favour of the slipper.'

8

The Race for Kabul

To Captain Oskar von Niedermayer and his companions, as they rode eastwards from Isfahan in July 1915, it seemed that the odds were anything but in their favour. Ahead of them stretched a 1,000-mile journey across some of the cruellest terrain on earth. To attempt, even in peacetime, to cross the great Persian desert at the height of summer would be seen by most travellers as foolhardy, if not sheer madness. But the Germans had little choice, for their orders, emanating from Kaiser Wilhelm himself, were to reach Kabul as soon as humanly possible. Apart from the punishing heat of the sun, and the choking, suffocating dust-storms, there was the eternal nightmare of having to find water and food for both men and horses. Then there were the scorpions and poisonous snakes, which made life a misery for both men and beasts. The grim wilderness harboured other dangers to travellers, too, notably the marauding bands of outlaws and brigands who lived by plundering caravans. Theirs would be particularly vulnerable to attack, for it was widely known to be carrying gold, arms and expensive gifts for the Emir of Afghanistan.

In addition to these age-old dangers and discomforts, there were others of an entirely different kind, which earlier travellers had been spared. Already, they knew, enemy patrols would be watching the routes leading eastwards from Persia into Afghanistan. In every village they halted at there would be spies and informers ready to betray them to the British or the Russians. With their progress thus watched, they would not dare halt long anywhere, however exhausted, for fear of ambush. And even when they reached the Afghan frontier, if they got that far, they might well be turned back on the Emir's orders, or even handed over to the British or Russians. The odds seemed to be stacked heavily against them, but this did not lessen their resolve. For they knew that if their mission succeeded, and Afghanistan joined the Holy War, then it would have a dramatic impact on the progress of the war, and on the destiny of the Fatherland.

Yet they could have been spared most of these dangers and discomforts by their chiefs in Berlin. Had Wassmuss not been allowed to abandon the mission, leaving it without anyone authorised to negotiate on behalf of the German government, then they would very likely have been safely in Kabul by now. As it was, precious time had been wasted. For instead of having to wait for Otto von Hentig and his two Indian companions, they could have left Isfahan weeks earlier, in the spring. They would thereby have escaped the terrible Persian summer, greatly speeding their progress, and enabling them to reach the Afghan frontier before the British or Russians had time to deploy spies and patrols to intercept them.

This delay had done little for the already strained relations between the military and diplomatic members of the mission. While it had now been agreed in Berlin that Niedermayer was militarily in command, and that Hentig and the two Indians were responsible for securing the mission's political and diplomatic goals, it is clear that both Germans considered themselves to be the overall leader, as their respective accounts show. Responsibility for this confusion, which had dogged the adventure from the very beginning, rested squarely with the organisers in Berlin who had failed to lay down a proper command structure, and whose instructions all along had been of the haziest.

The British, who had gleaned something of this disharmony and delay through their spies and wireless intercepts, could afford to feel smug. They had learned, during the Great Game years, about the realities and problems surrounding such joint military and political operations. Often this experience had been acquired painfully or expensively, as in the two Afghan wars and the Younghusband mission to Lhasa. For the

Germans it was an entirely new type of warfare, giving rise to stresses and strains and clashes of temperament. For the British it was reassuring to see that the great Prussian war machine, usually so hyper-efficient, could make such a mess of things, and its much-vaunted iron discipline be threatened by personal disagreements. Nonetheless, in the face of a common foe and uncertain dangers ahead, Niedermayer and Hentig agreed to set aside their differences and work together for the Emperor and the Fatherland. Even so, mutual antipathies continued to simmer not far below the surface.

Because it was harder to keep secret the presence of a large caravan and because, in such a sterile area as this, the daily task of obtaining enough food and water for the entire mission might have proved insuperable, it was decided to divide the mission into two groups, each travelling independently of the other, several days apart. Were it not for these considerations, it would obviously have been better to stick together for the month-long journey to the Afghan frontier, since this would have provided the maximum fire-power in the event of an attack by an enemy patrol or by armed brigands. However, it was agreed that the two parties would join forces again at a pre-arranged spot before making their final dash for the frontier. They would then decide how best this could be achieved. In all the entire mission consisted of around 100 men, all of them mounted. It was made up of a dozen or so German officers and NCOs, including several escapees from Russian POW camps, and an armed escort of Persian mercenaries hired from friendly chiefs. In addition, a number of officers and NCOs had been sent ahead of the leading party to reconnoitre the route and try to buy, with German gold, safe passage for them through the domains of brigand chiefs along the way.

Although Hentig, who led one of the two parties, also left an account of their hazardous ride eastwards, that written by Niedermayer, who led the other, is the more graphic. Travelling by night to escape what Niedermayer called 'the terrible fire of the Persian sun', as well as the attention of British spies, they frequently lost their way in the darkness. This brought other unexpected hazards. On their third night out of Isfahan they made a chilling discovery when they found themselves riding through 'hundreds of poisonous snakes which had come out to hunt'. After one horse had collapsed and died from a snake-bite, Niedermayer related, 'we had to send ahead men clad in leather leggings and armed with whips to clear the way'. The following morning, apart from their tracks in the sand, there was no sign of the snakes; instead the camp was crawling with giant scorpions which crept into the men's clothes to escape the heat. 'Every piece of clothing', Niedermayer wrote, 'had to be shaken carefully before we got dressed.' In addition, they were plagued by armies of insects of every kind. 'These', he added, 'live in incredible numbers in Persian houses, but appear not to worry the occupants who at intervals pick them out of their clothes, but refuse to kill them.'

The Germans found the heat hard to bear, the temperature in the shade on some mornings reaching 105 degrees Fahrenheit by 9 o'clock. Their precious supply of chocolate, and even their candles, had by now melted into solid masses. The going became even harsher after they entered the great salt desert, the dreaded Kavir, where the early morning temperature soared to an appalling 112 degrees, and a roasting hot wind blew mercilessly all day. 'It was a foretaste of what the nomads called the Hell of Persia,' wrote Niedermayer. 'If you looked at the sun it seemed pitch black, while if you turned your back on it the desert appeared snow white.'

At night they navigated between the rare, scattered water-holes simply by following the line of bleached skeletons of camels and other beasts which marked the trail. 'Only the camels and mules could stomach the evil-smelling water,' Niedermayer recalled. 'No amount of boiling improved it, and we had to quench our own thirst with the few water-melons we had left.' By now many of them, both Germans and Persians, were weakened by dysentery, slowing their progress even more. On one occasion, when the wind blew away their tracks, Niedermayer realised that some stragglers were missing, having lost the trail. He sent men back, who came upon them just in time, several already unconscious from thirst. The animals too were suffering severely from the heat and lack of water, particularly the horses, some of which had perished. But neither party had so far lost any men. However, the enthusiasm of the Persian escort was rapidly waning, for even those born in the desert were finding the pace set by the iron-willed Niedermayer punishing.

Then at last the weary travellers found themselves passing out of the great salt desert and approaching the small village of Chehar Deh, just over half way from Isfahan to the nearest point on the Afghan frontier. It was here that Niedermayer and Hentig had arranged to meet, with their respective parties, and decide how best to proceed. They had now ridden 300 gruelling miles, and were in desperate need of rest. For even if they reached the safety of Afghanistan, where no British or Russian patrols would dare pursue them, they still had a 500-mile ride ahead of them to Kabul. It was at Chehar Deh that they received their first definite information about the presence of British and Russian troops ahead of them, something they had previously merely assumed. More disturbing, though, was the news that the enemy were being deployed along the frontier in greater strength than they had expected. Because of this, and the likelihood of their having to fight for their lives, Niedermayer and Hentig decided to join forces for the remaining 200 miles to the frontier.

'In all,' wrote Niedermayer, 'we had no more than 15 or 20 trained soldiers, the rest being locally hired Persian escorts.' The latter, he knew, would be of little use against regular troops, especially those armed with machine-guns. 'We ourselves', he added, 'had no machine-guns or artillery, and our two wireless sets had been left behind in Isfahan. Somehow we had to keep our enemies guessing as to which route we would take.' Clearly they could not afford to linger at Chehar Deh. Every day that passed handed the enemy precious time in which to strengthen the cordon, and also to learn of their precise whereabouts and numbers. As it was, there were very likely British or Russian informers in the village. 'We therefore had to leave most circumspectly,' wrote Niedermayer, 'even at the cost of time-wasting feints and detours. All our fates would depend on the decisions and moves of the next few days.'

It was while they were debating those crucial moves that something happened that brought home to them their vulnerability and the need for extreme vigilance. One of the NCOs, sent out to try to buy meat for the party, stumbled by extraordinary chance on a leather bag full of money which he recognised as belonging to the mission's own small treasury. It had been concealed rather clumsily in an old mud wall, from where the thief clearly intended to retrieve it. The alarm was immediately raised, and one of the Persian servants was found to be missing. The suspect, Niedermayer recounted, was discovered in a tea-house smoking opium. 'He was dragged out and questioned. When he resisted being searched and tried to escape he was shot dead.' Later his horse was found, saddled up and ready for his intended getaway, together with evidence clearly showing how close a shave they had had. 'That very night,' Niedermayer wrote, 'he had intended to betray us to the Russians.'

*　　*　　*

In this remote Central Asian backwater, without a wireless set or any other link with the outside world, Niedermayer and his companions had no way of discovering what was happening elsewhere – least of all in the no man's land they were about to enter. In fact, the East Persian Cordon was still very far from complete, and in places virtually non-existent. The biggest gap lay around the mud-built town of Birjand, where the British and Russian sectors met, for this was the furthest point to which either of them had to get troops or supplies. Had Niedermayer and Hentig but known it, this loophole happened to lie at precisely the spot where they were preparing to make their final dash for the Afghan frontier. The defence chiefs in Delhi, however, were making desperate efforts to plug the gap, and urging the Russians to do likewise. Wolseley Haig, the British consul-general at Meshed, was ordered to enlist 150 former Indian Army soldiers from among the local Hazara tribesmen – old friends of the British from Great Game days – and use them to intercept the armed German parties. But this brought a protest from the Russians, who pointed out that Meshed, under the terms of the Anglo-Russian Convention, lay strictly within their sphere of influence. They promised, though, to dispatch Cossack troops to the region, and soon these were reported to be on the way. Even so, if the Germans were to be kept out of Afghanistan, it was clearly going to be a race against time.

From Kabul, so far as the British were concerned, the news was a little better, and the Viceroy, Lord Hardinge, was able to advise the Cabinet in London as follows: 'Emir has sent most satisfactory reply to my letters regarding approach of German agents to Afghanistan. He says it has never been the rule of the Afghan government to allow armed parties of foreigners to enter Afghanistan. If German parties enter Afghanistan they will be disarmed and interned until the end of the war.' The Viceroy added that the Emir, 'in a friendly postscript in his own handwriting', had reiterated his intention of maintaining Afghanistan's strict neutrality for the duration of the war. Reassuring though this was to the Viceroy and his advisers, they were nonetheless acutely aware that the Emir's promise held good only while he remained in control of his highly volatile and violent people. 'King Habibullah', reported one Englishman returning from Kabul, 'is our only friend in Afghanistan.' The rest were anti-British almost to a man. Like the Persians they were still smouldering from the humiliation of the 1907 Convention which had decided their destiny without either their knowledge or their agreement. Nor had they forgotten Britain's two invasions of their country, in 1839 and 1879, and the occupation of their capital. Were the Germans to succeed in reaching Kabul, it was clear that their message would not fall entirely on deaf ears.

But if the mood in Afghanistan at that time was largely pro-German, ironically it was anything but that in Turkey itself. Suspicions were growing over Germany's real intentions in the East, and particularly towards the Ottoman Empire. Before the war, the ruling triumvirate had been secretly boasting of using Berlin's money and technology to bring Turkey up to modern European standards as a military and industrial power. 'When that has been achieved,' one declared, 'we can say goodbye to the Germans within twenty-four hours.' As for the German-built Baghdad Railway, the Turkish sector could be nationalised the moment it was finished. Since then, however, the mood had changed. In the event of victory, it was being asked, would Turkey simply be absorbed into a new German empire, stretching from Berlin to Burma, with Kaiser Wilhelm as its Sultan-Emperor? Many Turks, faced by growing casualty lists and worsening shortages at home, were angry at the way they had been dragged into the war by the Germans and their friends at Constantinople. Few harboured any real hatred for the British, their traditional guardians against the Russians, frankly preferring them to their increasingly overbearing German allies.

In the Turkish capital, wild and ugly rumours began to reach the ears of Baron Wangenheim, the German ambassador, who had played a leading role in coercing the Sultan's largely unwilling government into the fray. In the bazaars, where there was a grave meat shortage, it was whispered that this was because, on Berlin's orders, all supplies were being sent to Germany. Indeed, very soon almost everything that went wrong was being blamed on the Germans. Fears began to spread through the German diplomatic, military and business communities that in the event of a major Allied victory a massacre of all Christians in the capital would result. And that clearly meant them and their families.

Already Wangenheim and his compatriots had seen for themselves how the unfortunate Christians of eastern Turkey, the Armenians, had reaped the whirlwind of the Holy War in the spring of that year, when Enver was looking for a scapegoat for his catastrophic and humiliating defeat by the Russians at Sarikamish. Indeed, only Wangenheim had been in a position to remonstrate with Enver and try to halt the appalling massacres and deportations that had followed. Cynically but frankly he had explained to a shocked Henry Morgenthau, the American ambassador, that Germany could ill afford to fall out with its Turkish ally by interfering in so sensitive a domestic matter. Not only did Enver need a scapegoat for his own military shortcomings, but also the hapless Armenians' homeland lay directly in the path of his grand design for a Turkish empire stretching from Constantinople to Kashgar. Germany's only concern at that moment, Wangenheim told Morgenthau, was 'getting on and winning the war'.

Nonetheless, growing American pressure over the fate of the Armenians, as word of the slaughter leaked out, soon began to worry Berlin. It was feared that this would inflame American opinion against Turkey, and with it Germany. The maintenance of American neutrality was crucial to Berlin's war aims, so around the middle of June Wangenheim began to change his tune. By that time, however, it was too late. The bloodletting was in full spate, and the German ambassador's protests that the Allies would make worldwide propaganda from it fell on deaf ears in Constantinople. Four months later, as though by divine retribution for his failure to act, Wangenheim was abruptly removed from the scene by a stroke at the age of 56. Today the man who dreamed of becoming Chancellor of the Kaiser's new post-war empire lies buried in the beautiful grounds of his former summer residence overlooking the Bosphorus, surrounded by others of his countrymen who died in the war which his intrigues had done so much to further.

In Constantinople, and throughout the Ottoman Empire, such intrigues had always been part of the natural order of things, and many other dark and perfidious dealings were afoot at this time. In December 1915, at the height of the Armenian massacres, an astonishing proposition was put to the Allies for halting the slaughter and ending the war with Turkey. It came from none other than Djemal Pasha, one of the triumvirate directing the war, then in Damascus from where he commanded the armies defending Turkey's southern flank. He offered, with Allied military assistance, to march on Constantinople, overthrow Enver, arrest his German advisers, halt the Armenian massacres and take Turkey out of the war. In return, he would be allowed to ascend the Ottoman throne himself as Sultan of a new Turkey, with Damascus as its capital. He would renounce for ever Constantinople and the Straits. These could either be ceded to Russia, which had long wanted them as an outlet to the Mediterranean, or be placed in the hands of an international commission. His domains would include Asiatic Turkey, Syria, Mesopotamia, Palestine and the Arabian peninsula. Both the Armenians and the Kurds, however, would be granted virtual autonomy within their traditional homelands, albeit under his supreme sovereignty.

But the Armenians could hardly expect to get all this for nothing, and the deal was also to include the payment, by wealthy Armenians outside Turkey, of a large sum of money. Some of this, it seemed, would go towards buying off those engaged in slaughtering and plundering the Armenian communities in eastern Turkey, and providing food and other immediate relief for their victims. The rest of the money would go into Djemal's own pocket, in the time-honoured fashion of the East, as his fee for arranging it all. To the Armenian leaders, desperate to save their people while any still survived, it seemed cheap at the price. In fact, it was through certain prominent Armenians, with high-level connections in St Petersburg, that Djemal had first put his discreet offer to the Allies.

This was a breathtaking piece of treachery against Enver and Talaat, his two fellow triumvirate members, not to mention a highly treasonable one against the Sultan. Djemal had chosen his moment well, moreover. For his offer came as the British and their allies were in the middle of their ignominious evacuation of the Gallipoli peninsula, their attempt to try to seize Constantinople having proved a ghastly and expensive failure. Here, Djemal knew, was their chance to save face. The British, at first, looked favourably at his offer. Quite apart from any need to redeem the calamity of Gallipoli, such a deal would remove any Turkish threat to Egypt, thereby freeing desperately needed troops for use against the Germans on the Western Front. The Russians too welcomed the offer, for it promised them what they had always wanted – Constantinople. At the same time it would enable them to divert troops from the Caucasus to Eastern Europe, where the war was going badly for them. Only the French rejected the proposal out of hand, for they themselves wanted Syria, with which they had enjoyed close links since the sixteenth century. They had no wish to lose it now to Djemal, despite his known liking for the French and dislike of the Germans, when it could become theirs as part of the booty of war in the event of an Allied victory.

The question of whether or not to pursue Djemal's offer was further complicated by the fact that the Allies had already begun to share out, on paper at least, the Sultan's domains in anticipation of eventual victory in the East. In April 1915, in order to stiffen Russia's resolution to remain in the war, it had been secretly agreed that Constantinople and the Straits would go to St Petersburg, together with part of eastern Turkey. The following month, as an inducement to the

Italians to declare war on the Turks, a portion of southern Turkey was earmarked for them. At the same time, the British had their post-war eyes on Mesopotamia, largely because of its oilfields, and also on Egypt and Cyprus which they wished to retain for strategic reasons. Nor was that all. In return for joining the Allied cause, Greece was being offered part of western Turkey in any post-war division of the Ottoman Empire, while other deals involving the Arabs and Jews were being considered in exchange for wartime assistance. It was clear, however, that none of these deals could be reconciled with Djemal's demands, as he wished to keep the Ottoman domains largely intact. Only the Russians stood to gain territorially from his offer, since they would get Constantinople earlier, and with certainty.

The Allies' agonising dragged on for weeks, but in the end Djemal's proposition was turned down. Britain and France preferred to gamble on eventually defeating the Turks, and thereby obtaining their maximum share of the spoils. Apart from the Russians, the real losers were the unfortunate Armenians, whose slaughter continued, and the thousands of Allied and Turkish soldiers whose lives were sacrificed on the battlefield during the long and bloody months ahead. Fortunately for Djemal, his double-dealing was never discovered by Enver and Talaat, and he continued to fight as their comrade-in-arms as though nothing had happened. For his part, Ambassador Morgenthau continued trying to intercede with Enver and Talaat on behalf of the Armenians, even suggesting that they might be found a new home in the American West. But his efforts proved futile, despite warnings from the Allied powers that the triumvirate would be held personally responsible. 'It's no use you arguing,' Morgenthau was told by Talaat, who was Minister of the Interior. 'The Armenians have openly encouraged our enemies. They have assisted the Russians in the Caucasus, and our failure there is largely explained by their actions.' Sadly for the Armenians, there was an element of truth in this. There were units of the Tsar's Caucasian army consisting entirely of Armenian volunteers who hoped, by assisting their Christian neighbour to defeat the Turks, to secure for themselves an independent homeland under Russian protection after the war.

From the German Embassy in Constantinople, meanwhile, the Holy War was being prosecuted with renewed vigour. Following Wangenheim's sudden death in October 1915, Max von Oppenheim, the Holy War's principal architect, had arrived from Berlin to take over the direction of the Kaiser's clandestine operations in the East. Large quantities of arms, gold and propaganda were soon being delivered to him by rail from Berlin for the use of his agents in Persia and, if things went well, in Afghanistan and beyond. Hitherto it had been virtually impossible to get such sensitive materials through, although a certain amount had been smuggled in by concealing it in the false bottoms of freight wagons. The free flow of supplies to Turkey had been interrupted by the neutrality of Bulgaria and Romania, which lay astride the only two rail routes, and also by the presence, athwart the most direct of these, of a hostile Serbia. But in the autumn of 1915, with the entry of Bulgaria into the war on Germany's and Turkey's side, and the overrunning of Serbia by German, Austro-Hungarian and Bulgarian troops shortly afterwards, a direct supply line between Berlin and Constantinople was at last opened. It was this, as it happened, which finally hastened the evacuation of Allied troops from Gallipoli, for it enabled desperately needed shells for the German and Turkish guns to be rushed to the front from Germany. Oppenheim's propaganda experts now hailed the Allied rout at Gallipoli as a great Holy War victory.

But not all German officers and advisers serving with the Turkish armed forces were convinced of the value, or even the wisdom, of trying to unleash a Holy War against the Allies. Many considered it a waste of valuable manpower and resources, and very likely to backfire on them. Indeed, because of such disagreements, senior German officers in the Turkish capital were frequently not on speaking terms with their diplomatic colleagues at the embassy. Nor was this view confined to the military. One stern critic of what he saw as von Oppenheim's cynical misuse of Islam was the Constantinople correspondent of the *Kölnische Zeitung*, Dr Harry Stuermer. In 1917, after obtaining asylum in Switzerland, he wrote a book called *Two War Years in Constantinople* in which he accused von Oppenheim and his colleagues of gross irresponsibility in unleashing 'the wildest fanaticism' against the forces of law, order and civilisation, and 'setting back by years' all that had 'so patiently and painfully' been won in the Muslim lands.

Stuermer claimed, furthermore, that the Holy War had attracted 'the scum of the earth' – would-be Niedermayers and Wassmusses who hoodwinked the German Embassy with their supposed expertise on the East into parting with considerable sums of money. Von Oppenheim and his staff, he alleged, had allowed themselves to be made 'the dupe of greedy adventurers who treated the embassy as an inexhaustible source of gold' in return for promising to spread the Holy War. Much of this had ended up in what Stuermer called Constantinople's 'low haunts', far from its intended destination. One such adventurer – a Russian-speaking German clerk from Baku, who offered to spread the Holy War among the Muslim peoples of the Caucasus – was given the rank of major and supplied with arms, money and propaganda with which to carry out his mission. 'Whole chests full of gold coins were sent to him to be distributed confidentially for propaganda purposes,' wrote Stuermer. Yet he failed to win a single convert to the Holy War, while the money seemingly was spent on financing his own opulent life-style in Constantinople on his return. Von Oppenheim, a genuine authority on the East, should have known better than to be deceived thus, Stuermer added. Yet he 'doled out thousands of marks from his own pocket – and millions from official funds' in support of what Stuermer called 'these false illusions'.

Whatever the truth of Stuermer's lurid picture of venality and incompetence in Constantinople, to the British the menace posed by the Holy War was becoming real enough. In large areas of Persia, almost daily, the Germans were tightening their grip and expanding their domain. Swelled by the influx of escaping POWs, the number of armed and able-bodied Germans and Austrians had by the autumn of 1915 grown to some 300 – according to British intelligence estimates. In addition, on the German payroll were around 1,000 Persian mercenaries, plus a number of Indian Army deserters and captured sepoys who had joined the Turco-German cause. So complete was Berlin's penetration of central and southern

Persia that no fewer than seven out of the seventeen branches of the British-owned Imperial Bank of Persia were in German hands, their treasuries having been plundered to help fund the Holy War. Telegraph offices, too, had been seized in many places by the Germans for their own exclusive use, and to deny them to the British. Virtual anarchy, deliberately fomented, now reigned throughout much of the country, with the pro-German Gendarmerie doing little or nothing to stop it.

Attempts, almost certainly German-incited, had been made on the lives of British and Russian consular officials, one or two of which had resulted in death or serious injury. It was also reported that Wassmuss had now moved his base of operations from the Bushire region back to Shiraz, in the interior, where he was officially supposed to be the German consul. Since both the Persian governor and the local Gendarmerie were known to be his friends, this augured ill for the small and wholly unprotected British Consulate there. Only in the Russian-controlled north of Persia, where German agents were being hunted down by the ferocious Cossacks, were they faring less well in their efforts to destroy Allied influence and drag the young Shah and his ten million subjects into the Holy War. Despite this, however, from the safety of the German Legation, the Minister, Prince Henry of Reuss, still had high hopes of ending Persia's neutrality, as will be seen. But already we have moved ahead of our narrative, and must return to the remote village of Chehar Deh, in the extreme east of Persia, where we left Niedermayer and his companions as they prepared to run the Anglo-Russian gauntlet towards the end of July 1915.

Cut off from all news of the outside world, the Germans knew nothing of the dramas unfolding in Constantinople, Teheran and elsewhere. Their sole immediate concern was to try to reach the Afghan frontier undetected. For once inside the Emir's domains they knew that they were reasonably safe from Allied pursuit. Although the British and Russians could arrogantly take the law into their own hands in the Shah's anarchic realm, in Afghanistan they would not dare to intervene. Such a move could hardly fail to incense the Emir, and further inflame the pent-up passions of his Anglophobic subjects. Indeed, that alone, without any German help, could spark off the very thing they had been sent all this way to bring about – the Holy War against British India.

Delhi's best hope, they knew, was to annihilate them before they could reach the frontier. Indeed, at that very moment, urgent messages were passing between London, Delhi and St Petersburg, and the scattered outposts of the East Persian Cordon, in a desperate effort to discover their whereabouts in this vast Tom Tiddler's ground. After a break of only eight years following the truce of 1907, and with Afghanistan and British India once more the flash-points, the Great Game was about to begin again in Central Asia.

9

Niedermayer's Bluff

The task of deciding how best to give the Allied patrols the slip now fell upon the sturdy and capable shoulders of Captain Oskar von Niedermayer. For not only was he in military command of the expedition, but he had also travelled widely in Persia before the war, and had once even stayed at the British Consulate-General in Meshed. The strategy he chose was to involve the use of decoys, feints and false information. If, even momentarily, he could lure the enemy patrols away from the main party's line of approach to the frontier, he believed they could slip through the hole this created in the net. Even so, if they were to reach the frontier before their pursuers realised they had been tricked and gave chase, his exhausted men and beasts would have to move at a punishing pace over the next 200 miles.

Niedermayer knew that he had to outmanoeuvre two distinct foes – the Russian patrols probing down from the north, and the British coming up from the south. At the same time he had to ensure that he had a clear gap ahead for the main party to make its dash through. He therefore briefed and sent off three small armed patrols. The first, which was intended to draw off the Cossacks, he dispatched to the north-east. The second, aimed at similarly deceiving the British, he sent to the south-east. A third patrol, consisting of a German officer – Lieutenant Wagner – and thirty armed Persians, was sent ahead to reconnoitre a route for the main party and to report back immediately they detected a gap. Meanwhile the first patrol, having led the Cossacks into following a false trail, would not attempt to catch up the main party, but would draw back and set up a secret base in the desert for those of the main party too sick to attempt the gruelling dash for the frontier. The second group, having with luck drawn off the British patrols, would try to reach Kerman, where they would join forces with Lieutenants Zugmayer and Griesinger. As part of this deception, all three patrols would spread misleading tales about their movements among any villagers or nomads they came upon, and also leave behind them, apparently in error, bogus secret papers designed to confirm these falsehoods.

Although Niedermayer's own men were tough and determined individuals on whom he knew he could rely totally, their Persian escort, who formed the bulk of the party, consisted of armed tribesmen of unpredictable loyalty, drawn into the Holy War by a heady mixture of German gold, religious fanaticism and a long-standing dislike of all things British and Russian. Confronted by well-trained Allied troops, very likely armed with machine-guns, they would almost certainly go to pieces and abandon their German paymasters to their fate. This clearly made the role of the lone officers leading the decoy parties particularly hazardous – just how hazardous, they would quickly discover.

By this time the British had somehow managed to find out through their network of informers that the Germans were already half-way to the Afghan frontier. Especially alarming was the discovery, in mid-July, that they had succeeded in crossing the great Kavir salt desert. Hitherto, from the earliest days of the Great Game when Napoleon and Tsar Alexander had together plotted to invade India through Persia, this had been regarded by British strategists as virtually impenetrable. But now an armed German party had crossed it, albeit at the narrowest point, in what was believed to be the first ever eastwards crossing by Europeans. The reaction in both Delhi and London was one of near panic. 'The Germans have a fairly easy path in front of them,' warned one senior Foreign Office official. 'Everything now depends on the attitude of the Emir,' wrote another; while a third noted: 'The Emir is sound, but he may be overridden.'

The Viceroy was no less gloomy. The day after learning of the Germans' alarming progress towards the thinly patrolled frontier around Birjand, he telegraphed London to warn them that the East Persian Cordon was not yet fully in position there and requested that Russian troops be rushed to the spot in the meantime. He further warned London that a second party was believed to be approaching the frontier from the direction of Kerman. His wire reached London at 2.20 a.m. Within hours the Foreign Secretary, Sir Edward Grey, had telegraphed the British ambassador in St Petersburg as follows: 'Urgent. German caravans numbering 196 persons, including 30 Germans and 15 Austrians are approaching Afghan frontier.' One group – Niedermayer's – was advancing from the direction of Chehar Deh, the other – Zugmayer's – from Kerman. If the Russians, who had troops in north-eastern Persia, could be urged to tackle the party approaching Birjand, where the two halves of the Anglo-Russian cordon met, then British troops would deal with those reportedly coming from Kerman. In the event, as will be seen, the Kerman threat proved to be a false alarm.

At the same time a report on German movements towards his frontiers was telegraphed to the Emir by the Viceroy, urging him to seize the Germans 'and their escort of hired assassins' if they slipped through the Allied cordon. The Viceroy further informed him: 'Wild stories are afloat in Afghanistan and among the tribes of the frontier that a Turco-German army is on the march towards India via Afghanistan. I need not tell Your Majesty how absolutely ridiculous and unfounded such stories are, since there are no Turkish forces in Persia at the present time, and no German or Austrian troops of any kind.' He suggested, however, that the Emir should publicly scotch such tales so that 'the more ignorant and credulous of Your Majesty's subjects may not be misled into thinking that these German parties, should they appear on your frontier, are the vanguard of a large force following.' Finally he reassured the Emir that, despite the lack of any clear-cut Allied victories so far, 'those who are best qualified to judge' had no doubt whatsoever as to the war's final outcome. With their vast superiority in manpower and economic resources, and their control of the high seas, the Allies could not in the long run fail to defeat both Germany and Turkey.

Meanwhile, though, to the frustration of the Viceroy and

his defence chiefs, the Russians seemed to be in no great haste to move their Cossacks into what the British perceived to be the weakest point in the East Persian Cordon. This lay immediately to the north of Birjand, where the British and Russian sectors met. The reason for this delay, it appears, was simply a question of priorities. The threatened infiltration of Afghanistan by German agents was rather less of a worry to the Russians than it was to the British. Furthermore, the Russians required every Cossack they could spare to protect their interests in northern Persia, where they were threatened by Turks, Germans and a hostile populace. But whatever the reason, the delay in filling the gap deepened the gloom in Delhi, as the secret files of the day clearly show. 'I'm afraid the Germans will get through unopposed. I don't see how this Russian force can catch them in time,' noted one mandarin on July 27, in a file labelled *German Agents in Persia*, just as Niedermayer was preparing to leave Chehar Deh. Nor was that all. A further cause for anxiety was the reported behaviour of the Russians towards the local populace – behaviour guaranteed to ignite Muslim fury against the Allies, and rally more converts to the Holy War. According to one tale which reached British ears, the Cossacks sent to reinforce the cordon had outraged local feelings by stabling their horses in a village mosque. 'So like the Russians!' noted one British official drily.

*   *   *

For all this British pessimism, Niedermayer and his companions were to enjoy no easy ride after leaving Chehar Deh, running into serious trouble almost immediately. After sending ahead his reconnaissance party under Lieutenant Wagner, and his two decoy parties to the north and south, he had advanced forty miles to the next village to await word from Wagner. As a precaution against informers he posted armed guards around the village to prevent anyone from leaving. While they waited, a secret courier arrived from Isfahan bringing encouraging intelligence on the progress of the war and some four-month-old German newspapers. But there was no word from Wagner.

Then, at last, they did get news – very bad news. Instead of finding the gap in the Anglo-Russian cordon he had hoped for, Wagner and his party had been attacked by a Cossack patrol fifty miles north of Birjand. Despite Delhi's worst fears, it was clear that the first of the Cossacks had arrived. The attack had taken place at night, enabling Wagner and his companions to escape, but with the loss of all their baggage, including some gold they were carrying. However, they had managed to inflict several casualties on the enemy, without suffering any themselves, and had now taken up a position thirty miles ahead of where Niedermayer was encamped. Ordered by him to rejoin his party so that they could consider their next move, they arrived next day in what Niedermayer described as 'a terrible state'. It transpired that they had been betrayed to the Cossacks by local Persians who may have been aware that they were carrying gold. Curiously, though, the Cossacks had not attempted to follow them, possibly fearing a trap of some kind. Nonetheless, Niedermayer knew they had little time to spare before more Cossacks began to arrive from the north, reinforced by British patrols from the south. They had to try to break out in the short time they had left, or their whereabouts would be discovered and the entire party would be annihilated where it lay half buried in the sand.

It was while they were thus deliberating that a column of unidentified horsemen was suddenly spotted in the far distance. Dust-devils and mirages were frequently being mistaken for approaching caravans, giving rise to false alarms. But careful scrutiny of this one through powerful binoculars convinced Niedermayer that it was no hallucination. However, there could be no way of discovering, until it was too late, whether it was hostile or friendly. Niedermayer gave immediate orders to his men to pack up as fast as possible. Hoping that they had not been spotted, and moving as cautiously as they could, they slipped away southwards across the desert. Fortunately it was evening, and darkness was falling rapidly. The gusting wind, moreover, which always sprang up at this time of day, quickly blew away all traces of their camp, as well as the trail they left behind them.

Niedermayer's plan, so far as he had one, was to try to squeeze through any gap which his scouts could find. This called for a succession of forced marches by night, stretching men and beasts to their absolute limit. Extreme vigilance was crucial, for the enemy had spies everywhere who would be instantly suspicious if they detected a large caravan travelling through the night towards the Afghan frontier. 'It was of vital importance not to light any fires,' wrote Niedermayer. 'Yet I had to intervene on many occasions when my Persian horsemen set fire to tufts of grass to light their opium pipes. Most of them were addicts and could only carry on this way.' They would halt, lie down and sleep blissfully for a while. Some they never saw again, for there could be no waiting or going back for those who failed to keep up the pace. At times, Niedermayer found himself almost envying the Persians their opium as the going got tougher. 'How fortunate they were', he wrote, 'being able to indulge in wonderful dreams. All we could dream about was immersing ourselves in pools of clear, cool water.'

Only the town of Birjand – just three days' march off – now lay between them and the nearest point on the Afghan frontier. Almost certainly there were British troops there by this time, while the Russians had long had a consulate in this remote mud-built town. Obviously it had to be avoided at all costs. But should they bypass it to the north, where they knew the Cossacks to be, or to the south, where the British were hunting for them? It was a nightmarish choice for Niedermayer, for their survival depended on his getting it right. Yet, as they approached the area of maximum danger, there was no possible way of finding out how the British and Russian patrols ahead of them were deployed, and therefore which of the two routes was likely to be the least hazardous. Niedermayer decided to take the northerly one. He had discovered from their Persian escort that the desert running northwards from Birjand was a notoriously harsh one, particularly in summer, with few if any wells. It was therefore the route that their pursuers might least expect them to take. With luck they would concentrate their thinly spread resources on the other, more likely approaches to the south of Birjand. After dispatching a small decoy group to the south-east, and circulating rumours that the main party would shortly be following it, Niedermayer and his companions instead turned the other way and disappeared into the hideously barren wilderness to the north.

*   *   *

By now Niedermayer's decoy parties and deliberately spread falsehoods had begun to have their intended effect, causing considerable confusion among those trying to monitor their movements, as British intelligence reports of the time clearly show. According to one, based on a lost (or so Delhi believed) German letter, some of the mission had already crossed into Afghanistan, thereby making further pursuit apparently pointless. This letter had almost certainly been 'mislaid' by Lieutenant Wagner on his northward feint. It fell into the hands of the British Consulate-General at Meshed, who in turn telegraphed its contents to Teheran, and thence to Delhi and London. Other disinformation planted on the British by Niedermayer had led them to overestimate wildly the number of Germans and Austrians, as against Persian mercenaries, making their way towards Afghanistan. One such report put the figure as high as 400. Finally, as we have already seen, the Viceroy had warned London that a second German force, led by the subalterns Zugmayer and Griesinger, was at that very moment heading towards the highly exposed and sparsely patrolled frontiers of southern Afghanistan and Baluchistan. Whether or not this also was the result of Niedermayer's efforts it is difficult to say. But one thing was certain, and that was that the Viceroy's fears were totally groundless. The two German officers, as will be seen, were stuck firmly in Kerman. Nonetheless, Delhi's concern led to the troops of the East Persian Cordon being even more extended, which is precisely what Niedermayer wanted.

In fact, as he and his companions toiled painfully across the desert somewhere to the north of Birjand, they had no idea of how Zugmayer and Griesinger were faring at Kerman, and were too concerned with avoiding enemy patrols to give them much thought. At one small water-hole, which turned out to be salt, they learned from nomads that two days earlier a British patrol had been there looking for them. 'The sun', wrote Niedermayer, 'was sheer torture.' Yet because of their need not to waste a moment in this region of maximum danger, they had to travel both by day and by night, thus stretching themselves and their animals to breaking point. Soon some of the escort could take no more. 'Several just dropped by the wayside,' Niedermayer recalled, 'and even I could hardly keep awake.' Others simply deserted, taking with them some of the party's precious water and spare horses after threatening the NCO in charge with their rifles.

Ahead of them now, just four hours' ride away, lay the main north–south road linking Birjand and Meshed. Eighty miles beyond that lay the Afghan frontier. Niedermayer guessed that the road would be regularly patrolled and closely watched by spies, for any party making for Afghanistan had to cross it. Extreme caution, therefore, was called for in approaching it, while the actual crossing would have to be made under cover of darkness. Niedermayer therefore sent ahead patrols to try to obtain a clear picture of the terrain and also report back on enemy activity on the road. Meanwhile, as they waited for them to report, he ordered a ruthless reduction of the party's baggage. Only the most vital equipment could be taken, in the interests of speed. The rest would have to be buried in the desert for possible retrieval later. Items thus jettisoned included the Kaiser's larger and heavier gifts for the Emir, as well as bales of Holy War propaganda. At the same time the men tried to snatch a little rest. However, it was not long before a messenger returned with news from Niedermayer's patrols. The road, it appeared, was clear, although an enemy cavalry unit had recently passed along it. They might soon return, so the crossing would have to be made swiftly.

'Our nervous tension overcame our exhaustion,' Niedermayer wrote. He and another officer now rode ahead and waited near the crossing point for the main party to catch up. By the time they arrived it was dark. No one spoke. 'On our flanks the scouts were listening for the slightest sound,' Niedermayer recounted. When he was totally satisfied that it was safe to move, he gave the order to cross. 'Like spectres', he wrote, 'we slipped across the road and disappeared into the eastern hills.' However, they were still far from safe. Although they had successfully crossed the most exposed point of their journey, they were not yet out of hostile territory, with another eighty miles to go. Furthermore, there was one final obstacle to be overcome before they were clear of the Anglo-Russian cordon. This was the so-called 'mountain path', thirty miles further east. It too was likely to be heavily patrolled, for alongside it ran the telegraph line used by the Allies to maintain contact with their cordon outposts in this remote region. Moreover, were they to discover that Niedermayer had given them the slip and crossed the main Birjand-to-Meshed road, then it would be here that they would try to waylay him, since it would be their very last chance before he and his party crossed safely into Afghanistan.

*   *   *

Had the Allies been able to concentrate all their forces, slender though these were, against Niedermayer, they might well have caught him by now. But not only did the British find themselves covering for the Russians to the north of Birjand until more Cossacks could be spared, they also firmly believed that a second German mission was on its way eastwards from Kerman. Indeed, that had been the intention of Zugmayer and Griesinger when, on July 4, they arrived in the town to raise the banner of the Holy War there. Fairly soon, however, they had run into unexpected difficulties. 'At the beginning the prospects were extraordinarily good,' Zugmayer reported to Prince Henry of Reuss, the German Minister in Teheran. 'We were greeted by the populace with rapture. Everyone saw in us a counterweight to the influence of the hated British and Russians, and to the oppression of the governor, his deputy and the chief of police, all of whom are in the pay of the British.' Every month, Zugmayer claimed, they received substantial bribes from the British consul there 'for betraying to him the activities of the Germans here'. This was almost certainly true, for as we know, the consul had been instructed by Delhi to use 'secret service funds' to try to combat German intrigues in south-eastern Persia.

But this British skulduggery was only one of their problems. Another lay with the Persian authorities in Teheran, who no doubt were being leaned on heavily by the British and Russians there. Ostensibly, Zugmayer and Griesinger had been sent to Kerman as German consul and vice-consul. Despite a succession of telegrams pressing Teheran for formal accreditation, this had failed to materialise. Without diplomatic status, the Germans had to send their telegrams *en clair* through the ordinary Persian telegraph service. This meant that they were read by the governor, who passed their entire

1. Kaiser Wilhelm II, who dreamed of unleashing a Muslim Holy War against the British and their allies throughout the East

2. Gobbling up the world – how British wartime propagandists portrayed the German Emperor's territorial ambitions

HIS MASTER'S VOICE.

The Kaiser (*to Turkey, reassuringly*). "LEAVE EVERYTHING TO ME. ALL YOU'VE GOT T
DO IS TO EXPLODE."

Turkey. "YES, I QUITE SEE THAT. BUT WHERE SHALL *I* BE WHEN IT'S ALL OVER?

3. Turkey as Germany's dupe – a *Punch* cartoon of November 1914

4. Sultan Abdul Hamid ('the Damned') of Turkey – befriended by Kaiser Wilhelm when all other European sovereigns and statesmen spurned him

5. Enver Pasha, Turkey's wartime military supremo and evil genius, who dreamed of carving out a great new Ottoman Empire for himself in Central Asia

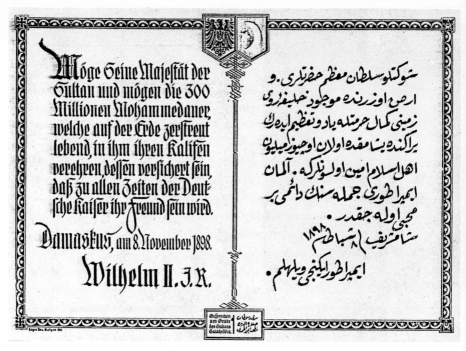

6. Kaiser Wilhelm proclaimed himself to be the protector of Muslims everywhere. This German propaganda postcard was circulated throughout the Islamic world.

7. Calling for a Holy War in Constantinople in November 1914 – the *fatwa* was read out i every mosque in the Ottoman Empire.

8. Setting the East ablaze. The cover of a German wartime magazine showing mullahs on the march

9. Tribesmen rallying to the call – as seen by a German war artist

10. The anti-British Indian revolutionary Vinayak Savarkar, who planned assassinations and bombings from his secret London headquarters. A Scotland Yard photograph

11. Har Dayal, Savarkar's Oxford-educated disciple, who founded the *Ghadr* revolutionary movement for the overthrow of the British Raj

Seine Hoheit

Asaf Jah Muzaffar-ul-Mumalik Rustam-i-
Dauran Arastu-i-Zaman Nizam-ul-Mulk
Nizam-ud-Daulah Nawab Mir Osman Ali
Khan Bahadur Fateh Jang
Nizam von Haiderabad

Euerer Hoheit beehre ich mich, hierdurch den Gruß der Kaiserlichen Regierung zu entbieten und den freundschaftlichen Gefühlen Ausdruck zu verleihen, die das Deutsche Reich Indien und seinen Fürsten gegenüber von jeher hegt. Seitdem die Engländer ihre Fremdherrschaft in Indien errichtet haben, haben sie ihr Bestes getan, um die indischen Fürsten und das indische Volk von jeder Berührung mit dem nichtenglischen Rußland abzuschließen. Andererseits hat Deutschland in sorgfältiger Beachtung der anerkannten Regeln des internationalen Verkehrs keinerlei Versuche gemacht, mit den indischen Herrschern in unmittelbare Verbindung zu treten.

Der von England und seinen Verbündeten, Rußland und Frankreich, in leichtfertiger Weise heraufbeschworene Krieg, der dem Dreiverband schon so schwere Verluste, Deutschland, Österreich-Ungarn und der Türkei

श्रीमान भगवत सिंह जी सग्राम जी ठाकुर साहिब गोंडल॥

श्रीमान को जर्मनसाम्राज्य की ओर से मैं प्रणाम करता हूं, और उस मैत्रीभाव को जो जर्मनसाम्राज्य की सर्वदे और उस के निवासियों के साथ रहा है प्रगट करता हूं। जब से अंग्रेजों ने हिन्दुस्तान में अपना राज जमाया है अन्हों ने पूरा प्रयत्न किया है कि भारतवर्ष के राजा और प्रजा का इंग्लेंड के बिना और दूसरे देशों के साथ कोई संबन्ध न हो। जर्मनी ने राजनीति के नियमों के अनुसार भारतीय राष्ट्रों के साथ परस्पर संबन्ध स्थापित करने का यत्न नहीं किया है॥

12. Lavishly produced letters like these captured ones were borne by German agents for delivery to Indian maharajas. Promising extravagant rewards, they sought to buy their wartime support.

13. Ambassador Wangenheim (*left*), who directed Holy War operations from his Constantinople embassy (*below*). He died there of a stroke in 1915 and is buried beside the Bosphorus (*right*).

Constantinople. *Ambassade d' Allemagne à Péra.*

14. The charismatic and ruthless German agent Wilhelm Wassmuss in Persian disguise (*left*). With anti-British tribesmen with whom he had forged close links before the war (*below*)

PERSIA. P 2339 / 315

POLITICAL

This Document is the Property of His Britannic Majesty's Government, and should be returned to the Foreign Office when done with unless required for official use.

RECEIVED 25 JUN 1915 POLITICAL DEPARTMENT

Copy to India 3 SEP 1915

Decypher. Mr. Marling (Teheran) June 24th 1915.
(d. 11.5 p.m. r. 8.40 a.m. June 25th).
No. 214.

German activity in province is increasing. Wassmuss is endeavouring to organise an attack by local tribes on Bushire: party of Germans strengthened by men locally recruited and Austrian prisoners of war who have escaped in some numbers from Trans Caspian viâ Meshed, is starting for Birjand and Afghanistan and another similar party under Zugmeyer and Griesinger for Kerman; Pugin is leaving for Meshed.

At Ispahan thanks largely to German connivance murderer of Russian Bank Manager is still at large and only satisfaction for outrage that Russia has obtained is exchange of Sirdar Motashem for Sirdar Ashja his own brother as Governor General, while I have not yet succeeded in getting Governor General removed from Fars. Fact undoubted Prime Minister is falling more and more under influence of pro-German democrats and though he makes profuse promises that he will check German intrigues nothing effective is done and there is now prospect that Farmafarma, Minister of the Interior, who is only member of Cabinet to show any degree of energy in that direction will be at instance of Turks and Germans transferred to Ministry of War which is nothing but a sinecure and where he will be of little practical use to us.

Prime Minister meets all representations for effective measures on the part of Persian Government with requests for the withdrawal of Russian troops and with threats to resign. He is well aware of Persia's difficult position. He is in difficult position.

This Document is the Property of His Britannic Majesty's Government, and should be returned to the Foreign Office when done with unless required for official use.

GREECE. P 2434

FILES ONLY.

Decypher. Mr. Bratislaw (Salonika)
D. 5.45 p.m. July 1st. 1915.
R. 10.15 p.m.

Following from Sir Mark Sykes for D.M.O. War Office Begins:

No. 3. Baron Oppenheim left Constantinople for the Interior about 10 days ago. Direction Konieh, Aleppo Mosul. Intention to raise pan-Islamic feeling against Great Britain. Addressed assemblies of Dervishes and religious notables at Constantinople and will do so elsewhere, preaches Monogawy, abandonment of Fez, and practice of skill in arms for public and war against Entente Powers. India Office may anticipate his activities in Persia about the middle of July. His propaganda not well received among Constantinople religious communities owing to his Jewish origin. He has large funds at his disposal and intimate knowledge of the country. Ends.

Repeated to Tehran & Cairo

RECEIVED 3 JUL 1915.

COPY OF TELEGRAM.

FROM Viceroy
DATED 11 August 1915
RECEIVED AT LONDON OFFICE

P 2930 / 1915

Foreign. Secret. German agents in Persia. Amir has sent most satisfactory reply to my letter regarding approach of German agents to Afghanistan. He says that it has never been rule of Afghan Govt. to allow armed parties of foreigners to tour Afghanistan. If German parties enter Afghanistan they will be disarmed and interned till the end of the war. In friendly postscript in his own handwriting Amir reiterates his intention to maintain neutrality during the present war.

Addressed to S of S for India and repeated to Tehran No 804. S.

RECEIVED 11 AUG 1915.

15. Secret British reports on the activities of German agents on the approach routes to Afghanistan and India

16. Safely in Kabul, Raja Mahendra Pratap, official head of the German secret mission – flanked by Otto von Hentig (*left*) and Captain Oskar von Niedermayer (*right*)

contents to his British paymasters, or possibly even destroyed them. This withholding of recognition by Teheran denied Zugmayer and Griesinger the right to fly the imperial German flag over the building they had chosen as their consulate. This, in turn, resulted in considerable loss of face for them locally. In a letter carried by a German NCO to Prince Henry in Teheran, Zugmayer complained bitterly: 'Our foes rejoice openly, scoff at the impotence of the German Legation, and wait only for the day when we have to withdraw in shame and derision.' He urged Prince Henry to bring pressure to bear on their behalf in Teheran, so that they could carry out their task of stirring up a Holy War against the British 'along the lines proposed by the Foreign Ministry and the General Staff' in Berlin. The days passed, however, without any tangible results or improvement in their position.

The two Germans' frustration was understandable enough. They had brought with them sufficient Holy War propaganda, in the form of virulently anti-British literature, to unleash half a dozen such insurrections. Carefully prepared by Max von Oppenheim and others in Berlin and Constantinople, and written in Persian, Pushtu, Urdu and other Asian languages, this consisted largely of leaflets, pamphlets and newspapers. These told of spectacular German and Turkish victories, both on land and at sea, and of catastrophic Allied disasters. One Hindustani leaflet claimed that the King of England had fled his throne and was on the run, and that British troops were deserting to the enemy *en masse*. Another, in Urdu, reported that the Russians had been heavily defeated in the Caucasus, that there was famine in St Petersburg, and that the Emir of Afghanistan had pledged himself to join in the Holy War against the Allies. Meanwhile, millions of Muslims throughout the East were flocking to the cause, including mutinying regiments of the Indian Army. These were but a few of the items of news dreamed up by the German propagandists and their Indian collaborators. To simple people, without any independent source of war news, this was heady stuff – but only if it could be got to them without further delay.

Prince Henry's seeming indifference to Zugmayer's problems is most likely explained by his own close involvement, at that precise moment, in a desperate piece of intrigue in

Teheran. By exploiting the pent-up feelings of the Persian people, and by making use of a highly emotive precedent dating back more than a thousand years in Muslim history, he hoped to drag the young Shah and his government into the Holy War. With Russian troops moving ever closer to the capital because of the growing threat of violence to the small Allied communities there, the feelings of ordinary Persians were running very strongly against them. Prince Henry's plan was to try to persuade the weak and vacillating sovereign, accompanied by many Persian notables, to perform what is known to Muslims as a *hejira*, or ceremonial flight to safety. Because the original *hejira* was made by the Prophet Mohammed, from Mecca to Medina in AD 622, this was calculated to stir up intense religious fervour among the volatile Persians, and make a fitting start to a Holy War. In the Shah's case, he would leave the royal palace in Teheran for the safety of the holy city of Qum, two days' ride southwards.

His widely publicised flight, which would be blamed on the infidel Russians, might be expected to arouse the nation's wrath and religious sensibilities and lead to a universal call for Persia to throw in its lot with Germany and Turkey. It was a clever game that Prince Henry played, for the more anxious the Allies in Teheran became, the closer the Russians moved to the capital. This, in turn, intensified anti-Allied hysteria, increasing the pressures on the Shah and his ministers to leave for Qum while there was still time. Prince Henry and his own staff – or so they proposed – would accompany the Shah to Qum, which would become Persia's Holy War capital. That, anyway, was the plan. However, with so much at stake, none of this could be explained to Zugmayer and Griesinger at Kerman for fear of the message being intercepted by the governor, or other hostile elements, and passed to the British. They would just have to be patient.

At the same time, in other parts of Persia, the Germans were further tightening their grip, especially in those regions where the Cossacks posed no threat, and where the local Gendarmerie officers were sympathetic to their cause. By now, with the aid of armed Persian mercenaries, the Germans had forcibly taken over several more branches of the British-owned Imperial Bank of Persia, and looted their vaults for

Holy War funds. And German arms and agents continued to pour across the frontier into Persia from Baghdad, bound for the base Niedermayer had set up at Isfahan. From there some of the arms, and the stolen British gold, were steered into the eager hands of pro-German Persian nationalists. Rabid extremists, styling themselves the Persian Democratic Party, they had vowed to rid the country, by violence if necessary, of all traces of British and Russian influence. It was in pursuit of this common foe that they had allied themselves to the Germans. Other smuggled arms, with more British bullion, made their way secretly southwards into Wassmuss's territory for distribution among the pro-German tribes there. By now the German 'Lawrence' was considered to be such a potential menace to British interests that his name was written in capital letters across the whole of south-west Persia on their staff maps.

Following his reverse at Bushire, Wassmuss had withdrawn into the interior to Shiraz, the capital of Fars province, where he had friends among the officers of the Gendarmerie. There, too, lay a temptingly soft British target for him in the shape of the small, isolated consulate. Already the consul – Major Sir Frederick O'Connor, who had once served as chief intelligence officer to Sir Francis Younghusband's Lhasa mission – had been instructed by his superiors in Teheran to destroy all his secret diplomatic codes but one. For it was pretty obvious that Wassmuss was hell-bent on avenging the humiliating raid by the British on the German Consulate at Bushire, and the arrest of the consul, Dr Listermann. Already two of O'Connor's staff had been murdered by the Wassmuss-led tribesmen. In September 1915, the British vice-consul at Shiraz, an Indian officer, was shot dead from behind by assassins while supposedly being escorted by troopers of the Gendarmerie. A few days later, one of O'Connor's *ghulams*, or mounted messengers, met with a similar fate. In fact, the Swedish officers of the Gendarmerie, officially there to protect the foreign communities and maintain law and order, made little attempt to disguise their pro-Wassmuss sympathies. Most of their Persian colleagues, moreover, were fervent members of the anti-Allied Democratic Party, and therefore shared this view.

Although O'Connor had a ten-strong Indian Army escort,

he knew that the consulate could not hope to fight off a determined attack by Wassmuss-led tribesmen, especially if they enjoyed the support of the Gendarmerie. All he could do was to warn his superiors of the dangers building up in Shiraz, and of the likelihood of their being seized as hostages, or even killed. He was urged, in reply, to try to hold on for as long as possible, although there was no way that reinforcements could be got to him from Bushire, since they would have to fight their way through hostile tribal territory, which would only add fuel to the fire. Were the consulate to be evacuated, however, this would be hailed – like the closing of consulates elsewhere in Persia – as a victory in the war against the infidels. The decision was left to O'Connor, who agreed to stay on. In view of the murderous forces ranged against them, and the hopelessness of their situation, it was a courageous decision. But it was one which he and the small British colony would soon regret.

In the meantime, news of a most unwelcome kind had reached Delhi and London. Niedermayer, Hentig, the two Indian firebrands and half a dozen German officers and NCOs had crossed safely into Afghanistan.

10

Audience with the Emir

Although the British had half expected it, the news that Niedermayer had given them the slip sent a chill through the corridors of Whitehall and Delhi. To their credit, though, they showed themselves to be good losers, freely conceding that it was a remarkable feat. 'The courage, skill and tenacity displayed by Niedermayer and his companions', wrote the official British war historian afterwards, 'are worthy of our highest admiration.' But what most astonished those British officers familiar with eastern Persia was the speed with which the Germans had travelled. Reporting the bad news to London, the Viceroy calculated that they had covered 255 miles in seven days. For badly exhausted men and beasts, suffering cruelly from thirst and hunger, who for a month and a half had struggled across some of the grimmest terrain on earth, this was a remarkable achievement. 'The Germans travel so fast', complained one British officer, 'that it is almost impossible to obtain adequate notice of their movements.' And yet the whole of eastern Persia was riddled with British spies and paid informers.

But without Niedermayer's iron-willed leadership, and his grim determination to outmanoeuvre the British and Russians, it seems highly unlikely that the party, or what was left of it, would have got through. 'We had to keep moving at all costs,' he wrote, 'to maintain what little lead we had.' At times, after their rare halts for sleep, he had to kick his men to force them on to their feet again. 'We had a hard task preventing tired or cowardly men from running away,' he recounted.

One after another the Persians threw themselves down on the burning sand, preferring to die rather than struggle agonisingly on. The Europeans, Niedermayer noted, showed themselves to have more physical and mental stamina than the Persians, though this is hardly surprising considering that the latter had little real commitment to the Holy War. Some German critics have accused Niedermayer of claiming more than his fair share of the credit for getting the party safely across Persia. However, in his own brief account of their journey, the firebrand Raja Mahendra Pratap, 'the Prince of India' and nominal head of the mission, unequivocally attributed their survival to Niedermayer's personal leadership and strategy.

The party, by this time reduced to what Niedermayer described as 'walking skeletons', finally reached the dried-up water-hole which marked the Afghan frontier late on the night of August 19, 1915 – exactly seven weeks after setting out from Isfahan. Through death or desertion they had lost half of their original number, though no Germans, Austrians or Indians had perished. Of the 170 horses and baggage animals they had started with, fewer than 70 had survived. But even now, although they had escaped death at the hands of the British or the Russians, the dangers were far from over. Men and beasts were desperately thirsty, not to mention hungry. If they were to survive, and not collapse through weakness, they had to find fresh water and food. Three hours after crossing into Afghanistan they came upon another water-hole. Although not totally dry, it was choked with camel dung. Nonetheless, their desperate animals drank gratefully from it. So too, after putting disinfectant in it, did Niedermayer and his companions.

Somehow they struggled on, hoping to reach some habitation where they could find food and water. 'How we managed to cover the next forty miles I do not myself know,' wrote Niedermayer. But at 5 o'clock the following morning, after travelling through the night, they came upon a deserted hamlet in the middle of the desert, today not even marked on the map. Hopes of finding a well here were soon dashed, and their thirst-maddened beasts were reduced to drinking salt water. Then, by a miracle, someone stumbled upon an abandoned irrigation channel still containing fresh water of sorts. 'Although it was teeming with leeches,' recalled Niedermayer, 'both men and animals drank their fill for the first time in many days.' The caravan was saved from death by thirst. They now had the strength to reach Herat, the Emir of Afghanistan's western capital, just two days' march away, where they hoped to make their first contact with the Kabul authorities.

Uppermost in the exhausted men's minds now was the crucial question of just how they would be received. Would they, as they hoped, be welcomed as saviours – the vanguard of an Islamic army which would help the Afghans finally to free themselves from British suzerainty? Or might they find themselves disarmed and interned under the laws governing neutrality? Or perhaps even be handed over to the British authorities in India – or simply turned back across the frontier into Persia to face once more their British and Cossack pursuers? Now that Niedermayer's task was over, political considerations such as these became the responsibility of Otto von Hentig, as representative of the German government, and his two Indian companions. Once the last of the Persian escort had been paid off, the party consisted largely of Europeans (albeit professing to have embraced Islam). Hentig decided therefore to send ahead the second of the two Indians, Mohammed Barakatullah, whose name was widely known throughout the Muslim world, not to mention to the British authorities. Indeed, his file in London described him as 'a highly dangerous individual' who was known to be working for the Germans. The task now set him by Hentig was to make immediate and friendly contact with the governor-general of Herat, and explain the reason for the mission's coming. He would inform the Afghan that they bore an important and urgent letter for the Emir addressed personally to him by Kaiser Wilhelm, as well as a number of gifts to be delivered to him in Kabul.

Despite his weariness and dishevelled appearance, Barakatullah carried out his task well, persuading the governor-general of the importance of the mission which was waiting on his doorstep. An armed escort, led by a colonel, was immediately dispatched to bring the party to Herat. The Afghans came upon the Germans and their friends recovering from their harrowing journey at a small village whose bemused inhabitants had never before set eyes on Europeans. Hentig and Niedermayer, who were anxious to enter Herat in a manner which would reflect well upon the Fatherland, would have liked to have remained there longer. Not only were they all exhausted, ragged and filthy, but several of the men were sick, one or two of them even delirious. But the colonel insisted that the governor-general's order must be obeyed, and that they must pack up and leave for Herat at once. After their experience of Persia's rather easy-going and compliant officialdom, such rigid insistence came as something of a shock to the newcomers.

Herat, however, which they entered on August 24, proved a veritable paradise to them after their long and painful weeks in the Persian desert. To reach the great walled capital of the Emir's western domains they rode first along the lush and fertile Herat valley, with beautiful orchards and gardens on either side, and overlooked by distant mountains. Everywhere it was cool and green. On arrival, they were escorted to the Emir's provincial palace. It was here, they were informed, that he stayed when visiting the province, and it was here that they would be staying while instructions were sought from Kabul as to the next move. Things looked distinctly promising, for the signs were that they were being treated as important guests of the state. A large table, weighed down with oriental delicacies, had been laid out for them by their hosts. 'With the intoxicating scents from the garden,' wrote Niedermayer, 'it was like a fairy tale.' Echoing him, Raja Mahendra Pratap recalled: 'For the moment we were able to forget all our recent hardships.'

During the next few days they remained on tenterhooks as they awaited news from Kabul. Finally, accompanied by a thirty-strong armed escort and mounted on a white charger, the governor-general paid them an official visit. After an exchange of gifts and formal courtesies, Hentig explained the reason for their coming and told the governor-general of the messages they bore from the German Emperor and the Ottoman Sultan for the Emir. The governor-general then informed them that arrangements were being made for them to leave Herat for Kabul, 400 miles to the east, in two weeks' time. In the meantime they would be provided with fresh clothes, horses and other necessities for the journey. 'At his own expense,' the Raja wrote, 'the governor-general sent a party of artisans – saddlers, blacksmiths, tailors and cobblers – to re-equip us and attend to all our needs.' In addition, they were presented with expensive oils, scents and soaps – unimaginable luxuries to men who had been unable to wash for weeks while struggling through dust-storms and sweltering heat. The Germans, it seemed, could feel well pleased with themselves. Everything appeared to be going according to plan.

*   *   *

Even before Barakatullah had been joined by the rest of the party in Herat, the British had learned from their spies of his arrival and cordial reception there. In addition to alerting the Emir to the news, they had immediately set about trying to discover how the Germans had managed to give them the slip, so that no others could follow. For they guessed that Niedermayer's party was merely the vanguard of further such parties which would attempt to reach Afghanistan if the signs were favourable. Indeed, so promising did these appear to the Germans that Niedermayer had already sent off a secret message to Isfahan suggesting that another German group should attempt to penetrate the Allied cordon before more enemy troops could be brought up to plug the gaps. The British, meanwhile, had dispatched an experienced intelligence officer from Birjand to try to establish the precise route Niedermayer and his men had taken, and ascertain who along the route had supplied them with food, water and guides. All he was able to discover, however, was that most village headmen in eastern Persia were open to offers from either side, and would sell themselves to the highest bidder – or to *both* bidders where circumstances permitted. But for the most part their sympathies lay with the Turco-German cause, if only because of their historic dislike of both the British and the Russians, who were now paying for their years of meddling in Persia's affairs during the Great Game era.

Meanwhile, in western Persia, German arms, funds and other materials continued to arrive from across the frontier in readiness for the coming Holy War against British India. This, Berlin believed, would very shortly be let loose by Hentig and his companions in Kabul, and by Prince Henry of Reuss in Teheran, through his machinations there. In addition to German arms, some 300 Turkish troops, wearing Persian caps and German badges, were reported to have reached Kermanshah, staging point for the main German base at Isfahan. Kermanshah, like Isfahan, was now virtually German territory, the British and Russian consulates having been long closed for reasons of safety. When the newly appointed Persian governor of Kermanshah, sent to try to curb German activities there, announced his intention of reopening the Allied consulates, he was warned bluntly by Prince Henry that if he persisted in this he would be forcibly prevented from taking up his new post. It was now estimated by the British that in Kermanshah alone the Germans had more than 1,000 men on their payroll, many of whom were destined for Isfahan and points east. Indeed, around this time – the autumn of 1915 – intelligence reached the British that two German parties were expected to leave Isfahan shortly to follow in the footsteps of Niedermayer and Hentig.

*   *   *

By now, thoroughly rested, the latter two officers and their party were on their way eastwards across the mountains from Herat to Kabul. Accompanied by an Afghan military escort, they travelled by the shortest but harshest route. A far easier, though rather longer, route would have first carried them southwards to Kandahar, and thence north-eastwards to the capital, thereby skirting the mountains. But clearly the Afghans wanted at all costs to prevent the mission from having any contact with the excitable tribesmen of the Indian frontier region, and to avoid news of their presence in Afghanistan reaching the latter's ears.

Normally the journey would have taken a month. However, by sometimes covering two stages in a day, they reached Kabul on October 2, with five days in hand. The first people to welcome them as they approached the capital were members of the Turkish community, 'easily recognisable', Hentig recalled, 'in their red fezzes'. They cheered the newcomers loudly, 'making us feel that we already possessed friends in Kabul'. Next to receive them as they drew closer to the mountain-ringed capital was an Afghan guard of honour, whose officers wore Turkish uniforms, and who welcomed them with a roar of '*Salaam!*' Word of their arrival spread swiftly through the capital, and excited crowds began to line the way. 'In the streets and from the roofs', wrote Hentig, 'they saluted us with shouts of joy. We could read on their faces the hope that, with our coming, a new day was dawning for Afghanistan.'

The party was now escorted to the Emir's comfortable guesthouse, known as the Bagh-i-Babur, which stood just outside the city and where they were to lodge as state guests. The views of the mountains around and the green valley below were magnificent, as were the Bagh-i-Babur's gardens and fountains. But their initial euphoria at all this was to prove short-lived, for they were quickly to discover that the Emir himself was away from his capital at that moment. He was, they learned, sojourning at his summer palace in the cool of the mountains. Moreover, he appeared to be in no great hurry to return to Kabul, which was just getting over a serious cholera epidemic. To men like Hentig and Niedermayer, impatient to make up for lost time and bring Afghanistan into the Holy War, this came as a bitter disappointment.

But while they awaited the Emir's pleasure, they set about winning converts to the Turco-German cause among the ordinary people of Kabul. Here they stumbled upon some unexpected allies. Living in the capital, they found, were two dozen Austrian soldiers – all of them ex-POWs who had escaped from camps in Russian Turkestan and made their way across the Oxus to neutral Afghanistan, where they had been allowed to remain. Among them were a number of skilled craftsmen, whom Hentig and Niedermayer immediately recruited for their hearts-and-minds offensive. Some of the men, for example, helped the Afghans to build a small hospital which, in Hentig's words, 'embodied the latest German hygienic principles of light, air and cleanliness' – concepts then entirely new in Afghanistan. One man, a peacetime sculptor, even adorned the hospital entrance with an appropriate and impressive piece of statuary, while another, a decorator, enhanced the interiors of the small operating theatre, the waiting room and the modest mosque attached to the hospital. Meanwhile, other ex-POWs with useful skills passed on the secrets of their crafts to local artisans. 'Above all, however,' wrote Hentig, 'the Afghans wanted to know about the outside world – especially how the war was proceeding, and its likely outcome and effects on them.' The Germans could hardly have asked for a better opportunity to spread word of the coming Holy War against British India.

There was, oddly, one other European living in Kabul at this time. He was an Englishman named Lynch, an engineer whom the Emir had engaged to set up a factory to make soap, candles and smokeless powder for cartridges. When the Germans arrived and began to spread anti-British tales among the populace, he decided to quit and return to India. On reaching Delhi he reported having frequently seen the Germans in the bazaar, though they never spoke. 'We just passed, growling like dogs,' he told the British authorities, who pressed him hard for any news of the mission. Yet although the Germans appeared to him to be treated 'like visiting royalty' by the Afghans, this was not how Hentig and Niedermayer were beginning to see it. As the days passed, with no word from the Emir and no answer to the several letters they had written to him, they began to feel uneasy. For at the same time their movements were becoming increasingly restricted. Once, when Niedermayer attempted to exercise his horse outside the guesthouse grounds, he was prevented from doing so by a sentry with a fixed bayonet. When he protested about this to the Afghan official in charge of them, he was told that their lives were thought to be in danger from British secret agents, and that they were being confined for their own safety. Naturally, the Germans did not believe a word of this.

Finally their patience snapped. They decided to embark on a hunger strike, and politely refused the succulent dishes offered them by the cook provided by their hosts. Although hardly recommended in Satow's classic *Guide to Diplomatic Practice*, this unorthodox tactic proved instantly successful among a people to whom hospitality is a sacred duty. Unnerved, no doubt, at the prospect of the emissaries of one of the most powerful nations on earth dying of starvation while ostensibly his guests, the Emir caved in. On October 26, more than two months after they first crossed into Afghanistan, three Rolls-Royces were sent to collect them from the guesthouse and convey them to the Emir's palace in the mountains. As the cars wound their way up into the foothills above Kabul, the Germans and their two Indian companions knew that the next few hours would decide the fate of the Holy War, and possibly even that of the entire war. For if, beginning with Afghanistan, they could eventually turn the whole of Muslim Asia against the British and the Russians, then an overall victory for Germany and Turkey was almost certain. It was an awesome responsibility which now faced them.

*   *   *

With so much at stake, the British had been far from idle all this time. For a start, they had been trying desperately to plug the gaps in the East Persian Cordon to prevent other German parties, reported to be on their way, from joining Hentig and Niedermayer in Afghanistan. But their most immediate fears were over the mischief which the latter two were now clearly hoping to foment in Kabul. For although the Emir had assured the Viceroy that he intended to remain faithful to his treaty obligations, and maintain strict neutrality, it was no secret in Delhi that he was surrounded by powerful individuals raring to settle old scores with the British. Nothing would delight them more than for the Emir to declare an all-out Holy War against India's infidel rulers.

Furthermore, for some time now the Indian government's intelligence services, under Sir Charles Cleveland, had been aware that the Germans were carrying with them highly inflammatory letters from the Kaiser and the Sultan urging the Emir to join them in the Holy War. If they could not prevent these from being delivered, they could at least try to upstage them by going one better. Hitherto, all diplomatic communication between the British government and the Emir had been via the Viceroy, in strict accordance with the terms of the treaty. But it was now decided that King George V, the British sovereign, should write personally to the Emir, in his own handwriting and on Buckingham Palace headed notepaper, thanking him warmly for his friendship and loyalty, and assuring him that an Allied victory was not far off. This departure from normal Anglo-Afghan protocol, moreover, appeared to place the two sovereigns on equal terms. To borrow a phrase from Kipling – who understood such imperial niceties – 'a throne sent word to a throne'.

But if King George V's letter, dated September 24, was to eclipse those of his rival sovereigns then there was little time to be lost. While it was being organised in London and rushed to Delhi the Viceroy telegraphed ahead to the Emir to advise him that the letter was on its way. It had been decided that it should be handed over to him with as much ceremony as possible. However, because under the treaty British officers and diplomats were barred from entering Afghanistan, the formal handover would have to take place at the last British post at the Indian end of the Khyber Pass. To emphasise the letter's extreme importance, the Emir was requested to send an official of appropriate rank to receive it. He immediately ordered a highly trusted Afghan noble to proceed to the frontier, accompanied by an armed escort in freshly tailored uniforms and bearing an impressive standard. They found the British party waiting for them at the pre-arranged spot beside a stream, attended by a guard of honour, in ceremonial uniform, from the Khyber Rifles. In a marquee which the British had erected, the King's letter was formally handed over amid much cordiality, after which the Afghan noble and his escort rode swiftly off to deliver it directly into the hands of the Emir.

Emir Habibullah, it is said, received the letter standing up, as a gesture of respect for its sender. So overwhelmed was the bearer by the burden of his responsibility, and so blinded by tears of emotion, that at first he failed to observe the Emir's hand reaching out impatiently for the letter. Nonetheless, he was duly rewarded for the alacrity with which he had carried out his task, while those who had escorted him and the historic letter each received a British-made Lee-Metford rifle, a trophy highly prized among Afghan tribesmen. The Emir now turned to reading the contents of the British sovereign's letter, to which Delhi had attached a translation to avoid any possible misunderstanding. For among such a volatile people that might mean the difference between war and peace, between Afghanistan joining the Holy War or remaining neutral.

Beginning with the words 'My Dear Friend', the King-Emperor's letter read as follows: 'I have been much gratified to learn from my Viceroy how scrupulously and honourably Your Majesty has maintained the attitude of strict neutrality which you guaranteed at the beginning of the war, not only because it is in accordance with Your Majesty's engagements to me, but also because by it you are serving the best interests of Afghanistan and the Islamic religion.' It went on to say that the writer was confident that the Emir would continue to pursue this course 'until victory crowns the arms of the Allies – a prospect which daily grows nearer.' By so doing, the letter concluded, the Emir would 'still further strengthen the friendship which I so greatly value, which has united our people since the days of your father, of illustrious memory, and of my revered forebear, the great Queen Victoria.' At the same time, in an accompanying letter from the Viceroy, the Emir was informed that it had been decided, in gratitude for his loyalty, to increase his annual personal subsidy by £25,000 – a sizeable sum in 1915. This was also intended, no doubt, to eclipse any similar inducement which the Germans might offer him. Such an inducement from them, however, would have to be very substantial, in view of the fact that the Emir already had in Delhi an unspent credit of £800,000, plus further investments in London. Nevertheless, with so much at stake, the British awaited his reply with considerable trepidation.

* * *

Meanwhile, the first of the Emir's audiences with his German and Indian visitors had taken place at his mountain retreat. Here, or so it seemed, the proceedings were safe from the attentions of the British intelligence services or any other interested parties. But were they? Years later – in an unsigned but clearly well-informed obituary of Sir Charles Cleveland in *The Times* – it was claimed that he had managed to penetrate the mission. I have not, however, been able to find any confirmation of this in the Indian government intelligence files of the time. Indeed, had one of Cleveland's agents been present at the meeting, then one might have expected a rather fuller account of it than the fairly sketchy one that the Viceroy did receive. As it is, to piece together what happened in the Emir's eyrie, one has to turn to the accounts left by Hentig, Niedermayer and Raja Mahendra Pratap, as well as to the German diplomatic archives.

The audience lasted all day, with a break for prayers and lunch. The most senior Afghans present were the Emir, his brother Nasrullah – who also served as Prime Minister – and Habibullah's son Amanullah, who would eventually succeed to the Afghan throne. Also in attendance were a number of senior ministers, court officials and advisers, most of whom, like Nasrullah and Amanullah, were known to be anti-British, and therefore likely to be sympathetic to the visitors. As the Germans and the two Indians drew up in their Rolls-Royces before the palace, which was really little more than a large bungalow, they had been startled to see a number of elephants tethered with chains outside. 'Expensive and unnecessary,' observed Hentig, 'these led us to conclude that the Emir considered himself to be one of the great lords of India.'

The proceedings opened with the formal presentation to the Emir of the letters from the German Emperor and Turkish Sultan, together with a number of small but valuable gifts, including gold watches of the latest design and finest workmanship. 'We also expressed our hope', wrote Hentig, 'of being able to present at a later date the larger gifts which we had left behind in Persia.' A slightly awkward moment then arose when the Emir asked why such youthful representatives, none of whom were out of their thirties, had been sent by the Kaiser and Sultan to discuss such important matters of state with him. Hentig explained that 'greybeards', or older men, would not have been able to endure the extreme hardships of the journey. The Emir also expressed surprise that the Kaiser's letter, unlike the Sultan's, was written on a typewriter, as though to question its authenticity. Again, Hentig was able to offer a satisfactory explanation. 'I pointed out to him', he wrote, 'that the Emperor was in his field headquarters, and that he had no scribes at his disposal there.' In fact, there are some slight doubts about this letter, since the original one bore Wassmuss's name as the mission's leader. It is just possible that some deft legerdemain had taken place somewhere along the line.

The Emir now asked what had brought them to

Afghanistan in the middle of a world war. Hentig explained that they had been sent by their Emperor to inform him that Germany, unlike Britain and Russia, fully recognised Afghanistan as an independent country, with the Emir as its sovereign, and wished to establish formal diplomatic relations with Kabul. For the Germans were aware that Britain's refusal to accept Afghanistan as a fully independent state, with its own foreign policy, was the cause of intense resentment among the proud Afghans, not excluding the Emir himself. Nonetheless, the latter remained poker-faced, his expression betraying no sign of how he viewed the Kaiser's offer.

It was next the turn of the Indian firebrand Mohammed Barakatullah, who claimed to represent the aspirations of his country's Muslim millions, to make his overture to the Emir on their behalf. He asked the Afghan ruler bluntly whether he was prepared, as an avowed Muslim, to lead his people in a Holy War to liberate the oppressed Muslims of British India. He asked him, too, whether he would allow German and Turkish troops to enter Afghanistan and join forces with his mujahedin, or holy warriors, for a combined invasion of India. The Emir's reply to the Indian's inquiry was wary but frank. While Afghanistan would not shirk its duty as a Muslim power, it was its misfortune to be squeezed between two giants, British India and Tsarist Russia. On the other hand, Germany and Turkey were far away. Although fanatical in the defence of their own country, his troops could not hope to withstand the full might of its two powerful neighbours. They had no experience of fighting against modern European armies equipped with the latest weaponry and employing sophisticated tactics. How, moreover, would he be able to pay his troops, for he would immediately lose his British subsidy, not to mention his funds banked with the Government of India? If he were to enter the fray as he was being urged to, he would first need arms, money and large numbers of German or Turkish troops. But how could these be got to him in view of the vast distances involved, the shortage of time, and the presence of the East Persian Cordon?

Unprepared for these demands from the Emir, Hentig and his companions found themselves at a loss as to how to answer. For they had no authority from Berlin or Constantinople to promise the Afghans any military or financial assistance, although these might come later if events moved satisfactorily. Their orders were simply to try to provoke the Emir, in a fit of religious outrage, to unleash his tribesmen against British India, while others fomented violent uprisings among the restive native population there. German or Turkish troops could only be brought in if Prince Henry of Reuss succeeded in his plot, which was being hatched at that very moment, to propel the Shah of Persia into the Holy War. Even then it was hoped to direct German-led Persian troops against British India, rather than German or Turkish ones, who were desperately needed elsewhere. For the principal attraction of the Holy War was that it would cost virtually nothing, whilst if it was successful it would force the British to tie up large numbers of troops on the frontier, or risk losing India.

The mission's first audience with the Emir, which went on late into the evening, now came to an end. The deliberations had been frank but friendly, with the Emir proving a wily bargainer, continually seeking to raise the stakes. 'This was no simple chieftain who could be dazzled with glass beads,' wrote Niedermayer. Indeed, the Emir had seemed singularly unimpressed by the gifts they had gone to such pains to deliver, or the promise of others – including a one-ton cinematograph – still to come. However, he had listened most attentively as Niedermayer argued the case, on military grounds, for an eventual German victory, and warned him how isolated he would find himself in that event were he to maintain his present friendship with Britain. Raja Mahendra Pratap and Barakatullah, both eloquent and persuasive speakers, had pointed out what rich territorial gains he would reap in the event of his helping to drive the British out of India.

But although he listened intently and asked many questions, the inscrutable monarch gave away few clues as to what he was really thinking. On the social level, however, he had behaved towards his foreign visitors with extreme cordiality. At the sumptuously laden lunch table which he had provided, he had sat between Hentig and the Raja, now and again serving them personally with choice morsels from dishes specially cooked and pre-tasted for him. 'The Emir's drinking water', Hentig observed, 'was taken from a locked silver samovar, the key to which was kept by a chamberlain.' The Emir's glass, he noted, was of a somewhat curious design. Covered by a crystal lid topped with a large ruby, it had a special opening for his mouth. An Afghan sovereign, it appeared, could take nothing for granted.

As they drove back to Kabul in the three Rolls-Royces that night, the members of the mission pondered the day's events. 'Our first encounter with the Afghan monarch had not been wholly unsatisfactory,' Hentig noted. 'At least the ice had been broken.' Their arguments, he knew, would take time to sink in. He was confident, moreover, that Nasrullah and other anti-British officials would continue to work on the Emir on their behalf behind the scenes. A promising sign was his agreement to hold further talks, including separate ones with the two Indians so that he could listen to their aspirations for their homeland. Like everything else in Afghanistan, these were to proceed at a leisurely pace over the coming weeks. The Emir, it seemed, was in no great haste to commit himself to Kaiser, Sultan, King or Tsar.

*　　*　　*

By this time wild accounts of what the Germans and Indians were up to in the Afghan capital were beginning to filter through the passes to a jittery Delhi. 'Extraordinary stories have reached us from Kabul,' the Viceroy advised London. However, he considered many of them to be greatly exaggerated, and remained confident that the Emir, despite the pressures on him, would not join the Holy War. On November 5, ten days after the Emir's first meeting with the mission, he went further. According to the Viceroy's sources, the Emir had flatly turned down their invitation to join the Holy War, telling them firmly 'that he could not break his alliance with the British Government'. This, as we know, was simply not true, although the Viceroy was happy to believe it. Nonetheless, he warned London that powerful individuals among the Emir's entourage were trying hard to force him to join the Holy War, 'but so far without success'. Other senior British officials were rather less sure of the Emir's steadfastness than the Viceroy, believing that the Afghan leader was simply biding his time until it was clear which side was winning the war.

Only then would he declare himself. It was significant that, although he had now had it for several weeks, he had not yet answered King George V's letter. What, they asked, was the Emir waiting for?

But then, early in December 1915, when the German mission had been in Kabul for two months, the Emir suddenly summoned to his palace the British Indian government's official Muslim agent in the capital. Leading him into his private office, he locked the door behind them so that they could not be disturbed. The Emir then told him that he had an important secret message for the Viceroy which could not be put in writing lest it fall into the wrong hands. It must be delivered by the agent in person. 'I am not a double-dealer,' he was to assure the Viceroy. 'I intend to stand by the British if I possibly can.' The British must not judge him by any individual actions which the pressure of public opinion and of those around him might force him to take. Nor should the Viceroy believe any wild rumours or bazaar gossip which might reach Delhi. Although he intended to remain faithful to his word, he could not risk showing, openly, any partiality for the British lest he be accused by his subjects of betraying the Faith.

The Viceroy, who was only too aware of the immense pressures the Emir was under, was relieved to receive this spoken message, for it went some way towards explaining why the Emir had not sent a written reply to King George V's letter. Nonetheless, there were others in Delhi who still suspected the Emir of playing for time, and therefore not wishing to put anything in writing lest it rebound on him later. Indeed, when he wrote asking for a large part of his accrued subsidies to be transferred from Delhi to Kabul, they began to assume the worst. The Viceroy, however, was not among them. 'In spite of differences of opinion in my Council,' he wrote, 'I determined to regard his promise as being made in good faith.' The funds were transferred, together with the Emir's promised increase.

If the terrible uncertainty over what was going on in the Emir's mind was worrying for the British, it was every bit as much so for Hentig and his companions in Kabul. For now, as the weeks passed, it was becoming clear to them that the Emir was not intending to embrace their cause, but was stalling, leaving himself free, or so they believed, to jump either way at the last minute. This was precisely what some of the Viceroy's less charitable officials were thinking. But the Germans were not proposing to give up that easily. There was far too much at stake to allow one man's obstinacy to wreck the Kaiser's grand design.

A brief coded report on the situation in Kabul was now prepared by Hentig and his colleagues. This was entrusted to a secret courier, a Persian, with orders to ride forthwith to Teheran, where he was to deliver it into the hands of Prince Henry, who was anxiously awaiting news of the mission's progress. But the courier, unknown to the Germans, had formerly been in Russian service. Instead, therefore, of riding straight for Teheran, he made for Meshed and handed over the message to Russian officials he knew there. Unable to read it, they passed it to St Petersburg, where it was eventually deciphered. Realising its significance, the Russians alerted the British ambassador, Sir George Buchanan, to its contents, which were then passed via the Foreign Office to the Viceroy.

The message, now several weeks old, informed Prince Henry that the mission had been cordially received by the Emir. However, it added that all hopes of inducing him to join the Holy War appeared doomed. The mission was therefore considering other ways of propelling Afghanistan into the war. With so much support for an anti-British jihad among the Emir's subjects, the dispatch of 1,000 Turks, plus those Germans already in Persia, might be all that was required to bring this about. The wording of the message was, perhaps deliberately, imprecise. It concluded with the words: 'Perhaps internal revulsion of feeling necessary here first . . . We are determined to go to any lengths.' To the Viceroy this could only mean one thing. The Germans were contemplating a *coup d'état* against the Emir, for if he refused to join the Holy War, then he must be overthrown. To the Viceroy, going 'to any lengths' meant assassination.

He at once wrote to the Emir to warn him of this threat to his throne, if not to his life. He enclosed the text of the German message, together with his own interpretation of its precise meaning. However, he took the liberty of retranslating the curious phrase about 'internal revulsion of feeling' as:

'Perhaps we shall find it necessary to begin by organising a *coup d'état.*' He told the Emir that the mission's request for a 1,000-strong Turkish force to be sent to join them was intended by the Germans to persuade 'a credulous and excitable populace . . . that this is the vanguard of a considerable Turco-German force'. However, as the Germans knew perfectly well, it was impossible for a force of any real consequence to cross Persia and reach Afghanistan. The ultimate aim of all this, the Viceroy continued, was to place on the Afghan throne 'someone more in sympathy with their wicked machinations than Your Majesty'. He concluded: 'I am perfectly confident that the success of such a plot is impossible, and that Your Majesty is perfectly secure. At the same time, I think it right that you should know what manner of men are your present guests in Kabul.'

What the Viceroy knew, moreover, but the Germans did not, was that the Turco-German force they had called for to help overthrow the stubborn Emir would not be forthcoming, since their message had never reached Prince Henry in Teheran. However, if the Kaiser's Afghan adventure had run into difficulties, other Holy War plots were being hatched elsewhere. Indeed, nearly 1,000 miles away in the mountains of southern Persia, the first of these was coming to a head at that very moment.

11

Wassmuss Pounces

Word that something had gone badly wrong with the small and isolated British community at Shiraz first reached the Legation at Teheran early in November 1915 from an engineer working on the Indo-European telegraph line. Although the cable linking Shiraz with the rest of Persia had been cut, he had learned from other sources that the eleven-strong colony had been abducted at gunpoint and carried off towards the coast. They included the British consul, Major Frederick O'Connor, the local bank and telegraph managers, two Englishwomen and two young girls. Their kidnappers, it appeared, were the very body supposedly there to protect them, the Persian Gendarmerie. They were acting, or so they claimed, on the orders of a group calling itself 'the National Committee for the Protection of Persian Independence'.

On receiving the report, the British Minister in Teheran at once demanded a full explanation from the Persian Foreign Minister, and the captives' immediate release. The authorities, however, denied all knowledge of the affair, and while awaiting further clarification the British Legation advised London that it was 'just possible' that the whole story was a German fabrication designed to damage further the already badly strained relations between Persia and Britain. If so, it would not be the first time that they had deliberately spread such wild rumours in the hope of plunging Anglo-Persian relations into a crisis and thereby propelling the Shah and his government into the Holy War.

But it quickly emerged that the telegraph official's warning was correct, and that the Gendarmerie had indeed arrested the entire British colony. This was supposedly on the orders of local Persian patriots, but it was soon to transpire that behind the move was Wilhelm Wassmuss, who by now was living among the tribes of the Shiraz region, freely distributing German gold, arms and alluring promises of rich rewards to come. The Shah, he assured them, was about to join forces with Germany and Turkey. This should hardly have come as any surprise to the British, for O'Connor had long been warning that Wassmuss was plotting such a move, and that both the local Gendarmerie and the tribal chiefs were totally in his pocket, having been bought with German gold.

O'Connor himself first discovered that Wassmuss had decided to strike shortly after breakfast on November 10, when one of his ten-strong Indian Army escort came running to him to report that parties of armed gendarmes had surrounded the consulate. Some, with machine-guns, had taken up positions on the flat roofs of houses overlooking the building, while another group with a field-gun had this trained on the gateway. At once O'Connor sent a runner to the British telegraph manager, whose office was next door, urging him to get a message through to Teheran, while he himself set about destroying secret documents and his remaining cipher. But his message crossed with one from the telegraph manager informing him that the line had already been cut.

'A single gendarme, carrying a white flag, then made his appearance at the consulate gate,' O'Connor recalled later. He bore with him a letter, in French, containing the following ultimatum: 'The arrest of yourself and of the English colony has been decided on by the Persian patriots. Half an hour, to count from the delivery of this letter, is granted you to take your decision.' If he and the British community surrendered then they would be moved to a small town between Shiraz and Bushire and held there until exchanged for Germans and others who had been taken prisoner 'on neutral Persian territory' and who were now in India. The two women and two girls in the British party would either be allowed to remain safely in Shiraz, or would be moved with the men and then sent under escort to Bushire. The choice was theirs.

'If after thirty minutes – and you will please note down the hour and the minute of the receipt of this letter on the envelope – you do not surrender, then the British consulate and houses will be bombarded,' it warned. If so, only he could be held responsible for the consequences – 'especially for the women' – of his refusal. The letter, which purported to come from 'the National Committee for the Protection of Persian Independence', concluded: 'As soon as you surrender, your houses will be occupied, and you will be given three hours to prepare for your departure. Mules – three for each prisoner – are being held at your disposal, and each of you may take one servant.'

O'Connor, an experienced soldier, knew that he had no choice but to surrender. They were heavily outnumbered and outgunned by those encircling them. The consulate building was not designed for defence – it stood in a garden surrounded by high walls without loopholes or parapets. 'But even supposing we had been in a position to defend the consulate itself,' he wrote, 'the rest of the small community were scattered here and there, and would have been left at the mercy of the revolutionaries.' The manager of the British-owned Imperial Bank, for example, lived with his wife and two young daughters a mile or so away. In view of this, O'Connor added, 'I wrote a reply accepting the terms of the ultimatum, under protest.'

During the half-hour allowed him by the ultimatum (which in the event proved to be only twenty minutes) O'Connor worked fast. In addition to destroying sensitive papers by soaking them in kerosene and making a bonfire of them in the garden, he also had a substantial sum of money in gold coins to worry about. Hiding this would clearly not be easy, for he knew that the building would be torn apart as the Persians searched it for valuables and for compromising papers and other evidence of British intrigue for their German masters. Nonetheless, he somehow managed to conceal the money, for subsequently it was recovered, but even in his memoirs, written fifteen years later, he does not reveal where he hid it. O'Connor was only just in time. 'Some twenty minutes after the delivery of the ultimatum,' he wrote, 'a Persian gendarmerie officer with a small escort marched up to the con-

sulate and informed me courteously that I was under arrest
and that he was now in charge of the consulate and all it contained.' He ordered O'Connor to prepare for an immediate
journey.

Closely watched by an armed gendarme, the British consul
went to his bedroom to pack a suitcase and change into riding
clothes. 'When I came out', he recounted, 'I found that the
gendarmes had carried the heavy steel safe out of my office,
and were preparing to lift it on to a bullock-cart.' He asked
them why they were taking it away, and they explained that it
was being moved to their headquarters where it would be
forced open. 'But I have the keys here,' O'Connor told them.
'It would be much simpler to unlock it.' The gendarmes gathered round the safe with scarcely disguised excitement, for
wild stories had been current of the consulate's immense
wealth. 'I opened the safe, which was of course empty, with
the exception of one or two Persian notes of small value, and
some worthless papers. It was a great disappointment to the
Protectors of Persian Independence, and the subsequent
frenzied search through the house and garden (which, I was
told later, was all dug up) failed to reveal either treasure or
arms.'

Their captors were clearly nervous, and although the ultimatum had promised three hours in which to prepare for
departure, word arrived from the Gendarmerie headquarters
that they were to leave at once. O'Connor was ordered to
mount his horse, which had been saddled. Then, accompanied
by his ten Indian troopers, who had been disarmed, he rode
out of the consulate under a strong escort of gendarmes. 'The
roofs of the adjoining houses', he wrote, 'were still occupied
by their pickets, armed with rifles and machine-guns.' Up the
road, trained on the consulate gateway, O'Connor saw one of
the Armstrong field-guns which he had ordered for the
Gendarmerie some months earlier, and which had been paid
for with money provided by the British government. From the
consulate they were taken to the Gendarmerie barracks which
were in the town itself. 'The main roads', O'Connor recalled,
'were guarded, and the people had been told to keep to their
houses. There were therefore no crowds.' However, as they
passed road-blocks and other posts manned by gendarmes

they met with shouts of 'Down with England!' and 'Long live Persia!'

At the barracks O'Connor found the rest of the British community assembled. In addition to himself, there were six other men, two wives and two young daughters – eleven of them in all. 'Within an hour,' O'Connor recalled, 'we were hustled off again, the men on horseback and the ladies in a carriage.' His Indian troopers and a handful of native servants accompanied them, together with a heavily armed escort. They were not told where they were being taken, but they noticed that they were on the road leading to the coast and to Bushire. As they passed the British Consulate, O'Connor observed that the Persian flag was now fluttering from the flagstaff, and that a machine-gun had been mounted over the gateway. Although Shiraz was the provincial capital, it appeared to be firmly in the grip of pro-German elements, and there was no sign of any intervention by the Persian authorities.

The journey took them four days. It was bitterly cold, and they spent the nights huddled together in squalid caravanserais along the route. They finally arrived at the fortress-town of Borazjun, the headquarters of a Tangistani chief who had thrown in his lot with Wassmuss and the pro-German faction in the Gendarmerie. Here they found Wassmuss himself waiting for them. O'Connor had first met him in Shiraz before the war, when the German had spent three months there, much of the time among the local tribes. He described Wassmuss as 'a blond, manly-looking Saxon of agreeable manners and genial character'. The two men had seen quite a lot of one another, and had even gone on short shooting expeditions together. It had been quite obvious, though, that the German was there to acquire intelligence and to make friends among the Gendarmerie officers and tribal chiefs on behalf of his government. 'But the prospect of German penetration into inland Persia,' wrote O'Connor, 'except perhaps of a commercial nature, seemed at that time so unlikely that, beyond keeping an eye on his movements, we did not take him very seriously, and our personal relations were of the friendliest.'

Now it was a very different Wassmuss who confronted O'Connor. The German, who had been living rough, was dressed as a Persian. He had grown a beard, and appeared to have adopted Islam. 'He expressed great regret', recounted O'Connor, 'that after our pleasant relations during the summer of 1913 matters should have come to this present pass.' But he had clearly not forgotten the blow to his plans, not to mention his pride, when he had been briefly captured by pro-British tribesmen, losing most of his possessions, including his code-book and carefully prepared Holy War propaganda. 'After all,' he told O'Connor, 'your people were responsible for my capture and that of my companions and caravan, and it was only by good luck and running a considerable risk that I escaped being carried off to India with the others.' He admitted, quite frankly, that there was an element of revenge involved in his seizure of the British and the holding of them as hostages against the release of his colleagues in India. However, he added: 'It's very bad luck that you should happen to be the victim after all our pleasant times together, but that is the fortune of war and can't be helped.' He said that they would shortly be handed over to the Tangistanis, who guaranteed their safety, and who would hold them at the remote village of Ahram, one of their tribal strongholds. They would remain there while negotiations proceeded over their exchange for the German and Persian captives. The two women and two girls, however, would be conducted to Bushire, as promised, where they would be handed over to the British by their gendarme escort. The ten Indian troopers would remain at Borazjun.

That afternoon the British party, still with their escort of gendarmes, set off for Ahram. They halted for the night at the half-way point, and the following day the two women and two girls left for Bushire, while the men were handed over to their Tangistani escort. As O'Connor and his male companions approached Ahram, the petty chieftain whose capital it was rode out to meet them. 'This worthy', wrote O'Connor, 'met us a few miles out from his stronghold, and after courteous greetings conducted us to his lair – destined to be our abode for the next nine months.' His lair consisted of a small mud fortress, parapeted and loopholed, and standing some forty feet high. Surrounding it was a twelve-foot-high outer wall. Inside this were two small courtyards. One was the preserve of the chief and his family, while the other was set aside for the hostages, plus the dozen ragged-looking guards who watched over them day and night. Wassmuss, they soon discovered, lived in a house in the village nearby.

'Here then', recounts O'Connor, 'we settled down to make the best of a monotonous existence. We were only some thirty miles from Bushire – so close that we could see the reflection in the sky of our warships' searchlights at night, and hear the sound of salutes fired on the King's birthday and other cere-monial occasions. We none of us imagined that the resources of the British Empire, whether diplomatic or military, would be incapable of extricating a British consul and a few subjects from such an ignominious captivity within a few weeks at most.' The pro-German chiefs, he added, were figures 'of the very smallest calibre, capable of mustering between them at most a few hundred quite unorganised riflemen'. The fortress at Ahram stood on a level plain within easy striking distance of Bushire, and presented no obstacles of a military nature. 'But the days slipped away into weeks, and the weeks into months,' he wrote, 'and no progress of any kind was made towards our release.' Fortunately, before being hustled away from Shiraz, one of their number had had the presence of mind to grab some playing cards and stuff them into his baggage. 'Bridge', wrote O'Connor, 'proved a perfect godsend.' Every evening, for the next nine months, they settled down to two rubbers which greatly helped to make the long stretches of boredom and the physical hardships of their incarceration more tolera-ble. Their only other distraction was to work out an elaborate plan of escape.

*   *   *

Within a few hours of the women and two children being delivered safely to Bushire, the British authorities there had obtained from them a full account of what had happened to O'Connor and his companions, and had telegraphed this to Teheran. For one of the women, the bank manager's wife, car-ried an urgent note from O'Connor describing events and spelling out their captors' demands. First, all the Germans and Persians seized by the British on Persian soil must be released. Second, funds belonging to the pro-German Tangistani chiefs which had been frozen by the British must be returned. And finally, the British must remove all their troops from Bushire. These demands, they insisted, must be met by November 24, just four days after the arrival of the women and children at Bushire. Otherwise, they warned, they would 'declare war' on Britain.

Urgent consultations followed between London, Delhi and Teheran, but it was decided, for the time being anyway, not to attempt to rescue the hostages lest, on the approach of a rescue party or punitive expedition, their captors simply cut their throats and take to the hills. There was another reason, too, for caution. Wild, but quite unfounded, rumours were being spread abroad that the Shah had joined the Holy War on the Turco-German side. Indeed, it was the Shiraz Gendarmerie's belief that he was about to declare war on the Allies that had led to their arrest, on Wassmuss's orders, of the British community. All this was part of a carefully orchestrated German plan emanating from Teheran. Here, it will be recalled, Prince Henry of Reuss was feverishly engaged in trying to bring off a coup which would finally force Persia into the war. This involved persuading the weak and vacillating young Shah, together with many of the country's leading figures, to perform a *hejira*, or ceremonial exodus from the capital to the holy city of Qum. The widely proclaimed reason for his flight would be the threat posed to the throne and to Persia's sovereignty by Russian troops who, to combat the growing danger of violence towards the Allied communities in Teheran, were gradually closing in on the capital. As Wassmuss struck, Prince Henry was negotiating a treaty with the Shah's largely pro-German ministers under which Berlin would provide them with arms and funds. Field Marshal von der Goltz, then in Constantinople, would take command of Persia's armed forces, including the Gendarmerie. A joint Holy War military base would be set up at Isfahan, already under virtual German control, and safely out of reach of the Cossacks. From here, with the hoped-for support of Niedermayer and Hentig's Afghans, the warriors of Islam would be unleashed against British India and Britain's interests in the Gulf.

By November 10, as O'Connor and his compatriots were being carried off from Shiraz, events were rapidly coming to a head in Teheran. For Prince Henry and his co-conspirators it was now or never. The Cossacks looked set to enter the city at any minute and seize him, his staff, their Turkish opposite numbers and the pro-German elements in the Persian government. Indeed, many of the latter had already left for the safety of Qum, where they expected to be joined at any moment by the Shah. There were signs, too, that the Germans were getting ready to move out of Teheran. Meanwhile, through their network of agents across the country, they were endeavouring, by means of rumours, bribes and other means, to incite the entire nation's wrath against the British and Russians. At the same time Prince Henry was loudly demanding that the Russians be ordered to halt their advance on a neutral Teheran. On November 13, the British Minister there warned Delhi in a telegram: 'The Germans are making great efforts to bring about movements in many parts of the country in their favour. Their object, of course, is to show the Persian government that the advance of the Russian troops has roused the whole of Persia against us.'

The following day the British and Russian ministers had a two-hour audience with the Shah at which they assured him that the Russian troops posed no threat to Persian sovereignty, but came only to protect the Allied legations and communities, which were threatened with violence from pro-German elements, and urged him to quash the inflammatory rumours which were being deliberately spread by Wassmuss and other agents of Prince Henry. 'We gave him to understand in unmistakable language', the British Minister reported, 'that if the Persian government did not act against the Germans, then Russian troops would undertake the task, and that if Persia allowed herself to be driven into war against us, the results to Persia and to himself would be disastrous.' However, their warning appeared to make little impression on the young ruler. 'His attitude', the British Minister told London and Delhi, 'was unsatisfactory and obstinate.'

Clearly they could not look to him or his government for any serious moves to halt German activities. The Cossacks, therefore, would have to do it for them. The Russian Legation immediately issued the following statement. 'The Imperial Russian Government has decided to put an end to the activities of the Turco-German agents who are scheming to drag

Persia into the war.' However, in a bid to allay deeply entrenched Persian fears of Tsarist intentions, the statement promised that Russian arms would not be used against the Persian people, but against the foreign enemy in their midst. 'Our forces', it concluded, 'have come with the sole purpose of maintaining order and protecting the foreign communities.' Realising that his time in Teheran was rapidly running out, Prince Henry and the rest of the German Legation staff left the capital on the afternoon of November 15, confident that the Shah would follow shortly.

Their hopes were soon dashed. At the eleventh hour, when he had actually called for his horse, the young Shah was persuaded by a much respected member of the royal family that to throw in his lot with the Germans, and let the Russians occupy Teheran, would almost certainly bring an end to the dynasty. In return for a last-minute undertaking that Russian troops would not enter the capital unless Allied lives there were threatened, the Shah agreed to stay. It had been touch and go, for the Germans and their allies had warned him that the Russians were intending to arrest him, and by the end he had hardly known whom to trust. But without the Shah as a figurehead, Prince Henry's plot collapsed, leaving the conspirators who had fled the capital exposed and isolated. Not long afterwards, the prince himself was ordered home, officially on grounds of ill-health, but in fact for his failure to deliver the Shah.

Although this was a major blow to German and Turkish hopes in Persia, the struggle was still very far from lost. From their new base at Qum the pro-German elements in the Persian government, calling themselves the Committee of National Defence, flooded the country with official-looking telegrams declaring that a revolution had taken place in the capital and that the British and Russian ministers had been forced to flee for their lives. As a smokescreen to cover their actual failure, the Gendarmerie attacked and seized the town of Hamadan, driving out the British and Russian consuls and plundering the vaults of the British-owned bank. At the same time rumours were spread that Field Marshal von der Goltz was on his way to Persia at the head of a large Turco-German force. Although quite untrue, these tidings helped to bolster the morale of the pro-German elements in Persia, and caused near panic among British defence chiefs in London and Delhi. In such a highly explosive situation, it was certainly not the moment to dispatch a military expedition to try to rescue O'Connor and his companions, since such a move would simply confirm, in most Persians' minds, German warnings about the Allied threat to their sovereignty. Similar considerations hampered Russian efforts to crush groups of German-led tribal levies and rebellious units of the Gendarmerie in the north of the country.

But if the Germans had suffered a setback over their bid to drag Persia into the Holy War, the British were about to face an even greater misfortune. Its tragic unfolding had begun, on November 22, 1915, on the banks of the River Tigris, in central Mesopotamia. There, thrusting up-river, a mixed British and Indian force had not long before captured the town of Kut from its Turkish defenders. Flushed by this success, it had then been ordered to march on the great Turkish garrison town of Baghdad, 100 miles further upstream. However, by the spectacular and ancient ruins of Ctesiphon, following an unbroken run of brilliant successes, the force suddenly found itself in grave trouble. For this time the Turks put up an unexpectedly determined defence, and by the end of the day the British had lost 4,500 men and the enemy some 9,000. Fierce fighting continued for a further two days, resulting in a Turkish withdrawal. Normally a commander would have seized on such an opportunity to pursue the retreating enemy mercilessly. But General Townshend, having lost so many men, and without any reserves, knew that he could not throw his utterly exhausted troops into battle again so soon. Moreover, with Baghdad now only twenty miles away, strong Turkish reinforcements would almost certainly be on their way. In view of this, he had no choice but to halt his advance until reinforcements could reach him from the south, which might take weeks. Yet if he dug in where he was, in the middle of a highly exposed desert, his troops risked massacre. His only option was to withdraw to Kut, eighty miles back down the Tigris, and wait there for reinforcements before advancing on Baghdad once more.

Townshend's men reached Kut on December 3, closely

pursued by the Turks. Four days later the British found themselves under siege. It was to last for five desperate months. Meanwhile, news of the unexpected retreat of this hitherto triumphant army came as a bombshell to the British people who had been led to believe that the capture of Baghdad, one of the great prizes of the war, was imminent. For its part, the hardpressed British War Cabinet had been counting on such a victory to offset bad news from just about everywhere else that winter. What with the evacuation of the Gallipoli peninsula by the Allies, the appalling casualty figures on the Western Front, the collapse of the Russian armies on the Eastern Front, and now this, there was little for people at home to celebrate that Christmas. But the British did have one success, even if few people knew about it at the time. This was the foiling of what became known as 'the Christmas Day Plot'.

12

The Christmas Day Plot

For some months now, it will be recalled, German agents and Indian revolutionaries had been secretly purchasing large quantities of small arms from dealers across the United States, a country then still not at war. At the same time, using German secret service funds, two vessels – the schooner *Annie Larsen* and the tanker *Maverick* – had been acquired for shipping the weapons across the Pacific to a rendezvous in the Far East. From there they would be smuggled into India, where revolutionary groups were eagerly awaiting their delivery. Unlike the earlier uprising in the Punjab, when impatient *Ghadr* leaders had struck prematurely, before arms could be got to them, this one was masterminded from Berlin as part of Germany's overall war strategy, and as such enjoyed the full support of the Kaiser's intelligence services.

The uprising, which aimed at seizing control of Calcutta, from where it would spread to every town and village in India, was timed for Christmas Day 1915, when it was reasoned that the British would be engaged in merry-making, and would therefore be caught off their guard. Ideally, it would coincide with the entry of both Afghanistan and Persia into the Holy War, or so it was still hoped in Berlin. To prevent the British from rushing in reinforcements from outside, and thus give the revolutionaries time to gain control of Calcutta, railway bridges were to be dynamited and telegraph lines cut. Using arms smuggled in from neutral Thailand, a second uprising was planned in neighbouring Burma, then part of British

India. At the same time, a vessel commanded by a German officer, and carrying armed Indian revolutionaries, would be sent to the remote Andaman Islands where veteran conspirators, including the hero Savarkar, were serving life sentences. The guards would be overcome, or even won over, and the prisoners freed to join in the bloody struggle for India.

The conspiracy, as we have already seen, involved the clandestine delivery by the *Annie Larsen*, sailing from San Diego in California, of 30,000 rifles and revolvers to a remote island off the Mexican coast. Here, away from the prying eyes of British intelligence, the weapons would be transferred to the larger, ocean-going *Maverick* for the long voyage across the Pacific to the Far East. On the island of Java, in the neutral Dutch East Indies, they would once more be off-loaded. Awaiting them there would be a number of small fishing boats chartered by the German consul for the final leg of their journey – delivery into the hands of the revolutionaries nicely in time for the Christmas bloodbath. Such then was the top-secret plan worked out between Berlin and those on the spot.

On March 8, 1915, weighed down with enough arms and ammunition to equip an army, the *Annie Larsen* had set sail for her island rendezvous with the *Maverick*. The schooner was running a little late, but with close on ten months to go, and with preparations in India and elsewhere well advanced, there seemed to be plenty of time in hand. In Calcutta the plotters had set up a bogus import-export business, calling itself Harry and Sons, to handle the arsenal's delivery and organise its distribution among the waiting revolutionary groups, while in Thailand similar arrangements were being made to receive those weapons intended for Burma. In addition, a further 5,000 rifles and 500 revolvers had been purchased in the Philippines by the German consul there, and a motor-schooner, the *Henry S.*, chartered to ship them across the South China Sea to a desolate spot on the coast of Thailand, together with two German-American weapons instructors. Finally, more weapons were being sought from nationalist sources in China for smuggling into India and Burma.

News that all these weapons were on their way had greatly boosted the morale of the Indian revolutionaries. This time, they were convinced, British rule in India would be brought to a bloody and humiliating end. That, in turn, would lead to the collapse of the entire British Empire, a ramshackle structure of which India was the linchpin. The plotters' hopes had already been raised by the near success, some months earlier, of Indian Army mutineers from the Singapore garrison in seizing control of the British colony there. Disaffected troops, their grievances inflamed by *Ghadr* propaganda, had risen against their officers, murdering forty of them and other officials. For some hours it had been touch and go for the British, but in the end, with the help of marines from Russian, Japanese and French warships patrolling nearby, the mutiny had been crushed and Singapore saved. Following a court martial, 2 Indian officers, 6 NCOs and 39 sepoys were executed by firing squads, while 15,000 spectators looked on. One NCO, who had been wounded during the fighting, had to be shot while bound to a chair. Many other sepoys were sentenced to transportation for life or long terms of imprisonment. Although there had been no serious planning behind the uprising, had it not been for the fortuitous presence of Allied warships the attempt might have succeeded. If Singapore could so nearly fall to a group of ill-prepared mutineers, then the seizure of Calcutta should present no great problem to well-armed and well-organised revolutionaries enjoying the backing of the Kaiser's intelligence services.

Equally encouraging to the conspirators in Calcutta were reports from the highly volatile Indian-Afghan frontier region of serious anti-British troubles among the Muslim tribes there. Already about 600 sepoys recruited from these parts had deserted from the Indian Army, while there had been many dismissals for misconduct. As a result an order had gone out that further recruitment from these tribes should cease forthwith. At the same time there had been a dramatic increase in trans-frontier raids by Afghan tribesmen. All this suggested to the plotters that when the moment came these fanatical and warlike people would eagerly join the banner of the Holy War and spill over into India. To organise that, however, was the task of their fellow conspirators now in Kabul, with whom they had no direct contact. So alarmed indeed was the Indian government by such a prospect that they had persuaded the War Cabinet in London to spare 'without delay' four battalions of British troops for dispatch to India for service on the frontier. For it was the Viceroy's view that the tribesmen feared only British infantry regiments, and held most native Indian units in 'utter contempt'.

But although in Calcutta the conspirators had some reason for optimism, they would have felt a lot less happy had they known what was going on elsewhere. Despite the careful arrangements of Captain Franz von Papen, the Kaiser's secret service chief at the German Embassy in Washington, the arsenal of weapons and ammunition intended for the Indian revolutionaries was still stuck somewhere on the far side of the Pacific. Indeed, neither von Papen nor his superiors in Berlin could say where precisely the shipment was at that moment. The *Annie Larsen*, her holds bulging with arms, had reached the island rendezvous all right. But of the tanker *Maverick* there was no sign and no word. Accounts of what followed vary somewhat, but it appears that the schooner waited at the island for a whole month, her captain becoming increasingly apprehensive at the lack of news of the tanker.

Fearing that the plot had been uncovered, and beginning to run low on food and water, the captain decided to head for the Mexican port of Acapulco, 800 miles to the south-east. There he managed to establish contact with the German consul in San Francisco, from where the *Maverick* was due to have set out for their rendezvous isle. He learned that the tanker's departure had been inadvertently delayed, but that it was now awaiting him at the rendezvous. He was ordered to return there as speedily as possible. But this time the heavily laden *Annie Larsen* ran into strong head winds. According to one version she never reached the island, being forced to abandon the voyage because of the weather. Another account maintains that she eventually got there, only to find that the *Maverick* had given up hope and left, after waiting for nearly a month.

The tanker, in fact, had set off westwards across the Pacific, hoping to pick up the scent of the elusive *Annie Larsen* somewhere on the way. She had stopped briefly at Hawaii to inquire about the schooner, but the Germans there knew nothing. At other islands she also drew a blank. This was not surprising, for having given up any hope of finding the *Maverick*, the schooner had put into an American port, where she hoped to receive further instructions from von Papen. By now the US authorities had become suspicious of the vessel's movements. On June 29 it was searched, and both it and its cargo seized. The German ambassador protested, but was overruled by the courts.

The *Maverick*, meanwhile, continued westwards towards the Dutch East Indies for her rendezvous there with the conspirators. However, her captain had no way of warning those expecting him of what had happened, and that instead of arms he was merely carrying bales of revolutionary literature plus half a dozen Indian freedom fighters on their way to join the insurrection. The task of receiving the *Maverick*, and handling the expected weapons, had been entrusted to two German brothers, both peacetime businessmen now turned wartime agents. Told to expect the *Maverick* during the first week in July, they planned to meet her just beyond Java's territorial waters. They therefore chartered a motor-launch and kept a twenty-four-hour vigil over the straits via which she was expected to approach Java. As the days passed without any sign of her, their hopes began to fade. Then, all of a sudden, they got word that she had arrived and put into a small port on a remote part of the coast. It was only then that they learned the truth about her failure to pick up the arms.

Although no two versions of the arms-for-India saga quite tally, this was far from the end of the story. As we have seen, the conspirators had other sources of weaponry. For a start there were the 5,000 rifles and 500 revolvers aboard the motor-schooner *Henry S.*, at that moment making its way stealthily across the South China Sea towards Thailand, which were to be smuggled inland to secret jungle depots close to the Burmese frontier. Then there were the arms for which the Indian revolutionaries were currently negotiating in China. The nationalists there had offered them a million rifles they no longer needed at $10 apiece. However, a German expert who had examined some of these dismissed them as antiquated and virtually useless. Finally a more promising source had been found in Yunnan, in south-western China. Initially it was decided to smuggle these into India and Burma by sea. But then it was discovered that the British had spies in all the ports along the southern Chinese coast, who would almost certainly have got wind of so large a movement of arms. Instead, therefore, plans were set in motion for carrying them out of China overland, using mules and ancient smuggling routes. This proved to be a prudent move, for the British had managed to discover – apparently from a notebook which had fallen into their hands – the name of the vessel the conspirators intended to use, and were maintaining a close watch on it. Meanwhile, the conspirators had come upon a third source of arms, including a large number of rifles and hand-grenades, in Sumatra, for which they were also negotiating.

In India, all this time, preparations had been going ahead to receive and distribute these weapons, and to give the revolutionary leaders some training in their use. They were determined that this uprising would not turn into a tragic fiasco like that in the Punjab. Secret revolutionary cells had been set up in the swampy and hilly regions to the east and north-east of Calcutta, where it was easy to conceal both men and arms. While the premises of Harry and Sons in the city was used as the movement's headquarters, elsewhere in the region other small shops and businesses were established as 'fronts' where freedom fighters could be recruited and funds and arms received. Contact had been made with disaffected elements among the Indian troops of the Calcutta garrison, whose co-operation was crucial if the plot was to succeed. If enough of them could be won over and induced to murder their British officers on Christmas Day, then others would follow suit, enabling the conspirators to seize control of Calcutta before Delhi and London realised what was happening. News of their victory would then spread quickly across India, encouraging other Indian Army units, and possibly the police, to rise and butcher their British oppressors. If their co-conspirators in Kabul had achieved their aims – and they had no way of discovering – then the tribes of the Afghan frontier, and perhaps the entire Afghan army, would join in the bloodbath. As one of the revolutionaries wrote years later: 'In those days everything seemed possible.'

*　　*　　*

While these final preparations were going on in India, in Kabul the Emir continued to stay his hand, being clearly in no hurry to commit himself either way. He had still not replied to King George V's letter, thereby causing much lost sleep in Delhi, where suspicions of his intentions were widely entertained. On the other hand, he had given Hentig and his companions little real hope that he was persuaded by their arguments. While he thus kept everyone guessing, there was really nothing more that they could usefully do other than wait and watch developments. Much, they knew, would hinge upon who, in the coming months, appeared to be winning the war. Clearly the wily Habibullah had no wish to find himself on the losing side.

The mission's lack of progress, and the prevailing air of uncertainty, did little for its morale or for relations between its German and Indian members. From the very start it had been an ill-assorted group, with no great love lost between Hentig and Niedermayer, while the Raja, nominally their leader, was proving to be a difficult companion, quarrelling with both Hentig and his Afghan hosts. The Germans had begun to lose faith in the ability of the Indians to deliver the promised revolution, despite their earlier assurances given in Berlin. For their part, it was beginning to dawn on the Raja and Barakatullah that Berlin was not remotely interested in India gaining independence, but simply in winning the war. Indeed, they were becoming increasingly suspicious that the Kaiser had his eyes on the throne of India for himself. While not openly severing relations with their German companions, they now determined to go it alone.

In October 1915 they were joined by a third Indian revolutionary – Maulvi Obeidullah, a Sikh turned Muslim – who had secretly made his way to Kabul from India with a handful of followers to join the Holy War which he believed to be imminent. Disregarding the Germans, the three Indians agreed to set up a revolutionary government in exile which would rule their homeland once victory had been achieved. Grandiloquently calling itself 'The Provisional Government of India', it nominated the Raja as its President, Barakatullah as Prime Minister and Obeidullah as Minister for Home and Foreign Affairs. Simultaneously the self-appointed triumvirate announced the formation of an 'Army of God', to whose banner they believed hundreds of thousands of tribesmen would flock the moment the signal went out from Kabul to drive the British from India. They still harboured hopes that the Emir, enticed by the promise of large tracts of northern India as his share of the spoils, would summon his people to join the Holy War. If not, then he would be swept aside by passions which he would be powerless to prevent. Once the torch of revolt had been applied to the tribal powder kegs along India's north-west frontier, they reasoned, then the ensuing conflagration would blaze out of control across the whole country, destroying every trace of British rule in its path.

But there was much to be done first if India was thus to be sent up in flames. Word of what was being hatched had to be got to tribal leaders along the frontier so that they would be ready when the moment came. Holy War leaflets extolling the Turco-German cause, and accusing the British of vile crimes against Islam, had to be prepared and distributed among the mullahs and elders of the region's many remote villages. For it will be recalled that they had been forced to abandon most of the incendiary literature they had set out with from Constantinople in the Persian desert when their very survival was at stake. Trustworthy couriers now had to be found to carry this propaganda from village to village, as well as agitators able to preach the Holy War in the languages and dialects of the Indo-Afghan frontierlands. For some time, as it happened, quite independently of the mission, itinerant Turkish firebrands had been at work among the border tribes, stirring up trouble for the British, and it was to them and other Turks living in Kabul that the Indians now turned. Indeed, given their deepening suspicions of Berlin's real motive for befriending them, the Raja and his compatriots found themselves looking more and more towards the Turks, rather than the Germans, as their allies.

That is not to say, however, that they spurned German help when it suited them. Before leaving Berlin they had been supplied with letters from the Kaiser to a number of Indian princes who, in the judgement of the German Foreign Ministry, were wavering in their loyalty to the British, and who might be persuaded, if the price were right, to turn against them. The letters promised the princes alluring post-war rewards if they would help to liberate India from British rule with the aid of their own private forces. In addition, in Constantinople the revolutionaries had been given similar letters from the Sultan, as Caliph, addressed to some of India's Muslim princes, urging them to perform their sacred duty and rally their subjects against the infidel British. The delivery of these highly seditious letters clearly presented considerable difficulties, for the recipients' domains lay within India's frontiers, and attached to their courts were British officers of the Indian Political Service who were there, among other things, to keep an eye open for any signs of treachery or other skulduggery.

What became of these letters is still something of a mystery. Hentig, in his memoirs, maintains that they were never in fact sent. But the Raja, in his, insists that they were. A trusted courier, he recounts, smuggled them across the frontier into India for onward transmission. Certainly a number of them fell into the hands of the British authorities (though it is a little unclear how) and these are to be seen in the old India Office archives in London. However, they and the Holy War leaflets were not the only such literature to emanate from Kabul at this time. For British frontier officers were soon to hear rumours of a mysterious letter circulating secretly among the tribal chiefs. Said to be signed by the Emir himself, it exhorted them to prepare themselves and their people for a Holy War against India, the signal for which would be given shortly. It was accompanied by tales of a German plan to march across Persia and Afghanistan and sweep triumphantly on into India, with the tribes at their back. All this was heady stuff to ignorant tribesmen, with little realisation of the vast distances involved, or of the fact that there were no German troops anywhere in the East who could possibly mount such an ambitious operation.

Although the Viceroy was fairly confident that the Emir's letter, if it existed at all, was a forgery concocted by Britain's enemies in Kabul, he was aware that in so volatile a region its repercussions could prove as explosive as if it had been genuine. To try to counter this, as well as similar propaganda emanating from Kabul, it was decided to demonstrate to the tribal hotheads what the consequences would be were they to join the Holy War. A grand *jirga*, or open-air meeting of 3,000 tribal leaders and elders was called at Peshawar, on India's north-west frontier with Afghanistan. Here they were informed by Colonel George Roos-Keppel, chief commissioner for the region, that Delhi had decided to reward their present loyalty by increasing their subsidies. After that, while a further 25,000 tribesmen looked on from the surrounding hillsides, they were treated to a bombing display by aircraft of the Royal Flying Corps. Few of the onlookers had ever seen an aeroplane before, let alone the terrifying destruction that these machines could, if angered, pour down on those below.

The effect of the demonstration was indeed salutary. 'Those bombing planes are worth at least 20,000 troops to you,' one tribal elder told Roos-Keppel afterwards. Further evidence of the impact they had made reached the commissioner shortly afterwards through an intercepted letter between two chiefs. Neither had witnessed the demonstration, but both were sworn foes of the British. 'I have heard remarkable things from the Mullah of Khema,' the letter declared. 'He says that the British have got machines at Peshawar which fly in the sky. God knows whether we can fight against such things or not, though the power of God is greater than such deeds of devils.' For a while, at least, the frontier remained unusually quiet.

*   *   *

Elsewhere in this shadowy game, however, things were far from quiet. In Calcutta, as they awaited the delivery of arms, the Christmas Day plotters were increasingly confident that before very long the city would be theirs. What they did not know was that their every move was being watched. Sir Charles Cleveland, head of the Indian security services, was fully aware of what was going on. The entire plot had been betrayed to the authorities. Curiously, there is no mention of this in the report of the Sedition Committee of 1918, set up to investigate the conspiracy and Germany's role in it. Details of the plot's betrayal were only revealed thirty years later by the Viceroy, Lord Hardinge, in his memoir of those times, *My Indian Years, 1910–1916*. 'It was in June 1915', he wrote, 'that a German officer in disguise landed at Singapore and was arrested by the military authorities. Among his papers was found a map of Bengal with certain marks on various points of the coast.' These, it transpired, were possible landing spots for arms. Also concealed on him was a secret code enabling him to communicate directly with Berlin, together with other compromising documents. His arrest, it appears, had resulted from a tip-off from the British authorities in the Dutch East Indies, from where he had just come.

The Viceroy immediately dispatched one of his most experienced police officers to Singapore, and after a prolonged cross-examination the German made a full confession. It was a curious tale, but one which convinced his interrogator. His name, he said, was Vincent Kraft. While serving on the Western Front he had committed some kind of an offence, the details of which he refused to divulge, but the penalty for which was death. Instead, however, he had been offered the alternative of undertaking what he described as 'a very dangerous mission' in the East, a region with which he was very familiar from before the war. His task, he revealed, was to organise an insurrection against the British in Bengal, for which both arms and money were being supplied by Germany.

'He gave us very full information of all the German plans,' wrote Hardinge, 'and as proof of his bona fides he continued under our supervision to correspond with his German superiors as though he was still free and active.' Twice he received from them substantial sums of money which were expropriated by the British authorities, and in due course he returned to the Dutch East Indies to join German agents operating from there who were unaware that he was now working for the enemy. After the war, the Viceroy added, Kraft asked that instead of being repatriated he should be allowed to emigrate to the United States with his family and with enough money to make a fresh start under a new identity. This was agreed to by his British spymasters, who helped him to disappear. Even in his memoirs, written in 1948, Hardinge was careful not to identify him, his name only emerging some years later when the secret Indian government archives of those anxious days were finally declassified. At the time, even in intelligence reports, he was simply referred to as 'Agent X'.

Had it not been for Kraft's arrest, Christmas 1915 might

well have ended in a bloodbath for the British community in Calcutta, even if the conspirators had failed to win control of the city. 'Immediate steps', wrote Hardinge, 'were taken to counteract the conspiracy.' The Royal Navy's routine watch for vessels trying to smuggle arms into India and Burma was greatly intensified, and British consuls alerted in the South China Sea area. But conspirators whose covers had been blown by Kraft were carefully shadowed rather than arrested, in the hope that they would thus implicate others involved in the plot. Even so they must have begun to wonder at times why so many things seemed to go wrong for no apparent reason.

In the middle of July, while on the way to deliver her cargo of rifles and revolvers to the revolutionaries in Thailand, the motor-schooner *Henry S.* had mysteriously broken down and been forced to put into port in Celebes, one of the Dutch East Indian islands, for emergency repairs. There, for no obvious reason, she was boarded and searched by Dutch customs officers who came upon, and impounded, the arms hidden in her hold. In fact, although the crew did not know it, the Dutch had been tipped off by the British about her illicit cargo. There was now little point in the captain proceeding with the voyage. However, one of the German-American weapons instructors on board decided to try to reach Thailand to warn the conspirators about the arms seizure. Not surprisingly he was quickly picked up by the British, and under interrogation eventually revealed the whereabouts of the secret jungle training camps and arms depots on the Thai-Burmese frontier. Soon afterwards, as a result of pressure from Delhi, the Thai authorities rounded up several hundred Indian and Burmese freedom fighters, thereby scotching Berlin's plan for an armed uprising in Burma.

As Christmas approached, the remaining strands of the conspiracy rapidly began to unravel. A second vessel known by the British to be heading for India carrying weapons disappeared mysteriously at sea. According to the Royal Navy she went down with all hands in a typhoon, but modern Indian historians believe that she was almost certainly sunk deliberately, as a result of information supplied by Kraft. The conspirators' arrangements for acquiring large quantities of rifles from southern China also appear to have come to nothing, though it is not quite clear why. So too did various other schemes, including the bold plan to send a vessel to the Andaman Islands to free the Indian revolutionaries incarcerated there. The latter failure comes as no surprise, however, when one learns that it was Kraft himself who was to have led this operation. Finally, on December 15, in a series of lightning raids in both Calcutta and Burma over 300 conspirators were taken into police custody. The great Christmas Day plot, aimed at ending British rule in India, had been crushed.

Nonetheless, so long as the Germans and Indians remained actively scheming in Kabul, the threat to India remained. Because of this, and the danger of their engineering the Emir's overthrow, London suggested that the Emir be urged to have the intriguers arrested and sent to India for safekeeping there. The Viceroy, however, was strongly opposed to such a move, fearing that any such precipitate action might disturb the present very delicate balance in Kabul, bringing things to a head and providing the Emir's opponents with a pretext for overthrowing him. He knew, moreover, that Habibullah was extremely astute and ruthless, and by far the best judge of how to outwit his foes.

The Emir, meanwhile, continued to hold discussions with members of the mission, although these never seemed to get anywhere, leaving Hentig and Niedermayer increasingly frustrated. However, he did make it clear that no amount of Holy War rhetoric, or extravagant post-war promises, would persuade him to take on, single-handed, his two giant neighbours, British India and Tsarist Russia. Anyone embarking on so hazardous an undertaking, he told them, would have to receive considerable military support from outside, including troops and artillery. His words could be interpreted as not wholly ruling out any possibility of his joining the Holy War if the circumstances were right. But whether, by dangling this faint hope before them, the Emir was simply keeping his options open lest the war take a sudden turn in Germany's favour, or merely stringing them along for other reasons, was far from clear to Hentig and his companions. By not giving them a definite no, and thereby allowing the pro-German elements around him to think that he might still be persuaded, he was perhaps hoping to stave off being overthrown or even assassinated. At the same time, he appeared anxious to keep the mission in Kabul, if only to keep an eye on their activities. Twice the Germans had threatened to return home, and each time they noticed that the Emir reacted by giving ground.

Then in December 1915, just as they were giving up any last hope of success and were once again threatening to pack up and go, all of a sudden the Emir gave them fresh cause for optimism. He indicated that he was prepared to consider a proposal they had made to him earlier for a treaty of friendship between Berlin and Kabul. Greatly heartened by the Emir's unexpected departure from his previous position, they now entered into discussion with him over the treaty's possible contents. This took much time, as perhaps the Emir intended. Finally, however, in the middle of January 1916, the draft treaty was ready. Under its terms, Germany agreed to recognise Afghanistan's full independence as a sovereign power, something which under her agreement with Britain she did not then enjoy. Germany would see to it, moreover, that Afghanistan would be fully represented at any post-war peace conference.

While the Emir gave no undertaking to enter the war, the Germans pledged themselves to supply him 'as quickly as possible, gratis and without return,' 100,000 rifles of the latest pattern, 300 artillery pieces, large and small, and other war materials needed to modernise the Afghan army. Berlin, furthermore, would establish and maintain a regular supply route across Persia along which would travel the promised arms and ammunition, plus military advisers, engineers and others. At the same time, Afghan officials would be sent secretly to Persia to negotiate further with Germany and Turkey. In addition the Emir would receive a payment of £10 million in sterling. Finally, in the event of Afghanistan deciding to enter the war Germany undertook to give her every possible assistance against the British and the Russians. Before the treaty could become effective, however, it had to be signed by both the Emir and the Kaiser's Foreign Minister, for Hentig had neither the seniority nor the authority to do so on the latter's behalf. Because of the great distances and difficulties involved, all this would take some time to organise, which may well have suited the Emir.

Even so, by going along with this, he clearly had very little to lose. After all, were the Germans or Turks ever to be in a position to supply him with this military hardware then it could only mean that they must be winning the war in the East. Otherwise it was mere wishful thinking by the Germans, and little more than an insurance policy so far as he was concerned. 'All in all the treaty appeared to be a mixture of bluff and meaningless concessions,' Ludwig Adamec observes in his study of Afghanistan's foreign relations. But although the treaty did not add up to very much, or pose any serious threat to British India, the mere suspicion of it at that time would have given the Viceroy apoplexy. The Emir, Hentig noted, was most anxious that no hint of the treaty's existence should reach the ears of the British or the Russians, whose combined wrath he did not relish. Indeed, on the very day he appended his signature to the treaty he instructed Delhi's Muslim agent in Kabul to reassure the Viceroy once again that he intended to remain strictly neutral. In the event, however, the British were not to learn of these nefarious goings-on until 1918, by which time it hardly mattered.

Hentig's satisfaction at obtaining the treaty was to prove short-lived. For within a matter of weeks the Emir had begun to perform a U-turn. Emissaries he had sent to Persia to conduct secret negotiations with the Germans were recalled to Kabul without explanation. At the same time, perhaps as a precaution against a coup or assassination attempt, he began to purge his court of officials known to be pro-German. Finally he informed the Germans that even if India were to go up in flames he could not consider joining the Holy War unless a Turco-German force of at least 20,000 men first came to his assistance – a logistical feat which both he and the Germans knew to be all but impossible. Simultaneously he replied at last to King George V's letter, reiterating his intention of remaining loyal to the British crown. The sighs of relief from the Viceroy and those responsible for India's defence were almost audible.

For Hentig and his companions it was clearly the end of the road. Although the Emir gave no reason for this sudden hardening of his attitude, it may well have resulted from news which reached Kabul at about this time. It was news of a major Allied victory in the East, and it effectively ruled out any possibility of a Turco-German force being sent to Afghanistan's assistance. For in February 1916, after successfully clearing Turks, Germans and their Persian sympathisers out of north-western Persia, triumphant Russian troops had thrust deep into eastern Turkey. There, after desperate fighting in terrible winter conditions, they had finally stormed the great Ottoman stronghold of Erzerum, guardian of the approaches to Constantinople, and hitherto considered impregnable. News of this Turkish catastrophe was to reverberate throughout the East.

13

The Storming of Erzerum

'The capture of the great fortress sent a thrill through the whole continent,' wrote M. Philips Price, the *Manchester Guardian* correspondent with the Russian forces. 'Every bazaar from Shiraz to Samarkand, Konia to Kuldja, began speaking of the mighty Urus who had taken Erzerum from the Osmanli.' For the sudden and unexpected surrender of this heavily defended enemy stronghold was the first Allied triumph in the Holy War between Cross and Crescent. 'Until then,' Philips Price observed, 'it was not clear who were to be the masters of the great road from Central Europe to Central Asia.' Now, it seemed, the Turks were on the run, and the conquest of Constantinople itself appeared attainable.

In that bitter winter of 1915/16, which had witnessed the humiliation of the Allied retreat from Gallipoli, the worsening plight of the beleaguered British garrison at Kut, and the bloody stalemate on the Western Front, Allied euphoria over this one solitary victory was perhaps understandable. Graphic reconstructions of the battle for snow-bound Erzerum, sketched by war artists who were not present, allowed readers to share this historic moment with their heroic Russian allies. 'The conquest of Erzerum was one of the most brilliant strategical episodes in the entire war,' wrote John Buchan. Indeed, so stirring were the accounts of it which reached London that when he used Erzerum's fall as the grand climax for *Greenmantle*, there was little he needed to invent – save for the presence of Richard Hannay and Sandy Arbuthnot.

The ancient garrison town of Erzerum, which has guarded the approaches to Constantinople for more than a thousand years, stands alone on a desolate plain surrounded by high mountains. Even today few people visit it in winter, so merciless is the cold, with temperatures sometimes plunging to 40 degrees below zero. Every winter wolves descend from the mountains, driven down by hunger and cold, and roam the suburbs and university campus in desperate search of food. Erzerum's winters are wretchedly long, with the first snows falling in October and lying, six feet deep in places, until the following April. The summers, correspondingly, are short and intensely hot. And as if that were not enough, Erzerum lies in the heart of an earthquake zone, and over the centuries these have cost the lives of scores of thousands of its inhabitants and wrought great destruction. It is not surprising that those nurtured in this harsh environment are capable of extraordinary endurance. While greatly admiring the courage and hardiness of the Russian troops he was accompanying, Philips Price conceded that Erzerum's defenders were every bit as stalwart. Many of them, moreover, had already been tempered in the crucible of sub-zero warfare, being survivors from Enver Pasha's disastrous attempt, the previous winter, to seize the town of Sarikamish and carry the banner of the Holy War into the Caucasus.

In February 1916, at the time of the Russian advance on Erzerum, the great Ottoman stronghold was ringed by a dozen or so outlying fortresses, strategically positioned in the surrounding mountains to control the passes and other approach routes by which an enemy might come. In winter it was additionally protected by the elements, the few roads leading to it being rendered impassable by heavy snowfalls. Some of these routes, moreover, carried those using them over passes 9,000 feet or more above sea level, presenting enormous problems where heavy artillery needed to be brought up to the front. During the 1880s, at the height of the Great Game between Britain and Russia, British military engineers had helped the Turks to modernise the garrison's defences, and not long afterwards a secret Russian report declared Erzerum to be unassailable without the use of siege artillery to take out the outlying forts. Later, when German military advisers replaced the British ones, further improvements were introduced, adding to the great eastern bastion's reputation for invulnerability.

The Russian advance on Erzerum, and eventually on Constantinople itself, had originally been planned for the spring. But then had come the devastating tidings of the Allied evacuation of Gallipoli, which overnight freed 50,000 battle-hardened Turkish troops for service in the east. It suddenly became clear that their arrival might not only halt the Russian thrust into eastern Turkey, but also turn the tide of the Holy War, threatening the Tsar's possessions in the Caucasus and Central Asia, and even India. The Grand Duke Nicholas, the Russian supreme commander in the Caucasian theatre, knew that he had little time to lose. The whole plan would have to be brought forward. He had to strike before Enver could bring up his reinforcements, even if this meant launching the campaign at the height of the cruel Turkish winter. But here the Russians had already secured one major advantage. In preparation for the advance, the Russian Black Sea fleet had systematically sunk most of the transport vessels used by the Turks to bring men and munitions to the Erzerum region via the port of Trebizond. This meant that from now on everything would have to be carried overland from Constantinople, which in winter could take anything up to six weeks. Moreover, with the nearest railhead no nearer than Ankara, the reinforcements would have to travel the last 500 miles along snow-blocked roads, most likely on foot and carrying their own food and ammunition. The Russians, for their part, could transport by rail both men and supplies from Tiflis all the way to Sarikamish, which was just eighty miles from Erzerum.

The Russian plan, drawing on 80,000 troops and relying heavily on surprise, was for a converging movement by three columns, attacking simultaneously from the north, south and east. Before the war, one of the Russian commanders, General Prejevalsky, had served for some years as military attaché at Erzerum. Speaking fluent Turkish, and dressed as a peasant, he had spent weeks wandering the region on foot or by pony. Unknown to the Turkish authorities, he had become intimately acquainted with the strengths and weaknesses of the surrounding forts, as well as with the best approach routes to the city itself. But rather than trying to destroy all the forts before fighting their way into Erzerum, because of the grave shortage of time the Russian generals decided to go only for those they judged crucial to its defence, even if this left their troops exposed to fire from the others.

The attack was launched on February 11, 1916. Initially it took the Turks totally by surprise, for they had never dreamed that the Russians would risk annihilation by exposing their troops to the merciless Anatolian winter which had destroyed Enver's 'Army of Islam' in the passes leading to Sarikamish. But the Turks quickly recovered, and fought stubbornly and heroically. They were old hands at winter warfare, moreover, and knew all the tricks. On the open ground before the forts they had dug a network of snow-trenches which in winter were invisible to an advancing enemy at more than 100 yards. In the forts themselves they had water for pouring down the slopes leading up to them, thereby covering the mountainside with huge sheets of unscalable ice. But the Russians, too, had some tricks of their own. For a start they decided to attack at night, despite the immense difficulties, for they guessed that the Turkish troops would be huddled together in the bottom of their snow-trenches to avoid freezing to death. They had come well prepared for such a move, moreover.

'The Russian soldiers', wrote Philips Price, 'were clad in white coats, so that in the darkness and against the snow they were invisible.' Creeping silently forwards, they managed thus to get within 250 yards of one of the forts before they were picked out by a Turkish searchlight. Immediately, a murderous hail of fire was directed down on them, wiping out one-third of the force in two terrible hours. But the rest struggled on until they were beneath the rocky outcrop on which the fort stood, which gave them some protection. Meanwhile, though the guns of the fort above could not reach them here, fire from a neighbouring one continued to rake their positions. By this time a heavy Russian artillery barrage should have opened up on the Turkish forts. The guns had not yet arrived, though, for those with the Herculean task of dragging them over the passes found themselves facing immense difficulties, as also had the infantry units of the main

force. Consequently the plan of attack was running dangerously late.

Only men inured to the sub-Arctic hell of the Russian winter, wrote Philips Price, could have attempted such a feat.
'The Russian troops had to cross mountain ranges with deep
snowdrifts at 10,000 feet, and go for at least three days cut off
from supplies of food, with nothing but the few crusts of
bread they could carry with them,' he reported. At first they
had tried to haul the guns over the mountains by sheer bodily
strength, but this had soon proved impossible. Instead, each
gun had to be dismantled so that the parts could be borne on
the shoulders of small groups of men. As it was, the merciless
cold proved too much for many of the troops, and during the
nights of February 12 and 13 over 2,000 of them died from
exposure or frostbite.

Meanwhile, early on the 13th, to save them from being mas-
sacred, the Russian troops pinned down beneath the Turkish
fort had been extricated from their highly exposed position
and withdrawn out of range of the enemy guns. However, with
no sign yet of the promised artillery support, and with every
chance of the Turks mounting a counter-attack, the Russian
commander ordered his men to try once more to penetrate the
enemy's defences. Again the Russians attacked at night, hoping to catch the frozen Turks off their guard. 'Immense difficulty was experienced,' wrote Philips Price. 'The snow lay in
drifts often five to six feet deep, and in places in order to move
the soldiers had to take off their coats and walk on them in the
snow, throwing them forward every three feet to avoid sinking
in up to their necks.' Silently and painfully the Russians thus
advanced all night, creeping ever closer to the Turkish snow-
trenches.

'At last,' wrote Philips Price, 'daylight began to break upon
this arctic scene, and through scuds of snow broken by the icy
wind the Turks saw a chain of dark forms slowly closing in on
them. They could hardly believe their eyes, for it seemed to
them impossible that a human army with rifles and ammunition could cross the country that lay in front of them.' They
realised with dismay that they were all but cut off, there being
only a narrow corridor through the snowfields along which
they could escape to the safety of the nearest fort. This they

succeeded in doing before the Russians, who greatly outnumbered them, were able to reach their trenches. But although
the Russians had gained valuable ground, they had still not
pierced the cordon which linked the forts. To achieve that
they required the support of those still making their way
across the snow-bound passes to the north-east. There was
nothing now for it but to sit tight and pray that their comrades
would arrive before the Turks counter-attacked in force and
drove them back.

It was around this time, according to some of the Russian
troops, that as the sun was setting a huge cross appeared in the
smoke-filled sky above Erzerum. This was seen by the devout
peasant soldiers as an omen in this war between Cross and
Crescent, and so it shortly turned out to be. For word reached
the forward troops that both the main body and the siege
artillery were now safely across the mountains. At the same
time a secret telegram was intercepted between the Turkish
commander and Enver Pasha warning that unless reinforcements could be got to Erzerum very soon the garrison was
doomed. An aerial reconnaissance of the Turkish positions
showed up serious weaknesses. With the Russian artillery now
in place overlooking Erzerum and the outlying forts, a heavy
bombardment commenced.

Outnumbered and outgunned, and with little hope of any
reinforcements reaching them in time, the Turks nonetheless
resisted ferociously, fighting off the Russian attacks again and
again. But gradually, exhausted by the relentless shelling and
repeated infantry and cavalry assaults, their resistance began
to weaken. Then, after a lucky shell exploded its ammunition
store, the first of the Turkish forts fell to the Russians. One by
one others followed, and it was now clear that the Turks could
not hold out much longer. Even so, as the Russian troops
closed in on them, they continued to fight. But then, on
February 15, a Russian airman on a reconnaissance flight over
the now blazing city reported signs of extraordinary activity in
the streets below, and also long baggage convoys beginning to
head westwards. General Prejevalsky, whose troops had got
closest to the city, was ordered by his commander-in-chief to
drive any remaining enemy out. The following morning,
escorted by a regiment of Cossacks, he rode into Erzerum only

to find the enemy gone, many of the buildings on fire, and the streets strewn with corpses.

Although officially accredited to the Russian army, Philips Price was not allowed to enter the captured city until the Grand Duke Nicholas had made his own triumphal entrance. As he approached the former Turkish stronghold, the British correspondent could see in the distance a thick pall of smoke hanging over it. But the eerie silence told him that the battle was over. On either side of the road, however, lay grisly evidence of its ferocity. Protruding through the snow he saw the humps of dead camels, the legs of horses, and men's faces 'with fezzes and little black beards, smiling at us the smile of death, their countenances frozen as hard as the snow around them.' That, he added, 'was all that was left of the *Drang nach Osten* in this part of the world.'

Mystery will always surround the fall of Erzerum, for it is possible that the garrison was betrayed to the Russians from within. T. E. Lawrence, then serving with the Arab Bureau in Cairo, claimed that he had secretly 'put the Grand Duke Nicholas in touch with certain disaffected Arab officers in Erzerum', via the War Office in London. Lawrence's claim, made after the war to the military historian Basil Liddell Hart, who was also his biographer, is not wholly inconceivable. There were certainly many disaffected Arab officers serving in the Ottoman armed forces who would have been happy to see an Allied victory. Lawrence's intelligence work in Cairo prior to the outbreak of the Arab Revolt in June 1916 brought him into contact with such dissidents, as had his pre-war travels in the Ottoman Empire.

The idea of such treachery, involving a stolen staff map pinpointing certain gaps in Erzerum's defences, is exploited to the full in John Buchan's *Greenmantle*. The crucial map is smuggled out of the city to the Grand Duke Nicholas at the Russian headquarters, with the aid of a traitor in the Turkish ranks. In the hands of the Russian staff officers its revelations enable them to seal the city's fate before the Gallipoli veterans can be thrown into the battle against them. John Buchan enjoyed high-level connections in both the British Cabinet and the War Office at this time, so it is not impossible that he heard that, in the words of Lawrence's biographer Jeremy

Wilson, 'something unusual' had taken place. Wilson also reminds us that, at the time of Erzerum's fall, Buchan was hosting an important Russian delegation to Britain. He might well have picked up a whisper of such goings-on from them. Lawrence himself, who asked Liddell Hart not to dwell on the involvement of an enemy within the garrison for fear of reprisals being taken against his family, told another friend, the poet Robert Graves, that '*Greenmantle* has more than a flavour of truth'. The truth will not be known, however, until the secret service archives of that period, which have a special 100-year embargo on them, are opened to historians. As a poignant footnote to the Russian victory it is worth recording that during their captivity prior to their murder by the Bolsheviks Tsar Nicholas and his family read *Greenmantle* and, according to a smuggled letter, were 'greatly cheered and comforted' by Buchan's stirring account of the Grand Duke's triumph.

The loss of Erzerum, coming so soon after the Turkish victory over the Allies at Gallipoli and thus partially eclipsing it, was a bitter blow to Enver Pasha, Turkey's military supremo. Although it was a wholly Russian victory, it was to give Allied morale a badly needed boost at a time when good news was in extremely short supply. Not only was the British garrison beleaguered in Kut in desperate straits, but there were fears in Cairo that with the collapse of the Gallipoli adventure Enver would turn the 50,000 troops thus freed against Egypt in an attempt to wrest back this lost Ottoman dominion. Although the Turkish defeat did nothing to relieve the pressure on Kut, it undoubtedly lifted the immediate threat to Egypt. From now on Enver would need all the troops he could spare to prevent the triumphant Russians from continuing their drive westwards towards Constantinople once the winter snows had begun to melt.

                    *   *   *

Unaware of any of this, or of the failure of their compatriots' bid to set Afghanistan ablaze, the Germans in Persia were meanwhile pressing on resolutely with their plans to spread the Holy War eastwards into India. Although they and their Persian sympathisers had been forced to flee Teheran, following their abortive attempt to win over the Shah to the Turco-

German cause, they continued to pursue Berlin's clandestine strategies from their widely scattered bases in central and southern Persia. Their most notable success had been the seizure as hostages of Major Frederick O'Connor, the British consul at Shiraz, and other members of the British community there. But despite Wassmuss's campaign of murder, terrorism and brigandage, which had turned much of southern Persia into a no-go area for the British, they still firmly held on to the ports of the Persian Gulf, so crucial to India's defence. Fears that Wassmuss might be planning further tribal attacks on Bushire and other British targets in the Gulf, however, forced them to maintain a larger military presence there than would otherwise have been necessary.

But perhaps more disturbing were the activities of Lieutenant Zugmayer, a tough pre-war Asiatic traveller, in the Kerman area, in south-east Persia, which lay uncomfortably close to both British Baluchistan and the highly volatile tribes of southern Afghanistan. At first he and his companions had encountered great difficulties with the local governor, whom they knew to be in the pay of the British, and who refused to allow Zugmayer to take up his appointment as German consul or to fly the German flag from the house they had rented as the consulate. Gradually, however, by means of bribes, promises and threats – not to mention an assassination – they had succeeded in strengthening their grip on the town. Finally, in December 1915, they had persuaded Persians sympathetic to their cause, aided by members of the pro-German Gendarmerie, to seize control of Kerman. The telegraph lines to Teheran were cut, and the small British and Russian communities, together with their consuls, were forced to flee for their lives. Zugmayer and his companions were now ready to light the fuse of religious fanaticism among the Baluchis and southern Afghan tribes.

In a region notoriously unstable, the prospects appeared promising. Already one Indian Army regiment recruited in Baluchistan had mutinied on learning that it was being sent to Mesopotamia to fight the Turks, and had murdered its commanding officer. Unaware of developments elsewhere, the Germans in Kerman had no reason to think that anything had gone amiss with Berlin's Holy War plans. For the final triumphant descent on British India, therefore, they believed that they would be joined by the Emir of Afghanistan's wild tribesmen, and by German-led troops sent by the Shah of Persia. Once inside India they would be hailed as saviours by the oppressed millions, whether Hindus, Muslims or Sikhs, with whom they would join forces under the banner of Allah to drive the infidel British from the country for ever. For in this remote corner of Persia, without radio or any other source of news, they had no way of knowing that Berlin's grand design for mass uprisings across India had been foiled by the British, and that most of the revolutionary leaders had either been hanged or imprisoned.

Zugmayer's plan was as follows. One group led by himself would head for Baluchistan, where they would spread word of the Holy War about to be launched against the British in India among the tribal leaders, at the same time distributing gold, rifles and inflammatory literature. They would aim to excite the tribesmen with visions of the loot they would amass were they to join the Holy War, and encourage them to plunder the British convoys bringing up vital supplies from Quetta to the troops of the East Persian Cordon. If these were cut off, then the British would be forced to reduce or withdraw their troops, which would expose the frontier to further German penetration. Meanwhile a second party, led by Lieutenant Seiler, the former German consul at Isfahan, would try to pierce the British cordon and reach Kabul, where they would make contact with Niedermayer and Hentig, and co-ordinate their final plans. On their way to the capital they hoped to spread word of the Holy War among the Afghan tribesmen along the route.

The two parties rode out of Kerman early in January 1916, heading east and south-east respectively. Seiler's task was the more hazardous, for not only did he have to dodge the British patrols and the spies they used to watch every well and village, he had also to cross a forbidding stretch of desert, though mercifully not in summer. Accompanied by two of his compatriots, and a number of armed Persian horsemen, he rode ahead of the rest of his party to try to reconnoitre a route to the nearest point on the Afghan frontier. Ten days later, after successfully crossing the desert, he and his companions reached a small village on the other side. Here they surprised and captured a British native agent assigned to report on their movements. But that night he managed to escape by cutting through the mud wall of the house in which they were holding him. In a matter of hours, Seiler realised, a British cavalry patrol would arrive and surround the village. Although his own party had ample time in which to get clear, the main group, unless quickly alerted to their danger, would almost certainly walk into an ambush. Seiler therefore dispatched a horseman to try to intercept and warn them. In the meantime, he and his companions took up a position on a ridge overlooking the village, from where they could observe the approach of the enemy and also, if the messenger failed to find them, the rest of his party.

The following day, guided by the native spy who had raised the alarm after his escape, a British cavalry patrol of a subaltern and fifty troopers reached the village. Discovering from the villagers that the Germans were hiding in the hills, they rode after them, trying to surround them. But Seiler and his men, also on horses, withdrew ever further into the hills, firing as they went. That night, leaving one of his officers, a Lieutenant Winkelman, to cover their escape by firing at the British in the darkness, Seiler and the others managed to slip through the net and away into the desert. But they left behind them four dead Persian tribesmen, another one mortally wounded, two injured baggage camels, several rifles and much of their equipment.

The next night a mysterious figure was spotted by the British sentries creeping silently towards the village. While one trooper covered him with a rifle, another leaped on him from behind. A fierce struggle followed, and the intruder had to be knocked semi-conscious with a rifle butt before he could be overcome. It turned out to be Lieutenant Winkelman, by now desperate to find food and water. 'He was a real sportsman,' observed one British officer afterwards, when it was realised that he had sacrificed his own liberty to enable his companions to get away. He was interrogated thoroughly before being sent to India, but beyond revealing that they had heard nothing from Kabul since Niedermayer and Hentig arrived there the previous summer, British intelligence reports show that he gave away little of value, and that much of what he did tell his questioners proved to be thoroughly misleading and inaccurate.

Nonetheless, allowing the British native agent to escape, rather than shooting him on the spot, had cost the Germans dear. Although Seiler and his party had managed to get away, the British were now fully aware of their intentions. For they had discovered from the villagers that Seiler's party was merely the advance guard of a heavily armed larger group of Germans and Persian mercenaries who were expected shortly. Reinforcements were hurriedly brought up to meet this threat. In the event, however, it never materialised, for the main party had run into serious difficulties. They had discovered that the small stockpiles of food and water which Seiler had arranged for them along the route had been plundered by local tribesmen. They were thus forced to return to Kerman, suffering severely from hunger and thirst. When he realised what had happened, Seiler saw that he had little choice but to abandon his attempt to reach Kabul and return instead to Kerman.

Lieutenant Zugmayer and his party, meanwhile, were busy stirring up mischief for the British among the Baluchi tribesmen to the south-east, and reports soon began to reach Quetta that the Germans were enjoying considerable success in recruiting them for the Holy War. Indeed, Zugmayer's prospects began to look extremely promising when he received a secret letter from a powerful Baluchi leader offering the Germans the full support of his tribe against the British. He proposed that Zugmayer send a trusted emissary to a small village close to the Indian frontier to hold further discussions there. Zugmayer immediately dispatched two of his officers to the village, intending to join them once initial agreement had been reached, after which a detailed plan of action could be prepared. One of the German officers was, like T. E. Lawrence, a pre-war archaeologist who spoke the language and had excavated in Persia. The two were royally entertained by their host, but soon the suspicion began to dawn on them that they were being duped. 'He was not so much a tribal prince, as we had been led to believe, but a robber chief,' wrote one of the officers afterwards. 'He wanted our weapons and our money in order to defeat his enemies.'

Disillusioned, they ended the talks abruptly, and headed back to join Zugmayer and break the news of their failure to him. However, on the way they were intercepted by their host's men and robbed of everything they possessed, being lucky to escape with their lives. Zugmayer and his companions now realised that they had been deluding themselves and were forced to accept that they had wasted their time having anything to do with the Baluchis. 'They are an impudent, underhand, dishonest and craven pack of curs, driven solely by greed,' observed one German bitterly. What one of the party had called 'our beautiful dream' of leading 'the brave Baluchis' in a Holy War against British India had ended in total failure.

The news from elsewhere in Persia was no better. They learned for the first time that Russian troops from the north had seized and occupied their stronghold at Isfahan, while even their own base at Kerman was no longer safe. The moment their two parties had left the town on their respective missions, the pro-British governor had managed to re-establish his authority there. In this, his hand had been greatly strengthened by news of the Russians' victory at Erzerum and the forcible expulsion of the Germans from Isfahan. Nor was that all. For Zugmayer and his companions now heard that following a visit to Persia, Field Marshal von der Goltz, supreme commander of German and Turkish forces in Mesopotamia and Persia, and one of the original architects of the Holy War, had abandoned his ambitious plan to lead a force of German-officered Persian volunteers against India. Disillusioned by what he had observed in Persia, he now saw no prospect of it succeeding. Most Persians, he warned Berlin, were only interested in Germany for its gold, and were the flow of this suddenly to cease then their devotion to the cause would likewise cease. As it was, they were already hinting that they could get better terms from the British.

Within two months of his return to Baghdad, the Field Marshal was dead, a victim of typhus. Today he lies in a grave beside that other Holy War fantasist, Ambassador Wangenheim, in the German war cemetery overlooking the Bosphorus in Istanbul. It was now clear that everything they, and their masters in Berlin, had hoped to achieve in the East by harnessing the forces of Islam to Germany's war machine was beginning to collapse. Already some of their former allies among the Persians and the Gendarmerie were showing signs of cold feet, causing the German officers and NCOs still in the country to feel increasingly isolated. Some of them, notably Zugmayer and his handful of compatriots in south-east Persia, were more than 700 miles from the nearest German or Turkish positions.

Besides the defection of many of their Persian friends, who had seen the writing on the wall, and realised that the Germans' promises of ridding them of the British and the Russians were hollow, Zugmayer and his companions now found themselves facing two new threats. Worried by reports of German activities in Baluchistan, the British had dispatched a tough and experienced frontier soldier to bring the restive Baluchis to heel. He was Brigadier-General Reginald Dyer, who was later to earn himself worldwide notoriety by ordering the Amritsar massacre. Although he had been given only 100 soldiers with which to pacify the tribesmen, Dyer spread ahead of him a tale that he was the advance guard of a 5,000-strong force which was coming to cleanse the region of German agents and punish anyone foolish enough to try to cross swords with the British. This bluff proved so successful that shortly afterwards Dyer's tiny force put to flight a 2,000-strong Baluchi raiding party, whose leaders only discovered afterwards that they had been hoodwinked. The presence of this new British force, operating to the south of the main East Persian Cordon, clearly posed a threat to Zugmayer and his companions were they to remain in the area.

At the same time, word reached them of an additional threat to their immediate safety. This was a British-led Persian force called the South Persia Rifles, commanded by Brigadier-General Sir Percy Sykes and, somewhat reluctantly, authorised by the Shah's government. Its purpose was to replace the pro-German Gendarmerie, which was now disbanded, and try to restore law and order in southern Persia. One of Sykes's first tasks, once the force had been recruited and trained, was to rid the region of all German agents and their local adherents. Those in the Kerman area were high on his hit-list. Thus sandwiched between Dyer's men and Sykes's,

Zugmayer and his companions knew that they had to move fast if they were to avoid capture.

They decided, therefore, to make for Shiraz, 300 miles to the east, which they believed still to be in the hands of Wassmuss and his local allies. From there, if the route to the frontier remained open, they would try to slip across it and reach Baghdad. Seiler and his party, who were still at Kerman, facing increasing harassment from the authorities, would make their way independently to Shiraz, perhaps joining forces with Zugmayer there for the final dash across the frontier to Baghdad and safety. Although both parties were well armed, they were repeatedly attacked by bands of Persian brigands, suffering considerable hardship and loss of life. Seiler's party, which had set out three days before Zugmayer's, finally reached Shiraz only to find it no longer in the hands of pro-German elements, and Wassmuss nowhere to be seen. After being relieved by the Persian authorities of all their gold and silver, as well as their weapons, they were then incarcerated. Much later Seiler managed to escape with two companions, and reports reached the British at Bushire that they had been spotted heading north in the direction of Kermanshah and the Turkish frontier, disguised as Persian tribesmen.

Zugmayer's party, in the meantime, had also faced repeated attacks by brigands as they struggled westwards, and several of their number, including the pre-war archaeologist, were carried off. The archaeologist was later handed over, unharmed, to General Sykes, who was somewhat startled by his request to be allowed to continue with his unfinished excavations. Zugmayer and a number of others managed to reach the town of Niraz, two-thirds of the way to Shiraz, before being detained, at Sykes's request, by the local authorities. From there they were taken under armed escort to Shiraz, where they were reunited with Seiler and other German officers and NCOs in the local gaol. Finally, following Seiler's escape, Zugmayer and the others were handed over to a British escort which took them to Isfahan, now under Russian military control.

In his memoirs, Captain Niedermayer wrote bitterly of the way his fellow Germans were treated by General Sykes's men: 'The prisoners were loaded into miserable carts, escorted by

250 soldiers armed with machine-guns and commanded by a British major.' During the journey, he claimed, their wrists and ankles were shackled with chains, while Sykes issued orders that anyone who tried to escape was to be shot on the spot. In point of fact, the British regarded the captives as terrorists, while Niedermayer looked upon them as heroes. When they reached Isfahan, Niedermayer alleged, the captives were 'mocked and abused' by the British consul and his staff, and 'photographed by the English ladies' in their shackles as though they were common criminals rather than prisoners-of-war. In Isfahan, which had not long before been their stronghold, they were handed over to a Cossack escort who, after removing their chains, took them northwards into Russia. At Baku, on the Caspian Sea, they were transferred to the small offshore island of Narghin, a sort of Russian 'Devil's Isle'. There they remained until the Russian Revolution the following year, when they were freed by the Bolsheviks.

'The month of April 1916', declares the official British history of the Great War, 'saw practically a total collapse of German hostile activities in Persia, and with it the discomfiture of their Persian dupes.' Not only had most of the latter now deserted the Turco-German cause, but many of the pro-German members of the Gendarmerie had been arrested, while the others were being recruited by General Sykes for the South Persia Rifles, entrusted with maintaining law and order in the British sphere of influence. Before very long both Shiraz and Kerman were firmly back in British hands, while the Russians controlled Isfahan and the other major towns to the north.

Only Wilhelm Wassmuss, skulking somewhere in the interior between Shiraz and Bushire, now remained at large. A man of iron determination, driven by a passionate dislike of the British, he showed no signs of giving himself up, or of losing his almost mesmeric influence over his Tangistani adherents. He possessed, moreover, a trump card. For he and his followers were still holding Major O'Connor and several other Britons hostage, six months after kidnapping them. And because no one knew precisely where he was, or where he might strike next, he remained a thorn in the flesh of the British authorities in the Gulf.

To Wassmuss the Holy War was still far from lost, and on April 29, 1916, there came news which must have greatly heartened him. After a siege lasting for five agonising months, the starving British garrison at Kut had surrendered to the Turks. More than 9,000 British and Indian troops who had set out up the Tigris to capture Baghdad were taken prisoner and marched off into captivity in Turkey. One of the most humiliating defeats ever suffered by a British army, it was immediately hailed as a great Holy War victory by Enver Pasha, who promptly proclaimed himself a *Ghazi*, or Muslim conquering hero.

14

The Million-Pound Bribe

It was the melting of the heavy winter snows in the mountains of eastern Turkey, hundreds of miles away to the north, which finally sealed the fate of the British garrison at Kut. Every year, since the very beginning of time, this has caused the mighty snow-fed Tigris to overflow its banks and flood vast areas of the low-lying Mesopotamian plain on either side. In biblical times it was this deluge which very likely gave rise to the story of the Flood and of Noah's Ark, which legend insists still lies somewhere beneath the snow and ice on the slopes of Mount Ararat. But in the spring of 1916, these same floods greatly hampered the progress of the 20,000-strong British relief force which was then desperately trying to reach the starving garrison in time. For as well as fighting off repeated Turkish attacks, the troops were having to contend with the steadily rising floodwaters. Soon it became all but impossible for the British commander, General Sir Fenton Aylmer, VC, to employ enveloping tactics against the enemy, or bring up his artillery, so restricted were his movements by the all-encircling waters. Nonetheless, Aylmer pressed on, determined to try to save the garrison, and with it the honour of the British Army.

During the first month of the siege, which had begun the previous December, morale among the British and Indian troops holed up in the small, mud-built Arab town had remained high. Despite heavy Turkish shelling, and repeated infantry assaults on his forward positions, General Charles Townshend, Kut's commander, was confident that he could hold out for another month at least, long enough, it was assumed, for the relief expedition to reach the beleaguered garrison. Both Townshend and Aylmer, as it happened, knew all about sieges from their earlier Great Game years. In 1895, Townshend had been the hero of the siege of Chitral, in northern India, where he had successfully held off attacking tribesmen for six weeks until the arrival of a relief force. Aylmer had served with distinction in the relief force, after winning the Victoria Cross by blowing open the gates of a native fortress which the British were besieging, thereby enabling it to be stormed. Ever since, the two officers had been close friends, making Aylmer more determined than ever to reach Kut while there was still time.

But as the days passed, and the relief party seemed to get no closer, the situation in Kut was becoming more desperate. Hopes of being relieved were fading by the day, as food supplies began to run out. Before long the defenders were forced to supplement their remaining rations by eating their transport animals, not to mention the town's skinny cats and dogs. At first, for religious reasons, many of the Indian troops refused to touch such meat. But in the end most agreed to do so after a special dispensation, obtained from their religious authorities in India, had been wirelessed to General Townshend. Even so, some of them still refused to eat the meat, and as there was nothing else they were issued with opium pills by the medical officers to assuage their hunger pains. Even the British troops had qualms where certain animals were concerned, albeit purely sentimental ones. Twice the garrison butchers sent back one mule, the much-decorated veteran of three frontier campaigns, although finally it too had to go into the regimental stew-pot.

The Turkish commander's strategy had been to leave sufficient forces around Kut to prevent a British breakout, while sending the rest of his troops down the Tigris to slow Aylmer's advance. For he knew that it was now only a question of time before the garrison was forced by starvation into surrender. Profoundly alarmed by Aylmer's lack of progress – he was still thirty miles south of Kut – and heavy losses, his superiors decided, on March 12, 1916, to sack him. His replacement was his own chief-of-staff, General George

Gorringe, for there was no way that anyone else could be got there in time. But by now the relief of Kut was a lost cause, with the Tigris still rising, and a scandalous shortage of river craft for bringing up artillery and ammunition, as well as aircraft for dropping emergency supplies to the doomed men. In the event Gorringe was to prove no more successful than Aylmer, and within a very short time he had suffered a severe mauling at the hands of the Turks, which brought the total number of casualties sustained so far in trying to relieve Kut to 23,000.

Two days later, however, on April 24, he made one last desperate attempt to get food and other vital supplies through to the town. Crewed by a handful of volunteers, and carrying sufficient provisions and ammunition to keep the garrison going for another month, the old river steamer *Julnar* was got ready to try to run the Turkish gauntlet. Every effort possible was made to maintain secrecy over what would otherwise be a suicide mission for those on board. To try to protect them from the murderous fire they knew they would face from either bank the moment they were detected, the vessel was reinforced with steel plates and sandbags. Alas, these precautions were to prove in vain, for it appears that she had been spotted either by Turkish spies or by a reconnaissance aircraft while being prepared for the twenty-five-mile dash up the Tigris. She had not proceeded far, therefore, before she came under heavy fire. In spite of this, the *Julnar* sailed bravely on towards Kut, her hull and superstructure riddled with holes. At 1 a.m. a radio message was received from Townshend to say that heavy firing had been heard from a spot about eight miles down river, and after that silence. The following morning a reconnaissance aircraft confirmed the worst. The gallant *Julnar*, and those of her crew who had survived, were in Turkish hands. She had finally been halted by steel hawsers which the enemy had stretched across the river. Victoria Crosses, both of them posthumous, were subsequently awarded to the vessel's captain and pilot, while the survivors were also decorated.

Meanwhile, in London, an even more desperate attempt was being planned to try to save the starving garrison. Lord Kitchener, the Secretary of State for War, had come up with a

THE MILLION-POUND BRIBE   215

breathtakingly unorthodox scheme for persuading the Turks
to release their fatal grip on Kut. In the face of vigorous opposition from other senior British officers and Foreign Office
mandarins, who condemned the idea as dishonourable,
Kitchener proposed offering the Turks an enormous bribe to
let the garrison go. The sum he had in mind was £1,000,000, a
staggering amount of money in those days, and sufficient to be
shared by all those, including Enver Pasha himself, who would
be involved in so delicate a decision. Under the terms of the
offer, the British and Indian troops thus freed would not be
used against the Turks for the rest of the war. From the point
of view of the Turks, who had suffered heavy casualties in the
battle for Kut and Baghdad, it would free men and resources
for their defence of eastern Turkey against the Russians.
Kitchener, who had long experience of the ways of the East,
and knew of Enver's fondness for money, believed that the
offer stood a sporting chance when all else had failed.

Amid great secrecy, the proposition was put to the Turkish
commander, Khalil Pasha, a nephew of Enver's. He did not
immediately respond, which raised British hopes. Meanwhile
three British intelligence officers with experience of the Turks
were chosen to handle the ransom negotiations which it was
hoped would follow. One of them was Captain T. E.
Lawrence, then serving with the Arab Bureau in Cairo. They
were ordered to proceed immediately to Basra and from there
to General Gorringe's headquarters aboard a steamer moored
in the Tigris. Contact having been made with the Turks, the
three officers were escorted under a white flag across no man's
land to Khalil Pasha's headquarters. The Turkish general
proved courteous and hospitable. However, he was dismissive
over the offer of money, even when the amount was doubled.
Clearly, Enver had vetoed it. Having shortly before lost
Erzerum to the Russians, and with it considerable face
throughout the East, he desperately needed a victory. To him,
at that moment, the surrender of Kut by the British before the
whole world was beyond any price.

Townshend's capitulation came the following day, on April
29, after he had ordered the guns to be spiked, the launches to
be blown up and all remaining stores burned. Finally, before
smashing his radio transmitters and hoisting the white flag

over the town, he sent out one last message. 'We cannot hold on any longer,' he declared. 'We have done our duty, and recognise that our situation is one of the fortunes of war. We thank General Gorringe and all ranks of the Tigris force for the great efforts you have made to save us. Goodbye and good luck to all.' It was the last that was heard from the garrison. After a siege lasting 143 days, breaking all previous records in the history of modern warfare, Kut had been starved into submission. The following day more than 3,000 British soldiers, 6,000 Indians and hundreds of non-combatants, all desperately weak from hunger or illness, were marched northwards into captivity in Turkey, from where many of them were never to return.

Enver's triumph over Kut was to prove somewhat short-lived, however, for within a year the town was back in British hands, with Baghdad also in the bag a fortnight later. Nor did Kut's humiliating surrender prove to have quite the devastating impact on public opinion in the East that the British had feared, if only because the wartime censors were able to stifle news of it in the Allied press and throughout the colonial territories. It was argued by some, moreover, that by holding out for nearly five months the garrison had tied up enemy forces which almost certainly would have been directed against Egypt or other British or Allied interests in the East. But this, as everyone knew, was mere rationalisation. There could be no disguising the magnitude of the disaster, so soon after the Gallipoli débâcle, or the military incompetence which was to blame for it.

*   *   *

If Niedermayer and Hentig, then both still in Kabul, had entertained any hopes that the evacuation of Gallipoli by the Allies, and now the surrender of Kut, might restore their fortunes with the Emir, winning him over as an eleventh-hour convert to the Holy War, then they were to be sadly disappointed. It quickly became clear to the Germans that, come what may, he did not intend to shift his position, and that they were now simply wasting their time staying on in Kabul. Despite all their efforts, their only achievement during their many months in the Afghan capital had been to induce the Emir to sign a treaty of very dubious value or practical utility.

And already he was beginning to show signs of going back even on this. Yet he appeared happy, eager in fact, to allow the Germans to remain in his country. For not only were the energetic Niedermayer and his companions advising him on how to modernise his army and train his troops along the latest Prussian lines, but Habibullah was thus able to keep a close watch on what they were up to. Furthermore, as the Germans were only too uncomfortably aware, when the right moment came they would make a valuable gift from the Emir to the Viceroy of India. Clearly it was time to get out.

Nevertheless, it must have been with intense disappointment that they now prepared to leave Kabul. Had they succeeded in their mission of bringing Afghanistan into the Holy War, and of unleashing the full fury of the Emir's forces against the British in India, they might well have changed the course of the war. Indeed, their names, like that of Lawrence, might have been remembered to this day. As it was, they had suffered great hardship and faced innumerable perils, only to see it all collapse in failure. Their sole concern now, however, was how to run the Allied gauntlet and get home. They knew that the moment they departed the Emir's domains, where the ancient laws of hospitality protected them, they would once more become fugitives, with the British and the Russians, not to mention marauding brigands, in merciless pursuit of them.

They finally left Kabul on May 21, 1916, nearly ten months after first entering Afghanistan. To improve their chances of survival, and of evading capture, they decided to split up into more than one party, each making its way home independently and by a different route. Niedermayer chose to head westwards, taking his chance once again with Persia, while Hentig rode eastwards through the Pamirs towards Chinese Central Asia. Shortly before the war, he had served as a diplomat in Peking, and he now hoped to put his knowledge of the country to good account. Based on the old Silk Road town of Yarkand, Hentig planned to make as much mischief as possible for the British and Russian communities in this isolated region. If he could stir up the local Muslims against them, then he could start his own small-scale Holy War there, forcing the dispatch of troops to the spot to protect British and Russian citizens and other interests. Finally, he could make his escape across

China to the German Legation in Peking, where he would await further orders from Berlin.

After a two-month ride which took him to the Oxus river and then along the Wakhan corridor to the Chinese frontier, Hentig reached Yarkand where he immediately began to spread wild rumours about the war's progress aimed at damaging Allied prestige. He also circulated reports that several hundred German soldiers had already arrived in Afghanistan, and that many more would follow. At the same time he set about organising tribal raids into northern India and Russian Central Asia, obtaining weapons for this purpose by purchasing them illegally from Chinese government arsenals.

Word of Hentig's activities quickly reached the ears of the British and Russian consul-generals in Kashgar, the regional capital, a hundred miles away. Alarmed, they at once called upon the Chinese authorities to arrest Hentig and his companions for violating the country's neutrality. Fearful of using force against this small but formidable German party, the Chinese governor ordered Hentig to halt his activities or face arrest and imprisonment. But ignoring this, Hentig instead set out for Kashgar, causing consternation among the unprotected British and Russian communities. For although his intentions were uncertain, rumours preceded him that he was planning to attack their consulates. The governor was now forced to act, and troops were sent to seal off the town's several approaches.

The Germans were finally located just fifteen minutes away from the British Consulate-General. At first Hentig threatened to fire on the Chinese troops if they tried to stop him. However, he and his men were heavily outnumbered, and in the end were forced to lay down their weapons and surrender. They were then taken to the governor's residence where, guarded by 100 armed troops, they were kept prisoner in the garden while the Chinese agonised over what was to be done with them. Eventually, under heavy escort, they were taken to Peking. From here, travelling via the United States and Norway, Hentig finally reached home some time in 1917, whereupon he found himself dispatched once more to Constantinople, this time to serve in the German Embassy there.

Niedermayer, meanwhile, had undergone some hair-raising

experiences which he had been extremely lucky to survive. On reaching the town of Herat, where he and his companions had first entered Afghanistan, he ordered Lieutenant Wagner and the rest of the party to remain there with the expedition's baggage and secret papers while he tried to reach Turkish territory. From there he would seek further instructions from Berlin, which he would try to communicate to them in Herat. For he guessed, quite correctly, that the British would have learned by now from their spies in Kabul of the party's departure for home, making penetration of the East Persian Cordon by the entire group extremely hazardous.

After dying his beard red and disguising himself as a Turcoman, Niedermayer set out on a journey which turned out to be even more harrowing than his outward one the previous summer. This time, so as not to ride straight into the arms of the East Persian Cordon, he took a different route. Accompanied by a hired Turcoman escort, he first struck northwards into Russian Central Asia, before turning westwards, thereby skirting the top end of the cordon. But he had not gone far before his escort deserted him, leaving him to the tender mercies of the local Turcoman brigands. He was robbed, badly injured and left dying of thirst and starvation. Had it not been for his exceptional toughness of body and spirit, and the kindness of ordinary shepherds and nomads, he would almost certainly have perished. As it was he had to beg in order to survive. Eventually, having made his way back into Persia, he reached Teheran, though he dared not linger there for fear of recognition. Pushing quickly on, in September 1916 he finally reached the safety of Turkish territory, where he was ordered to return to Germany. In Berlin he was hailed as a hero and decorated in person by the Emperor, who invited him to stay at the royal palace so that he could hear his story at first hand, and discuss with him the situation in the East.

At this point, nothing whatsoever had been heard of Hentig. It began to be assumed therefore that he and his companions must have perished. When, months later, Hentig did finally reach home, he discovered to his anger that all the credit for their daring, if unsuccessful, venture had gone to Niedermayer. Even the British accepted this version. 'Niedermayer's mission', wrote Sir Percy Sykes, with whom he had stayed in Meshed before the war, 'was a complete failure. But his courage and initiative were remarkable.' A longrunning antipathy was to develop between Niedermayer and Hentig, only ending in 1984, when the latter died, in his ninety-seventh year. Niedermayer had perished, nearly forty years earlier, in a Soviet prison. As an officer commanding German troops of Turkic origin, he had been jailed by the Nazis for criticising Hitler's *Ostpolitik*, only to fall into the hands of Russian troops at the end of the war. After lengthy interrogation by KGB officers at the Lubyanka prison in Moscow, he was sentenced in 1948 to twenty-five years in a Soviet slave camp for alleged war crimes. He died that August, aged 63, while in solitary confinement, tapping a last message to a German doctor in the next cell to say that he was gravely ill. Even today, among German historians, the debate rumbles on over what went wrong with the Afghan adventure. Much of the blame, it is clear, lay with the German High Command and Foreign Office for not making it clear from the start which of the two men was in overall command of the mission. Had they done so, then the reputations of two brave and resourceful officers, whose activities caused the British grave anxiety, need never have been besmirched by petty jealousy.

But we have moved far ahead of our narrative. At Herat, it will be recalled, Lieutenant Wagner had been left behind with the rest of the party and its baggage with orders from Niedermayer to await further instructions. After weeks had passed without any word reaching them, they assumed that Niedermayer must be dead or have been captured. In fact, it seems that Berlin's messages had simply failed to get through. Despairing of ever hearing, though, Wagner and his five remaining companions decided to try to run the enemy gauntlet and get home. Leaving the expedition's secret papers and codes in a locked steel trunk in the care of the friendly Afghan governor, they set out westwards. Disguised as Afghans, they succeeded in slipping through the Russian section of the cordon, only to find themselves attacked by hostile Persians. In the ensuing battle only Lieutenant Wagner managed to escape and eventually reach Turkish territory. The rest were captured and, after very rough handling, turned over to the

Russians. They notified the British, who sent a patrol of Indian cavalry to collect the prisoners for transfer to India. 'It was snowing hard and extremely cold,' recalled the young British officer commanding the escort. 'The prisoners were standing against a wall, their hands tied behind their backs, blue with cold and terror, and exhausted by hunger.' Their Russian guards, he added, were of Mongolian appearance – 'a wild lot of slant-eyed villains'. The Germans seemed extremely relieved at being parted from them.

Aside from the two Indian firebrands, Raja Mahendra Pratap and Mohammed Barakatullah, who had stayed behind in Kabul, only Wassmuss now remained at large. But as his supplies of gold – most of it plundered from the vaults of British banks – dried up, so too did the fervour of his Persian devotees. There was a growing suspicion among them, moreover, that he had all along been hoodwinking them with his extravagant promises and imaginary conversations by wireless with the Kaiser in Berlin, and even with the Emir of Afghanistan in Kabul. As the months passed, more and more of his followers began to melt away. He still held his one trump card, the British hostages, but even they, although he did not realise it, were beginning to slip from his grasp.

In addition to their obvious propaganda value, Wassmuss had seized the hostages in the hope of trading them with the British for certain Germans who were being held in India. Accordingly, although he personally read all the correspondence first, he allowed O'Connor to communicate by letter with the British in Bushire so that the terms for such a deal could be worked out. But what Wassmuss did not realise was that O'Connor, a former Indian Army intelligence officer, had devised a way of secretly communicating with his superiors by means of these letters. For this, he employed invisible ink made from powdered alum dissolved in water. His biggest problem, he recalled afterwards, 'was how to inform our friends at Bushire in the first instance that we were planning to communicate with them by this means.'

In case one failed, he came up with two solutions. First – in Morse code on a tiny scroll of paper – he wrote a brief message explaining his intention. This he persuaded an Indian carpenter working on the fort to deliver to his opposite number in Bushire, promising him that he would be generously rewarded when he did so. A minute hole was then drilled in the man's wooden plane, and the message inserted into it. 'A scrap of putty sealed the end of the hole, and a smudge of dirt rendered it invisible,' wrote O'Connor. At the same time he informed the unsuspecting Wassmuss that he intended to learn Italian – a language he knew the German did not speak – in order to fill in the long hours of boredom. With Wassmuss's permission he wrote to a woman living in Bushire who he knew spoke Italian, asking her to try to obtain three books for him. These were: *Rascaldate sul Fuoco, La Parte Bianca* and *Di Questa Lettera.* Translated, these invented titles read: Heat over the fire . . . the white part . . . of this letter. Wassmuss was completely fooled by this, and allowed the letter to be sent.

Both of O'Connor's messages, as it happened, were received and understood in Bushire, and thereafter a regular secret correspondence was maintained. By this means O'Connor was able to inform his colleagues on the coast about a bold escape plan which the hostages were working on. In return they were sent a map and instructions regarding the best route to a secret rendezvous point where they could be picked up by an armed rescue party. They were even sent a compass – 'soldered up in the middle of a box of Huntley & Palmer's Mixed Biscuits', O'Connor recalls. In the end, though, the plan had to be abandoned because of the physical condition of one or two of the hostages, which would have made it impossible for them to trek thirty miles over difficult terrain in the darkness, very likely pursued by armed horsemen.

As for going without them, O'Connor wrote: 'We could not reconcile ourselves to leaving them behind to face further imprisonment and possible, and indeed probable, ill-treatment at the hands of our semi-savage gaolers.' Already one of their number – Pettigrew of the Indo-European Telegraph Department – had died of a heart-attack, and they had buried him in a grave just outside the fort. This had happened earlier on in their imprisonment, when an armed patrol from Bushire had approached to within a few miles of the fort and there had been a brief exchange of shots. 'The Khan and his followers', wrote O'Connor, 'became unusually excited, and ordered us all into the courtyard for immediate execution. But later, when our troops had withdrawn, they quietened down, and the Khan was afterwards very apologetic about it all.' Nonetheless, it was to prove too much for Pettigrew.

But O'Connor's secret correspondence with Bushire was not the only thing going on behind Wassmuss's back. Unknown to the German, discreet negotiations were proceeding between the British at Bushire and the Tangistanis guarding the hostages. The British were offering, among other inducements, to free sixteen Tangistani prisoners they were holding in exchange for Wassmuss's British captives. They also undertook to reopen the routes to the Gulf which they had blocked in order to deny the rebels access to the coast and therefore crucial supplies. Gradually, O'Connor noticed, the Tangistani chief's attitude to the hostages changed. 'As time went on,' he wrote, 'and no help came from Germany, and the permanent menace of our troops at Bushire remained, he came to realise that he and his friends were backing the wrong horse.' He began to grant them extra privileges. Already they were allowed to take exercise and to receive newspapers from Bushire, although Wassmuss insisted on seeing the latter first, as they were his sole source of war news. But now they were permitted by their guards to bathe once a week in the irrigation channels watering the fields around the fort. Having hitherto been denied any bathing facilities, the hostages were extremely grateful for the use of what O'Connor termed 'these muddy ditches', in view of the oppressive heat they were exposed to within the mud walls of their prison.

At last, in the summer of 1916, after interminable haggling, terms for their exchange were agreed between the British and their Tangistani captors. To the anger and dismay of Wassmuss, whose objections were ignored, no Germans were included in the deal. The handover was arranged for the evening of August 10, when both sides would bring their captives to a previously arranged spot. As O'Connor and his companions left the fortress with their Tangistani escort they were joined for a while by Wassmuss himself. 'He rode alongside me for some distance, explaining his attitude towards us, and admitting that our release was a serious blow to his plans,' O'Connor wrote. While he had every reason to feel ill-will towards Wassmuss, O'Connor – later to become Colonel Sir Frederick O'Connor – confessed to a sneaking sympathy for the lonely German. 'His life must have been very arduous, and one of constant danger,' he wrote. 'Wassmuss lived in extreme simplicity in the native manner, on native food, and rode continuously about the country, from place to place and from tribe to tribe, in every extreme of climate, and always at the mercy of those treacherous, fanatical people.'

As they approached the rendezvous, the two parties halted half a mile apart, as had been agreed. O'Connor recalled: 'An emissary from each side then rode across to verify the number of the prisoners before the actual exchange took place, while we sat chatting happily with our captors awaiting the return of our messenger.' It was at this point, when things appeared to be proceeding smoothly, that an unexpected hitch occurred. Due to confusion over his name, it now transpired that one of the key Tangistani prisoners was missing. 'When this news leaked out', O'Connor wrote, 'there was a scene of great excitement – the tribesmen rushing about and shouting, declaiming against the incorrigible perfidy of the British, and threatening to shoot us all out of hand.'

Eventually, when the Tangistani chief had succeeded in calming his men down, it was agreed that O'Connor, as the senior British hostage, would return to the fort until the missing man was found and delivered safely to Bushire ready for exchange. In the event, this was to take a further ten days. 'But the conditions were now very different,' O'Connor recalled. 'The Khan impressed upon me that I was no longer to regard myself as a prisoner, but as an honoured guest.' Finally, after being held hostage for more than nine months, he set out once again for the coast. 'The Khan himself rode with me for a few miles,' wrote O'Connor, 'when we bade each other farewell.' That evening at sunset, accompanied by a Tangistani escort, he reached Bushire, where he received a tumultuous welcome.

Wassmuss was to remain at large in Persia for the rest of the war, still trying vainly to stir up the tribesmen into attacking British targets. Thus single-handedly challenging the might of the British Empire, he continued to be a nuisance. At the very end of the war, his dream finally shattered, he was seized by the Persian authorities and handed over to the British in Teheran. There he briefly managed to escape, but was quickly recaptured. Lord Curzon and others wanted to have him tried for war crimes, but finally he was allowed to return home to Germany. Some years later, haunted by the knowledge that he had exploited and betrayed the simple Tangistani tribesmen among whom he had spent the war, he returned to southern Persia to try to teach them modern farming methods and thereby raise their wretched living standards. But the experiment ended in disaster, and Wassmuss went back to Germany where not long afterwards he died a broken man – penniless, disillusioned and friendless. Aged only 51, he had more than paid for his failure.

In the summer of 1916, however, there still remained one final twist to the Wassmuss story. When he first rode into southern Persia to launch his campaign there against the British, it may be recalled that he was seized by pro-British tribesmen. Although he had managed to escape, fleeing barefoot across the desert, he was forced to leave all his possessions behind, including documents and papers. Following a rudimentary search, these had been sent to London where they were deposited in the basement of the India Office and forgotten. But then, by chance, their existence, and the circumstances of their capture, reached the sharp ears of Admiral Sir Reginald Hall, Britain's wartime Director of Naval Intelligence, whose orbit included the breaking of enemy ciphers. Acting on a hunch, he immediately ordered all Wassmuss's belongings to be brought to him. A swift search revealed what he was looking for – the German wartime diplomatic code-book.

It was an astonishing coup, and it explained why Wassmuss had appeared so anxious, at the time of its loss, to recover his baggage. But the momentous consequences of Admiral Hall's discovery still lay months off. In the meantime, a dramatic new development had split the loyalties of the Muslim world right down the middle, finally putting paid to any remaining hopes which Berlin or Constantinople might still have had of turning the wrath of Islam against the Allies.

On June 10, 1916, the Grand Sherif of Mecca and Guardian of the Holy Places of Islam thrust a rifle through the window of his palace and fired a single shot at the Turkish barracks opposite. It was the long-awaited signal that the Arab Revolt against the Sultan's rule had broken out.

15

The Tide Begins to Turn

The Arab Revolt, which aimed at ending 400 years of Turkish occupation, had begun with high hopes. The Grand Sherif of Mecca, Emir Husain, who was a direct descendant of the Prophet, had originally planned the uprising amid great secrecy for August 1916. But he had been forced to bring it forward by two months because of fears that the Turks might have got wind of it, and be intending to depose him for refusing to join the Holy War and plotting with the British against the Sultan. For it was learned that a powerful Turkish column, accompanied by a formidable German mission, was at that moment on its way southwards towards Mecca. Already the Turks had hanged scores of Arab nationalists whom they suspected of plotting against them. In addition to fears for Husain's own safety, it was believed by the British that the Turco-German force might threaten their vital coaling station at Aden, and at the same time establish strategic links with German troops in East Africa, with whom they were engaged in a bitter struggle.

Husain had originally told the British that he was confident that some 100,000 Arab troops – nearly one-third of the Sultan's front-line forces – would desert to his standard on hearing of the revolt. But although Husain's ill-trained irregulars managed to seize Mecca, the Turks held firmly on to the important city of Medina, refusing to surrender. Fears now began to arise that the Turkish garrison there, which had ample supplies of food and ammunition, might fight their way through the surrounding Arab forces, seize Mecca and hang the Grand Sherif. Although the Arabs were good guerrilla fighters, they were terrified of being bombed from the air or of being shelled. After a few weeks the Arab Revolt looked dangerously near to collapse. The British realised that they would have to offer Husain more than post-war promises and moral support if they were to save the situation.

It was at this point that a handful of carefully chosen British officers – including T. E. Lawrence, who was later to immortalise both the Arab Revolt and himself through the intoxicating prose of his *Seven Pillars of Wisdom* – were seconded by military intelligence in Cairo to the Emir Husain's forces. For it was realised that what the insurrection most urgently needed, if it were ever to represent a serious threat to the Turks, was skilled leadership, expert advice and regular contact with GHQ Cairo. An immediate priority was to prevent the Turks from bringing up more troops, artillery and other supplies to the besieged city of Medina via the Hejaz Railway. Completed, under German supervision, only eight years earlier, this line was originally designed to carry pious Muslim pilgrims to the holy sites of Mecca and Medina, but also with an eye to Turkish strategic needs. On the latter count, it was now paying dividends. For without modern explosives, and the knowledge of how to use these, the Arabs could only make hit-and-run raids against passing trains, which were heavily armed with machine-guns and infantry escorts.

This deficiency Lawrence and his fellow officers were quickly able to put right, blowing up troop trains, bridges and railway stations, and instructing the Arabs in this new art. At the same time, Muslim Egyptian gunners (infidel British ones being ruled out so close to the holy places) were landed by the Royal Navy on the Red Sea coast, while the warships' own guns joined in the bombardment of the Turkish positions. Later, British aircraft were used to strafe both the enemy and his lines of supply. Communication between the British officers with the Arab forces and Cairo was provided by the Royal Navy. Gradually, with this and other help, the Arab Revolt once again began to gather momentum, spreading northwards along the route of the pilgrim railway towards Aqaba and, eventually, Damascus. However, not everybody approved of Britain's sponsorship of the Arab Revolt. The principal objectors were the mandarins at the India Office in London and in Delhi. They had tried, in vain, to argue that such active encouragement of rebellion against the Turks, if seen to succeed, might stir up similar feelings against British rule among restive Muslims and Hindus in India. The very thing that the Holy War strategists in Berlin and Constantinople had so signally failed to achieve, the British now risked bringing about for them.

If the Arabs believed that they were fighting for independence, however, they were in for a shock. For the Allies, as we know, had already secretly agreed among themselves how the Ottoman dominions were to be divided up in the event of Turkey's defeat. Constantinople would go to the Russians, while the most desirable of the Arab lands were to be shared out between the two other main victors, Britain and France. The British would get most of Mesopotamia – including Baghdad and Basra – as well as Transjordan and northern Palestine, while Syria, Lebanon, Cilicia and Mosul would go, directly or indirectly, to the French. There were, admittedly, vague references in the agreement to the establishment of 'an independent Arab State, or a confederation of Arab states'. Precisely what this would consist of was not spelled out, however, and even it was to be divided into British and French spheres of influence.

Nor was that all. Not long afterwards, also as a result of wartime expediency, one further promise was made over the division of the spoils. Anxious for Jewish finance, scientific skills and political support in the United States, the British Foreign Secretary, Arthur Balfour, wrote to Lord Rothschild, a leading British Zionist, pledging his government's support for the setting up of a Jewish national home in Palestine after the war, provided that the rights of 'existing non-Jewish communities', meaning the Arabs, were safeguarded. The Arab Revolt leaders, of course, were privy to none of this, putting their trust in pledges which they considered had been made to them by the British High Commissioner for Egypt, Sir Henry MacMahon, on behalf of the Allies, in return for rallying to their cause rather than to the Holy War decreed by Constantinople.

Before long, though, as the whole world knows, these conflicting promises would come home to roost, their bloody and bitter consequences haunting us to this day. The truth was to emerge when the Bolsheviks seized power in Russia and rummaged through the Tsarist diplomatic archives. There they stumbled on the texts of a number of secret treaties between the Allies, including the Anglo-French plan for the division of the Arab lands. To the intense embarrassment of the Allies, they immediately published these, repudiating those entered into by the Tsarist government. Seizing upon this evidence of British and French perfidy, the Turks flourished it before the Arabs. By this time it was too late, though, for the triumphant Arabs, riding on General Allenby's right flank, were well on their way to Damascus, which they dreamed of as their new capital. However, the story of the Arab Revolt, and its unhappy post-war consequences, is too well known to need retelling here, and anyway does not really form part of this narrative. We are more concerned with the no less momentous events taking place at this time to the east, rather than to the south, of Constantinople. For it was there, less than a month after the Arab Revolt broke out, that the Turks and the Germans threw away their greatest, and last, chance of igniting a Holy War in Asia.

*   *   *

Two months after the Niedermayer-Hentig mission left Kabul for home, a series of native uprisings against Russian rule suddenly broke out in Central Asia. During the next six months, more Russian blood was spilled than in the entire conquest of the region the previous century. Although there were reports of mullahs calling for a Holy War, and talk of Turkish agents at work among the Muslim populace, the uprisings appear to have been spontaneous, arising from specific fears and grievances. But had the Germans been aware of what was brewing in Russian Turkestan, only 400 miles to the north, they would no doubt have hastened there to try to take charge of things instead of heading disconsolately homewards. For this might have been the very spark which they had failed to ignite in Afghanistan. Skilfully directed, it might have been fanned into a conflagration which would have engulfed much of Muslim Asia. As it was, by the time word of trouble across the Oxus river began to reach Kabul, they were far away and out of hearing.

The immediate cause of the troubles was the highly emotive issue of conscription. Hitherto, the native peoples of Central Asia had been exempt from military service. But early in 1916, because of the heavy casualties suffered by Russian troops on the Eastern Front and in Turkey, it was decided to draw on the Muslim population to provide, not soldiers, but labourers to build defensive works, thereby freeing Russian troops from non-combat duties. This change of policy was justified by the argument that the Tsar's European subjects were shedding their blood to protect others who were not being called upon to make any sacrifice on behalf of the country.

It was thought wise in St Petersburg not to conscript Muslims by age group, as was usual for military service, lest fears were aroused that they were being called up to fight on the battlefield, and also because in Central Asia no birth records were kept. It was agreed instead to introduce quotas for each town and village, leaving it to the mullahs and elders to choose those they considered suitable. In this way, it was thought, trouble would be avoided, and a 250,000-strong labour force would be raised from a non-Russian population of over 3 million. Accordingly, small recruiting teams of local Muslim officials were appointed in each region to prepare lists of those eligible for call-up, while quotas were worked out for every town and village which they were required to fulfil.

These quotas, however, were not based on population figures alone. For a critical consideration in the whole operation was the harvesting of Turkestan's huge cotton crop, vital to both the local economy and the war effort. In order to avoid any disruption, it was decided to reduce the burden on the cotton-producing areas by raising the numbers of conscripts to be provided by the non-cotton regions. But despite this, to many small farmers the loss of just one son or worker at harvest time could be catastrophic, especially with the cotton price frozen by the government at an artificial low, while the price of food soared out of control. This was not the only source of resentment, though, among families subject to the call-up. Word soon began to get around that wealthy families were able to purchase exemption for their sons by bribing those entrusted with producing the draft rolls. Indeed, subsequent investigations revealed that this malpractice took place on a vast scale. There was also widespread fear over the use the young conscripts would be put to once they had left their towns and villages. Partly due to problems in translating Russian military terms into the local Turkic tongues, wild rumours began to spread that the men were being sent, without any military training, into the front line as soldiers, or to dig trenches under enemy fire on the battlefield.

The first official announcement of the conscription plan had been received by the Muslim population in glum silence. However, Russian officials soon detected a growing feeling of unease and hostility towards them. One Russian colonel in Tashkent reported hearing rumours that there was to be a Muslim uprising timed to coincide with a religious festival on July 18. Even some Muslim families were beginning to feel nervous. 'The well-to-do natives of Tashkent and Samarkand', he recalled, 'started to remove their families from the city, and to conceal their most valuable possessions.' Word also reached the Russian authorities that secret native emissaries had been sent southwards into Afghanistan to seek assistance from their co-religionists there. Secret police reports of the time abound with shadowy references to outside agitators spreading dissent among the Tsar's Muslim subjects. But fears of foreign interference in Central Asia had long haunted the Russians, beginning with the British in the Great Game era, and continuing with a Pan-Turkish scare emanating from Constantinople in the 1890s. It is quite possible, though, that some of the Holy War leaflets produced in Berlin and Constantinople had found their way across the Oxus. One such tract intercepted by the Russians declared: 'The time has come to free ourselves from infidel rule. The Caliph has powerful allies. This war was sent by God to give Muslims their freedom, so those who do not join in are the enemies of God. If force of arms is not used against the infidels now, then we will never be free.'

The first sign of trouble came on July 4, when an angry mob attacked and stoned a police station in a town to the east of Samarkand in an attempt to seize weapons. They were finally driven off after thirty had been killed or wounded by the defenders. But from then on, as word spread quickly from village to village in the Samarkand region, the violence grew worse and more frequent. Its victims included many of the native officials engaged in preparing the call-up registers, who were either murdered or forced to flee for their lives, their homes being burned. Similar outbreaks now began to occur in other parts of Turkestan, where again the hatred of the mob was directed against those officials who had done the Russians' bidding. In some towns there were calls for a Holy War to be declared.

Seeing that the isolated Russian communities, whose menfolk were mostly away at the war, were now seriously threatened, the authorities in Tashkent, the region's military and administrative headquarters, at once placed the whole of Turkestan under martial law. Cossack units were rushed to the main troublespots with orders to crush the uprising before it turned into a full-scale revolution or Holy War. To try to delay their arrival, the rebels tore up the railway lines and cut the telegraph links with Tashkent. But armed only with primitive weapons, and without either proper leadership or an overall plan of action, they were no match for the merciless Cossacks. Had Niedermayer and Hentig directed their clandestine energies towards Turkestan rather than Afghanistan, then it might perhaps have been a different story. As it was, Muslim resistance was quickly and ruthlessly stamped out in all the main population centres.

Not content with that, however, the Russians were now out for blood, determined to teach the ungrateful Muslims a lesson they would never forget. One man who managed to escape the Cossacks' orgy of vengeance later told a Soviet investigating team: 'The Russian commander ordered his troops to shoot and burn. They descended on the villages, shooting whoever they met, raping the women and perpetrating other bestialities. They set fire to our homes and crops and carried away the harvested grain.' On August 20, the Governor-General of Turkestan toured some of the most trouble-hit areas. Assembling the mullahs and elders, he told them: 'You all deserve to be hanged, but we are sparing your lives so that you may be an example to others.' Seeing that further resistance to the call-up was futile, the Muslims now resignedly accepted it, although the Russians agreed to delay its implementation until the cotton crop had been harvested. Finally,

on September 18, the first party of young conscripts left
Tashkent by train for European Russia, the vanguard of
thirty-six such trainloads to be dispatched over the next
month or so.

In the more remote parts of the Tsar's Central Asian
domains, however, the troubles were still far from over. To the
north and to the east, among the largely nomadic Kazakhs and
Kirghiz, the uprisings had begun in much the same way as
elsewhere, as word reached these distant communities. But
with few troops within reach to deal with them, they were to
last much longer and prove more violent. Until relief columns
could be got to them from Tashkent and other garrison towns,
the Russian settlers had to organise their own militias. Some
of these European peasant farmers, who came of tough pio-
neering stock, saw the disturbances as a godsend – an opportunity to drive the Muslims from prime agricultural land
which they had owned for hundreds of years. Attacked by the
better-armed and well-organised Russians, thousands of
Kazakh and Kirghiz tribesmen were forced to flee for their
lives, abandoning their livestock, and in some cases even their
children and old people. Elsewhere, the settlers got the worst
of it, the luckier ones escaping to the relative safety of the
nearby towns, leaving their burned-out farmsteads behind
them.

By the middle of August, having pacified the more central
parts, the first Russian relief columns began to arrive in the
Kazakh and Kirghiz regions, bent on punishing the troublesome tribesmen. Once more a bloodbath was unleashed on the
long-standing Russian colonial philosophy of 'the harder you
hit them, the longer they remain cowed.' By the end of
December, the last flickering of resistance had been brutally
extinguished, and as elsewhere the Kazakhs and Kirghiz now
meekly accepted conscription. In all, throughout the whole of
Turkestan, nearly 4,000 Russian civilians had perished, plus
some 200 soldiers and officials. Furthermore, an estimated
9,000 Russian farmsteads had been destroyed. Just how many
Muslims lost their lives will never be known, although it is
thought to have gone into the tens of thousands. The picture
is complicated by the wholesale flight of Kazakhs and Kirghiz
across the mountains into Chinese Turkestan to try to escape

from the bloodshed. Many of them perished from exposure or starvation on the way, and others while trying to return. One Soviet expert calculated that the Muslim population of Russian Central Asia fell by one million during the war years, largely as the result of the events of 1916.

Despite the widespread suffering that the uprisings had brought upon the Muslim population, the authorities in St Petersburg were determined to punish those they regarded as the ringleaders. A series of trials followed. In all, more than 300 Muslims were sentenced to death, and many times that number to imprisonment or banishment. Anxious not to create martyrs, however, and also to begin some kind of reconciliation between the two communities, the Russians commuted all but fifty of the death sentences to life imprisonment, and reduced many of the other sentences. Corrupt officials, including Russian ones, were punished, and new and fairer laws introduced. To try to relieve the now desperate food shortages, large quantities of cheap grain were brought in by train from other parts of Russia. Soviet scholars subsequently sought to explain, in Marxist terms, the real reasons for the 1916 uprisings. Were they anti-Russian, or merely anti-Tsarist? Were the Muslim leaders genuine progressives trying to cast off their colonial shackles, or simply feudal religious reactionaries in pursuit of power for their own ends? And were there outsiders – Turks, Germans or other imperialists – involved? The answers changed frequently, depending on Moscow's current ideological line on colonialism.

For a while, following the suppression of the uprising, Central Asia remained quiescent, though not for very long. Within less than a year it was to find itself in the grip of even bloodier events following the outbreak of the Russian Revolution, but that we will come to in due course. In the meantime, despite the continuing stalemate on the Western Front, the tide of war elsewhere was beginning to show signs of turning in the Allies' favour.

*　　*　　*

Ever since the humiliating surrender of General Townshend to the Turks at Kut the previous April, British forces in Mesopotamia had been quietly preparing their revenge. Great pains were taken this time to make absolutely sure that there could be no repetition of the same fatal mistakes that had left Townshend's men stranded at the mercy of the Turks. When, in December 1916, the British were ready once more to advance up the Tigris towards Kut and Baghdad, it was with a far more formidable army than that led by the unfortunate Townshend. For a start, with 150,000 men, it was many times larger. But equally important it was commanded, not by a soldier whose experience was limited to Indian frontier campaigns, but by one of the finest fighting generals in the British Army, Sir Stanley Maude, who had earned his spurs in action in the Sudan, the Boer War, at Gallipoli and on the Western Front. For both the British and the Turks, the War Cabinet was aware, there was a great deal at stake in the outcome of this campaign. While many people had never heard of Erzerum until it fell to the Russians, almost everyone knew of Baghdad, the legendary city of the 'Thousand and One Nights'. If it could be wrested from the Turks after nearly four centuries of Ottoman rule, then this would do much to restore Britain's prestige in the East, while gravely injuring that of an enemy still riding high from the victories at Gallipoli and Kut.

But in addition to its psychological value, Baghdad's capture would have very important strategical consequences for the Allies. It would enable Maude's troops to join forces with Russian units then in north-western Persia. Once Baghdad was theirs, they could together seal off, once and for all, the routes leading eastwards through Persia towards Afghanistan, India and Russian Central Asia. This would free troops, in India anyway, for deployment elsewhere. But if Russian units were to take part in the capture of Baghdad, it called for close liaison between Maude, advancing up the Tigris, and his Russian opposite number closing in from the west. This was not easy, for all signals had to travel by a circuitous route – in Maude's case first to London, then to St Petersburg, and finally down through Russia and the Caucasus to Persia. Nor was it helped by the growing sense of unease now gripping a Russia already on the brink of revolution, and beginning to undermine the morale of the armed forces. As Philips Price of the *Manchester Guardian* reported: 'The powers of darkness were tightening their grip upon Russia during the autumn and winter of 1916 . . . The gulf between the rulers and the ruled was widening every day, and the only question was: when would the crash come?'

General Maude knew little of this, however, as he began his advance up the Tigris. At first, though his forces outnumbered those of the Turks by nearly four to one, his progress was slow. Ably commanded, the enemy resisted the British every inch of the way. The stalwart Turkish infantryman, as every soldier knows, is formidable in defence, and here he was well dug-in in strongly prepared positions – indeed so much so that no fewer than four Victoria Crosses were won during the next three months while trying to dislodge him. Gradually, though, Maude's superior tactics and numbers began to tell, and on February 24, 1917, aerial reconnaissance revealed that the Turks had begun to withdraw from Kut. Even so, their rearguard continued to fight ferociously, thus enabling most of the defenders to escape before the British entered the town. Townshend's earlier surrender there had at last been avenged. But fearing a repetition of his ill-fated dash for Baghdad, the War Cabinet were extremely hesitant about allowing Maude to press straight on, lest he too walk into a similar trap. Only after repeated assurances from Maude that he was now facing a broken army did they finally agree.

Maude's confidence was swiftly vindicated. On March 10, six days after advancing northwards from Kut, a curious red glow was observed over Baghdad from the British forward positions. The Turks, it soon became evident, were systematically destroying everything of any military value, just as Townshend had in Kut. Rather than allow his army, already badly mauled, to be totally destroyed, the Turkish commander, outnumbered and outgunned, had decided to abandon Baghdad. Here he had an unexpected stroke of luck. Just as Maude's troops had fought their way to within three miles of the city's suburbs, their advance was suddenly halted by a choking dust-storm which completely obliterated everything. It was as if a genie had been released from a bottle in this city of oriental fairytales, and had spirited the defenders away.

'The whole of the Tigris Army had been looking forward

with eagerness to reaching Baghdad,' declared the official British history of the campaign, 'and during the last few days, when it had been in sight, there had been many instances in which officers had been obliged to restrain the ardour of their men, anxious to be among the first to enter it.' Now their moment had come. Early on the morning of March 11, kilted troops of the Black Watch occupied the railway station – terminus of the still-unfinished Berlin-to-Baghdad railway – and reported that the city appeared to be empty. Other units soon confirmed this, and by noon the Union Jack was fluttering over the citadel, having been raised by an officer who had crossed the Tigris by coracle. It was, according to the official British war historian, the thirtieth time that Baghdad had fallen to a conqueror in its long and bloody history. The name of General Maude was thus added to those of Nebuchadnezzar, Alexander the Great, Cyrus and Harun-al-Rashid, the eighth-century hero of the *Arabian Nights*.

The capture of Baghdad was a spectacular triumph for the British, providing a war-weary public at home with a badly needed tonic. To the troops, however, it proved to be something of a disappointment in view of Baghdad's exotic and romantic reputation. 'Viewed from a distance, especially in the early morning or evening light, the city among the palm and orange groves, with its shimmering blue and gold domes and minarets and its fine river foreground presents a fair picture,' declared the official history. But proximity quickly dispelled such notions. The rotting corpses of men and animals lay everywhere, while the streets ran with hundreds of diseased and half-starved dogs. Stinking rubbish was piled everywhere in the labyrinth of narrow, winding alleyways between the dilapidated houses of mud-brick. The shops in the bazaar were shut and empty, having been plundered by hordes of Arab and Kurdish looters the moment the Turks had gone. Many buildings, too, were on fire, including parts of the citadel. The powerful new German wireless station, used for direct communication with Berlin, had been blown up shortly before Baghdad fell.

But if the reality proved disappointing to Maude's troops, he himself suffered an even greater disappointment. He had hoped that the fleeing Turks would be crushed between his forces and those of the Russians. Of the latter, however, there was neither sign nor word. The Turks had been able to escape northwards towards Mosul, where no doubt they would regroup. Had they been destroyed, as had been intended, then they would no longer have posed a threat to Baghdad. This would have freed a major part of Maude's force for deployment elsewhere, thereby possibly hastening the war's end. As it was, Maude had to advise London that he must keep his entire force, so that he could pursue the Turks northwards lest they bring up reinforcements and try to regain the city.

Baghdad's loss, after so many years of Ottoman occupation, was a bitter blow to Enver's pride, which had become greatly inflated as a result of the earlier Turkish successes at Gallipoli and Kut. On hearing of Baghdad's capitulation, he at once ordered its recapture, whatever the cost, and began to assemble a large force with which to achieve this. In the event, it was to be needed elsewhere. To the Germans, too, the seizure of Baghdad by the British came as a severe blow to their plans. Field Marshal von Hindenburg, Chief of the German General Staff, admitted in his war memoirs that its loss 'killed many German dreams'. The *Drang nach Osten* had begun promisingly enough. In two years of war Germany and Austria-Hungary had gained control of a vast corridor of territory which now linked them directly with Constantinople and the Ottoman Empire beyond. This included Poland, Serbia and the greater part of Romania, all of which they had conquered, plus Bulgaria, the hitherto missing link, which had decided to throw in its lot with them.

Running the entire length of this great strategic corridor – stretching 2,000 miles from west to east, and safely beyond the range of British naval guns – was the Berlin-to-Baghdad railway. This mighty project had become, in the eyes of the world, the symbol of the German Emperor's ambitions in the East and the main instrument for their accomplishment. In fact, at the time of Baghdad's fall, the railway was all but complete save for some tunnels still to be blasted through the mountains of south-eastern Turkey. The news, therefore, was a devastating blow to the Kaiser's hopes, as well as to his pride. For, before the entire world, the railway's much-vaunted terminus had fallen into the hands of the very power whose monopoly of the East it was intended to destroy. But there was even worse news to follow before the spring was out.

*   *   *

By this time, the Allies had begun to see that, as things were, they could not hope to win the war outright. With the bloody stalemate on the Western Front, they would eventually be forced to negotiate for peace, which might simply provide Germany with a much-needed breathing space. Only one thing now could really tilt the balance in favour of the Allies, and that was the entry into the war of the United States of America, with its vast manpower, wealth and other resources. But so far neither President Wilson nor the American people had shown any stomach for the fight, although they were happy to supply Britain and her allies with munitions and food. In February 1915, to try to sever this transatlantic life-line, Germany had decided to launch an all-out submarine campaign against the Allied merchant fleets. That May, the British liner *Lusitania* was sunk with the loss of 1,198 lives, 114 of them American. An angry Wilson had obtained a grudging German apology, compensation for the families, and a promise from Berlin that 'liners will not be sunk without warning and without safeguarding the lives of non-combatants, provided the liners do not try to escape or offer resistance.' For a while the attacks were more selective, although American lives continued to be lost, leading to further American warnings and further German promises.

Early in 1917, aware that the submarine blockade was not achieving the desired results of paralysing American trade with the Allies, the Germans decided to intensify the campaign by including as targets vessels of any nationality found inside Allied waters, American ones included. They knew that this would almost certainly bring America into the war, but they banked on crippling the Allied war effort before this could have any effect. 'Give us only two months of unrestricted submarine warfare,' declared Arthur Zimmermann, the German Foreign Minister, 'and we shall end this war and make peace within three months.' However, in case his calculation proved wrong, Zimmermann had another trick up his sleeve which would delay any American intervention long enough for his submarine terror to work. In the event of America declaring war, he would see to it that Washington was faced with a major crisis on its own doorstep.

On January 16, 1917, shortly before the Germans announced their intention of unleashing all-out submarine warfare, Zimmermann sent a top-secret coded telegram via his ambassadors in Washington and Mexico to the Mexican President inviting him, on the declaration of war by America, to join in on Germany's side. Mexico and America had long been at loggerheads, and twice since 1914 the Americans had taken punitive action against their neighbours who demanded the return of Texas, New Mexico and Arizona, which had been conquered by the United States in the middle of the previous century. If the Mexicans agreed to enter the war on Germany's side, Zimmermann promised them help in recovering their lost territories during the post-war peace settlement. The telegram also sought Mexico's help in trying to induce Japan, then one of the Allies, to change sides and attack America in the Pacific.

Because of its immense importance the telegram was sent by three different routes, for wartime communications were subject to frequent disruption, and the Germans' own transatlantic link had already been severed. One of the channels which the unconscionable Zimmermann decided to use was the private wire of the US State Department, access to which had been trustingly granted to him in order to speed President Wilson's peace-making efforts. Because the telegram was in code, and the Americans were then neither code-breaking nor reading other governments' diplomatic correspondence, Washington was unaware of its sinister contents. However, Zimmermann had not reckoned with the British intelligence services, who were considerably less scrupulous than the Americans over such matters.

In his enthusiasm to get his message to the Mexicans as soon as possible, Zimmermann failed to take into account the fact that telegrams from the American Embassy in Berlin went by overland line to Copenhagen, and thence via Britain by transatlantic submarine cable to the United States. He was totally unaware, therefore – as indeed was the British government – that all correspondence sent by this route passed through the hands of Admiral Hall's naval intelligence staff. Hall, it will be recalled, was in possession of the top-secret German diplomatic cipher which he himself had found when rummaging through Wassmuss's captured baggage. He had also discovered that the Germans, seemingly unaware that the cipher had been compromised, were still using it. Why Wassmuss had so signally failed to warn Berlin of its loss is mystifying, though perhaps he feared Zimmermann's wrath, or trusted that the British would fail to find or recognise it among the vast quantities of propaganda literature which he had also had to abandon when he gave his captors the slip. He had certainly gone to great lengths to try to recover his baggage at the time, which had somewhat puzzled the British on the spot, and led to Hall's hunch over its possible contents.

The highly sensitive, and unquestionably illegal, task of reading intercepted diplomatic telegrams was carried out in what was known simply as Room 40 – a specially set up code-breaking unit, composed of brilliant if eccentric intellectuals, within Hall's main naval intelligence-gathering organisation. Their remarkable skill at reading intercepted wireless messages, it was claimed, made any German surprise attack impossible. It was on January 17, the day after Zimmermann sent it, that two of Hall's cryptologists set to work on the infamous telegram. One of them was a peacetime clergyman, the Reverend William Montgomery, the other a young publisher, Nigel de Grey. Armed with Wassmuss's code-book, they managed to get the gist of it, although this was made more difficult by the fact that the Germans were now using a slight variant of the captured code. Recognising the political significance of what was emerging before their eyes, they immediately alerted Hall, who at once saw that this damning evidence of German perfidy was precisely what was needed to shock America into the war. For not only did the Zimmermann Telegram, as it has come to be known, reveal Germany's plot to embroil Mexico and Japan in its machinations, it also disclosed Berlin's decision to launch indiscriminate attacks on American shipping with its submarine fleet. Altogether it was dynamite, but it also presented Hall with an extremely sticky political problem.

If it was to have the desired effect on American public opinion, clearly Washington would have to be shown the evidence of Zimmermann's skulduggery. Reasonably, lest the State Department suspect it of being a forgery, they would want to know how the top-secret telegram was obtained. To reveal this would be to admit that the British were intercepting traffic between American embassies and the State Department. Even Hall's own government was unaware of precisely what Room 40 was up to. Regardless of the telegram's contents, the disclosure of how it was acquired would almost certainly trigger the mother and father of a row between Washington and London. To spare this embarrassment, and the damage it might do to Anglo-American relations, Hall knew he had to find some other way of getting his hands on another copy of the telegram, thereby saving him from having to reveal his guilty secret.

For two weeks Hall held on to the telegram, speaking to no one of it, while he pondered possible solutions to his quandary, and while his code-breakers struggled with the passages they had so far failed to decipher. Although President Wilson continued to express hope that involvement in the conflict could be avoided, there was now a distinct possibility that America might enter the war, as the Allies desperately hoped, before the U-boat terror was unleashed. If so, then it would not be necessary for Hall to produce his telegram, or at least not have to explain how he had obtained it. But while the world waited to see which way America would jump, Hall found the solution to his problem. Discreet inquiries revealed that the most likely way for the German ambassador in Washington to pass Zimmermann's coded telegram to his opposite number in Mexico City would be by the normal commercial telegraph system. After all it was in a top-secret code, and both the United States and Mexico were neutral countries. Indeed, if Zimmermann's instructions were to be acted upon swiftly, there was really no other or better way open to him. If so, Hall reasoned, there must be a copy of the telegram filed in the central telegraph office in Mexico City. As so often, Hall's hunch proved right, and by fair means or foul a copy of it was obtained for him by the British ambassador. To Hall's delight, it was found to be in Wassmuss's original code, and not in the more difficult variant of it, suggesting that the German ambassador in Washington was aware that his colleague in Mexico did not possess the updated version. This enabled Hall's code-breakers to decipher those passages which had hitherto defied them, and freed his own hands to reveal the perfidious telegram to his chiefs in the War Cabinet.

Meanwhile, as all this was going on, there had been two further developments. On January 31, as forecast by Zimmermann in his telegram, Berlin announced to the world its plan to wage indiscriminate submarine warfare against American and other neutral vessels engaged in delivering supplies to the Allies. As a result, uncertain what to do, large numbers of vessels bound for Britain and elsewhere sought refuge in their nearest port while awaiting advice from their governments or owners as to how to proceed. Obviously this had the effect of slowing, if not halting, the flow of badly needed supplies to Britain and her Allies, which was precisely what the Germans wanted. Three days later President Wilson severed diplomatic relations with Germany, and their respective ambassadors returned home. However, there was still no sign that Wilson was prepared to join in a war that neither he nor the vast majority of his fellow Americans wanted. The War Cabinet in London now decided that there was only one way left to force his hand and to jolt the American public out of its complacency. And that was to reveal personally to President Wilson Admiral Hall's evidence of Germany's treacherous intentions towards his country.

On February 23, Sir Arthur Balfour, the British Foreign Secretary, asked the American ambassador to call on him at the Foreign Office as he had something of the greatest importance to impart to him. Balfour was later to describe the moment when he handed the piece of paper bearing the decoded telegram to the American as 'the most dramatic in all my life'. Shaken by what he read, and convinced by Balfour of its authenticity, the ambassador alerted the State Department in Washington shortly to expect from him 'a telegram of great importance to the President and Secretary of State'. He then sat down to write a dispatch describing how the British intelligence services had obtained the telegram from Mexico City sources, and how they had used the code captured from Wassmuss two years earlier to decipher its contents. On reaching the State Department his dispatch and the telegram were delivered to the White House and taken up to the President. The British had feared that he might dismiss the telegram as a forgery or hoax, but they need not have worried. He was reported, by one who was present while he read it, as displaying 'much indignation'. For the telegram clearly showed that while purporting to talk peace with Wilson, Zimmermann was all along secretly plotting against the United States.

So that it could be claimed as an American intelligence coup (for the British did not want the Germans to realise they were reading Berlin's diplomatic traffic), the Americans managed to secure for themselves a second copy of the telegram from the Mexico City telegraph authorities. State Department experts, using the Wassmuss code lent them by the British, then decoded this, yielding an identical text. On March 1, the damning telegram was released by the Associated Press wire service to newspapers throughout America. The headlines told the whole story to a stunned nation. US BARES WAR PLOT, declared the *Chicago Daily Tribune*. WILSON CONFIRMS GERMAN WAR PLOT, echoed the *Boston Journal*. GERMANY ASKS MEXICO TO SEEK ALLIANCE WITH JAPAN FOR WAR ON US, reported the *New York Tribune*, adding, in a sub-heading: MESSAGE FROM ZIMMERMANN TO MEXICO REVEALS ASTONISHING PLOT TO ATTACK FROM BORDER IF AMERICA GOES TO WAR – TEXAS, NEW MEXICO AND ARIZONA PROMISED AS REWARD. CONGRESS FACES WAR DEMAND. It was a sensational disclosure, and it was to have a profound effect on the American public who by now had begun to realise that war with Germany was inevitable.

But still Wilson appeared to hesitate, although he ordered that American vessels proceeding into the war zone should be armed. It was only after five American merchant ships had been sunk by U-boats, with the loss of American lives, including women and children, that he abandoned any remaining hopes of achieving a peace settlement between the warring powers. Armed neutrality, as he had called it, gave way to a determination to defeat Germany. On April 6, confident that he had the backing of the entire nation, President Wilson declared war on Germany, though not on Turkey, with which America had no quarrel.

Historians are still not agreed over what precisely propelled America into the war, but the interception, decoding and publishing of the Zimmermann Telegram by Admiral Hall's intelligence staff unquestionably played a major, possibly determining, role. Without recourse to Wassmuss's abandoned code-book, however, they could not have pulled off their brilliant coup, in which case Zimmermann would have kept his secret, while America's entry into the war might have been even longer delayed, possibly to the point where the Allies would have been compelled to negotiate for peace. Almost certainly Wassmuss never learned what the loss of his code-book cost his country, for by the time its role in the affair came to light he was dead. Had he known, though, this arch-champion of German expansionism would have been appalled. For it could be argued that his failure to warn Berlin that the code might have fallen into British hands may indirectly have cost Germany the war. Although the dispatch of American troops to France was still a long way off, the comforting awareness that this dynamic new power, with its huge manpower and resources, was now on their side, lent the war-weary Allies new heart. And when American troops and aircraft did finally arrive in France it was just in time to turn the tide against the exhausted German armies.

But in the spring of 1917, while the Americans were still agonising over whether or not to throw in their lot with the Allies, even more momentous events were taking shape in Russia. They were to bring renewed hope of victory to the Germans and Turks at a time when they had all but abandoned their dreams of together conquering the East. In India, however, these ominous new developments were to strike fresh fears into British hearts at the very moment when they thought that the Turco-German threat was over. A new chapter was about to open in the unending story of the Great Game, one which was destined to change the entire course of history.

MELTDOWN

'The British imperialists tried to prove with
their propaganda that Turkish and German
troops, after seizing Transcaucasia, would cross
the Caspian Sea and burst into Turkestan.
There they would be joined by more than
100,000 German and Austrian POWs, after
which they would move into Afghanistan and
India. Intervention in Russia was thus
explained by the need to defend India.'

Leonid Mitrokhin, *Failure of
Three Missions*, Moscow, 1987

16

The Great Russian Collapse

The Russian Revolution of March 1917, which gradually led to the collapse of Tsarist forces everywhere and the end of the country's participation in the war, undoubtedly saved the Turkish armies from annihilation in the East. Had the 70,000-strong Russian Caucasian army joined forces with General Maude's 150,000 men north of Baghdad, as originally planned, then the badly mauled and demoralised Turkish army would have been crushed in the vice thus formed. As it was, the Turks were given a crucial breathing space which enabled them to regroup, thereby postponing the collapse of the Ottoman Empire for a further eighteen months.

Even without the Revolution, though, the effectiveness of the Russian forces had been severely reduced by the cruel eastern Turkish winter, during which both sides had had to abandon the struggle simply in order to survive. On the exposed mountainsides entire units were frozen to death, while everywhere frostbite took a steady toll of limbs and lives. With supply lines from Tiflis and Kars badly disrupted, Russian troops in some areas were reduced to living off half a pound of bread a day, eked out with soup made from the boiled-down flesh and bones of donkeys, dogs and cats. Disease, including typhus, was also adding to the casualties. Morale, too, was beginning to deteriorate, accelerated perhaps by rumours circulating among the troops of deepening troubles at home and on the Eastern Front in Europe. By the first week in March, when food riots triggered the Revolution in

St Petersburg, leading to the abdication of Tsar Nicholas II, more than a million men were said to have deserted. Exhausted by the terrible demands of the war, which showed few signs of ending, and bitterly resentful of the Tsar's autocratic rule, people of all classes were fast approaching the point where they could take no more. Indeed, the fall of the Romanovs, after more than three centuries on the throne of Russia, was mourned by few, while their replacement by Kerensky's provisional government was welcomed by the vast majority of Russians, regardless of class or political persuasion.

Nowhere was the news from St Petersburg greeted more enthusiastically than in the Caucasus. When word of the Tsar's overthrow reached Tiflis on March 15, the response was instantaneous and tumultuous. The entire fabric of Russian imperial authority began to collapse, reported Philips Price of the *Manchester Guardian*. 'First the police vanished from the streets; then the government offices closed down; then bands of revolutionaries and students arrested all the remaining gendarmes and seized the premises of the secret police, where they arrested the chief and his wife.' Three days later a mass meeting was held in the city's main square to celebrate the Revolution and to decide on the future. It was, Philips Price wrote, 'one of the greatest days in the history of the Caucasus', with people riding in on horseback and in bullock-carts from distant villages in the mountains. As well as thousands of Georgians, Armenians and Azerbaijanis, 'there were wild mountain tribesmen – Lesgians, Avars, Chechens and Swanetians – in their long black cloaks and sheepskin caps.' For centuries they had lived in the remote recesses of the Caucasus, under their own feudal chieftains. 'Many of them did not know whether they were subjects of the Tsar of Russia or the Sultan of Turkey. Yet they had come across miles of mountain tracks out of curiosity to confirm the rumours they had heard.'

Soldiers from the Tiflis garrison, including officers on horseback, poured into the great square, eager to celebrate the news, and determined to have their say. Next, carried shoulder-high, came political prisoners, recently freed from the dungeons of the local gaols, where many of them had been languishing since the abortive revolution of 1905. Three times, amid wild cheering, the Marseillaise was played by the town's several bands. 'Every head was bared,' Philips Price reported. 'The mountain tribesman took off his shaggy fur hat, and the long hair of the Russian student fluttered in the breeze.' The troops, who a few days earlier had sung 'God Save the Tsar', now presented arms to the stirring revolutionary anthem. Democracy was on the lips of every speaker who addressed the eager crowd that Sunday afternoon, and hopes of peace filled everyone's hearts. All prayed that Russia would very soon be out of the war which had left so many bereaved. Finally the historic meeting broke up amid euphoric scenes, unprecedented in the region's bloodstained past, as ancient foes embraced one another and vowed eternal comradeship. The multitude who had attended it hurried back to their towns, villages and army barracks, bringing with them the latest tidings of the momentous events which were taking place in St Petersburg and spreading throughout the great Russian Empire.

Philips Price, a Gloucestershire landowner and pre-war traveller in Central Asia, had been profoundly affected by what he had witnessed of the war, first on the Eastern Front in Europe and then for nearly two years in the Caucasus and eastern Turkey. Like many liberal-minded people at that time his sympathies lay with the Russian masses whose suffering he had witnessed 'as they marched like sheep to the slaughter', and he welcomed the end of the Tsar's oppressive rule and the coming of the Revolution. He believed, like many others, that he was witnessing a new dawn in Russia. 'The shots fired on the banks of the Neva', he wrote, 'echoed far and wide across the plains of the Ukraine to the Cossack steppes, over the snowy peaks of the Caucasus to the bleak plateau of Armenia, and across the Caspian to the sandy wastes and fertile oases of Turkestan. The people have at last seen the light, and have freed themselves from the darkness of the middle ages.' Shortly afterwards he left the Caucasus for Moscow and St Petersburg to report on the stupendous developments there.

In the light of this revolutionary turmoil and uncertainty in the Caucasus, not to mention among the High Command in St Petersburg, it was hardly surprising that the Russians had

failed to keep their rendezvous with General Maude in
Mesopotamia. Yet while their advance westwards towards
Constantinople, which had followed their taking of Erzerum,
had by now petered out, in eastern Turkey the Russian armies
continued to hold the line. Indeed, Kerensky's new government had optimistically given Britain and France solemn
assurances that Russia would stay in the war and faithfully
honour its obligations to its allies. After all, as one of the
rewards for helping to defeat the Turks, the Russians had
been promised Constantinople, the warm-water outlet they
had so long coveted. Moreover, at this point, the revolutionary
virus was still largely confined to the troops in the rear areas,
notably the Tiflis garrison, as Philips Price had witnessed. It
would not be until the Bolshevik *coup d'état* of November
1917 that the Russian armies on the eastern Turkish front
finally collapsed, the troops heading home lest they arrive too
late to receive their due share in the promised redistribution of
land.

In the Caucasus, meanwhile, the principal revolutionary
and ethnic groups had met together in Tiflis, the Georgian
capital and former Tsarist military headquarters, and had
formed a caretaker government calling itself the Transcaucasian Commissariat. Consisting of Mensheviks, Social
Revolutionaries and other groups – but no Bolsheviks – it
sought to preserve the Caucasus from all-out anarchy and ethnic violence. Its twelve-man cabinet was composed of three
Georgians, three Armenians, three Azerbaijanis and two
Russians, with a Georgian president. Styled commissars, each
had his own portfolio, ranging from war to agriculture, education to supply. Most of the population were more than satisfied with the Kerensky government, which had swept away all
vestiges of the hated Tsarist regime, and the new
Transcaucasian Commissariat refused to recognise the
authority of the Bolsheviks when they seized power in St
Petersburg and proclaimed themselves Russia's legitimate
rulers.

In a region so steeped in bloodshed and intercommunal
strife, such unity of purpose was a remarkable achievement.
However, the Transcaucasian Commissariat's writ was not
universally accepted throughout the Caucasus. In the great oil

town of Baku, on the Caspian Sea, the Bolsheviks had managed to gain the upper hand under the charismatic leadership of Stepan Shaumian, a close friend of Lenin's and himself a veteran revolutionary. Refusing to bow to the authority of Tiflis, Baku declared its allegiance to the new Bolshevik regime in St Petersburg (or Petrograd, as it had been renamed on the outbreak of war to shed any Germanic stigma). In addition to this, there was a further internal division which threatened both the Tiflis government and, in particular, the Baku government. Whereas the Georgians and Armenians, both ancient Christian peoples, were just about able to co-exist, the Muslims and Armenians in Baku and surrounding Azerbaijan had a long and bitter history of mutual hostility which had led to frequent massacres and counter-massacres. This was something which the Tsarist authorities at times had not been averse to encouraging, having found that setting these intensely volatile peoples at one another's throats made them easier to govern.

Now, with the collapse of Tsarist rule in the Caucasus and the melting away of the Russian armies in eastern Turkey, the Muslims of Azerbaijan realised that their chance had come. Although they had neither the arms nor the organisation to wrest power from Shaumian and his fellow Bolsheviks in Baku, they could see that the door was wide open to the Turks, their co-religionists and ethnic cousins, to whom they were strongly sympathetic. Were a Turkish army to advance into the Caucasus towards Baku, they would find, waiting to welcome them, a fifth column a million or so strong. Further east, moreover, in Central Asia, were several million more Muslims similarly sympathetic to the Turks. In 1916, as we have seen, they had tried and failed to free themselves from Russian rule. Like their Azerbaijani neighbours, they too would readily welcome a Turkish army which promised to liberate them from infidel rule, whether Tsarist, Bolshevik, Menshevik or Social Revolutionary.

Such a Turkish advance would not only threaten the survival of Shaumian, himself an Armenian by birth, and his fellow Bolsheviks in Baku. The prospect also chilled the blood of the large Armenian population, whose numbers had been greatly swollen by refugees fleeing the war in eastern Turkey.

But they were not the only ones with cause for concern. Were the Turks, not to mention the Germans, to march into the Caucasus and thence into Central Asia they would pose a very grave threat to India. Even the infiltration of a handful of Turkish or German officers, preaching the heady gospel of Pan-Turkism or Holy War, might achieve what Niedermayer, Hentig and Wassmuss had failed to bring about, now that there were no Russian troops to crush such a move. Once ignited in the Caucasus or Central Asia, the flame might spread southwards through Persia and Afghanistan to India.

The British had been somewhat slow to see what was going on in a region hitherto the responsibility of St Petersburg. Indeed, they had allowed themselves to be lulled into believing that all was well on the eastern Turkish front. 'Russia is a big country, and can wage a war and manage a revolution at the same time,' a senior official in St Petersburg had assured the British military attaché. As a result, the speed of events in the East following the Bolshevik coup had taken the War Cabinet in London by surprise. With the disintegration of the Russian armies in eastern Turkey, a large and totally undefended gap had suddenly appeared in India's defences, and already reports were beginning to reach London that Muslim freedom fighters were attacking Russian units returning home from Turkey and seizing their weapons.

Shortly afterwards, the Allies received what they angrily perceived as a further stab in the back from the Russians. On December 3, 1917, in the burned-out Polish city of Brest-Litovsk, German and Bolshevik negotiators met to try to hammer out a separate peace between their two countries. Both parties were equally eager to see Russia out of the war – the Bolsheviks because they saw it as a quarrel between imperial rivals and they wished to concentrate on building a new society along utopian lines, and the Germans because it would enable them to switch large numbers of their troops to the Western Front in time for their planned spring offensive. It was an altogether strange gathering. 'Fate had decreed', wrote the historian John Wheeler-Bennett, 'that the representatives of the most revolutionary regime ever known should sit at the same table as those of the most reactionary military caste among the then ruling classes, that a Bavarian nobleman, a

Knight of the Golden Fleece and a Prussian major-general should negotiate on equal terms with a group of Bolshevik leaders but lately returned from exile, and from whose clothes the reek of dungeons had barely been banished.'

The Germans presented their opposite numbers with harsh terms, demanding the surrender of Poland, the Ukraine, the Baltic provinces, Finland and the Caucasus, as well as the return to Turkey of the garrison town of Kars and surrounding areas captured by the Russians. By means of brilliant debating tactics, the chief Bolshevik negotiator, the then little-known Leon Trotsky, prevaricated, stringing out the talks for nine weeks, in the hope that the Revolution would spread to Germany and Austria, thereby ending the war without any loss to Russia. But angered by his delay in signing the treaty, the Germans had resumed their advance, finally forcing Lenin to order acceptance of Berlin's terms, though in the event they came to naught following Germany's defeat. In the meantime, however, Russia's opting out of the war was having profound repercussions in London and Delhi.

The nightmarish prospect of a Turco-German army pouring through the Caucasian gap was bad enough. But that was not the only thing preying on the minds of British defence chiefs just then. In prison camps scattered across Russian Central Asia were 40,000 able-bodied German and Austrian troops captured by Tsarist forces in eastern Europe, who now found themselves free after being abandoned by their guards. Here, ready to menace India, was an entire army in the making. Indeed, reports were already reaching Delhi that some of their officers were trying to organise them into a fighting force ready to link up with a Turco-German spearhead advancing through the Caucasian gap, or to act independently if arms could somehow be got to them. The collapse of the Russian armies brought a further fear. 'The streets of German cities were in darkness,' wrote General Ludendorff, second only in the German military hierarchy to Hindenburg. Aircraft and U-boats were severely restricted in their movements. What Germany desperately required was oil. If they could get their hands on Baku, with its huge oilfields, the situation could be transformed. In addition, to the east of the Caspian Sea in Turkestan were 200,000 tons of harvested raw cotton, used in the manufacture of explosives and uniforms. At all costs, it was agreed in Delhi and London, these vital war materials had to be kept out of the enemy's hands.

There could be no question, however, of sending troops to plug the gap, for there were none to be spared, and anyway there was no way of getting them there in time, if at all. The nearest British troops were Maude's men in Baghdad, but they could not be used since this would leave Baghdad vulnerable to recapture, and anyway they would first have to fight their way through 500 miles of Turkish-held territory, capturing Mosul on the way, to reach the Caucasian gap. And even if they managed this, how could they be supplied? The War Cabinet was not prepared to risk another disaster like Kut by over-extending its forces again. To make matters worse, General Maude himself was suddenly struck down by cholera, dying three days later in the very house in which Field Marshal von der Goltz had died of typhus just eighteen months before. It was hardly the moment to rush into any hazardous new enterprise. Yet somehow the Caucasian gap had to be closed while there was still time.

The War Cabinet could see only one way of achieving this, and that was by persuading the local population to form militias and defend their own homelands. The British, for their part, would provide them with the necessary funds, training and encouragement, and arms and ammunition would have to be obtained from Russian units hurrying back from eastern Turkey. As it happened, the British already had a handful of officers on the spot who were able to organise all this. These were members of a small wartime mission attached to the Tsarist Caucasian headquarters at Tiflis. After the Revolution they had stayed on, trying to persuade the Russians to continue resisting the Turks, while anxiously watching the rapidly deteriorating situation around them. But because the mission lacked the money required to finance the militias, and to pay for locally acquired arms, the task of providing this and somehow getting it up to Tiflis fell to the British minister at Teheran, nearly 600 miles away. Meanwhile, in London and Delhi, staff officers were looking at other ways of blocking the expected Turco-German advance.

Nor was this the only hole left in India's outer defences by the collapse of the Tsarist armies. The Russian-manned northern sector of the East Persian Cordon had suddenly ceased to exist as the troops made for home, leaving Afghanistan once more vulnerable to enemy infiltration. This gap, 300 miles wide, had somehow to be filled, and the only way to do that was by extending northwards to the Russian frontier the patrols and outposts of those units manning the British sector, thereby stretching them even more thinly. Protests from Teheran about this further British incursion into Persian sovereign territory were simply brushed aside. With so much at stake, and the Persians themselves still wavering in their loyalties, the British were in no mood to take risks.

The first task of the British mission at Tiflis was to try to determine who among the various ethnic and religious groups in the Caucasus were most likely to offer serious resistance to an invader, and therefore be worthy of Allied support. Of the three principal nationalities, the Azerbaijani Muslims, with their pro-Turkish leanings, obviously could not be relied upon, and indeed would have to be watched. The Georgian Christians, while hostile towards the Turks, had worrying historical links with the Germans dating from the early nineteenth century. In fact, on the outbreak of war German agents had been infiltrated into Georgia to try to exploit these, though without any success. Moreover, the Georgians were a fiercely nationalistic people who were likely to resist anyone threatening their newly won freedom, secured after suffering more than a century of Tsarist domination. They were therefore judged to be worth cautious support, especially against the Turks.

The most obvious candidates for British support were the Armenian Christians, whose ancient homeland lay directly in the path of any Turkish advance towards Baku, giving them a compelling reason for resisting their historic foe. Many of them, moreover, had served in the Tsar's forces and had shown themselves to be capable of fighting fiercely and determinedly, spurred on by both their dread of the Turks and St Petersburg's promises of independence of some sort within the Russian Empire after the war had been won. Any such hopes had now collapsed, but the Armenians, as one British

intelligence officer put it, 'had every reason to fight to the bitter end', for clearly the Turks would be bent on revenge for
what they saw as Armenian duplicity in siding with the Allies.
Indeed, already, as the Russian troops streamed away from the
front around Erzerum, Armenian irregulars were replacing
them in the trenches in a desperate attempt to hold the line,
while efforts were being made to transfer to the Caucasus
other Armenian units serving elsewhere.

While the unfortunate Armenians clearly had everything to
lose from a Turkish victory, they also had everything to gain
from an Allied one. For already President Wilson and other
Allied leaders were urging that the Armenians be given an
independent state in eastern Turkey after the war as compensation for their suffering and as a reward for their loyalty to
the Allied cause. Such a move was strongly supported by the
British, although this was not without an element of self-
interest. For at that time, in December 1917, the War Cabinet
was far from confident that a cessation of hostilities would
necessarily see Turkish and German long-term ambitions in
the region broken. In a secret memorandum it urged the
establishment of an Armenian state as 'the only barrier against
the development of a Turanian movement that will extend
from Constantinople to China, and provide Germany with a
weapon of even greater danger to the peace of the world than
the control of the Baghdad Railway.' While with hindsight this
can be seen as verging on paranoia, it was in fact no more than
a resurgence of the old nightmare that had haunted British
cabinets ever since the early days of the Great Game.

Despite the enemy hammering at the gates of the Caucasus,
and the formation of a multi-national provisional government
– the Transcaucasian Commissariat – the British mission officers in Tiflis trying to organise local resistance soon found
themselves in a quagmire of ethnic rivalries and jealousies. Its
complexities, though beyond the scope of this narrative, were
to make their task doubly difficult and dangerous. By providing one faction with funds and other assistance, they were
immediately seen as aligning themselves with its cause, and
thus threatening those of its rivals. To make matters worse, it
was also evident that any British or Allied interference in the
Caucasus, even for the strict purpose of safeguarding the

strategic approaches to India, would be regarded by the Bolsheviks, both in Baku and in the Kremlin, as a hostile act motivated by colonialist ambitions. In fact, the War Cabinet had already begun to regard the Bolsheviks, who had so treacherously left the Allies in the lurch and sold out to the Germans, as enemies pure and simple. Maintaining good relations with them, therefore, was viewed as being of secondary importance to securing India's frontiers. Furthermore, Lenin's own grip on power at that time appeared extremely tenuous, and the betting among analysts in London was that his revolutionary government would last no longer than had Kerensky's. But none of this made it any easier for those who had to deal with the Bolsheviks on the spot.

It was into this seething cauldron of different nationalities, languages, religions, aspirations and fears that there was now plunged an individual destined to play an extraordinary, often bizarre, role in this narrative. His unenviable task was to distribute British gold among the various rival factions, while still trying to maintain good relations with those who got none. In a region so riven by hatred, jealousy and mistrust – and no less so today – this might appear little better than suicidal. But the individual chosen, 40-year-old Major Aeneas Ranald MacDonell, diplomat turned intelligence officer, was more than usually qualified to attempt it.

For seven years he had served as British vice-consul in Baku, and before that had lived there for a number of years. He was therefore closely acquainted with the peoples, politics, languages and customs of the Caucasus, where, in Baku alone, were to be found no fewer than forty-five different nationalities and ethnic groups. He was also on familiar terms with most of the leading figures in this polyglot community. All this was to prove invaluable to him in the turbulent weeks and months ahead. But MacDonell possessed one other attribute which perhaps enabled him, more easily than most, to grasp the explosive complexities of Caucasian tribalism. For MacDonell was a highlander by birth, like so many of the *apparatchiks* and others with whom he would have to deal, and moreover, as twenty-first hereditary chief of Glengarry, he was himself a clan leader of ancient lineage.

In December 1917, with the agreement of the Foreign

Office, MacDonell was given the rank of major and seconded to the British military mission in Tiflis for 'special duties'. It was to mark the beginning of an adventure from which he was lucky to escape with his life.

17

Caucasian Powder Keg

Major MacDonell reached Tiflis by train from Baku to find the Transcaucasian capital alive with wild and conflicting rumours concerning its likely fate. Threatened from the west by the Turks, from the north by the Germans, and from within by the Bolsheviks, its immediate prospects looked bleak. Not only was the Transcaucasian Commissariat, the temporary government, largely powerless, but the people themselves had no real will to resist. Turkish, German and Bolshevik agents walked the streets quite openly, making little attempt to conceal their allegiance, confident that no one had the authority to arrest them. 'An atmosphere of the darkest uncertainty prevailed,' MacDonell recalled. 'News from the fronts of Europe was meagre, that from Russia alarming and always contradictory.' Even the British military mission had only the sketchiest notion of what was going on, the few telegrams reaching them being mostly indecipherable. 'Only the Georgian aristocracy seemed certain of anything,' MacDonell reported. 'They were certain they were going to be wiped out, by whom it did not matter. But until that somebody appeared they meant to have a good time and get rid of any money they had left. No one seemed to care a damn.' The town was full of loafing soldiery, and the cafés, hotels and night-clubs of the fashionable Golivinsky Prospect were filled with officers in splendid uniforms and beautiful, dark-eyed Georgian women. 'As long as the wine and women lasted,' recounts MacDonell, 'the Georgians were content to enjoy them.'

Cut off from London and the rest of Russia, the British mission's sole lifeline was the railway by which MacDonell had travelled up from Baku, from where contact of sorts could still be maintained with Teheran. But even this was subject to severe disruption in the wake of the Revolution and the subsequent collapse of the Russian Caucasian army. With most of the locomotives and rolling-stock commandeered by the fleeing troops, few trains were still running. MacDonell's own journey had taken thirty-six hours instead of the usual six. As a diplomat he was used to travelling in some comfort up to Tiflis, but those days were now over. It was every man for himself. As a result, the train was perilously overcrowded, with many passengers forced to clamber on to the carriage roofs or ride the buffers. MacDonell, sitting on his suitcase and hardly able to move, was grateful to find a place in a luggage wagon which he shared with some sixty other passengers, including families with young children. Except when the train halted and they could climb down on to the track, their sole sanitary arrangements consisted of one communal bucket which was periodically emptied over the side. During the momentous times ahead, MacDonell was to get to know every yard of this 300-mile stretch of the line. For it would be used for smuggling the secret funds dispatched by Teheran to finance those still resisting the enemy. However, if the gap in India's outer defences was to be plugged, it had quickly to be decided how and to whom this money was to be distributed.

To try to avoid becoming entangled in the region's bitter internecine wrangles, the British decided that the money should be distributed to their chosen candidates by General Lebidinsky, the Russian officer still nominally commanding the Caucasian army. 'It was evident from the first', MacDonell wrote afterwards, 'that nothing could be hoped from the Georgian Army, whose infantry were mostly Bolshevik, while its cavalry declared its intention of only guarding its own territory.' The most obvious candidates, as we have seen, were the Armenians, who were still holding out against the Turks in their ancient homelands around Erzerum and Trebizond. One million roubles were therefore paid to them via General Lebidinsky – supposedly in great secrecy. But news of the payment quickly reached the ears of their principal rivals, the Georgians and the Azerbaijanis, who were furious. MacDonell blamed the leak on 'the chattering tongues of the Armenians . . . who boasted that the primary object of the British mission was to assist them.' To try to placate the Georgians and the Azerbaijanis, they too were offered funds if they would continue to man the Turco-Caucasian front alongside the Armenians.

It was a forlorn hope. Some Georgian commanders happily pocketed the money, insisting that they still remained loyal to the Allies and, as they vowed to MacDonell, 'much preferred killing Turks to enjoying wine, women and song'. However, they quickly proved themselves to be 'very bad soldiers', MacDonell recalled. The Azerbaijanis, for their part, turned the British offer down flat and withdrew their remaining troops from the front. They had no wish to fight their co-religionists and ethnic cousins, the Turks, whose help they might very soon be glad of. Their immediate concern was to protect their territorial interests against those who threatened them. For a start that meant the Bolsheviks, whom they saw as merely yet more Russian colonialists in a new guise. Already the Bolsheviks, led by Stepan Shaumian, the 'Caucasian Lenin', had virtual control of Baku, the richest and largest city in the Azerbaijani heartland. To make matters worse, Shaumian was an Armenian, and already there were alarming signs that, at his instigation, Armenian nationalists and Bolsheviks in Baku had reached an accommodation clearly directed against the Azerbaijanis.

In the event this was understandable, for the Azerbaijanis had been quick to accumulate weapons in anticipation of trouble ahead. They had achieved this, for the most part, by forcibly relieving the home-going Russian troops of theirs. In January 1918, in one bloody ambush alone, they had attacked a troop-train between Baku and Tiflis and, after killing 1,000 Russian soldiers, had made off with 15,000 rifles and large quantities of ammunition – to the great consternation of the Bolsheviks and Armenians. It was this accumulation of arms that had enabled the Azerbaijanis to spurn the British offer, with its unacceptable strings. Altogether, the situation in the Caucasus was extremely confused, not to say explosive. As the weeks passed, it was to deteriorate rapidly.

By now MacDonell was travelling regularly back and forth between Baku and Tiflis on what he called 'my little train'. This consisted of three carriages – a sleeping car, a dining car and another for his official escort. On the Baku-to-Tiflis run he carried large quantities of roubles for eventual distribution to the Armenians and others. These were skilfully concealed behind mirrors, inside ventilators and in various other nooks and crannies. For MacDonell was anxious to keep all knowledge of what he was up to from the Azerbaijanis. Because the money was largely going to their ancestral foes, the Armenians, there was a grave risk of the train being attacked and robbed. On the return journey, from Tiflis to Baku, he often smuggled human contraband – mostly men and women wanted by the Bolsheviks or others, who were desperate to escape into Persia. Many were former Tsarists and their families fleeing the wrath of the Revolution.

As the situation in the Caucasus worsened, the journeys became more perilous. On one they were attacked by hostile Azerbaijanis, who raked the train with rifle and machine-gun fire, fortunately ill-aimed, for they sustained no casualties. The small escort had been given strict orders not to retaliate. 'Wise instructions,' MacDonell wrote later. 'One shot fired into that mob would have meant no rails at the next station, a concerted attack by thousands of armed Tartars, and the end of ourselves and the little train.' But that was not the last of his adventures on the Baku-to-Tiflis railway. For a while he was joined in his clandestine work by Captain Edward Noel, a British intelligence officer sent from Persia in February 1918 to try to discover what precisely was going on in the Caucasus, now almost totally cut off from the outside world, and gauge what resistance, if any, the Allies could expect to a joint Turco-German thrust towards the Caspian and beyond. Together he and MacDonell travelled up from Baku on what was to be the last of the rouble-smuggling expeditions.

By now MacDonell's special train had shrunk from three carriages, with their own locomotive and armed escort, to just one carriage attached to the rear of the occasional passenger train still braving the route. Nonetheless it was stuffed with concealed roubles which Noel had brought with him from Teheran. 'Our journey took three days, and was full of adventure,' MacDonell wrote. They had not gone far when suddenly the engine left the line. Someone had removed a rail. It took the combined efforts of railway workers and passengers to get it back on the track, and only after a delay of many hours did they set off once more. The next obstacle came in the person of a drunken Russian officer who, after introducing himself as Count Potopsky, joined the train at a wayside halt, making himself at home in MacDonell's carriage. 'He then informed us', MacDonell recalled, 'that he had joined the Revolutionaries, and harangued us on the liberties of the people.' Somehow the Count had discovered that they were carrying large quantities of concealed roubles, for he next declared that he intended to prevent them from reaching Tiflis 'with money for the reactionary forces'.

Because he was so obviously drunk, MacDonell and Noel did not take this threat very seriously. However, at the next halt the Count tried to seize control of the engine, with the intention of taking the train back to Baku. 'We put him off at the next stop,' MacDonell recounts, 'but that was not the end of the Count. He managed to persuade a train-load of troops returning from Tiflis to put about and give us chase. Then followed a most exciting four hours over a rickety track.' At one point their pursuers got so close to them that they were able to fire into the back of MacDonell's and Noel's carriage. Fortunately the Count and his Bolshevik friends literally ran out of steam, forcing them to abandon the chase before they could get closer still. Had they caught up with their quarry, and found the funds destined for those still loyal to the Allies, it would have boded ill for MacDonell and Noel. More than likely they would have been shot on the spot as imperialist agents, which is precisely what they were.

Like others who had observed Noel in action, MacDonell was profoundly impressed by his total disregard for danger. 'Noel', he wrote, 'was a regular officer trained in political intelligence work. He was, I think, one of the bravest men I ever met.' He appeared to be wholly without fear or concern for his own personal safety. 'The alarming thing about Noel', MacDonell added, 'was that he so easily instilled these qualities into others.' Before very long, as we shall see, Noel was going to need every bit of that courage to see himself through an experience which might have broken lesser mortals. However, that is to move ahead of our narrative, for he and MacDonell were still not yet finished with the railway. Having escaped by the skin of their teeth from one lot of foes, it was now their misfortune to fall into the hands of another. This time it was pro-Turkish, anti-Armenian Azerbaijanis, who had set up their own unofficial government at Elizavetpol, which lay half-way along the railway between Baku and Tiflis.

'Our train was held up,' wrote MacDonell, 'and Noel and I were detained under guard.' MacDonell was only too glad to let Noel, a professional to his fingertips, take charge during their interrogation, which was to last two days. Their inquisitor, who appeared to be a Turkish intelligence officer posing as an Azerbaijani, accused them of smuggling arms and money to the Armenians. 'For two days,' recalled MacDonell, 'I watched a very clever piece of bluff.' Sensing uncertainty in their interrogator, Noel demanded that the train be searched. This, of course, was the very last thing they wanted. Noel, however, insisted, but stipulated that the Persian consul-general should be present while the search was carried out. The Azerbaijanis approached the Persian diplomat, who strongly advised them, as a new and inexperienced government, not to risk insulting and thereby angering so powerful a nation as the British. Noel, who spoke fluent Persian and had considerable experience of the Persian character, had rightly calculated that the diplomat would at all costs wish to avoid becoming personally involved in a row with the British government. 'On the following day,' wrote MacDonell, considerably relieved, 'we were allowed to continue our journey to Tiflis.' For buried among his dirty clothes were no fewer than two million roubles. But even now their adventures on the Baku-to-Tiflis run were not quite over.

On reaching Tiflis, then still nominally the Caucasian capital, they found that so far as the Allies were concerned the situation had worsened considerably. By now all remaining hope of persuading anyone – whether Armenians, Georgians or Russians – to send troops to the front had collapsed. One by one, during the spring of 1918, Erzerum, Trebizond, Van and Kars surrendered to the Turks, who now appeared to be consolidating their forces along the pre-1914 frontier before launching their final thrust into the Caucasus. 'To add to the confusion,' wrote MacDonell, 'the various outlying tribes all over the Caucasus were busy declaring their independence and setting up so-called republics.' Small wars were in progress everywhere, as faction fought faction and ancient scores were bloodily settled. The Georgians were even talking of inviting in the Germans, if only to protect them from Turkish occupation. Clearly the smuggling of further funds to Tiflis was now pointless, not to mention, as MacDonell and Noel had discovered, extremely hazardous. The small British military mission made preparations to escape northwards across the mountains lest the Germans arrive and take them prisoner, while MacDonell and Noel decided to return to Baku where there was crucial work to be done if the Turco-German advance was to be halted, and the threat to India lifted.

There could be no question this time of simply attaching MacDonell's carriage to the next train leaving for Baku, for there were no longer any such trains. With much of the route now in the hands of the Azerbaijanis, who regarded all trains as ripe for plunder, traffic had all but ceased. There was no road fit for vehicles, and anyway there were no vehicles which could have made the journey. Apart from the railway, the only other way was by horse, and with the whole region in the throes of a bloody civil war that was no less dangerous. It was then that MacDonell and Noel learned that the Bolsheviks in Tiflis were planning to shoot their way through. Led by an armoured train, no fewer than seven troop-trains, carrying 10,000 armed soldiers, were about to set out for Baku, now a Bolshevik stronghold. A passenger train was scheduled to bring up the rear, and it was to this that MacDonell and Noel managed to obtain permission to attach their carriage. This may appear surprising in view of the brush they had had with the drunken Russian count and his Bolshevik friends on the way up. But evidently that had been an isolated incident. So far, the British military mission and members of the small foreign diplomatic community had found themselves treated reasonably correctly by those Bolsheviks they encountered. After all, these were still early days. Until very recently the British and Russians had been close allies, and contrary orders had not yet been issued by Moscow, which was even then feeling its way. Stalin's infamous directive of July 1918 ordering the arrest of all Allied military missions and foreign businessmen in the Caucasus still lay several months off. However, had the local Bolsheviks known who was sharing the carriage with MacDonell and Noel, the consequences for the two British officers might have been very grave indeed.

According to their passports, the two passengers were the Reverend and Mrs Jesse Yonan, an American missionary and his wife. The former was said to be seriously ill, and on his way home to the States, his wife meanwhile nursing him. Their meals were always served to them alone in their compartment, and few other passengers saw them during the five-day journey to Baku. The Reverend Yonan apparently spent much of his time asleep. The truth about the couple was rather different. The ailing missionary was really a senior Tsarist officer, General Polovtsov, for whose capture dead or alive the Bolsheviks had offered a considerable reward. For it was General Polovtsov who, in July 1917, had crushed Lenin's first attempted coup against the Kerensky government, thereby forcing Lenin to flee to Finland, and earning himself a place high on the Bolshevik death list. Anyone found assisting him or his wife, Lenin had decreed, would face a mandatory death sentence.

The passports on which the general and his wife were travelling were perfectly genuine ones which had once belonged to the Reverend and Mrs Yonan, both of whom were thought to be dead. MacDonell had managed to acquire them through murky contacts in the Tiflis underworld, where virtually anything could still be obtained at a price. No one besides he and Noel was aware of the couple's real identity, but even with their false passports it was crucial that they remained out of sight. Although they had done everything possible to change their appearance, had they allowed themselves to be glimpsed they might well have been recognised. For many of the Bolshevik troops on the accompanying trains had, not long before, served under the general's command. Now, unwittingly, they were about to help him and his wife to escape by escorting them through this hazardous, strife-torn region to Baku, from where the fugitives hoped to reach Persia by ship. Indeed, many of the troops would be killed during the several days of fierce fighting ahead, as anti-Bolshevik Azerbaijani tribesmen tried desperately to prevent them from reaching, and so reinforcing, Baku.

The nine trains, led by the armoured one, now steamed out of Tiflis station at a steady 15–20 m.p.h., and with a half-mile gap between each. With the exception of the 'neutral' British carriage, which bore the Union Jack, the trains all flew large hammer-and-sickle flags and bristled with machine-guns, sharpshooters and look-outs. This weird procession, wrote MacDonell, 'seemed to stretch like some huge centipede from horizon to horizon'. Meanwhile, as he and his companions prepared to run the gauntlet with their unlikely escort, elsewhere on the Holy War battlefield fresh moves were afoot.

* * *

In London, it will be recalled, the War Cabinet was frenziedly engaged in trying to plug the Caucasian gap before the Turks and Germans could make use of it to infiltrate, or even march, eastwards towards Afghanistan and Turkestan. The efforts, on the spot, of MacDonell, Noel and other members of the British military mission in trying to shore up India's furthermost outworks with the liberal use of gold were intended merely as a stop-gap. In the meantime, London and Delhi had been hastily putting together a rather grander scheme for frustrating Turco-German moves against India, although Soviet historians would subsequently maintain that their secret aim was to crush Bolshevism in the Caucasus and absorb this oil-rich region into the British Empire.

The British master plan involved the dispatch, during the spring and summer of 1918, of three special missions to what defence chiefs saw as the three most vulnerable sectors of the approach route to India. The smallest of these missions, led by Colonel F. M. Bailey, an experienced political officer and pre-war Tibetan explorer, consisted of only three officers and diplomats. It was to be sent to Tashkent, in Russian Turkestan. Not only was this the headquarters of Bolshevik activities in Central Asia, but also concentrated in this area were large numbers of German and Austrian POWs recently freed by the authorities there. It was Bailey's urgent task to ascertain Bolshevik intentions towards India, and also to try to prevent the ex-POWs from combining with an advancing Turco-German force, or even with the Bolsheviks, and thereby threatening the stability of Afghanistan and ultimately India. Bailey's extraordinary adventures among the Bolsheviks during the next sixteen months have been chronicled in full in an earlier book of mine, *Setting the East Ablaze*, and are therefore not repeated here. However, the other two missions, aimed explicitly at halting an enemy thrust through the Caucasus, are central to our narrative, for they were to find themselves in the thick of things as the crisis deepened.

One of these missions was led by Major-General Wilfred Malleson, a veteran military intelligence officer, and consisted of a handful of officers and NCOs, plus a small detachment of Indian troops serving as escort. Malleson's orders were to proceed to Meshed, at the northern end of the East Persian Cordon and close to the Russian frontier, and from there to keep a careful watch on developments in Transcaspia, through which an enemy might advance eastwards from Baku. He was also to try to make friendly contact with those elements across the frontier willing and able, with British help, to resist a Turco-German incursion. If the need arose, moreover, he was to deny an invader the use of the Transcaspian railway by destroying it. For without access to this it would be virtually impossible for an enemy to transport a large force eastwards across the waterless Karakum desert. 'In actual fact,' one Soviet historian has alleged, 'Malleson's task was to overthrow the Bolshevik government in Turkestan by directly bringing in British troops and by supporting internal counter-revolutionary forces. Initially, the mission was to prevent the Bolsheviks from obtaining control over the western section of the railway line, and the Caspian port of Krasnovodsk.' Its ultimate aim, he charged, was to bring to the spot 'forces sufficient to seize not only Transcaspia but also the whole of Central Asia'.

The other mission, commanded by Major-General Lionel Dunsterville, a Russian speaker, was to consist of an advance party of a dozen officers and NCOs. Initially it was ordered to proceed from Baghdad through north-western Persia to Tiflis to take over from MacDonell and his companions the task of persuading the Armenians and others to resist the Turks and

Germans. In due course, as fast as they could be recruited, a further 400 officers and senior NCOs would be sent to Tiflis to join them in training the local levies to fill the gap left by the disintegrating Russian forces. In the event, following the hasty departure of the British mission from Tiflis on May 3, and the approach of the Germans to the Georgian capital through the Ukraine, this idea was abandoned. Instead, Baku was to be the point where the enemy would be resisted, and Dunsterville and his team were ordered to proceed there. But again there were problems. Not only was Baku in the hands of the Bolsheviks, who were utterly opposed to the presence there of British troops (whom they suspected of coming to overthrow them), but the mission's route through the mountains of northern Persia was blocked by large numbers of hostile tribesmen trained by German and Turkish officers, and determined to stop them. Dunsterville's mission was never intended or organised as a fighting force. Indeed, had they attempted the journey, his small advance party of a dozen or so officers and NCOs, plus a handful of drivers, would have been slaughtered to a man.

It was clear to Dunsterville that without reinforcements it would be impossible for the mission to seize the southern Caspian port of Enzeli, from where they hoped to sail for Baku. Moreover, were it to get around that they were carrying sacks of gold with which to finance resistance to the Turks, it would be suicidal even to remain where they were, on the easily ambushed road to Enzeli. He decided therefore to withdraw to a safe distance, to the Persian town of Hamadan, while they awaited the arrival of the reinforcements from Baghdad, 300 miles away across the mountains. From Hamadan, by means of secret agents and Russians fleeing from the Bolsheviks, he endeavoured to keep in touch with developments in Baku, and also to monitor the Turkish advance. At the same time, lest the Turks turn their attention to Hamadan, he recruited and trained local Kurdish and Persian levies, whom he planned to lead as a guerrilla force if the need arose. Besides this there was little else that he could do as he waited impatiently for the reinforcements which would enable him to fight his way through to Enzeli. He was only too aware that all this time the Turks were pushing on towards Baku, and that there was now a grave risk that, as with Tiflis, now all but in German hands, they would again be too late.

*   *   *

Little of this was known to Major MacDonell or Captain Noel as they and their escort of seven troop-trains proceeded cautiously towards Baku. During the first day after leaving Tiflis they had encountered no resistance, but next morning they entered territory occupied by pro-Turkish Azerbaijanis – or Tartars, as they were then usually called. It was now that the bloody struggle to prevent the Bolsheviks from reaching Baku commenced. 'The enemy, native tribesmen led by Turkish officers, were entrenched in the foothills about a mile from the railway,' MacDonell wrote. To prevent them from coming any closer, they were engaged by the field-guns mounted on the armoured train. However, they also held the railway station ahead and had to be driven out of there before the trains could proceed. The troops detrained and, under cover of artillery fire from the armoured train, attacked the station. 'Fighting around the station and in the village lasted for about four hours,' MacDonell tells us. Finally, after the station had been set on fire, the enemy were forced to abandon it, and the trains were able to advance once more. The enemy continued to fire at them from the nearby foothills, but they were too far off to do much damage. As their train passed safely through the blazing station MacDonell and Noel saw that it was littered with corpses.

From now on, MacDonell recalled, 'every station had to be taken by storm', as they advanced deeper into Azerbaijani-held territory. The fiercest battle was for Elizavetpol, the half-way point between Tiflis and Baku. 'It was a whole day', wrote MacDonell, 'before the station was taken and burned. We could not get through it until the flames had subsided enough to let us pass, but not enough to let the enemy reoccupy it.' Indeed, so intense was the heat that it blistered the paintwork of the coaches. Earlier, despite its heavy escort, the passenger train had come under fire, and suffered a number of casualties. They included the driver and stoker, both of whom had been wounded, but who carried on most bravely, and later were rewarded by their grateful passengers with a generous

17. The Emir of Afghanistan, whose tribal armies the Germans hoped to unleash against British India

18. The iron-willed Captain Niedermayer (*centre*), who gave the British the slip, but who quarrelled with von Hentig over their respective roles

19. General Lionel Dunsterville, commander of the British Baku mission (*right*), on his way there across Persia

20. Armenian recruits being taught to use rifles for the coming defence of Baku against the Turks

21. The battle for Baku. Front-line defenders watching for the advancing Turks

22. A corner of a foreign field. The first British casualty is buried beside the Caspian.

23. Major Ranald MacDonell, British diplomat turned intelligence officer, sentenced to dea[th] by the Baku Bolsheviks after his escape to Persia

24. Captain Edward Noel, DSO, British intelligence officer condemned to be shot by Persian nationalists, but instead kept in chains for many months

25. General Polovtsov, Tsarist officer, wanted by the Bolsheviks. He was smuggled out of the Caucasus disguised as an American missionary by MacDonell and Noel.

26. A rare picture of Captain Reginald Teague-Jones, the British intelligence officer who was forced to change his identity and disappear after being accused of murdering twenty-six Bolshevik heroes

27. Stepan Shaumian, leader of the doomed Baku commissars, with his wife and young sons in happier times

28. The Shaumians' home in Baku, where MacDonell played trains with one of the commissar's sons. It later became a Communist shrine.

С. Г. Шаумян   М. А. Азизбеков   П. А. Джапаридзе   И. Т. Фиолетов

Я. Д. Зевин   И. В. Малыгин   Г. Н. Корганов   М. Г. Везиров

Г. К. Петров   А. М. Амирян   М. В. Басин   С. Г. Осепян

Э. А. Берг   В. Ф. Полухин   Ф. Ф. Солнцев   А. А. Борьян

И. Я. Габышев

М. Р. Коганов

Б. А. Авакян

И. П. Метакса

И. М. Николашвили

А. М. Костандян

Как братская могила Степана, Алеши и других не знает ни армянина, ни грузина, ни татарина, ни еврея, так и бакинский пролетариат не знает никакой национальной розни. Вожди бакинского пролетариата как при жизни не различали трудящихся по национальности, так и после смерти они, как бы демонстрируя великую идею межнационального мира и солидарности, находят покой все в единой могиле... Вечная память великим учителям!

Г. К. ОРДЖОНИКИДЗЕ

С. А. Богданов

А. А. Богданов

И. А. Мишне

Т. М. Амиров

29. Bolshevik Valhalla – portraits of all twenty-six Baku commissars, shot by their revolutionary rivals in the Karakum desert. Shaumian is at top left.

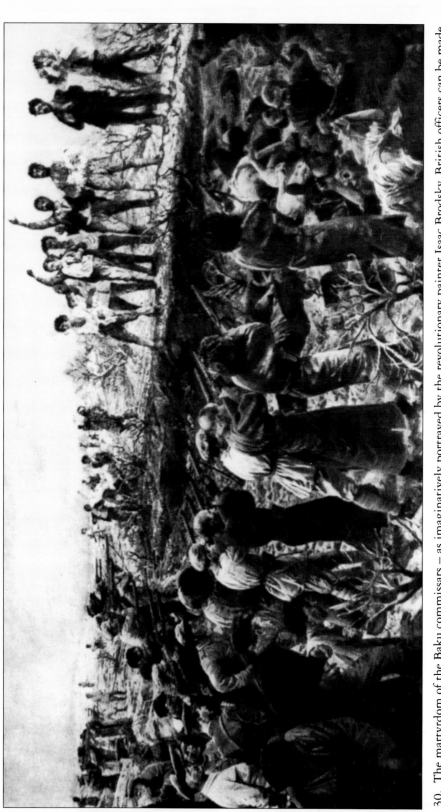

30. The martyrdom of the Baku commissars – as imaginatively portrayed by the revolutionary painter Isaac Brodsky. British officers can be made out on the left.

31. The execution spot. Monument to the dead commissars – its inscription blames the British interventionists for their murder – in the heart of the Karakum desert (*far left*). The desolate place on the Transcaspian railway where the twenty-six were dragged from the train (*left*)

32. Destruction of a myth. It took a revolutionary sculptor twenty-five years to complete this red granite relief of the commissars' martyrdom (*left*). One January night in 1990, an enraged Muslim mob destroyed all traces of it (*below*).

donation. The American missionary, or more correctly General Polovtsov, had a lucky escape as he lay on his bunk. 'I was awoken by a loud explosion quite close to me,' he recalled in his memoirs. 'I even thought at first that somehow my revolver had gone off accidentally. But I soon found that there were holes in both walls of the carriage, just above the berth I was lying in.' From then on, he observed, 'the majority of passengers in our train preferred lying flat on the carriage floor to occupying comfortable seats and bunks.'

Their adventures were still far from over. That night their train ran into the back of the one in front, completely blocking the line. As a result, after disentangling their engine from the wreckage, they were obliged to retrace their steps until they came upon some points where they could be switched to the other track. By this time, unaware of what had happened, the armoured train and those carrying their escort were well on their way to Baku. 'We were now alone and unarmed,' wrote MacDonell. 'Liaki, the last stronghold of the enemy, lay ahead of us, and it was there that we would have to take in water for our engine. We were by now many hours behind the troops, and we steamed slowly towards Liaki not knowing what we were going to find.' All seemed quiet as they rounded the last bend. The station was deserted – 'the first we had seen not in flames,' MacDonell noted.

Leaving the driver to take on water, he and Noel walked into the nearby village. 'It was a ruin,' MacDonell recalled, 'with the dead lying in the streets and the dogs sniffing at their corpses.' Then, through binoculars, they suddenly spotted men advancing towards the village in formation. Clearly they were soldiers. 'They were perhaps two miles away, and slowly but surely encircling us,' wrote MacDonell. Hurrying back to the station, they warned the driver of the need to get moving. But there was no hurrying him, nor any way of cutting short the refuelling. MacDonell and Noel could see that it was going to be touch and go. Trying to look as calm as possible, they paced up and down the platform, saying nothing to the other passengers. Had they alerted them, they would have mobbed the driver, further delaying him. 'Those were anxious and exciting moments,' wrote MacDonell, 'but at last the engine had its fill.' The train began to move, slowly gathering speed.

'By now the Tartars were in the village,' MacDonell wrote. Seeing their quarry escaping, they started shooting. 'We ran through their fire as we crossed the bridge a few hundred yards from the station,' he added. Soon they were safely out of range. But it had been a very close run thing.

Despite the dangers, the journey was not without its moments of frivolity and even euphoria. At times during those five days and nights they were held up for many hours on end, and Edward Noel recalled playing poker for high stakes and drinking champagne 'mixed with the crackle and roar of burning stations'. Whenever there was a battle ahead, he wrote, 'the more adventurous climbed trees and endeavoured with field-glasses to make out what was happening'. Even so, for most of them, it was with considerable relief that they finally steamed into Baku, hours behind the last of their escort. However, although the delay had caused them much anxiety, it at least meant that the station was no longer swarming with soldiers, thereby reducing the risk of someone recognising General Polovtsov and his wife as they were spirited off to the relative safety of MacDonell's home.

The problem now arose, though, of how to smuggle the fugitives out of Baku, which was under strict Bolshevik control, and into neighbouring Persia. For both of them would require exit visas, which would mean presenting themselves to the authorities – 'many of whom', wrote the general afterwards, 'knew me well'. MacDonell decided to take a gamble. Reverting to his official position as British consul, he himself went to those issuing exit visas and explained that the elderly missionaries were too exhausted and shaken by their dangerous rail journey to come in person. Yet, as American citizens, they were anxious to get home as soon as possible so that the husband could receive specialised medical treatment. MacDonell was taking a grave personal risk in all this, for diplomatic immunity counted for little in those turbulent times and death had been decreed for anyone assisting or sheltering the Polovtsovs. But his gamble paid off, and he returned with their passports containing the vital stamps. Meanwhile he had discovered that a tramp steamer was due to leave Baku shortly for Enzeli, and had managed to obtain berths on it for them. That night, under cover of darkness, the two Russians slipped aboard the vessel unnoticed. Although he had enjoyed their company during their hazardous days together, it was with considerable relief that MacDonell observed: 'I was glad to surrender my charges to the care of Providence.'

Sailing with the Russians to Enzeli was Captain Noel. From there he hoped to reach General Dunsterville to report to him in detail on the chaotic situation in the Caucasus. He then intended to return to Baku, now the focal point of British concern, to continue with his intelligence work there. The Polovtsovs were eventually to reach safety. Noel, however, was less fortunate.

18

Bloodbath in Baku

From all that one can discover about him – and that is surprisingly little – Captain Edward Noel reminds one uncannily of John Buchan's brilliant but elusive hero Sandy Arbuthnot. Indeed, Noel might easily have stepped from the pages of *Greenmantle*, the novel in which Sandy first surfaces. The real-life Noel and the fictional Sandy have much in common. Like Sandy, Noel was born of an aristocratic family, his grandfather being the Earl of Gainsborough. Like Sandy, he was an outstanding linguist, fluent in Persian, Arabic and Russian, and in his element among Asiatic peoples. Like Sandy, he was a fine horseman and deadly shot, fond of venturing into remote and dangerous places, and given to adopting disguises. Noel appears to have been totally fearless – Gertrude Bell speaks of his 'flawless courage', and others bear this out. Eternally on the move, his wartime journeys were to earn him the coveted MacGregor Medal, awarded for explorations 'contributing to the defence of India', and dating from the Great Game era. According to Sir Arnold Wilson, one of Noel's chiefs, his 'amazingly rapid movements' across difficult terrain made him a legend among Persian tribesmen, while his subsequent adventures on the North-West Frontier were to earn him a similar reputation there. 'Wherever he served,' recalled Sir Basil Gould, another of his contemporaries, 'he became a name, always roaming with a hungry heart.' However, to Soviet historians of this period he became, more prosaically, 'the British spy Noel'.

He had first come to the notice of the authorities, as a young

Indian Army subaltern a few years before the war, somewhat accidentally. It was strictly forbidden at that time for British officers to enter Persia without authorisation from the Political Resident – something rarely granted. Ignoring this, and hoping not to be found out, during one of his leaves Noel slipped into the country disguised as an Armenian. However, his presence was soon detected by Sir Percy Cox's network of spies, and Noel was summarily marched before the great man and asked to explain himself. The episode could have ruined his career, but Cox was impressed by the young officer's boldness, not to mention his fluent Persian. Instead of punishing him, the astute Cox gave him a severe dressing-down and immediately loaded him with work in the Residency, thereby depriving him of the remainder of his leave. Soon afterwards, on Cox's recommendation, Noel was transferred to the élite Political Department, the traditional breeding-ground of Great Game players.

Even at that stage in his career, legends began to grow around the youthful Noel. Once, short of money to finance his home leave, he worked his passage as a stoker in the furnace heat of a ship's boiler-room as it steamed up the Red Sea in the height of summer. And twice, in 1909 and 1910, he bicycled all the way from England to India, sleeping in Bedouin camps and Turkish villages, and attracting swarms of small boys all wanting to try out his bicycle. 'The key to Noel's character', wrote one contemporary, 'was that if anything was said to be impossible he felt obliged to have a go at it.' But he also had a first-class brain, and his chiefs had a high regard for his abilities as a political officer, assigning him tasks of great complexity.

Sir Arnold Wilson declared that Noel's wartime adventures 'would fill a good sized book', and expressed the hope that he would one day write it. Another former colleague described him as 'a man of fabulous achievement'. Yet, like Buchan's Sandy, Noel remains elusive. He kept no diary and wrote no memoirs, and the intelligence reports of the times yield little, or have been withheld by the Foreign Office as 'still too sensitive'. Even Noel's brother, now dead, who himself served as an intelligence officer in Persia, could tell me little, while an advertisement seeking information brought no response.

Thus, sadly, most of the details of Noel's many adventures died with him in 1974. However, he did leave an account of one of his exploits, which befell him immediately after he disembarked from his Russian tramp steamer at Enzeli on March 18, 1918. It was one which few would wish to emulate. Indeed, it very nearly proved to be Noel's last.

* * *

Noel intended to slip unnoticed out of Enzeli and make his way southwards across the mountains to Hamadan, where General Dunsterville and his small mission were impatiently awaiting reinforcements from Baghdad. Enzeli itself was in the hands of the Bolsheviks who, officially anyway, were behaving fairly correctly towards foreigners, including Britons. Noel was not therefore anticipating any trouble from them. The trickiest part of his journey lay in the seventy-odd miles of mountainous terrain lying to the south of Enzeli, for this was firmly in the hands of the armed Muslim tribesmen blocking Dunsterville's advance. These Persian tribesmen, nicknamed 'Jungalis' – or 'Junglies' by the British – after the dense vegetation characterising this region, numbered around 3,000 and were led by a colourful individual called Mirza Kuchuk Khan. A passionate Persian nationalist, who had sworn to rid his country of all foreigners, he had nonetheless gratefully accepted military assistance from the Germans and the Turks. As a socialist and revolutionary, he had also established friendly links with the Bolsheviks. His principal foes had been the Tsarist forces which, until the Revolution, had occupied large parts of northern Persia. 'He had defied them with considerable success,' wrote Noel. 'His method was to fall on Russian convoys or isolated outposts, but to retire into the forests if opposed by regular forces. Since the Russian collapse he had gained greatly in numbers and prestige, and had become more daring.' Although the port of Enzeli was controlled by the Bolsheviks, this did not appear to worry him as they had assured him that they had no territorial ambitions towards his country. Kuchuk Khan's Jungalis, like the Bolsheviks, were not yet engaged in hostilities with the British, although they were bitterly opposed to Dunsterville's presence in Persia. The resourceful Noel therefore believed that he could run the Jungali gauntlet without much difficulty, although he does not tell us precisely how he intended to do this. In the event, however, it was hardly relevant.

Unknown to Noel, the Bolsheviks in Baku had become suspicious of his activities there, and had sent a warning to Kuchuk Khan that he was on his way to Enzeli. Noel realised, too late, that he was in danger while lunching with an old friend, the director of Customs at Enzeli, from whose home he was making arrangements for his journey southwards. One of the Persian servants hurried in to report that half a dozen armed Jungalis were downstairs asking to see Noel's host. Their leader demanded that Noel be handed over to them at once. Resistance was out of the question, but Noel just had time to toss a diplomatic bag containing a secret cipher into his host's large Russian stove. As soon as it was on fire he slammed the doors on the stove and went downstairs to face his captors. He was escorted to a nearby house where he was guarded by four Jungalis while arrangements were made to move him elsewhere. From the room in which he was held he could see the harbour jetty where several vessels were being unloaded by Russians. Noel realised that if he was going to escape he must do so now, before he was moved to somewhere more secure. He decided to make a sudden break for it, and hare down the quay towards the nearest group of Russians. Speaking excellent Russian, he hoped then to throw himself on their mercy in the few moments he would have before his guards caught up with him.

'Waiting till I saw a fatigue party of some twenty or thirty Russians pass about two hundred yards from my temporary prison,' wrote Noel, 'I pushed aside my guards and made a run for it.' He reached the Russians well ahead of his pursuers and catching one giant by the beard he shouted: '*Save me from these Persians!*' At first it looked as though he was saved, for the Russians agreed to take him to their commissar. 'But on the quay', Noel continued, 'were many hundreds of Persian porters who were busy loading the ships, and who now left their work and gathered to watch the fun.' The Jungalis, moreover, were not prepared to surrender their prisoner. 'A tug of war ensued,' wrote Noel, 'in which I was the rope. The porters joined in with zest, and I gradually felt the Russians give way. Dishevelled and battered, I was hurried away to the water's edge. There I was put in a boat and rowed out across a narrow lagoon to a Jungali post on the other side, where there was no danger of Russian or other interference.'

Noel's immediate feeling was one of intense regret that he would now miss out on the momentous events which were taking shape in the Caucasus and elsewhere in Central Asia. 'I would no longer be taking a hand in what seemed to me the making of history,' he wrote, 'and the wildly exciting game of occupying the Caucasus and creating a belt of new states from the Black Sea to the Pamirs. In those days such undreamed-of things were materialising. The world was in flux and everything seemed possible.' His first escape attempt had failed, but he was already planning another – 'impelled by the thought that I was still close to the outside world, whereas in a short time I should doubtless find myself on the way to God knows what jungle seclusion.' Noel had quickly noticed that his captors had got out their opium pipes and had begun to smoke them. He realised that if he could keep them at it long enough eventually they would become so doped that they would be incapable of giving chase.

'Their supply of opium', he wrote, 'seemed limited, but to offer them money to buy more would be too blatant.' So he asked them if they would buy some for himself. They appeared astonished, but readily accepted his money. During his travels among the Persian tribes Noel had tried smoking opium before, and was therefore familiar with its effects. He had somehow to give the impression that he was succumbing to the drug without actually doing so. After a while, therefore, he began to simulate the opium smoker's characteristic cough, suggesting that he had reached the point of 'kaif', the Persian term for a 'high'. When he judged the moment right, and his captors' resolve appeared sufficiently weakened, he intended to get up and casually wander outside as though wishing to relieve himself, trusting that they would no longer insist on escorting him. But any such hopes were suddenly dashed with the arrival of a Jungali officer and escort. 'My guards shuffled sheepishly to their feet,' Noel recalled. 'The officer rebuked them sharply, then ordered me to collect my belongings and follow him to a boat.' Moments later they put out to sea.

'All through that night', wrote Noel, 'I was rowed steadily across a series of lagoons. Towards dawn we drew in to the shore and landed at a wooden jetty. My escort found us ponies and we rode through a forest of high trees and thick under-growth.' Everywhere was enveloped in mist, making it difficult for Noel to work out in which direction they were travelling. After riding for some hours they halted at a tiny hamlet consisting of half a dozen huts grouped around the house of a local landowner. Having no prisons of any kind, the Jungalis had instead decided to hold him in this remote spot while his fate was decided. Only now did he discover the reason for his seizure. The Jungalis, he learned to his horror, were planning to try him for genocide.

*   *   *

Shortly after Noel's departure, Baku had erupted into blood-shed. The Jungalis, it appeared, now held him personally responsible for the massacre of several thousand of their fellow Muslims at the hands of the Armenians. To understand how this came about, it is necessary to look briefly at the events leading to this bloody turmoil. Shortly after hearing of Noel's capture, MacDonell, then still in Baku, received a message asking him to call urgently on one of the leading Muslim figures in Shaumian's left-wing coalition. Although calling itself the Baku Soviet, it included Muslims and others who were neither Bolsheviks nor necessarily sympathetic to their aims. After discussing, somewhat circumspectly, the general political situation with his Muslim host over tea and biscuits, MacDonell rose to go, wondering why he had been invited in the first place. He was soon to find out. Reaching into his desk, the Azerbaijani drew out a bundle of papers. From these he extracted an envelope. MacDonell at once recognised it as one he had given to Noel to post to his wife immediately he reached the safety of the British lines. Apologising for opening it, MacDonell's host handed it to him, saying that it had been found to contain nothing compromising. The letter, he said, had been discovered by the Jungalis, together with other papers, among Captain Noel's possessions. The other papers, however, were highly compromising. 'They clearly show', he told MacDonell, 'that you and he were involved in the escape of General Polovtsov from the Bolsheviks.' With a suspicion of a smirk, he added: 'This would be a serious matter for you if it reached the ears of Shaumian and his commissars.'

MacDonell hardly needed to be told this. He asked the Azerbaijani whether he proposed to inform Shaumian. 'No,' he was told. 'Not unless you attempt to carry out any of Noel's schemes.' This put him on the spot, for he had already been instructed to do just that, now that Noel was out of action. His task was, in his own words, to 'devise or create a situation' that would enable General Dunsterville to enter Baku and organise its defence against the advancing Turks. In effect, this meant arranging the overthrow of those members of the Baku Soviet, including Shaumian, who opposed British military intervention, not to mention those Muslims eager to welcome the Turks as their liberators from Russian rule. 'At the time,' MacDonell observed, 'the task looked pretty hopeless.' However, he assured the Azerbaijani that if the British government had any such intentions it would hardly entrust them to 'one as unskilled as myself' when it had at its disposal a highly efficient secret service. And so they left it, with MacDonell uncomfortably aware that his diplomatic cover had been partly, if not entirely, blown. Flight was out of the question. Not only would he be closely watched, but even if he reached Enzeli he would almost certainly meet with the same fate as Noel. Anyway, his orders were to remain in Baku while there was still hope of keeping it out of the hands of the Turks.

As it happened, MacDonell need not have worried. Baku was now suddenly gripped by events which drove all other thoughts from men's minds, regardless of their political or ethnic affinities. The question of Polovtsov's escape became past history, while the threat of British intervention was momentarily forgotten. Survival became the principal concern of the various factions. The crisis came as no surprise, however. Although Shaumian had managed to forge a coalition between his own Bolsheviks, the Armenians and the city's Muslims, it had from the start been an exceedingly fragile one, rent by fears, suspicions and jealousies. Whilst willing, for reasons of expediency, to form temporary alliances, the principal factions had widely conflicting aims. There was no love lost between any of them, least of all between the Azerbaijanis and the Armenians. Baku, not for the first time in its history, was a powder keg, merely waiting for the match to be applied to it. The explosion came in April 1918.

Alarmed by the growing military strength of the Armenians, to which British funding had undoubtedly contributed, the Baku Muslims had secretly sought help from their co-religionists elsewhere. Among those who responded were units of the all-Muslim Savage Division, which had until the Revolution formed part of the Tsarist forces. Flushed by their success in overthrowing the Bolshevik garrison at the Caspian port of Lenkoran, some detachments now set sail for Baku. Their arrival, on March 30, caused great consternation among both Bolsheviks and Armenians. When officials were sent down to the dockside to try to discover what their intentions were, they were driven back by gunfire, a number of them being killed. Eventually, however, the newcomers were disarmed by a stronger Bolshevik force. But then more units of the Savage Division arrived and on April 1, in MacDonell's words, 'the Baku cauldron boiled over'.

No one really knows who fired the first shot, but very soon the city had become a battlefield, with trenches and barricades being hastily prepared everywhere. Russian gunboats in the harbour, whose crews were mostly sympathetic to the Bolsheviks and their leftist allies, joined in against the Muslims, mercilessly bombarding their quarter of the city, and wreaking terrible carnage and destruction. But it was the Armenians who decided the issue. At first they proclaimed their strict neutrality, and refrained from taking part in the struggle for control of Baku. They withdrew their forces to the Armenian quarter and deployed them purely for self-defence. But their neutrality only lasted for the first few hours of the battle. Under intense pressure from the Dashnaks, an extremist Armenian nationalist group, their leaders joined forces with the Bolsheviks against the Muslims. It was a decision they would pay for dearly before six months were out. 'For three days it was touch and go as to who would get the upper hand,' wrote MacDonell. 'But at last the Tartars and the Savage Division were beaten back, and by the fifth day not a single Muslim of any importance was left in the town, and few of their houses were left standing.' Some 10,000 armed

Muslims, together with a handful of former Tsarist officers, had been soundly beaten by 6,000 Bolshevik and 4,000 Armenian troops.

One British witness to the slaughter was Ida Dewar Durie, the wife of a British officer serving with the military mission in Tiflis. As it looked more and more as though the Germans would shortly take over Tiflis, she had left for the seeming safety of Baku, together with other Allied wives and civilians. She was staying in the Hôtel d'Europe, anxiously awaiting word of her husband Robert, when she found herself caught up in the battle for Baku, which she watched from her bedroom window. In a letter to her family she described what she, and another Englishwoman sharing her room, saw as the battle ebbed and flowed in the streets around the hotel and shells from the gunboats shook the town.

'Curiosity and excitement kept us recklessly glued to the window most of the day.' Through the cracks in the shutters of their darkened room they saw the gleam of rifle barrels in windows and other vantage points up and down the street, while from a rooftop above them a Maxim machine-gun fired ceaselessly all day. The hotel itself, she went on, 'wore a ghastly, deserted, squalid appearance, its dark, shuttered hall and staircase remaining packed with nervous people who bolted back up the stairs at the least alarm.' The hotel stood in a part of the town held by the Bolsheviks, and 'perspiring, red-faced, breathless' soldiers rushed in and out, periodically barking 'desperate orders hoarsely down the telephone'.

Across the road from Mrs Dewar Durie's room was a hospital run by the Swedish Red Cross, already full of wounded German and Austrian POWs from the Eastern Front. Now the staff found themselves having to deal with local casualties too. 'Every few minutes a dead or wounded man was dragged in by his feet and head. For the first time I looked down upon ashen faces smeared with blood, the hair black and ragged, and standing on end.' Their colouring reminded her of the faces of the dead 'in the huge battle pictures I had seen at Versailles long ago'. One wounded man was very nearly dropped as firing suddenly broke out, startling those lifting him out of the car which had brought him. All the wounded delivered to the hospital appear to have been Bolsheviks or

Armenians, for Mrs Dewar Durie makes no mention of seeing any Tartar casualties, except for the dead, who were strewn about the streets in scores. Indeed, periodically search parties would comb the hotel 'hunting for Tartars who had eluded them', and once she witnessed two Muslims being dragged roughly along by a party of Bolsheviks. 'As I looked, and without a second's warning, the group halted, and the prisoners were shot in the head.' Their executioners then wrenched off their boots and tossed their corpses into the gutter, where they remained for two days.

Occasionally the staff of the hospital opposite came out and washed away the blood from the entrance. But eventually, as more and more cases arrived, they gave this up. Some of the stretcher-bearers, she noticed, were German and Austrian POWs, 'who worked splendidly'. Despite the fighting, an unending stream of men, women and children passed by below carrying huge bundles of possessions and bedding. Aged and aristocratic-looking ladies were being helped along by friendly soldiers, while one young girl, shrieking hysterically, was brought into the hotel to recover. After resting awhile, she was hustled on again by her wealthy-looking but distracted parents, her harassed, grey-haired mother 'imploring her to bear up'. Other groups consisted of Tartar prisoners, their armed escorts holding aloft white flags on their bayonets. By this time there was a desperate shortage of food everywhere, and Mrs Dewar Durie and her companion were reduced to a diet consisting almost entirely of bread, cheese and Caspian caviar, for the hotel restaurant had long ceased to function. The shops in the street below had been looted, and Mrs Dewar Durie saw one hungry soldier, supposedly guarding the hotel, 'flit across the street and do a little looting on his own account'. She was somewhat embarrassed when shortly afterwards he generously offered her some of the biscuits he had stolen.

By now the Muslim leaders could see that they had no hope of overthrowing the Bolsheviks and their allies and seizing control of Baku. They had unwisely taken the Armenian declaration of neutrality at face value, and had also been badly taken aback by the savagery of the naval bombardment. Rather than face total massacre, they therefore sued for peace.

Urged by Lenin to show restraint towards the ethnic groups whom the Bolsheviks sought to win over to their cause, Shaumian agreed to a ceasefire. But the Armenians, seeing that at last they had their ancient foes on the run, were now out for vengeance. The fighting thus continued, until virtually the entire Muslim population had either been driven from the city or been slaughtered. By the fifth day, although much of the city was still ablaze, all resistance had ceased, leaving the streets strewn with dead and wounded, nearly all of them Muslims.

From her window, Mrs Dewar Durie watched grimly as the corpses were collected from where they lay and flung unceremoniously on to carts. 'Some of the bodies', she wrote, 'were practically naked after the looting. Officers could be seen roughly searching their pockets, snatching out notebooks and papers soaked in blood, their own hands and arms red to the elbows.' Although the shooting was now over, the worries of those in the hotel were not. In the Muslim quarter, its flames fanned by a gale which had suddenly sprung up, a huge fire was raging out of control. Mrs Dewar Durie was told that it had been deliberately started by the Bolsheviks and Armenians in order to drive the Muslims out of their positions. Were the wind to change direction, and blow from the north, they were warned, then the hotel would be in the path of the flames. Desperately tired after several nights without sleep, they now packed up their belongings, ready to flee to the sea-front. 'Until midnight,' she wrote, 'we watched the semi-circle of flames now so close to us. Then, gradually, the wind began to die down, and we knew that another peril had passed us by.' However, a further two months were to go by before she was reunited with her husband at Vladikavkaz, 100 miles north of Tiflis, where the British military mission was now based. Even then her troubles were not over, for the mission were taken prisoner by the Bolsheviks, and she was forced to flee in disguise.

With the collapse of the Muslim revolt, the Baku Soviet had been saved. Shaumian reported at once to Lenin: 'For us the results of the battle were brilliant. The destruction of the enemy was complete. We dictated to them the conditions, which were signed without reservation.' While Azerbaijani sources claimed that as many as 12,000 Muslims, including old men, women and children, had been killed, Shaumian insisted that no more than 3,000 had died. But he admitted that the participation of the Armenian units 'lent the civil war, to some extent, the character of a national massacre', adding that 'the Muslim poor suffered severely'. However, he went on to reassure Lenin that those Muslims who had not fled Baku 'are now rallying around the Bolsheviks'. With the revolt crushed, and the Armenians, who had themselves suffered many casualties, thus weakened, Shaumian set about tightening his grip, politically and militarily, on the city. Arguing that together they would be better able to resist the Turks, whose war aims clearly went beyond their gains under the terms of the Brest-Litovsk treaty, he persuaded the Armenians to merge the best of their units with his. Even so his power barely extended beyond the city limits. For most of the surrounding region, including the crucial rail link, was still firmly in the hands of the pro-Turkish Azerbaijanis, resulting in desperate food shortages for the city's inhabitants. As one historian subsequently put it: 'Baku was a Bolshevik island in the midst of an anti-Bolshevik sea.'

*   *   *

It was immediately after the crushing of the Baku Tartars that Captain Edward Noel found himself accused by his Jungali captors of being personally to blame for the slaughter. Arraigned before three judges at a sort of revolutionary court martial, he demanded proof of this wild claim from his accusers. 'To my dismay,' he wrote, 'my judges turned on me triumphantly with the counterfoils of my cheque-book which had been removed from my pocket after my abortive attempt to escape in Enzeli.' This was the cheque-book which had been used to pay British subsidies to the Armenian units who continued to resist the Turks. Although the money had been secretly channelled to them via the Russian military authorities, the stubs revealed the damaging truth only too clearly. Noel cursed himself for having failed to consign the compromising cheque-book, as well as the code-book, to the flames at his host's home when his captors had come for him. He now tried to protest his innocence, arguing that he had had nothing to do with the massacres, and had been nowhere near at the time.

His accusers would have none of it, and pressed home their case even more remorselessly. 'Had I not paid large sums to the Armenians? Had not the massacres taken place a few days later? Had I not taken great care to leave Baku before they started?' Brushing aside Noel's answers, his judges declared that the evidence against him was overwhelming. 'I was clearly guilty of the murder of thousands of Muslims,' he recounted. The three judges then solemnly announced their verdict. Sentencing Noel to death, they told him that he would be shot at dawn the next morning.

19

Captain Noel's Bizarre Adventure

While Noel was pondering his fate in a jungle prison somewhere in northern Persia, MacDonell found himself faced with the task of single-handedly persuading the Bolsheviks to allow the British to help them save the city from the Turks. For it had become clear by now that the territorial ambitions of Enver Pasha, whose desk bore portraits of Napoleon and Frederick the Great, had not been dimmed in the least by his defeats at Erzerum and Baghdad. It was obvious, at least to the British, that he had no intention of settling for the gains granted him at Brest-Litovsk. It was increasingly evident that he aimed to make Baku his, although this was in clear violation of the treaty. During the anxious days and weeks that now followed, MacDonell was to find himself increasingly entangled in a web of intrigue and treachery as he played his hazardous and solitary game.

Since his departure from Tiflis for Baku, the political scene in the Caucasus had been changing rapidly and dramatically. By the end of May 1918, any remaining pretence of Caucasian unity had collapsed. In rapid succession, Georgia, Armenia and Azerbaijan declared their sovereign independence, both of one another and of Moscow. The Georgians, fearing liberation by the Turks, had pre-empted this by inviting in German troops. Berlin required no second bidding, not only recognising the new state but also sending troops to help protect its frontiers. The Armenians, whose ancient homeland and newly proclaimed capital, Erivan, lay in the path of the advancing Turks, continued to resist them, although they knew that very soon, as the enemy brought up more troops, they would have to sue for peace or face total annihilation. The Tartars, on the other hand, looked eagerly towards the Turks, seeing them as saviours who would liberate them at last from their ancient oppressors, the Russians, and from their new ones, the Bolsheviks. With Turkish help, they dreamed of making Baku their new capital, having first wreaked bloody vengeance on the Armenians for their role in the slaughter of the city's Muslims. In the meantime, they continued to harass from the rear those Armenian units still resisting the Turkish advance.

These bitter internecine rivalries were not just confined to those whose homelands lay in the path of the enemy. Another rift had already started to open up between the Turks and their German allies. From the beginning, as we know, there had never been much love lost between them, though hitherto they had largely been able to paper over any cracks. Now, however, faced by the prospect of acquiring crucial war materials and new territories in and beyond the Caucasus, an intense rivalry had begun to develop between them which threatened to undermine their common war aims. The most desirable of these prizes, in the short term at least, were Baku's huge oilfields. Oil was desperately needed by both the Turks and the Germans to fuel their war machines, which were becoming increasingly oil-dependent. In competition with them both for Baku's oil and other economic resources was Lenin, who badly needed them to revive Russia's tottering economy, devastated by four long years of war, not to mention the disruption caused by the Revolution. For this reason alone, he was utterly opposed to allowing British troops into Baku. Despite the British government's assurances, he was convinced that once they were there they would never leave, and would eventually absorb the entire region, together with its raw materials, into the British Empire. Even the Turks, were they to succeed in taking Baku, would be easier to get rid of in the end than the perfidious British.

Fearful of losing out to the Germans, Enver had already begun to transfer Turkish units from the Palestine front to the Caucasus in readiness for his advance on Baku. Such large-scale troop movements took weeks to organise, though, thereby giving Baku a temporary reprieve. The withdrawal of these badly needed units from Palestine was to help seal the fate of those Turkish and German troops left to defend Palestine and Syria against General Allenby, whose forces had captured Jerusalem. Berlin objected strongly, but to no avail. German worries about Turkish bad faith now began to deepen. Enver, once engaged in the Caucasus and in Central Asia, might drop out of the war on other fronts, perhaps even making a separate peace with the Allies, thus leaving Germany in the lurch. Moreover, were a race to develop between the Germans and the Turks for the raw materials of the Caucasus, the former were at present in no position to compete, for every German soldier who could be spared was needed in France or elsewhere. Berlin therefore sought to persuade Enver to hold back, proposing that a joint force, with a largely token German presence, be dispatched to keep Baku out of British hands. The sharing out of Baku's oil, and the region's other resources, could then be resolved on a commercial basis with Moscow by means of diplomacy. But Enver was determined to let no one interfere with his dreams of creating a new Ottoman Empire in Central Asia, and would have none of it. He ordered the preparations for a Turkish advance on Baku to go ahead without delay.

Such then was the situation in the Caucasus when, in the spring of 1918, MacDonell set about his all but impossible task of trying to persuade Chairman Shaumian, leader of the Baku Soviet, to invite General Dunsterville to help organise the city's defences. Dunsterville and members of his mission, it will be recalled, were at that time held up in northern Persia, impatiently awaiting the arrival of reinforcements from Baghdad. For his advance on the Caspian port of Enzeli, from where he hoped to sail for Baku, was blocked by Kuchuk Khan's Jungalis who, somewhat incongruously, were simultaneously allied to the Turks, the Germans and the Bolsheviks, effectively ruling out any question of negotiating a safe passage through. At last, early in June, Dunsterville's reinforcements began to arrive across the rough mountain tracks. Shortly afterwards around 1,000 British and Gurkha troops, supported by light artillery, attacked the Jungali positions, inflicting heavy casualties on the numerically superior Persian nationalists. The road to Enzeli was now open. However, beyond establishing a base there, there was little more that Dunsterville could do other than wait to see whether MacDonell could change Shaumian's mind. In the meantime he set about trying to discover what had become of Noel, of whom nothing had been heard since his disappearance three months earlier.

*   *   *

In fact, despite being sentenced to be shot, Noel was still very much alive. After his trial he had been taken back to his jungle prison for what he assumed would be his last night on earth. It was clear, however, that his gaoler and single guard felt sorry for him. The night, Noel wrote, was cold, 'so they piled up the brazier with charcoal, and fanned and blew till the embers cracked and glowed.' Then they produced three opium pipes, one of which they offered to Noel, holding it to his lips because his hands were tied. A long silence followed, during which the two men began to exchange knowing looks. Noel could sense that something was in the air. One of them then turned to him and said somewhat mysteriously: 'Gather up your heart, for tomorrow will be different from what you now fear.' He then looked expectantly at his companion, as though for help. 'Yes,' said the other, 'it will be alright. They don't really intend to shoot you. It is all done to frighten you and make you confess.' Nonetheless, Noel wondered whether they were not telling him this merely to cheer him up.

The next morning the same three judges who had sentenced him to death arrived with a dozen armed Jungalis. 'The senior judge asked me whether I was now prepared to save my life by making a full confession. I repeated my previous explanation. I was taken out of the house. I tried to catch the eye of my gaoler of last night, but he resolutely looked away.' Two hundred yards from the village was an open field with a row of trees at one end. Noel was led up to one of the trees, while twenty paces away the firing-squad was drawn up facing him. All this time the judges urged him to confess. It had been their intention, Noel believed, to maintain their pretence to the very last moment, convinced that in the end he would crack. But the plan went wrong. Suddenly a messenger rode up bearing a letter, which he handed to the senior judge. Clearly he had got his cue wrong, and should have waited until the order to fire was about to be given. The judge looked perplexed, but opened the letter. 'After a brief hesitation,' wrote Noel, 'he announced that he had received orders that my execution should be postponed.' It was not a reprieve, however, merely a stay of execution. The judges and the firing-squad now rode off, and Noel was led back to his prison, where the smile on his kindly gaoler's face clearly said 'I told you so.' As soon as they were alone, he whispered to Noel that his nightmare would not be repeated. Indeed, it was the last that Noel would see of the judges or hear of the massacre charge. His ordeal, however, was far from over yet.

Escape plans now occupied Noel's mind once more. 'Among the sentries who watched over me was one who was very forthcoming,' he wrote. After a while the man offered to help him escape. 'He and I were to slip out of the house together when his turn of sentry-go fell in the middle watches of the night.' He would lead Noel by forest paths to a point from where he could reach General Dunsterville's lines. But the journey would require food, and this would mean money. Noel gave him most of his remaining cash, while he himself began saving bread from the daily ration given him by his captors, concealing it in a recess which he found inside the chimney of the room in which he was held. But as the days dragged on, and his co-conspirator kept producing excuses for delaying the escape, Noel began to get suspicious. When finally he asked Noel for his watch to help finance the escape plan, he refused. The next thing he knew was when a number of armed Jungalis arrived and seized his secret cache of food. Then they ordered him to pack up his possessions and be prepared to leave that evening.

'Soon after nightfall I was blindfolded and mounted on a shaggy pony. We set off from the village and plunged into the forest. After travelling for some hours the bandages were taken from my eyes and I was told I could dismount.' Noel found himself in a small clearing in the forest, where stood a solitary peasant's cottage. He was to be placed in the custody of the owner and his family. So confident were the Jungalis that no European could possibly escape through the dense forest from this lonely spot, which was even more remote than his previous village prison, that they decided to leave him without guards. Nonetheless, they warned him that were he foolish enough to attempt to run away 'I should be found in the morning within half a mile of the house, hopelessly entangled in the thorn brambles.' If he managed to escape these, he risked being sucked into the bog. Either way he would not get far, and would quickly be rounded up.

In fact, after taking a good look around, Noel decided his prospects of escape were better from here than from his previous prison. From the house, which stood on ten-foot piles, he could see in the far distance, beyond the belt of dense forest, a range of snow-capped peaks. 'If I could get to the mountains,' wrote Noel, 'I should be out of the country of Kuchuk Khan and among friendlies. I must make for those mountains, for I calculated that there could not be much more than ten miles of forest between me and the foothills.' Nor was that all. 'My last quarters', he observed, 'were in a populated district. There I was much further from the foothills, and there was little chance of finding my way undetected, quite apart from the question of eluding the guards. Here, on the other hand, escape from the house was easy, and few people if any would be encountered in the forest.' He concluded: 'I refused to believe that I could not make my way through the ten miles of forest, however difficult they might be. Once I had reached the foot of the hills I had only to follow up a valley and I should soon be out of the jungle country and among the nomad tribesmen, who I felt sure would help me on my way.'

The only precaution which those in charge of him took to prevent him from escaping was to take away his shoes at night. These were placed in the safe-keeping of a man who slept on the ground immediately underneath the house. Alongside him slept the family dog. 'My problem', wrote Noel, 'was how to get hold of my shoes.' As part of the plan he was evolving, he began the habit of taking a stroll around the clearing every evening just before dusk. On returning, he would take off his shoes and place them precisely where their guardian put them before lying down to sleep. 'What I planned to do was to tie the shoes together by their laces, and fish for them with a string and hook through a hole in the floor of my room.' The hook he fashioned from a piece of bent iron which he picked up, but obtaining the string was more difficult. Finally he persuaded those in charge of him to give him a needle and cotton with which to repair his clothes. 'I laboriously plaited the cotton into string,' he wrote, 'until I had a sufficient length.' Other problems included the lack of a compass and the question of a disguise. In the absence of the former, he hoped to navigate with the aid of the stars, while a chance conversation he overheard gave him an idea for a cover which would explain what a strange European was doing alone in the forest. It appeared that shortly before the war a local Persian landowner had sold a large area of the forest to an Armenian timber merchant who had been unable, because of the war, to start operations. 'It occurred to me', Noel observed, 'that I could pass myself off as the Russian agent of the Baku Armenian who had been sent to discover the state of the forest.' He endeavoured to instil in his memory the names of some of the individuals he had heard being discussed in connection with the deal.

He was now all but ready to go. Only one problem remained. How, in total darkness, would he find his way through the almost impenetrable forest without any kind of illumination? In this remote backwater there was obviously no possibility of obtaining a torch. The only solution was to wait for the full moon, which meant delaying his escape by another ten days. But there then followed a week of heavy and continuous rain, making travelling on foot virtually impossible, for the forest was already full of treacherous bogs. Noel had no choice but to postpone the whole venture for a further month, until the next full moon. Although this was disappointing, it did have one advantage. The weather was steadily becoming warmer, making sleeping out in the open forest less punishing. At last, both the weather and the moon were just right. Stuffing his spare clothes into his bedding to make it appear that he was still occupying it, Noel crept down the ladder from the attic where he slept into the large living-room below.

'All around,' he wrote, 'the family lay wrapped in their blankets or just sprawled out asleep. I tiptoed through them, picking my way so as not to tread on anyone. A board creaked and I waited. No one moved. At last I reached the hole in the floor, and lying flat I fished for my shoes, drew them up and tiptoed back across the room.' He then slid silently down the pole which served as a staircase, and headed swiftly towards the forest. There was just enough light from the moon for him to see his way and avoid colliding with the trees. 'I was keyed up with excitement,' he recalled. 'I was on the way home.' Navigating by the moon, he made good progress. 'But so excited was I at my success,' he recounts, 'that I paid no attention to the brambles and thorns through which I had to tear my way. It was only after an hour or more that I realised that the flannel trousers I was wearing had been ripped into shorts, and that my legs were a mass of tears and scratches.' Even so, his exhilaration was so great that he felt neither pain nor fatigue.

By now he was well away from his captors, with no sign of pursuit. Then, suddenly, he ran into an unexpected obstacle. Before him stretched a wide strip of rice fields which would have to be crossed. Unfortunately, to keep wild boars and other animals off the precious crop, nightwatchmen were strategically positioned around it. 'Many of these men had dogs, which began to bark as they heard and scented me,' wrote Noel. Immediately, they started to call out to one another and move towards him. 'I made one or two frantic rushes,' Noel recounts, 'floundering through mud and water, but all the time the dogs and the circle of watchmen were closing around me.' Before long he found himself cornered in a bramble thicket, surrounded by snarling dogs and men threatening him with cudgels. A very swift and convincing explanation was called for if he was not to be torn to pieces by the dogs or have his skull broken by the angry cudgel-wielders.

Noel hastily told the men the story that he had concocted about his being the Russian agent of the Baku timber merchant, adding that he had somehow got lost in the forest. To his immense relief, not to say astonishment, the men accepted his explanation, their mood changing instantly from hostility to sympathy. He was given fresh directions and allowed to continue on his way. But his exertions and abrasions now began to take their toll. 'I found myself borne down by a devastating weariness. I seemed scarcely to have the strength to drag my feet out of the mud, which clung to my shoes like glue. The going was appalling. Thorny undergrowth, mud, water.' But when dawn broke he could see that he had made good progress, for he was now nearing the foothills. As a result of scratches from poisonous thorns, however, his legs and feet were badly swollen. 'In the end', he wrote, 'I had to split open my shoes with an old razor blade to allow my continuing at all.' He had by now left behind him the cruel thorn bushes and bogs, and reached the foothills. Utterly exhausted, he lay down to sleep. When he awoke it began to rain. But very soon, he knew, he would be clear of Kuchuk Khan's domains, and safe.

All that day he struggled on, snatching some more sleep in an empty wood-cutter's hut he chanced upon. His progress was now very slow, due to his fatigue and injuries, and by the evening he had still not found anywhere to spend the night. Then all of a sudden he stumbled on a well-worn pathway, which he knew must eventually lead to a habitation of some kind. Minutes later, in the darkness, he saw a house. 'I entered,' he wrote, 'and found a number of Persians sitting round an open fire in the middle of the room, drinking tea. I recognised dimly that they were muleteers.' Noel realised that, by good fortune, he was in a *chai-khana*, or inn, where travellers could obtain rest and refreshment. 'The owners of such shanties are accustomed to all sorts and conditions of travellers,' he noted, 'so no one paid any particular attention to me.' He still had on him a handful of small coins, with which he purchased some hot milk. He also had left the remains of the stale bread he had stored up for the journey. Having thus eaten, he then lay down, utterly exhausted, 'on the divan of boards which ran round the room and served as a bed for all and sundry'. It was a fatal miscalculation. As he wrote afterwards, the *chai-khana* was clearly on a regular caravan route, and would therefore attract his pursuers. But he was too tired at that moment to consider such dangers.

'I was awakened', he recalled, 'by pairs of rough hands. I tried to get up, but was seized and held down as though I was a savage animal.' A torch was shone on him, and he recognised the man holding it as his gaoler, from whose house he had just escaped. 'He was wildly excited,' wrote Noel. 'I could hardly blame him. If I had escaped he would have been for it. Kuchuk Khan would never have believed that I could have got away through the forests without his help.' His gaoler had at first been afraid to admit to Kuchuk Khan that Noel had escaped, and had sent two of his men off to try to follow the Englishman's tracks. Meanwhile he raised a posse of his friends to join in the pursuit, but after a mile or two they lost the trail. It was sheer chance that had decided them to follow the caravan route which Noel had stumbled upon. Indeed, his gaoler subsequently told him, they had all but given up hope of finding him when they decided to search the *chai-khana*.

To make quite sure that Noel could not make another break for it during the night, his captors now bound him hand and foot. When, however, he pointed to his badly torn and swollen legs, they agreed to loosen the ropes around them. They also brought him tea. For despite their initial anger on recapturing him, wrote Noel, they were kindly men. He had, it will be recalled, earned an almost legendary name among the tribes to the south, as well as among his fellow officers, for the remarkable speed with which he could cover difficult country. His captors, who believed their jungles to be virtually impenetrable to anyone other than themselves, appeared equally astonished, and asked him 'by what sorcery' he had got so far. 'My feat', he wrote, 'had obviously greatly raised me in their estimation.'

Because he was clearly unable to walk, when dawn broke they mounted him on a pony and led him back in the direction from which he had so painfully come, though not to the house from which he had escaped. 'For some days', he recalled, 'I remained in a large village while my feet were treated with a salve of herbs. Then, one morning, I was mounted on a pony and led by three armed men for some hours through the forest until we reached a small clearing occupied by a poor peasant, his wife and a large family.' But this time they were taking no risks. 'As soon as I had dismounted,' Noel recounts, 'a pair of large and heavy iron horse shackles were produced and locked round my ankles. These hobbles were the kind used for horses let out to graze, and prevented practically all movement. They were terrible things. But I found that by tying a piece of rope to the middle of the chain joining the two ankle rings, and taking the weight of the chain in my hand, I could with great care move at a snail's pace without seriously hurting my ankles.' At night he was made to come into the modest house in which the family dwelt, and there the chain joining his feet was passed around a wooden post, making escape all but impossible.

However, to make doubly sure that Noel did not try to escape again, perhaps by some sorcery while everyone else was slumbering, a 20-year-old youth was ordered to sleep alongside him. In addition, a light consisting of a wick floating in a bowl of vegetable oil flickered all night just a few feet away. 'The days passed with terrible monotony,' wrote Noel. 'There seemed little if any hope of escape.' With nothing else to do he spent hours analysing the reasons for his failure at the last attempt. He cursed himself for his haste. He should have waited until the weather was warmer, when nights spent out in the forest without any covering would have been more bearable, and when there would have been plenty of wild fruit to live off. Moreover, he should have travelled more slowly. He would not then have torn his feet to pieces on the thorns nor have had to seek shelter in the *chai-khana*, which had proved his undoing.

As the weeks passed, without any news or contact with like minds, Noel had to endure 'the hell of solitary confinement'. For a man of his temperament, being both shackled and isolated was 'terrible and devastating', and he feared that he might go mad. 'I repeated to myself every scrap of song, verse or declamation that I could remember.' He also whiled away the days and nights by studying the wildlife around him. He noticed that at night 'dark, large bugs, like brown lady-birds' emerged from the woodwork and made a bee-line for him, but showed no interest in the youth asleep beside him. Instead of killing the bugs and counting their corpses, one night he decided to vary the game. He intercepted one bug which was making for him, and placed it on his sleeping companion. 'But the creature came straight back to me,' he noted. 'I repeated the process many times before I broke the bug's determination.' This time it remained on his companion. 'I expected to see him wake,' Noel wrote, 'but the only sign he ever made of being conscious of the bug's attentions was a slight twitch in his sleep.' However, by means of puerile games such as this, Noel endeavoured to maintain his reason and morale during those long and excruciating months since his seizure on

March 18. He could only guess at how the war was going for the Allies.

* * *

In fact, from London, things were still looking distinctly gloomy. True, the German U-boat and Zeppelin offensives had been neutralised, and American troops were on their way across the Atlantic to join the Allied armies in the field. But on the Western Front in the spring of 1918 the picture was bleak. For there, on March 21, General Ludendorff had unleashed a massive and brilliantly orchestrated thrust designed to smash the deadlock and drive the Allies from their entrenchments. Until then every attempt to end the bloody stalemate had failed at dreadful cost to each side, and minimal territorial gain. Ludendorff's offensive, employing more than sixty divisions, including those now switched from the Russian front, was directed principally against the British army, which he judged to be the most vulnerable. With the American troops not yet ready for battle, the German general knew that this was his last chance of destroying the enemy, or at least their will to go on fighting. He came very close to succeeding, for during the next four months of bitter fighting his troops were to inflict nearly one million casualties on the Allies and take 225,000 prisoners. His advance, moreover, was to bring him to within thirty-seven miles of Paris.

However, that spring, British anxieties were not confined to the Western Front. The War Cabinet, as we have seen, was gravely concerned about the threatened Turco-German breakthrough in the Caucasus, the gateway to Central Asia. Persia, too, was now giving cause for alarm to those on the spot. Officially Teheran was still neutral, but there were powerful anti-British elements within the Shah's cabinet, as well as among some of the tribes. Their hand had been greatly strengthened by reports of Ludendorff's early successes, and a growing belief among many ordinary Persians in that last spring of the war that a German victory was now inevitable. Under pressure from these elements, the government in Teheran denounced the British military presence in Persia, declaring that it both threatened the country's independence and violated its neutrality. This military presence included General Dunsterville's mission, the East Persian Cordon and the British-officered South Persia Rifles recruited and commanded by Sir Percy Sykes. The latter force, which had replaced the pro-German, Swedish-officered Gendarmerie, had been set up to rid the country of the groups of armed German agents who had virtually taken it over, and to try to restore law and order. This British move had followed repeated warnings to Teheran that if the Shah's government could not protect Allied lives and interests within the country, the British would do it themselves.

Encouraged by the German victories, and by the hasty departure of the Tsarist forces from the north of the country, the Persian government now demanded that the South Persia Rifles be disbanded. This the British refused to do until Teheran could guarantee the safety of Allied citizens and property. But Teheran's denunciation of the South Persia Rifles as a foreign force imposed on it against its will was a signal for a wave of anti-British feeling in many parts of the country. In April, serious troubles broke out within the ranks of the South Persia Rifles. Several British officers were murdered, and there were mutinies and large-scale desertions. Those mutineers and deserters who were caught were summarily executed on Sykes's orders. But the troubles persisted, and indeed spread, with one entire tribe declaring war on Britain. It was even rumoured that Niedermayer was on his way back to Persia to try to rekindle the embers of the Holy War, causing Field Marshal Sir Douglas Haig, an old India hand now Commander-in-Chief on the Western Front, to recommend the military occupation of all Persian towns to protect India's frontiers. In the event this was to prove unnecessary. For after several most anxious months, with the aid of reinforcements rushed to Bushire, Sykes was able to stamp out rebellion within his own ranks, as well as the threat to British lives and interests posed by the hostile tribes.

Throughout the spring of 1918, feverish debate continued within the British War Cabinet, its newly formed Eastern Committee and the military hierarchy over the strategy and policy which should be pursued in the territories lying between the advancing Turks and Germans and British India. There was also considerable disagreement, not to mention confusion, over precisely what was happening there. Some

wanted Dunsterville to proceed to Baku, with or without
Bolshevik approval, and organise its defence while there was
still time. They looked upon the Bolsheviks as little more than
the hired agents of German expansionism. Others, however,
still believed that some kind of collaboration might be
achieved with them over keeping the Turks out of Baku – or at
least, with the help of the Bolshevik fleet, in preventing them
from crossing the Caspian and reaching Krasnovodsk, start-
ing-point of the militarily crucial Transcaspian railway. Yet
others saw Tabriz, which in May 1918 was on the point of
falling to the Turks, as a more immediate threat than Baku,
fearing that instead of waiting until they had captured the latter, the Turks would thrust eastwards across Persia from
Tabriz. With the Russian garrisons long gone, there was now
nothing but General Dunsterville's small force, plus his
locally recruited levies, between the advancing Turks and
Afghanistan. Indeed, it was reported that Enver's own half-
brother, Nuri Pasha, was already on his way to take command
of the triumphant march eastwards. Among other wild
schemes proposed for halting the Turks was the dispatch of a
small team of British officers to Baku to blow up the oil-wells,
and the deployment of Japanese troops (whose government
had offered their services) to help plug the gap. One senior
officer in London had even suggested arming the Afghans, an
idea hastily scotched by Delhi which considered these unpredictable neighbours quite threatening enough with those
weapons they already possessed.

Soviet historians have always insisted that behind all this
lay an ingeniously thought-out British master plan. Instead of
the confusion, vacillation, poor intelligence and muddled
thinking which were the reality, they perceived the continuation of a sinister strategy which had been pursued by London
ever since the days of the Great Game, a fresh opportunity for
which now suddenly presented itself. 'Revolution and civil
war in Russia', wrote the Cold War historian Leonid
Mitrokhin in 1987, 'seemed to create all the conditions necessary to fulfil the age-old dreams of the British strategists.' It
was their aim, he insisted, 'to capture Transcaucasia, annex
the Caucasus from the new Soviet state, and turn the area into
a colony', without any regard for the wishes of the inhabitants.

Under the guise of defending British India, Mitrokhin claims, Dunsterville's orders were to secure a foothold in the Caucasus. Then, with the assistance of counter-revolutionary forces, he was to overthrow the Baku Soviet and seize control of the whole of the Caucasus, the Caspian Sea and all surrounding regions. To help him achieve these unscrupulous aims, the Russian-speaking British general was accompanied by 'forty Ford vans loaded with gold and silver'. In addition, 'experienced agents' had been sent ahead to prepare the way for him. Foremost among these, he adds, was Major MacDonell, 'the British consul and agent in Baku'.

20

Alone among the Bolsheviks

While MacDonell would have laughed at being described as 'an experienced agent', he had nonetheless been far from idle since the seizure of his unfortunate colleague Noel. Indeed, a great deal had been going on in Baku, where the former British consul now found himself alone among the Bolsheviks. His immediate instructions were to try to persuade the obdurate Shaumian to accept British military assistance while there was still time. There was only one thing for it, he decided, and that was to call personally on this all-powerful figure at home, where they could speak in privacy. He was also anxious to find out whether Shaumian had learned of his own complicity in the escape of the wanted Tsarist general Polovtsov – a crime, it may be recalled, which carried a mandatory death sentence.

'I visited Shaumian late one night in his own flat,' MacDonell recounts. 'The door was opened by his small son aged ten. I explained who I was. The small boy made a grimace . . . then retired a few paces.' He began to harangue MacDonell in a loud voice. 'You bourgeois . . . you damned parasite of the possessing classes,' he declaimed shrilly. The outburst brought Mrs Shaumian hurriedly to the door. 'After some laughter,' wrote MacDonell, 'I was ushered in to the presence of the great man.' He found the revolutionary sunk in a deep chair poring over a thick file which he laid aside as MacDonell entered. 'The room', wrote MacDonell, 'radiated middle class contentment. At one end of the big table was laid Shaumian's supper. At the other end were school books lately studied by the small boy. On a chair were some garments for repair, hastily set down as Mrs Shaumian left the room. It seemed impossible to imagine that this homely family was headed by a violent revolutionary ready to destroy all who stood to counter his theories. Yet it was true.'

Shaumian received his visitor warmly, rising at once from his chair and producing a bottle of wine. Although the two men were aware that they were political adversaries, they seemed to hit it off. Shaumian may well have found MacDonell's dry sense of humour and down-to-earth approach something of a relief after being engaged in earnest debate all day long with his fellow revolutionaries. For unlike most of his Bolshevik colleagues, Shaumian was a well-educated and sophisticated man, and was very likely glad to have someone like MacDonell to talk to. 'I think he liked me,' the British officer concluded, 'although I felt that he considered me of little significance as an opponent.' It is evident, too, from MacDonell's account of the extraordinary times which followed, that he held Shaumian in high personal regard, especially for the determined way in which he tackled the desperate food shortages in the now isolated city. Unlike many other Bolsheviks, moreover, Shaumian believed in achieving his aims through persuasion rather than through the use of terror.

It was Shaumian himself who had first raised the question of British intervention. 'Is your General Dunsterville coming to Baku to turn us out?' he asked MacDonell accusingly. When MacDonell assured him that Dunsterville, as a soldier, had no other aim than to help him to defend the city against the Turks, Shaumian retorted mockingly: 'And you really believe that a British general and a Bolshevik commissar would make good partners?' Without waiting for MacDonell's answer, he went on: 'No! We will organise our own forces to fight the Turk.' In vain MacDonell tried to argue with him, but it was evident that Shaumian believed that Red Army reinforcements were on their way to Baku from Bolshevik-held Astrakhan, at the northern end of the Caspian Sea, and therefore British help, with its political dangers, was not needed.

One useful thing did emerge, however, from MacDonell's first meeting with the Bolshevik supremo, and that was the reassuring discovery that Shaumian appeared not to have learned of his role in the escape of General Polovtsov and his wife. If Shaumian was aware of this, then he showed no sign of it, telling MacDonell that he would be happy to see him at any time. But he would not allow him to send messages in diplomatic code, as he had always previously done as British consul, over Baku's only radio link with the outside world. From now on, Shaumian insisted, everything must be sent *en clair*. It was obvious that he wanted to know what MacDonell was telling his superiors about the situation in Baku and elsewhere in the Caucasus, not to mention what instructions he was receiving from them. MacDonell quickly warned Teheran to tell London only to send him messages which they would not mind the Bolsheviks reading, and that nothing in code would be delivered to him.

Almost at once MacDonell ran into trouble over Shaumian's new ruling. At London's request he had prepared a detailed report on the situation in Baku, including a summary of his interview with Shaumian. But it appeared that the Bolshevik chief had already begun to have second thoughts about his rejection of the British offer of help. MacDonell recounts: 'Shaumian refused to transmit the cable, and after two days' delay presented me with his own version.' In this he demanded guarantees that were he to accept assistance then the entire force would come under the command of the 'Baku Soldiers' Committee'. This would have the power to dismiss individual officers and men, including even Dunsterville himself, and also to conduct courts martial, while the city's overall defence would continue to be organised by Shaumian's own military advisers. Although MacDonell knew that these terms would be wholly unacceptable to London, he nonetheless had no choice but to pass them on without comment. What he did not know was that even now, as he was pressing Shaumian to accept British help, there was still strong opposition in some military circles at home to allowing Dunsterville to proceed to Baku at all. For it was feared that it might prove a death-trap, another Kut. Although Dunsterville himself was eager to go, believing that there was still a fighting chance of saving the city from the Turks, at the time when Shaumian stated his terms the final decision had still not been made. His demands, in any case, were ignored, being regarded as preposterous.

MacDonell soon became aware that even among the Bolsheviks there were some who saw in Dunsterville their only hope and advocated inviting him in on terms acceptable to the British, while the Armenian leaders in Baku were for it to a man. But Shaumian was a formidable leader and stern disciplinarian who brooked no dissent from those around him. He was known, moreover, to enjoy Lenin's personal confidence and friendship. His view therefore prevailed. Nonetheless, sensing doubts, MacDonell persisted in trying to change his mind whenever he saw him, which was frequently. 'I remained a welcome visitor – except at mealtimes,' MacDonell recalled. 'For it was not considered the thing to feed at a friend's house, as you ate up a ration.'

He and Shaumian's young son were now firm friends. 'Often while his father read through piles of documents we would play with his toy railway. I was usually the deposed Grand Duke, who had become a shunter. I was always sworn at and sometimes hit over the head for making mistakes, or for being late with the food train. Once I was executed. I often marvelled how Shaumian could work through all the din we made, but he said he would not have the children out of the room for anything. They were to him a greater inspiration than all his ideals.' Shaumian appeared to MacDonell to require no sleep. 'After the family had retired to bed,' he remembered, 'I would listen for hours to his discourses and theories on the Perfect State, in which each member of the community would work for the whole, as did the individual cells of the healthy human body.' Fierce arguments ensued, occasionally lasting until dawn.

It was at this time that MacDonell first became aware that plots were afoot in Baku to overthrow Shaumian and the Bolsheviks and call directly on the British for help. Indeed, it was even whispered that some of the Bolshevik naval crews were considering sending warships to Enzeli to fetch Dunsterville and his men. Fewer and fewer people now believed, as Shaumian still appeared to, that some 6,000 Bolshevik troops and 4,000 Armenian ones would be capable of defending the city against the Turks when they launched their long-expected attack. These anti-Shaumian plots presented MacDonell with a dilemma. Up to now, his orders had simply been to try to persuade Shaumian to change his mind about rejecting British offers of help. But because all coded instructions from London or Teheran had now ceased, his superiors had no way of keeping him up to date with developments at their end, or of issuing him with fresh directions. Certainly nothing had been said about trying to overthrow Shaumian if he continued to be obdurate. However, although he had no wish to see any harm befall Shaumian or his family, MacDonell realised that London's best interests would be served if the Bolsheviks were replaced by those more amenable to Dunsterville's coming. All he could do in the meantime was to watch developments closely while continuing to try to persuade Shaumian to see reason.

Now, all of a sudden, things began to happen. 'Late one morning, while I was having breakfast after an all-night sitting with Shaumian,' MacDonell recounts, 'a young girl rang my front door-bell.' The visitor, who looked somewhat dishevelled, introduced herself as Marie Nikolaievna. She asked MacDonell if she might speak to him in private. On entering, she handed him a letter from the head of the British military mission formerly in Tiflis, but now relocated 100 miles to the north, safely out of reach of the Germans. Its author, who emphasised that he could not vouch for the bearer, informed MacDonell that she had offered to act as a secret courier. The letter, which carefully avoided saying anything remotely compromising, simply updated MacDonell on the mission's present whereabouts. Marie, whose face struck MacDonell as possessing 'a look of very fixed determination', informed him that she was about to start working for the Bolsheviks as a typist and also carrying messages to their outposts. In fact, she told him, she planned to use this as a cover for her real activity, which was to spy on the Bolsheviks and thus help to bring about their downfall. 'She declared herself ready to die for her Emperor,' wrote MacDonell, 'and assumed that I too had similar sentiments.' Clearly she was offering him her services as a spy. 'I thanked her,' he wrote, 'and told her that I had every intention of remaining alive.'

Marie was angered by this. 'You think me a Bolshevik spy,' she declared. MacDonell had no reason to think otherwise, and continued to act with extreme caution. 'I assured her', he recounts, 'that the British had no other motive than to help the party in power to keep the Turk from Baku, and that therefore spying was unnecessary.' This again angered Marie. 'That declaration of yours', she told MacDonell scathingly, 'is almost becoming a slogan!' Highly suspicious now, MacDonell quickly asked her how she knew that he had ever said this before. As far as he could recall he had only ever uttered it to Shaumian himself. It was the joke of the town, she told him. It was said that he repeated it to Shaumian three times a day. That, thought MacDonell, somewhat chastened, was embarrassingly close to the truth. 'Indeed,' he added wryly, 'I was getting a little tired of it myself.' Nonetheless, he was most careful not to lower his guard for a second, lest Marie be an *agent provocateur* sent by Shaumian to discover his real intentions.

She now leaned forward across his desk and pleaded with him passionately. 'Why', she asked, 'do you not get rid of them? The Bolsheviks will always be your enemies.' There were, she assured him, hundreds of Tsarist officers in hiding in the town, and thousands of loyal Russian workmen on the oilfields. In addition, there were the pilots of the aviation school, all of whom were royalists and simply waiting for a leader. 'Raise them,' she begged, 'and turn out this scum!' But MacDonell repeated what he had already told her – that the British government had no intention of interfering in Russia's domestic politics. Marie stared at him for several seconds without saying anything. Then she asked him whether he was absolutely certain of this. 'I nodded,' he wrote, 'and she suddenly burst into tears.' Until then, MacDonell tells us, he had firmly believed her to be a Bolshevik agent sent to spy on him. 'But now', he went on, 'her tears seemed too genuine.' He decided to take the risk.

When she had dried her tears, MacDonell suggested that she might assist him by carrying some letters for him while travelling for her Bolshevik chiefs. 'Just ordinary reports', he assured her, 'that anybody can read.' Marie smiled. 'You still don't believe in me,' she chided. 'But if it is messengers you want, I can arrange hundreds, all girls like myself.' She told him that a network of such girls, all fervently anti-Bolshevik,

served as couriers throughout Russia, carrying instructions
and dispatches for the Tsarist cause. To escape notice, they
often travelled with groups of refugees or peasants on the
move. 'We, the schoolgirls and students, are organising the
communications which will save Russia and our brothers,' she
told him.

'Marie Nikolaievna', MacDonell wrote years later, 'proved
to be one of those wonderful Russian women who often make
one feel ashamed of being a mere male. True to her promise
she organised a regular service of communications which later
came to be of vital importance to myself and my work. These
girls turned up from time to time, sometimes in the guise of
beggars asking for food, sometimes peddling small wares.
They carried messages in the soles of their shoes or in the
leather buttons of their coats and other hiding places. Some
were hardly out of their teens – little heroines who do not
appear in the history books.' When, finally, Baku fell to the
Turks, MacDonell was much concerned for her safety. But, to
his relief, he spotted her with a group of Russian officers on
the boat taking them all to safety. 'When we reached Enzeli,'
he wrote, 'she disappeared, and I never heard of her again.'

Marie was not MacDonell's only secret visitor at that time.
A succession of mysterious Tsarist officers and others called
on him to offer their services in what they believed to be his
anti-Bolshevik activities. 'Many of them', he wrote, 'were
obviously Bolshevik agents who wanted to know what I was
up to, but the majority were probably genuine.' However,
towards them all he acted with extreme caution. He suggested
that they offer their military skills and experience to the
Bolshevik authorities responsible for the defence of Baku,
explaining that this was what General Dunsterville hoped to
do if Shaumian were to invite him. One former Tsarist colonel
was so outraged by MacDonell's suggestion that he threatened
to thrash him if he did not apologise. But MacDonell could
not afford to take any risks. As it was, such goings-on caused
him great embarrassment. 'These visits from former Tsarist
officers', he wrote, 'naturally placed me under suspicion.'
Shaumian began to grow cool towards him, suggesting that if
he had anything important to impart to him he should do so
at his office and not his home. 'I missed those pleasant visits

to his family,' MacDonell recounts, 'and was sorry I could no longer play at being the deposed Grand Duke with his small boy.' His own small sons, together with his wife, had long before been sent home to the safety of England.

'I was now carefully watched,' he recollected. 'Being shadowed gives you an odd feeling in the middle of the back.' Even years later, he added, this uneasiness returned if anyone walked behind him for long. The Bolsheviks were not yet very practised at it, although they had evolved a system of 'passing you on' when they thought you had spotted your shadow. Sometimes MacDonell, who was very fit, would deliberately set out to exhaust his pursuers, leaving them sweating in the afternoon heat while he ducked into the Hôtel d'Europe for an iced drink. 'Poor little devil,' he wrote of one of his victims. 'His coat was over his arm, his shirt was undone and he was fanning himself with his hat.' MacDonell could not resist asking the unfortunate man whether he had enjoyed his walk. It had taken them through the more distant and hillier parts of the town where MacDonell knew that his shadow would not be able to pass him on to a colleague. Indeed, he had mischievously halted several times to allow his puffing pursuer to catch up, lest he be obliged to withdraw from the game. 'I think', wrote MacDonell, 'that he longed to shoot me.'

By this time, unknown to MacDonell, London had finally lost patience with Shaumian and had decided to take a far tougher line with him. The first that MacDonell knew of this was on July 10, when a young British intelligence officer arrived in Baku disguised as a Persian-Armenian trader. Captain Reginald Teague-Jones had been sent by General Malleson, head of the British intelligence mission in Meshed, to try to obtain a picture of precisely what was going on in Baku, and also to brief MacDonell on the War Cabinet's new strategy. 'He told me', recalled MacDonell, 'that the new policy of the British and French governments was to support the anti-Bolshevik forces . . . It mattered little whether they were Tsarist or Social Revolutionary, so long as they were prepared to oust the Bolsheviks.' This was, in effect, a declaration of war against the Bolsheviks, even if Moscow was not officially informed of it. Needless to say, it was to have profound implications for MacDonell and other British officers who thus found themselves operating behind Bolshevik lines, and for none more so than for Captain Teague-Jones, who was destined to play an extraordinary role in the momentous events which were soon to follow.

Teague-Jones, as MacDonell was quick to see, was a professional to his very finger-tips. If ever a man was born to be an intelligence officer it was surely he. His childhood and upbringing remind one a little of Kipling's Kim, the orphan who was recruited and trained for his future calling in the Great Game while still only a boy. Like Kim, his origins are somewhat obscure, although his father, a language teacher, appears to have died when Teague-Jones was only 13. Because his mother, who had two other younger children to bring up, now found herself in straitened circumstances, kindly friends living in St Petersburg offered to take young Reginald off her hands and see to his education. Having early displayed a gift for languages, he was sent to a German-run school in the Tsarist capital which specialised in languages. Here he rapidly acquired fluency in German, Russian and French, not to mention first-hand experience of revolutionary politics – at the age of 15 he was nearly crushed to death by an excited mob during the 1905 Russian revolution.

On returning home to Britain, he spent a further two years at London University – studying what I have been unable to discover – before proceeding to India in 1910. There, at the age of 21, he joined the Indian Police, where he soon found himself engaged in frontier intelligence work, sometimes in disguise, while adding Persian and other Asiatic languages to his already formidable linguistic armoury. His unusual talents did not go unnoticed by his chiefs, and very soon he was transferred to the Foreign and Political Department of the British Indian government, an élite body which had in the past schooled many of the most celebrated players in the Great Game. It was here that Teague-Jones was working when war broke out. Again he was transferred to make best use of his gifts, this time to military intelligence in the Persian Gulf. As the Baku crisis deepened, with the consequent threat to India, he was seen as the ideal individual to send there to find out just what Shaumian was up to, and how best he could be dealt with.

'Teague-Jones's energy and enthusiasm were amazing,' MacDonell recounts. 'In spite of my twinges of conscience about my relations with Shaumian, he carried me with him. War is war, and a dirty business anyway. I would willingly have handed everything over to the trained hands of Teague-Jones.' But his visitor was anxious to get back to Meshed, so that he could report to Malleson. 'The one fact that was really important', Teague-Jones noted in his journal, 'was that the Turks were making steady progress towards Baku.' Only the Armenians and anti-Bolshevik factions were prepared to fight them. The following night, still dressed as an itinerant trader, he took the ferry back across the Caspian to the small port of Krasnovodsk. From there he intended to hurry eastwards by rail, and finally by pony, to Meshed. But first he had some urgent business to attend to in Krasnovodsk. He found the wooden jetty thronged with anxious townsfolk desperate to learn the latest news from Baku, where many of them had friends and relatives. Had the town fallen yet? How long could it hold out for? How close were the Turks? But Teague-Jones had no time to waste. Pushing through the crowds, he made straight for the town.

His concern was over the huge stockpiles of raw cotton, the principal export of Russian Central Asia, which overflowed from every spare railway wagon, goods yard, siding and way-side station between Krasnovodsk and Tashkent. A small mountain of it, neatly stacked in bales, lined the quay in the port, where it awaited shipment to Astrakhan, at the northern end of the Caspian. An essential ingredient in the manufacture of certain explosives, as well as having other vital wartime uses, the cotton was desperately needed by the Germans and Turks. The Bolsheviks, moreover, were known to be equally anxious to turn it into hard cash. In Baku Teague-Jones had learned of the presence in Astrakhan of a German mission whose task it was to purchase as much of the cotton as they could get hold of. He had also learned that the Bolshevik authorities in Baku and Krasnovodsk had agreed to make available vessels to ship the cotton to Astrakhan without delay. Teague-Jones knew that he had to move fast if he was to frustrate the German plan.

At first he had toyed with the idea of destroying the cotton on the quayside himself by pouring oil on some of the bales and setting fire to them that night. This would also have had the effect of destroying the entire port, thereby preventing any further exports of cotton. But it would at the same time have reduced the unfortunate population of this isolated town to starvation, so Teague-Jones set about trying to find some other solution. He had been given the name of a senior Russian shipping official who was known to be secretly anti-Bolshevik, and he immediately went to call on him. At first, after Teague-Jones had revealed his identity, they discussed the general situation, with the Russian questioning him on what was going on in Baku. Impressed by the man, whom he felt he could trust, Teague-Jones now came straight to the point of his visit.

There were, he learned, three vessels in port actually loading cotton at that moment. Two of these, if not all three, would be ready to sail at around midnight, whereupon their place at the quayside would be taken by two other vessels which were standing by. Others were expected shortly. How, Teague-Jones asked, could the vessels be prevented from sailing? The Russian scratched his head. There was no easy answer, he said. Teague-Jones urged him to try to think of some way of stopping the cargo from leaving. Suddenly the man's face brightened. 'I have an idea,' he said thoughtfully. 'It's only an idea, but it could work.' But could he introduce a friend, a man who was totally trustworthy, into the plot? Seeing little alternative, Teague-Jones nodded. The Russian now explained his ingenious plan.

His friend, it transpired, worked in the Krasnovodsk radio station, then controlled by the Bolsheviks. He had been kept on there because he was the only man in the town who knew how to repair the transmitter when it broke down, which was often. This was crucial to his scheme, as Teague-Jones would see. For if the loading of the cotton was to be halted, this had to be done – or appear to be done – officially. Orders for the shipment of the cotton had come from the Bolshevik authorities at Astrakhan. Any contrary orders, therefore, must also emanate from there – or appear to. Furthermore, they must come by radio, for this was the only direct means of communication between the two towns, which lay 500 miles apart. It was here that his friend would come into the plot. A message was now sent to him inviting him to join them.

The Russian's plan was for the wireless station at Krasnovodsk to receive an urgent signal from Astrakhan ordering the loading of cotton to cease forthwith. This, of course, would be written by themselves. Shortly after that, before the authorities in Krasnovodsk had time to question the order, the transmitter would go out of action. As this frequently happened, it would not arouse any undue suspicions. The breakdown, needless to say, would have been arranged by their friend, who would then be called upon by the Bolsheviks, as usual, to try to repair it. 'Not only will we cancel the shipment of cotton,' declared the Russian, 'but we'll send the ships away so they won't be available when the wireless is working again.' But how, Teague-Jones asked, would the fake message be fed into the flow of incoming signals? Their friend from the wireless station came up with the answer. One of the signallers who handled the incoming traffic he knew to be strongly anti-Bolshevik. For a suitable inducement he would almost certainly agree to 'receive' their fake message and pass it to the authorities in the usual way.

Their next step was to compose a plausible message. 'I know exactly how to word it,' said their fellow conspirator, 'for I have seen many of them coming through lately.' The Krasnovodsk Soviet Executive Committee, he went on, would be ordered to halt the loading of all cotton immediately, as all available vessels were to be kept in readiness for the transport of oil and petrol to Astrakhan. Ships already loaded were to be unloaded immediately and then sent on to other ports. But he expressed fears for his own safety if the Bolsheviks eventually discovered the truth. Here Teague-Jones was able to reassure him. 'If the worst came to the worst,' he told him, 'you could slip across into Persia, where our people would look after you.' Teague-Jones now looked anxiously at his watch. Time was running short. There was a danger that the vessels might finish loading earlier than expected, and sail for Astrakhan before the midnight deadline. He drew out a knife and carefully slit open the lining of his coat. From it he withdrew a wad of ten-rouble notes. This was the bribe which was to be given by their friend to the signals clerk. With a wave of his hand, the man hurried off in the direction of the wireless station.

'That afternoon,' Teague-Jones noted in his journal, 'the wireless station broke down. The last message to come through was a peremptorily worded order to the Krasnovodsk Soviet Executive Committee to cease loading cotton and to off-load any that had already been loaded.' There was much grumbling and argument over the reason for this sudden and unexpected reversal of plan, not to mention the heavy loss of revenue. Wild rumours began to circulate through the town that the vessels were really needed for the evacuation of Baku, or for transporting General Dunsterville's force there from Enzeli. But no one in Krasnovodsk dared to disobey an order from Astrakhan. As a result not a single bale of cotton left the port. And by the time the Bolsheviks and the Germans did discover what had happened, they were in no position, as will be seen, to do anything about it.

Having thus accomplished his task, Teague-Jones was anxious to get back to Meshed as quickly as possible to report on the situation in Baku and Krasnovodsk and along the railway line running eastwards across the desert. He therefore caught the following afternoon's train to Kaahka, 400 miles away, from where he would ride southwards across the mountains into Persia. He knew the route well, for this was the way he had come. But this time he took with him what little food he could buy in Krasnovodsk, knowing that there would be none available on the train or along the route. For on the outward journey he had gone without a proper meal for the best part of five days, as well as having to sleep on filthy and crowded station floors.

It was along the Transcaspian railway, Teague-Jones knew, that the Turks and possibly the Germans would advance eastwards towards Afghanistan and northern India were they to capture Baku and cross the Caspian to Krasnovodsk. If this happened, the British mission at Meshed had orders to try to destroy the railway before the enemy could make use of it. However, they had no detailed maps of the line which could be used to spot its most vulnerable points. As his train crawled slowly eastwards through the shimmering heat of the Karakum desert, Teague-Jones kept a careful, though discreet, watch for any culverts or bridges which could be dynamited if the need arose. But the line had been built at the height of the Great Game, by Russian military engineers, with this kind of threat ever in mind, and he noticed few weaknesses which could not be repaired in a matter of hours.

Twenty-four hours later he steamed into Ashkhabad, the capital of Transcaspia, where he was greeted with startling news. Two nights earlier, on July 12, the ruling Bolsheviks had been overthrown in a coup. As a result the town was still in considerable turmoil. However, during his brief halt there he was able to discover what had happened. The local anti-Bolsheviks, led by Russian railway workers who lived in barracks in the town, had seized an arms store and helped themselves to the weapons it contained. These they had distributed freely to all and sundry, whereupon an armed mob had marched on the Bolsheviks' headquarters. A number of officials had been shot dead, while nine others who had been tyrannising the populace were hanged. A new provisional government calling itself the Ashkhabad Committee was being formed at that very moment, while his train was taking on water at the station. Its political leanings were still far from clear, although it consisted entirely of European Russians, mostly Social Revolutionary railway workers, who were the Bolsheviks' principal rivals for power at that time. Although claiming to represent the interests of the Turcoman Muslims, the Committee included none among its numbers, considering them to be too unsophisticated to understand revolutionary politics.

The overthrow of the Bolsheviks at Ashkhabad was, of course, a development of enormous importance to the British, and Teague-Jones knew that there was no time to be lost in getting word of it to General Malleson at Meshed, and thence by telegraph to Delhi and London. But what he did not know, as his train continued slowly towards Kaahka, was that the repercussions were already being felt elsewhere. Word of the Ashkhabad uprising had quickly spread along the line to Merv and Krasnovodsk, where the Bolsheviks had met with a similarly bloody fate. Four hours after leaving Ashkhabad, the train reached Kaahka, where Teague-Jones left it. From Krasnovodsk he had wired ahead asking for mules to meet the train for the ride southwards into Persia, but he found that the telegram had never arrived. In the bazaar, however, he was introduced to a muleteer who agreed to take him, for an extortionate sum, to Meshed. Teague-Jones set himself a target of two days for the journey, little more than half the time it had taken him when travelling up from Meshed ten days earlier, although the muleteer insisted that this was impossible. The sun was already setting when they left Kaahka for the Russian frontier.

It was to prove a punishing journey. After the searing heat of the desert it was cruelly cold in the mountains, even in July. Aware that the intelligence he bore was getting staler by the hour, Teague-Jones drove the mules and their owner mercilessly on. At times he rode, at others he walked, dragging and kicking the beasts in his determination to maintain the pace and prove the muleteer wrong. Then at last, in the far distance, he saw the lights of the Persian town. Two hours later, shortly before midnight and utterly exhausted, Teague-Jones rode through the ancient gateway into Meshed. It had taken him two days. He now headed for the British consulate, where General Malleson's intelligence staff were quartered.

21

The Plot

In Baku, meanwhile, as the Turks fought their way ever closer to the beleaguered city, MacDonell found himself being drawn into a desperate plot that summer to overthrow its Bolshevik rulers. Soviet historians have accused him – 'acting on the orders of British intelligence' – of personally being behind the conspiracy. Although his superiors in London were anxious to see Shaumian fall, it does not appear that MacDonell was the actual brain behind the plot. All the same, as he himself admits, he was intimately involved in it. With London's full approval, he attended a secret meeting of the ringleaders – mainly ex-Tsarist officers and Social Revolutionaries – and also contributed towards the financing of the plot from the two million roubles of British government funds he had concealed in his house. Furthermore, as he reveals in his memoirs, he was involved in plans, also authorised by London, to destroy Baku's oil-wells rather than let them fall into Turkish hands.

Despite all this, however, MacDonell was unhappy about the hasty way in which the coup was being organised. 'Every Tsarist captain', he wrote, 'had gazetted himself colonel or general, and the whole thing was rather like a comic opera.' The ringleaders, mainly Georgians, were anxious to exclude the Armenians, whom they disliked and distrusted. The Armenians, they argued, would be quick enough to turn against Shaumian the moment the coup looked like succeeding. MacDonell tried to persuade the conspirators to delay their plans until General Dunsterville could be fully informed of what was going on. It would take time, he pointed out, for British troops to reach Baku from Enzeli, during which almost anything might happen in a beleaguered and divided city without proper leadership or an organisation capable of running or defending it. But there was no stopping the hot-headed conspirators, who were united only in their fear of what the Turks would do if they captured the city, and their opposition to the Bolsheviks.

A day was fixed for the coup, giving MacDonell little choice but to go along with it. The plan was for the oilfield workers to call a strike and gather *en masse* on the Baku seafront, where speakers would denounce Shaumian's failure to prepare properly for the coming Turkish onslaught. Then they would vote unanimously in favour of calling on the British to come to Baku's rescue. While those troops and police still loyal to Shaumian were fully occupied in trying to control the unruly oil-workers, several hundred armed Russian ex-officers, said to be in hiding in the town, would suddenly rise, surround the Bolsheviks' headquarters, and seize Shaumian and his entourage. It had meanwhile been arranged that the naval crews in the harbour and members of the aviation school would join in, thereby deterring anyone from rallying to Shaumian's cause. Finally, once it was clear that the coup had succeeded, armed Armenian troops would be deployed on the streets and at key points in the town to maintain law and order. Because he enjoyed good relations with the Armenian leaders, it would be MacDonell's task to bring the Armenians in at the right moment. As for the Muslim population, they were no longer a factor, for those who had not been killed in the recent massacre had mostly fled into the countryside ready to welcome the advancing Turks.

'The following days', wrote MacDonell afterwards, 'were perhaps the most enthralling in my life. We were all now involved in a very dangerous and exciting game.' If everything went according to plan, then it looked as though Shaumian was doomed, and that General Dunsterville and his troops would soon be in Baku. Then, all of a sudden, disaster struck. On the day before the coup, one of the principal conspirators was arrested by the Bolshevik secret police. MacDonell saw him being taken away under guard. 'It was a bad moment,' he confessed. 'I feared that he might give some sign of recognition, so I disappeared into a shop.' The crucial question now was whether the man, a Russian colonel, would reveal all in what MacDonell called 'the persuasive atmosphere of a Bolshevik prison.' If he did, then they were all as good as dead. Then came still worse news when it was learned that two lesser figures in the plot had also been arrested, and that certain individuals' names and other compromising material had been found on them. However, at this late stage, there was no way of knowing how much the Bolsheviks had discovered. It was therefore decided to proceed with the plan, but to keep news of the arrests secret lest others involved in the conspiracy lost their nerve and failed to act. 'Our safety', wrote MacDonell, 'depended on the immediate success of the coup – after which there would be no Bolsheviks to arrest us.'

By this time he had managed to get a message through to Dunsterville advising him of what was happening, and it was now just a question of waiting until ten o'clock the next morning, when the oil-workers were due to gather on the seafront, and seeing what transpired. 'I well remember standing by the open windows of my drawing-room overlooking the bay,' MacDonell recounts. 'I could see the fleet lying at its moorings perhaps half a mile away. The old gunboat had steam up when I first looked out shortly after dawn, but at half-past nine the ships were still moored to their buoys and I could see no movement on board.' Yet he knew that if they were to take up their positions by ten o'clock they would very soon have to be under way.

From where he watched, however, he was unable to see the waterfront where the mass demonstrations were due to take place at any moment. 'Ten o'clock, the fateful hour, approached and passed. I listened for the crackle of rifles. I listened for the acclamations of those thousands of workers who were to demand the presence of the British. But no sound broke the silence, and the fleet remained at its moorings.' Then, all of a sudden, a pinnace left the harbour and headed towards one of the warships. Through his binoculars MacDonell watched some men go aboard. 'They were not sailors,' he noted grimly, 'they were police.' It was now quite clear that the plot had been betrayed.

At half past ten, MacDonell could bear it no longer, so he walked down into the town to try to discover what was going on. 'The streets were full of patrols, soldiers and police,' he wrote. But the shops were all open as though nothing had happened. On the seafront, though, where the oil-workers should have been, he came upon a little wooden rostrum, 'such as demonstrators always carry for their speakers', lying abandoned. He hurried on to the hotel where one of the leading conspirators was staying, only to learn that the man had left suddenly for Krasnovodsk by the early morning ferry. There was no sign of the substantial sum in roubles which MacDonell had passed to him in a pigskin suitcase. Proceeding further, he gradually learned more of what had happened. It appeared, as he had feared, that one of the detainees had spilled the beans to his Bolshevik interrogators. As a result, during the night, a number of key conspirators had been arrested, including some of the Tsarist officers who were to have attacked Shaumian's headquarters. When that morning the oil-workers had tried to march into town they had found their way barred by armed Bolshevik troops, and their leaders had been arrested. Indeed, most of the principal plotters had now either been arrested or had simply vanished. This left MacDonell feeling highly exposed, and expecting a visit from the secret police at any moment.

At first, however, the Bolsheviks appeared to ignore him, unaware perhaps of his role in the plot. Instead, the officially controlled Baku press directed its fury against the 'Tsarist counter-revolutionaries' whose evil schemes had been foiled 'only by the perspicacity of the Bolsheviks and the indomitable will of the workers'. No mention was made of any British involvement, perhaps for fear of encouraging the growing number of ordinary people who would have welcomed General Dunsterville's intervention. Meanwhile, Shaumian was sending increasingly desperate telegrams to Moscow asking for Red Army troops to be sent to defend Baku. His Armenian units, he reported, had so far put up a gallant and spirited resistance to the advancing Turks, but were now becoming demoralised. This, he claimed, was due to 'English agitation' and to the 'cowardice' of some of their commanders who were calling for Dunsterville's assistance. 'I ask you earnestly to hurry,' Shaumian begged Moscow. But apart from fulsome praise from both Lenin and Stalin for so steadfastly refusing British help, all he received were 170 cavalrymen from Ashkhabad and a further 780 troops from central Russia to be added to the 20,000 Armenians who, less than 100 miles to the west, were trying to hold the approaches to Baku. Yet ranged against them were nine fully equipped Turkish infantry divisions, who outnumbered them by at least three to one.

By this time, as Shaumian's interrogators gradually extracted from their prisoners the details of the abortive plot, the finger of suspicion began to point more and more at MacDonell. The first warning he received of this was when he discovered that his telephone had been cut off. Also there was no longer any pretence of discretion over shadowing him. 'Men were posted within sight of my front door,' he wrote, 'and they followed me about quite openly.' When he tried calling on Shaumian at home, as though nothing had happened, he was turned away by a rough-looking sailor guarding the door. From then on, as MacDonell found himself caught up in an ever more bizarre succession of events, things began to move fast.

First, via a trusted source, he received a terse message simply asking him to be certain of being at home the following morning. The next day at noon a visitor arrived at his back door. The caller, at first sight, appeared to be an itinerant dealer in oriental rugs, which MacDonell was well known to collect. MacDonell invited him in, whereupon he spread out a number of fine rugs on the floor for inspection. But then, after looking furtively around to make certain that no one else was present, he held out his hand to MacDonell and introduced himself. 'I am Colonel Martev,' he declared. Next, he took off one of his high leather boots and thrust his hand into it. There was a faint click from within the boot, and the colonel withdrew from inside it a folded note. 'My own invention,' he remarked with obvious pride, patting the side of the boot before pulling it on again. He handed the note to MacDonell, who quickly read it.

It was from one of the leading conspirators, a Russian priest whom he trusted implicitly. It warned him that the Bolsheviks were divided over whether or not they should arrest him. 'The majority, it seemed, were for arraigning me before a revolutionary tribunal,' MacDonell wrote, 'but Shaumian and some others were against it.' The note instructed him to attend, quite openly, a party at a certain address that night, where he would receive further news and advice. Followed by his shadow, who took up position opposite the house, MacDonell rang the front-door bell that evening and was invited in. After a somewhat frugal meal, for food was desperately short, MacDonell's host invited him into another room to admire some of his Persian rugs. But instead he immediately led him through to the rear of the house where a ladder took them on to the roof. 'There was no moon and it was very dark,' MacDonell recalled. 'My feet seemed to sink deep into the soft pitch with which the roof was covered. Once I nearly fell headlong over a telegraph wire. We turned to the right, then an electric torch flashed for an instant about ten yards ahead of us.' They then descended another ladder, at the foot of which a young girl was waiting. Not a word was said, and no explanations given, but the girl led MacDonell to a dimly lit room in which he could see, laid out on a bed, a Bolshevik soldier's uniform. Motioning to him to put this on, she then led him and his host down the back stairs of the house to a street exit, by which they left.

Having, by this somewhat elaborate means, shaken off MacDonell's shadow, the two men walked through the darkness to another house, several minutes away. MacDonell wondered what his Foreign Office chiefs would say if they could see him now, dressed in the uniform of a Red Army private. Arriving at the house, they were greeted by a middle-aged Armenian woman. A passer-by would merely have thought that she was welcoming home her soldier-son. Ushering them in, she led them to an upstairs room where three men, none of them known to MacDonell, were clearly awaiting them. One of the three, acting as spokesman, explained to MacDonell that he would now almost certainly be arrested by the Bolsheviks and put on trial. His friends, however, had made very careful arrangements to ensure that the case collapsed. The Bolsheviks, he said, would offer him a lawyer to handle his defence. He was to accept this offer, for the man was, in fact, a friend. The spokesman then briefed him on the strategy which had been worked out with his lawyer, and which he was to follow meticulously. After that he was taken back to the first house, where he was allowed to change into his own clothes, before returning via the roof-tops to the party. This was now breaking up, for the ten o'clock curfew was approaching. 'I left with the other guests', MacDonell recalled, 'and was immediately picked up and followed home by the unsuspecting ruffian who had shadowed me to the party.'

Very soon afterwards, as MacDonell's mysterious friends had warned, he was arrested. 'I had just finished my evening meal,' he wrote, 'when a large black car containing the head of the secret police and three soldiers drove up to my door.' They were polite and apologetic, explaining that 'Comrade Shaumian' wished to see him urgently. On arriving at the Bolshevik headquarters MacDonell was escorted into a large room where several rows of chairs faced a long table covered with a cloth of revolutionary red. Seated at the table were Shaumian himself and several other Baku commissars, earnestly discussing some papers which lay before them. A number of people sat expectantly in the chairs facing the table, while others, including soldiers, sailors and workers, came or went or stood talking in low voices. MacDonell's escort reported their arrival to Shaumian, whereupon his guards were dismissed and he was ushered forward to the table and given a chair.

Carefully avoiding MacDonell's gaze, Shaumian told him that they wished to put to him 'certain questions' regarding recent events in Baku, and his connection with them. Immediately MacDonell demanded to know why he, still officially a British diplomat, had been arrested, since this was in contravention of international law. Looking somewhat embarrassed, Shaumian assured him that he was not under arrest, and that the soldiers had been provided merely for his own protection. He then asked MacDonell if he would like to be legally represented. Remembering his instructions of the previous night, MacDonell said that he would, and asked innocently whether he should send for his own lawyer. Shaumian assured him that this would not be necessary, as they would provide him with an excellent one. At that, an Armenian stepped forward and introduced himself to MacDonell, before leading him to a table at the far end of the room.

Here they were joined by two Bolshevik officials who were to question him, after which it would be decided whether there was a case against him. If there was, then this would be heard by the Baku Revolutionary Tribunal. This body, MacDonell had discovered, had already sentenced one of the principal conspirators to death, and put a price on the head of the one who had escaped (with MacDonell's roubles) on the Krasnovodsk ferry on the morning of the coup. He, however, was only there for questioning, he was assured. 'I expressed my gratification at this subtle distinction,' MacDonell recalled wryly. In the course of his interrogation, he told the two officials that his explicit instructions from his government were to try to persuade Shaumian to accept British help in defending Baku from the Turks. Had the British government wished to engineer a coup, he added, they would hardly have employed him, a total amateur in such matters, when no doubt they had plenty of professionals on whom they could call. As for those who had been arrested, it was hardly surprising that he knew some of them, since he had lived in Baku for years. He had no reason to suspect, however, that any of them were involved in plots against the Bolsheviks. The two official investigators took careful notes of all this.

'Now', MacDonell wrote, 'came the lead I had been told to expect.' Handing him a bundle of typed documents said to have been found in the possession of the man who had been sentenced to death, his lawyer asked him whether he had ever seen them before. MacDonell studied them very carefully, while the others looked on in silence. He was not long in finding what his friends of the previous night had told him to look out for. 'The machine that typed these', he told his interrogators, 'occasionally jumps a space after the letter B, and the middle bar of the letter E is damaged.' Hardly expecting what was to follow, the two men agreed. MacDonell then drew from his pocket the letter, signed by Shaumian and handed to him by the chief of police, requiring his presence at the inquiry. Pointing to identical defects in this, he now dropped his bombshell. Staring the two officials in the face, he declared: 'All these were typed in this office.'

The two men were clearly thunderstruck. Snatching up the papers, they carefully compared the typefaces. 'Impossible!' one of them gasped incredulously. 'On the contrary,' MacDonell answered, adding that the discovery gave credence to the rumours that Shaumian himself had engineered the plot in order to demonstrate his strength in crushing it and to find out who was secretly opposed to him. There was a long and embarrassed silence. Presently his lawyer asked him: 'That will be your line of reply?' MacDonell nodded. The three men then hastily rose from the table and retired to another room, where they were immediately joined by Shaumian and several other commissars. A Red Army soldier had evidently been ordered to keep a close eye on MacDonell while they deliberated, for he moved appreciably, though discreetly, closer to where MacDonell sat alone while his fate was decided.

Finally, after a long interval during which they were obviously devising a strategy, Shaumian and his colleagues emerged, and MacDonell was invited to take a chair before the long table. Here, after he had been given a glass of tea and some biscuits, he was asked a succession of questions about himself. All these were innocuous enough, none of them referring in any way to the plot, or to his suspected role in it. The reason for this was fairly obvious to MacDonell. The public seats behind him were filled by an audience which had come expecting, or at least hoping, to witness something pretty sensational. The last thing that Shaumian wished them to hear was MacDonell repeating his damaging allegations about the source of the counter-revolutionary documents, for this would be around town in no time. Just how his mysterious friends had arranged this, MacDonell never discovered, although it very likely saved his life. For it had clearly forced Shaumian and the members of the revolutionary tribunal on to the defensive, making the proceedings little more than a face-saving exercise. 'The whole thing tailed off miserably,' MacDonell wrote, 'and shortly before one o'clock in the morning most of the public chairs were empty.' At around half past one he was told that he was free to go home, though he was warned that he must not leave Baku or attempt to communicate with General Dunsterville.

The secret police chief who had arrested him now drove MacDonell home through the empty streets in his own car, this time without the armed soldiers. 'I was too tired and nervy to exchange many pleasantries,' MacDonell wrote, 'but it was evident that he had something to say, so I invited him in to try a whisky and soda – the one thing I was really longing for myself.' When he was quite sure that there was no risk of his being overheard, the police chief, who had once served the Tsar in a similar role, advised MacDonell that he would be wise to leave Baku as soon as possible. Indeed, if he wished to join General Dunsterville at Enzeli, he might be able to help him to leave Baku secretly. 'He then spoke of his card debts,' MacDonell recounts, 'and his difficulty in meeting them.' Taking this to be a hint, MacDonell asked if he could possibly help him out. 'He immediately protested in horror,' wrote MacDonell, 'saying that this smelt too much of the old regime.' The signal was nonetheless pretty clear to Mac-Donell, who decided to pursue it further.

Gradually the police chief's protests began to weaken, and a few days later it was all fixed up. 'Two hundred pounds of the British taxpayer's money', wrote MacDonell, 'enabled him to pay off his card debts, and me to go aboard the steamship *Tula* bound for Enzeli.' After his new friend had called off his shadows, MacDonell slipped aboard the vessel the following morning, but carrying no luggage. A trusted member of the ship's crew took him down to the engine-room where he was concealed in a small recess behind the boiler, out of sight of any of the passengers or crew. There MacDonell had to wait all day in the suffocating heat until the vessel sailed. Only then was he able to leave his hiding-place and retire to a deck cabin where he hung out his sopping, and only, set of clothes to dry. The following day, looking more like a dervish than a British diplomat, he disembarked at Enzeli, where he immediately proceeded to the British headquarters there. General Dunsterville was then at Kazvin, where the bulk of his small force was encamped. Arrangements were at once made to convey MacDonell there so that he could report to the general at first hand on the latest situation in Baku, and subsequently to the British minister in Teheran. 'It was good to be among one's own people again,' MacDonell wrote thankfully, after so many anxious weeks of playing the Great Game against the Bolsheviks.

Just how thankful he had reason to be he learned a few days later when listening to a news bulletin broadcast by the Bolshevik-controlled radio station at Baku. An orderly had run over from the British receiving station to say that his name was being continually mentioned in a Russian-language broadcast, and would he come over and translate it. 'I gathered from it', he wrote, 'that after my disappearance a full-dress trial had been staged.' In his absence he had been found guilty and sentenced to be shot. 'I regret to say', he added, 'that some others who were not absent had also been sentenced.' In retrospect, it seems very likely that Shaumian, wishing to avert a serious showdown with the British, who after all had troops nearby, had deliberately allowed MacDonell to escape revolutionary justice, and that his debt-ridden police chief had turned this to his personal advantage. Either way, MacDonell was extremely lucky to have escaped with his life, while others had paid dearly with theirs.

Not long afterwards, on July 31, an even more sensational piece of news from Baku reached British ears. Shaumian had finally been overthrown. As fears over his failure to prepare to defend the city against the fast-approaching Turks turned to near-panic, more and more of his former supporters had deserted him. Finally, by 259 votes to 236, the Baku Soviet had resolved to turn to the British for help. Shaumian, bitterly angry, declared that he and his remaining supporters would have no part in this, and that they would withdraw forthwith from both the Soviet and from Baku itself. 'With pain in our hearts and curses on our lips,' he declaimed in an emotional order of the day, 'we who had come here to die for the Soviet regime are forced to leave.' Then, loading all the weapons and ammunition they could gather aboard a number of vessels in Baku harbour, and taking with them all their troops and supporters, they set sail for Astrakhan, the only port on the Caspian still in Bolshevik hands.

On Shaumian's departure, control of Baku passed swiftly and bloodlessly into the hands of the Social Revolutionaries who called themselves the Centro-Caspian Dictatorship. Consisting mostly of Russians, they also enjoyed the support of the Armenians. In full agreement over their need for British help, they immediately sent an urgent appeal to General Dunsterville to come to Baku while there was still time. Simultaneously they dispatched fast naval vessels in pursuit of the fleeing Bolsheviks with orders to arrest them and escort them, together with the desperately needed arms they had removed, back to Baku. This was swiftly accomplished, and Shaumian and his fellow commissars were now reported to be languishing in one of the city's gaols, which until very recently they had controlled.

General Dunsterville's long-awaited moment had finally arrived. While his staff officers hurriedly commandeered suitable vessels for shipping Dunsterforce, as it was officially called, to Baku, MacDonell was found a new uniform to replace the clothes he had escaped in, and sent ahead to advise the Centro-Caspian Dictatorship that help was on its way. The race to try to save Baku and its precious oilfields from falling into Enver's hands was on at last.

22

The Battle for Baku

'The view of Baku from the sea', wrote General Dunsterville, 'is most imposing.' In the centre of the town, surmounted by a gleaming golden orb and cross, rose the distinctive dome of the Russian Orthodox cathedral. Stretching along the corniche, looking out across the Caspian Sea, were rows of handsome buildings, once owned by wealthy families who had made their fortunes here. For at the end of the last century, Baku had been one of the wealthiest cities on earth. The discovery of vast oilfields in this remote corner of the Tsar's empire had brought entrepreneurs and adventurers of every nationality rushing to the spot. Experts calculated that Baku had enough oil to heat and illuminate the entire world. So sodden was it with the stuff that one had only to toss a match into the Caspian off Baku for the sea to catch fire and burn for several minutes.

For a few short years the town became a Klondyke, where huge fortunes were made or gambled away overnight. Baku's new rich, some of them barely literate, built themselves palaces of great opulence on the seafront. Famous European luxury stores opened branches on Baku's elegant new tree-lined avenues, along which ran smart horse-drawn trams. Well away from all this were the great oilfields, with their forests of wooden derricks running down to the sea on either side of the town. Here, in shanties, lived the army of oil-workers, and everywhere there hung the sickly sweet smell of crude oil which lay in glistening black ponds where it had leaked from the drillings. At one time Baku's oilfields were producing more oil than all the wells in the United States.

But when, on August 17, 1918, the British disembarked in its sleepy port, only the ghosts of this once opulent past remained. The millionaires, like the Swedish-born Nobel brothers, had long departed, the elegant European-owned stores were shuttered up, and the horse-drawn trams no longer ran. In the aftermath of the war and the Revolution, Baku must have looked much like Shanghai after the Communist takeover in 1949, though its decline had begun long before the war or the Bolsheviks' coming to power. A series of marathon strikes in the oilfields, the result of miserable working conditions, had crippled the industry, often reducing the flow of oil to a trickle. Bloody ethnic strife, leading at times to massacres, and violent repressive action by the Tsarist authorities had caused further damage to the industry. Lacking confidence in Baku's future, the oilfield owners saw little point in investing in the latest technology. The war had served to isolate the town still further from the international market, leaving it to depend instead on the subsidised domestic one. All in all this had hastened the once-rich city's demise, playing into the hands of the revolutionaries with their heady new gospel, and paving the way for Shaumian's short-lived Baku Soviet, and now for the grandiose-sounding Centro-Caspian Dictatorship.

As General Dunsterville's vessel approached the quayside on that summer morning, he and his staff officers were carefully studying the terrain on which the battle for the town would be fought. Behind Baku, overlooking it on three sides, were high, barren hills, and somewhere behind these were the Turks. If they had artillery, and could get it up on to these heights, then they would be able to pulverise the town, and with it Dunsterville's small force, at will. At all costs the Turks had to be prevented from securing the high ground if Baku, and its precious oilfields, were to be saved. Dunsterville's most immediate task, however, was to discover the present dispositions of the Turks, as well as of the defending forces. It was for this reason that he had sent ahead MacDonell, followed by a small advance party, which had now been in Baku for several days.

No sooner had Dunsterville's vessel, the *Kruger*, docked

than he received an urgent message from the five-man Centro-Caspian Dictatorship asking when they might meet him. At the same time the officer commanding the advance party came aboard to brief him on the immediate situation. They had arrived to find the front line virtually undefended, with a Turkish thrust expected the following day. Clearly the local commanders and their troops were looking to the British to take over the fighting from them. Perhaps MacDonell had done his work too well, for it quickly became evident, Dunsterville wrote later, that the townspeople were expecting 'ship after ship' to pour out British troops on to the quayside. When the tiny advance party of the Hampshire Regiment had disembarked they had been bitterly disappointed. 'And yet,' wrote Dunsterville, 'the mere sight of these fine-looking soldiers inspired them to the extent that, when the Turkish attack took place the following day, every man in the town seized his rifle and rushed to reinforce the firing line, with the result that the Turks were thrown back in confusion.'

The British advance party had also found Baku's line of defence, which formed a nineteen-mile-long crescent around the city, to be woefully positioned. 'Rifle pits are so badly sited', they reported to Dunsterville, 'that the occupants can only shoot into the air.' There were neither barbed-wire entanglements nor any communication trenches. Yet in some places the Turkish forward positions were little more than a mile away. Supposedly manning the city's defences were 10,000, largely half-hearted, local volunteers. Of these, 3,000 were Russians and 7,000 Armenians. All had rifles, but few had received any proper military training. Most felt that they had already risked their lives enough, while some were even for holding talks with the enemy. As for those Muslims remaining in Baku following the recent massacre, most if not all of them were ready to welcome the Turks, and therefore represented a potentially dangerous fifth column, or enemy within.

The actual enemy, vanguard of Enver Pasha's 60,000-strong 'Army of Islam', consisted of 14,000 battle-hardened Turkish troops, with reinforcements expected in due course. Once Baku was in their hands, they planned to carry the banner of the Holy War across the Caspian into the Muslim lands beyond, liberating the Turkic peoples dwelling there, and carving out of the Tsar's former domains a new Ottoman Empire over which Enver aimed to rule as Sultan. Already the forward Turkish positions were dangerously close to the town, the advance party warned Dunsterville. 'Enemy batteries, with aeroplane observation, could at any time bombard the harbour and destroy shipping,' they reported, 'especially if they bring up heavy guns.' Fortunately, as yet, there was no sign of the latter. In the meantime, while they awaited the arrival of Dunsterville and the main force, the advance party had been moved into the most vulnerable sectors of the front line.

If the people of Baku had been disappointed by the size of the advance party, then they were hardly reassured by the sight of the rest of the British force as it disembarked on the quayside. For altogether Dunsterforce never amounted to more than 1,000 fighting men. Their task, it will be recalled, was not to try to defend Baku themselves, but rather to shape the Russian and Armenian volunteers into a force capable of holding off the Turks until reinforcements could be spared from elsewhere. At worst, they might be able to hang on until the British were able to build a small makeshift naval force which, if Baku fell, could prevent the Turks from crossing the Caspian to the vital railhead at Krasnovodsk. To this end, a handful of Royal Navy officers had accompanied Dunsterville. It was their task to try to obtain suitable vessels, fit them with British guns, and use them to gain control of the Caspian. Two quite separate vessels had already been requisitioned for evacuating Dunsterforce in a hurry if the Turks succeeded in overrunning the town before the British had time to establish themselves. These were tied up, with armed guards on board, beside the *Kruger*.

A tour of the battlefield, meanwhile, had quickly convinced Dunsterville that the situation was even worse than he had been led to believe. If the Turks, with their overwhelming numbers, were to make a really determined assault, then he knew that nothing could save Baku, however bravely and resolutely his own troops and the local volunteers fought. Indeed, the only possible explanation for the Turks holding back was either that they were awaiting further reinforcements, or that they believed that the British had landed a large force at Baku. If the latter was the reason, then it would only be a matter of time before they discovered the truth, alerted to it most likely by the 'enemy within' – their Muslim friends in Baku, from whom little could be concealed.

But if in Baku the picture looked gloomy, in the summer of 1918 elsewhere the war news was better than it had been for a long time. On the Western Front, General Ludendorff's great offensive, which had brought his troops to within thirty-seven miles of Paris, had been halted, and the sixty divisions he had thrown against the Allies hurled back. His master plan to break the long deadlock on the Western Front had rebounded catastrophically. August 8 – the day of the Allied counter-attack – proved to be the turning point of the war in Europe, and was subsequently described by Ludendorff as the German army's 'day of mourning'. During the following weeks the Allies were to win victory after victory, albeit at very heavy cost, as they broke through the German defences at many points. To the German troops, who had been assured that the Allies were on their last legs, the enemy's resources seemed inexhaustible and their advance unstoppable. Even the Kaiser was now secretly admitting that his dreams of world domination had been destroyed and that he had made a terrible miscalculation. Nevertheless, the war in Europe still had a further three months to run, although the outcome was becoming more certain every day. At the same time the news from the other main theatre of war, Palestine, looked equally encouraging. Amid reports of bitter rifts, even violence, between the Turks and their German advisers, General Allenby was preparing his forces for a massive drive northwards towards Damascus.

All this, though, was of little comfort to General Dunsterville and his meagre force as they prepared to face overwhelming Turkish odds on the barren heights around Baku. From there, 600 miles from the nearest British garrison at Baghdad, they saw virtually no prospect of their receiving any reinforcements, or of being relieved if they found themselves trapped. Nonetheless, as they grimly set about their task of preparing Baku's defence, they did find a few things to smile about. There was their first encounter with caviar, still

fairly plentiful in this Caspian port, which the troops nicknamed 'fish jam'. Then there was the curious affair of the
German military mission. Believing the city had already fallen
to the Turks, a small group of German staff officers arrived in
the harbour aboard a vessel from further up the coast and
asked to be taken to the Turkish headquarters. They had been
informed by their allies, it transpired, that they intended to
take Baku on a particular date, and had therefore set out from
Tiflis accordingly. Discovering their error too late, they were
arrested by a British subaltern armed with a revolver and
handed over to the Baku authorities.

Finally there was good news about Captain Noel, who had
long been feared dead. He now suddenly turned up in Baku,
with an extraordinary tale to tell, after finally being released
by his Jungali captors. They had been forced to come to terms
with the British following their resounding defeat by
Dunsterville's troops. It was agreed that Noel, who had been
kept in shackles lest he try to escape again, would be
exchanged for Jungali prisoners held by the British.
Embarrassed at having to return him in such poor physical
condition, Kuchuk Khan, the Jungali leader, gave orders that
he was to be given special rations to try to restore some of the
weight he had lost in his jungle prison. Only then was he to be
handed over. This created something of a problem, for Noel
was naturally of lean build, unlike most Persians, and therefore, in his captors' eyes, appeared to be making very slow
progress. 'Yet before I could hope for my release,' Noel wrote
later, 'I would have to reach the Persian standard of plump-
ness, which is very plump indeed.' Worried by Noel's seeming
lack of progress, Kuchuk Khan dispatched one of his lieutenants to investigate. Noel explained to him that, by and
large, the British were a skinny race, and eventually succeeded
in convincing him that 'all the feeding in the world would not
make a fat man of me'.

Two days later, on August 27, he was handed over to the
British at Resht, near Enzeli, 'still wearing the septic rags in
which I had lived for five months'. Despite his privations,
Noel immediately asked to be sent to join Dunsterville at
Baku, the scene of his earlier adventures with MacDonell,
where he thought his local knowledge might prove useful.

There was another motive, too: 'I was eager to make up for all my lost time, and to be in at the death.' In the bazaar at Resht he managed to find a high-necked Russian blouse, an embroidered belt to go round his waist, trousers and some long black leather boots. Finally, he bought a tall black felt hat. 'Next day', he wrote, 'I reached Baku, and looking like a Bolshevik commissar reported to General Dunsterville.' The dauntless Noel immediately put up a plan for a daring raid on the Turkish lines of communication in an area with which he was familiar. Dunsterville, who judged the venture 'extremely hazardous', nonetheless considered that it stood a fair chance of success, and agreed to let Noel have a go. But it called for careful planning and, fortunately for Noel perhaps, it was overtaken by events. Subsequently Noel was awarded a DSO for the various shadowy activities he had been engaged in during the war, an unusual distinction for a junior officer.

Nor was he the only young British intelligence officer to turn up in Baku determined not to miss out on the great drama about to unfold there. Another was Captain Teague-Jones, whom we left riding into Meshed to report to his chief, General Malleson, on the situation in Baku and Krasnovodsk, as well as the overthrow of the Bolsheviks in Ashkhabad. He had volunteered to return to Ashkhabad to find out more of what was going on there, and to try to ascertain the attitude of its new rulers towards the British. On reaching the town, dressed once again as a trader, he immediately made contact with the Ashkhabad Committee, as the new anti-Bolshevik authorities now called themselves. 'They looked exactly what they were, typical railway workers, dirty and unshaven and obviously very frightened,' Teague-Jones later wrote in his journal. 'Fate and circumstances had driven them to lead a revolution. The tyranny of the Bolshevik regime had driven them to desperation. They had risen and overthrown their late tyrants, and now were just beginning to realise that they were alone.' After questioning Teague-Jones about the strength of the British forces in northern Persia, they asked him anxiously whether they could hope for any help from Britain if the Bolsheviks sent troops against them from the Red Army garrison at Tashkent.

Explaining that he could not speak for his superiors in

London and Delhi, Teague-Jones promised to telegraph their plea to General Malleson at Meshed, who would undoubtedly seek the advice of his superiors. This he did, and discussions were to follow between Malleson and representatives of the Ashkhabad Committee. These, in turn, led to the dispatch to Transcaspia of a small force of British Indian troops from the East Persian Cordon. For with the Turks very likely to capture Baku, followed by the railhead at Krasnovodsk, India's defence chiefs were most anxious to keep the regions beyond in friendly hands, especially now that the Bolsheviks were viewed more and more in London as pawns in a German-inspired plot against the Allies, and therefore totally untrustworthy. Having thus set up contact between the anti-Bolshevik authorities in Ashkhabad and Malleson, Teague-Jones pressed on to Krasnovodsk, to find out what was going on there since the Bolsheviks' overthrow. Finally, he caught the ferry across to Baku, ostensibly to report to Malleson on the latest situation in the beleaguered town, but in fact because this was clearly the best possible place for any ambitious young officer to be. Very soon he found himself co-opted on to Dunsterville's staff, entrusted with setting up an intelligence unit, complete with a network of spies, having conveniently forgotten about Malleson.

Since their arrival, General Dunsterville and his staff had been frantically trying to reorganise the local Russian and Armenian units, and buttress their determination to resist the advancing Turks. They had been dismayed to find innumerable committees replacing the normal command structure. They also found that entire sections of the front would be left undefended while the soldiers attended political meetings or retired to the town to have afternoon tea with their womenfolk or families. Very few trenches had been dug, and when the defenders were urged to remedy this they replied: 'Why should we dig ourselves in? Only cowards do that. We want to fight!' Periodically, Dunsterville recounts, they would line up in a row and discharge their rifles in the air as though hoping to frighten the enemy. 'They frequently did this when there was no sign of an attack, and when the nearest Turk was behind cover some 3,000 yards away,' he added. Although fiercely anti-Bolshevik, the army was nonetheless a revolutionary one. Lacking a single effective leader, it was without discipline, laws, regulations or punishments. Orders could be obeyed or ignored at will.

While acknowledging that the hardy Armenian villagers living in the mountains of eastern Turkey had, and were still, resisting the enemy with great courage, Dunsterville bluntly accused their soft, town-dwelling cousins in Baku of cowardice. This cowardice, however, was understandable, Dunsterville added. 'He was not a soldier by instinct or training, but just an ill-fed, undersized factory hand. A rifle was pushed into his hand and he was told to go and fight. He had no equipment, no proper instructors, no decent officers and no regular arrangements for food supply. As he sat in the trenches with the bullets whistling by and the shells bursting overhead, he knew that most of his mates had skulked back to town and were having tea with the girls. So why shouldn't he go too?' Under such circumstances no troops on earth could be expected to display much valour, the general added.

On discovering the pitiful state of the city's defences and its supposed defenders, the Russian-speaking Dunsterville had immediately pressed the five-man Centro-Caspian Dictatorship to give him sole overall command of Baku's defence, but this was firmly refused. When he suggested that one of them should be chosen as their leader, they unanimously insisted that none of them felt able to shoulder such a responsibility. For their part, they expressed anger and disappointment at the size of the British force, claiming that they had been misled into expecting many more troops. Relations between Dunsterville and the five were thus strained from the very beginning, making co-operation more and more difficult as the days passed and the Turks fought their way closer.

But it was not only Baku's land defences which led to rifts between Dunsterville and the Dictatorship. His efforts to create a makeshift Caspian navy met with strong objections from the Dictators, who opposed any idea of a British naval presence in Russian waters. They proposed instead that the light naval guns which were already on their slow journey up from Baghdad should be mounted on their own vessels to replace the Russian-made ones which were now almost out of ammunition. With these they would then undertake to protect

Dunsterville's sea communications – his only ones – with Enzeli, and also, in the event of Baku falling, to prevent the Turks from reaching Krasnovodsk. However, with such totally unpredictable individuals in charge, there was no possibility of Dunsterville agreeing to this. As a result, his small naval staff only succeeded in acquiring two suitable vessels for conversion, in addition to the *Kruger* and the two others earmarked for evacuating the force in an emergency. Such was Dunsterville's frustration in the face of this unending obstruction that at times he was sorely tempted to overthrow the five and take control of the city.

And if that was not enough, he now encountered another irritation – the loss of his newly acquired intelligence officer, the truant Teague-Jones, whose services in organising a spy network were already proving invaluable to him. For if Teague-Jones had conveniently forgotten about General Malleson at Meshed, the general had certainly not forgotten about him. Very soon Malleson was demanding his return. At first the hard-pressed Dunsterville had turned a deaf ear to Malleson's entreaties. But what he did not realise was that Malleson, too, was facing a serious crisis, 500 miles to the east. For at that very moment Bolshevik troops from Tashkent were on their way by rail towards Ashkhabad, determined to restore Moscow's rule there by greatly superior force of arms. In response to desperate pleas by the rebel Ashkhabad Committee, an Indian Army machine-gun detachment, consisting of forty Punjabis led by a British officer, had been rushed to a spot near Merv, 200 miles east of Ashkhabad, where the Committee's own meagre forces were preparing to resist the Bolsheviks. A few well-directed bursts of machine-gun fire from the Punjabis, however, had scattered the astonished attackers. Though little more than a skirmish, this was the first time that British and Russian troops had fired on one another since the Crimean War.

Delhi, as we have already seen, was extremely anxious to keep Ashkhabad out of Bolshevik hands, and further detachments of British Indian troops from the East Persian Cordon were on their way to the Ashkhabad region to try to bolster the Committee's slender forces. Captain Teague-Jones's presence was therefore urgently needed in Ashkhabad so that he could report back to Malleson on developments there and co-ordinate military operations with the Committee. As a result of a sharp order from Delhi, Dunsterville was given no choice but to return him to Malleson's command. On August 24, disappointed at missing out on the coming struggle for Baku – not to mention being parted from an attractive young Russian girl he had just met – Teague-Jones left by ferry for Krasnovodsk, from where he caught the train once more to Ashkhabad.

*   *   *

Two days after Teague-Jones's departure, a 1,000-strong Turkish force, supported by artillery and cavalry, launched a determined assault on the weakest sector of Baku's defences. Their aim, it was clear to the British, was not to try to take the city, but to tighten their stranglehold on it in preparation for the final assault. Because of the extreme unreliability of the Baku volunteers, the key points on this part of the front were now permanently manned by British troops, in this case by a company of the North Staffordshire Regiment. For most of that day they succeeded in holding off the advancing Turks with rifle and machine-gun fire as they waited in vain for the Armenian reinforcements which had been ordered up. Four successive waves of attackers were thus driven back, but there was still no sign of the Armenians who were to have harried the enemy's flanks. 'The local troops stuck to their usual role of interested spectators,' wrote Dunsterville bitterly.

A desperate attempt was now made to rush British troops to the spot instead, but they arrived too late to save the Staffordshires' positions from being overrun. The losses were very severe. Dunsterville was informed that night that only about half a dozen men had succeeded in getting back. The company had lost every one of its officers, and eighty men. The Turks had achieved their objective, forcing Dunsterville to establish a fresh line of defence even closer to the town. 'But had the attack fallen on local troops,' he wrote, 'there would have been nothing to check the Turkish advance into the heart of the town. The splendid gallantry of this company of the North Staffords saved Baku on this occasion.'

By now the Turks had brought up more artillery and had begun to bombard the city centre. Here stood the Hôtel

d'Europe, which the British had commandeered as their headquarters, and it soon became clear that this had been singled
out for special attention. Shells were also falling around the
Kruger in the nearby harbour. 'The shelling of my ship, the
Hôtel d'Europe and the town generally was now becoming so
accurate that I could only believe that the enemy had a direct
telephone line from the town, with an operator within a hundred yards of myself,' recalled the general. But an intensive
search of the area failed to uncover anything. Finally the hotel
was so badly damaged that Dunsterville had to move his headquarters to another hotel. This, too, was soon reduced to little
more than rubble, forcing the British to move once more.
Their suspicions that there was a spy in their midst subsequently proved to have been justified. Shortly after the war
was over MacDonell was greeted by a Turkish colonel who
asked him whether he remembered the red-bearded Tartar
who sold the British fodder for their mules. MacDonell
replied that he remembered him clearly. 'Well,' said the
colonel with a smile, 'that red-bearded old Tartar was me.'

A second major Turkish attack was launched on August 31,
five days after the first. Under cover of darkness they had
managed to drag a dozen machine-guns to within 500 yards of
a British hill-top position. This was held by another company
of the North Staffordshire Regiment, some eighty men in all,
for it had been judged an obvious target for the Turks. The
Turkish machine-guns, protected by bullet-proof shields, had
been skilfully positioned so that they could rake the British
entrenchments from the side. But they too were vulnerable to
attack from the flank or from behind, and troops from the
Baku garrison were immediately ordered up to the front to
help deal with them. Meanwhile, a murderous fire was being
directed by the Turks against the defenders, killing the subaltern commanding the company among others. When it
became clear that once again the Baku troops had no intention
of coming to the assistance of their British comrades, the order
was given to the latter to withdraw in order to save them from
annihilation. Shortly afterwards another British unit, this
time a company of the Royal Warwickshire Regiment, had to
be hastily withdrawn in the face of an overwhelming enemy
when Armenian troops supposedly protecting its flank sud-

denly melted away. As a result, Baku's already dangerously overstretched line of defence had once more to be shortened and redrawn still closer to the city. It was now painfully clear to Dunsterville and his staff that unless the 10,000 troops of the Baku garrison could be persuaded to fight alongside their 1,000 British comrades, the city was doomed, and with it Dunsterforce.

The general, who had personally watched the Baku soldiery – 'with their backs towards the enemy' – heading rapidly away from the front line, decided to give the Baku authorities one last chance of getting a grip on their men. Otherwise he knew that he would have no choice but to try to evacuate his own troops by sea and recommend to the Dictators that they surrender the city to the Turks in the hope of thus preventing any further bloodshed. Already panic was setting in among the civilian population. Vessels crowded with Armenian and other refugees, terrified by the Turkish bombardment, were leaving Baku for Krasnovodsk to escape the fury which they knew would be unleashed if the city fell. They were only too aware that the massacre of the Baku Muslims five months earlier had still to be paid for in blood.

That evening Dunsterville wrote an urgent letter to the Dictators describing what he had seen with his own eyes of their soldiers' cowardice, and pointing out the futility of attempting to defend Baku, 'with troops who have no intention of fighting'. By return he received an invitation to attend an emergency meeting of Baku's Council of War that same evening. 'The entire room was filled with members of the various committees,' he wrote afterwards. Apart from the Dictators and their military advisers, there were the Armenian National Council of Baku, workers' delegates, soldiers' delegates, sailors' delegates and peasant deputies. Each had a different plan for the city's salvation, their representatives expounding these at great length. Each, in Dunsterville's view, was equally futile. One sailor spoke for a full hour, repeatedly declaring that they would all fight to 'the very last drop' of their blood. It was perfectly clear to Dunsterville and his staff that this was simply rhetoric, and that nothing would change. At 1 a.m. they finally departed in despair, 'leaving the assembly to continue their futile discussions'.

By now, short of some miraculous and unexpected development, Dunsterville had made up his mind to evacuate his
force at the earliest possible opportunity, before the Turks
broke through the remaining defences and swept into the city.
Already reports were reaching him of heavy Turkish reinforcements hastening towards Baku, and of other units being
diverted to sever the Baghdad-to-Enzeli road, thereby cutting
his lines of supply and communication, and preventing British
reinforcements, had there been any, from reaching him. Amid
the greatest secrecy, his staff officers immediately set to work
on a plan for the evacuation of the entire British force by sea.
While these preparations were afoot, the British troops continued to man the weakest sectors of the front, as though
nothing was amiss. At the same time it was clear that the
Turks were building up their forces for the final push which
would deliver Baku to them, and which everyone knew could
not now be far off.

Then, quite unexpectedly, a monumental piece of luck came
Dunsterville's way. It was provided by an Arab officer (one
account says an Armenian) serving with the Turkish army,
who deserted and secretly crossed over to the British lines. He
brought with him the precise date when the Turks planned to
launch their all-out onslaught against Baku. He told
Dunsterville's intelligence officers that the attack was scheduled for the early hours of September 14, in just two days'
time. But he was not able to tell them whereabouts on the
fourteen-mile-long defensive line it would be delivered.
Normally such vital intelligence arriving in this manner would
have been treated with the utmost suspicion, even bearing in
mind that neither Arabs nor Armenians had any reason to love
the Turks. However, this particular officer, as it happened,
was known personally to one of the Dictators, who vouched
for his absolute trustworthiness. His information, Dunsterville wrote, was invaluable 'as it enabled us to have all our
troops on the ground', even if they had to guess where the
attack would fall.

The Turkish onslaught began, as the deserter had forecast,
in the pre-dawn darkness of September 14. First came a heavy
artillery barrage, which was followed by an advance by massed
infantry, some eight to ten battalions in all, against defensive

positions around a gash in the hills colourfully known as Wolf's Gap. Because of their commanding situation, these should have constituted the most easily defended sector of the city's defences. Yet within an hour or two the Baku forces holding them had been driven out by the Turks. 'They were now actually in possession of the heights immediately above the town, within hundreds of yards of its outskirts,' wrote Dunsterville. 'It was incredible that this strongest portion of the whole line should so easily have fallen to the enemy, especially when all troops had been warned of the impending attack.' Any further advance by the Turks into the town was now halted, for the time being anyway, by Dunsterville's own men. However, they lacked the numbers necessary to drive the Turks off the heights, and it would only be a matter of hours, Dunsterville knew, before the enemy had manhandled their artillery up there. 'And once they were there,' he wrote, 'the harbour lay at their mercy.' It was crucial, therefore, that the British evacuation should be completed before this happened, lest the vessels packed with troops and wounded become sitting targets for the Turkish gunners.

Detailed plans for the great escape had already been issued to company commanders and other officers. Only the final go-ahead from Dunsterville was now needed to set the whole operation in motion. But beyond ordering the vessels being used in the evacuation to stand by, even at this late stage he stayed his hand. He still hoped that the Baku forces might be persuaded to save themselves from almost certain massacre by launching a counter-attack and driving the Turks from the vital heights around Wolf's Gap. It would have taken very little, he wrote later, to repulse an enemy 'who had been kept at bay for twelve hours after gaining the key position'. Any such hopes were quickly extinguished as word reached him that all attempts to rally the Baku troops had failed. Now, if his own men were not to be annihilated as well, he knew that they must leave the doomed city immediately. Otherwise Baku would become another Kut, whose fate cannot have been far from his thoughts as he summoned his staff together for the last time. Indeed, although he did not know it, rumours were beginning to circulate in London that all was lost, and that Baku had already fallen to the Turks.

Shortly before 5 p.m. Dunsterville gave the order to evacuate the town. It was a carefully phased operation, carried out under cover of darkness in the hope that the enemy would not realise what was happening until it was too late. The strictest secrecy had also to be maintained for another reason. 'When the news of our intended withdrawal spread round the town,' wrote Dunsterville, 'the entire population would regard us as enemies, and my troops would have to fight their way through the streets to the ships.' He also feared that the Dictators would order their naval vessels to fire on them as they sailed away, although in the dark they would be less vulnerable. To guard against his men being attacked by a mob on their way through the town, he ordered armed pickets to be placed, as unostentatiously as possible, on street corners, while all entrances to the harbour were to be strongly defended.

The withdrawal of troops from the front line was to begin at 8 p.m. It would start with the Warwicks and the Worcesters on the right. Their retirement would be covered by the Staffords on the left, who would have to remain in position for a further hour until the others were safely aboard. Meanwhile, the sick and wounded were being carried on board two small vessels, the *Kurst* and the *Abo*, which had been turned into makeshift hospital ships. They would sail away into the darkness, hopefully unnoticed, when the last of the casualties from the clearing stations were safely aboard. The dead and the missing would have to be left behind, the former where they had been buried by their comrades. Last to leave would be the 1,200-ton *Kruger*, which was to carry the bulk of the troops, and a fourth vessel, the 200-ton *Armenian*, which was earmarked to serve as a floating ammunition dump, carrying away as much of their unspent arsenal as could be saved. One direct hit by a shell on this, it need hardly be said, would be enough to flatten most of the town, and very likely blow the *Kruger* out of the water too.

By a stroke of good fortune, just as the sun set, a sudden lull descended over the battlefield. After fourteen hours of continuous fighting, both sides were utterly exhausted. Not only did this greatly facilitate the stealthy withdrawal of Dunsterville's troops from the front line, but it also meant that there were no last-minute casualties to be carried down to the harbour in the darkness. The *Kurst* and the *Abo* were thus now able to set sail for Enzeli. 'Their instructions', wrote Dunsterville, 'were to offer no resistance to any serious opposition, to comply with all orders in case of a meeting with the fleet, and to explain that the steamers held sick and wounded only.' In the event, both vessels got clear of Baku without attracting any undue suspicions, reaching Enzeli the following day.

By 10 p.m. the withdrawal from the front had been completed without either the Turks or the Baku authorities getting wind of it. But then, just as the last of the British troops were safely aboard, word began to spread quickly through the town that they were leaving. The first that Dunsterville knew of this was when a mounted soldier of the Baku forces galloped up to the entrance to the wharf where the *Kruger* was berthed and demanded to know what was going on. 'Why are you deserting us?' he shouted angrily. 'Stop these movements immediately.' Then, turning his horse round, he raced off to raise the alarm. Moments later two of the Dictators arrived and breathlessly demanded to see Dunsterville. They warned him that any attempt to withdraw his troops would be regarded as treachery and would be punished accordingly. Unable to see Dunsterville's men, who by now were out of sight below decks or shielded by the darkness, they then told him: 'If you have removed any of your troops from the firing line, you are to send them back to their original positions at once.'

Dunsterville reminded them that he had warned them earlier that unless their own troops were prepared to offer effective resistance he would have no choice but to evacuate his men, who had never in the first place been sent to defend Baku but rather to help them to defend their own city. 'My troops', he told them, 'have sustained the fight throughout the day for sixteen hours without relief, or any real support from your troops, who have done little of the fighting. Under such circumstances I refuse to sacrifice any more of their lives in a vain cause.' As for returning them to the front, he added, 'I will give no such order. I sail at once.' Furious at this, one of the Dictators told him: 'Then our fleet will open fire on you and sink your ships.'

He and his companion now turned on their heels and made for the gangway. One of the general's staff whispered to him:

'Why not arrest them and take them along too?' But Dunsterville was opposed to hostage-taking, and instead gave orders for the *Kruger* and the ammunition ship *Armenian* to weigh anchor. He knew that it would take the Dictators time to agree among themselves what action to take, and then to get orders to the fleet, some of whose crews had become very friendly towards the British troops who had tried so hard to help them. Furthermore, the two vessels would be leaving with all lights out, while the gunboats had no searchlights since these had been commandeered for use on the front. Given a good start, the *Kruger* and the *Armenian* would be quite difficult to find and fire at with accuracy in the dark.

By 11 p.m. everything was ready, and Commodore David Norris, the senior British naval officer, gave orders to cast off. Their main concern was the guardship, which they could not avoid sailing past. They could only hold their breath and pray that those on watch would not spot them in the darkness as they slipped stealthily away. 'All went well', Dunsterville wrote, 'until the critical moment when we were right opposite the guardship, creeping along behind a row of barges at anchor.' Then, to everyone's utter horror, all the *Kruger*'s lights suddenly came on. In his memoirs Dunsterville was to blame it on 'an ill-wisher among the crew', although they never discovered the culprit. Immediately, a demand was signalled to the *Kruger* from the guardship's bridge. 'Who are you? Anchor at once,' it ordered. Ignoring this, Norris now headed for the open sea at full steam. The guardship opened fire, but the shells fell short. Very soon the *Kruger* was safely out of range, and Norris knew that their speed was sufficient for them not to fear pursuit by the antiquated Russian gunboats.

But their secret was now out, and somewhere in the darkness behind them, still to run the gauntlet, was the *Armenian*, the floating bomb, which appeared to have been held up for some reason. She was commanded by Colonel Alfred Rawlinson, who had volunteered for this hazardous task. His father, Sir Henry Rawlinson, had been one of the leading players in the Great Game, and he had inherited his taste for risky exploits. With the guardship now fully alerted to what was happening, Dunsterville could only fear the worst for

Rawlinson and his small crew. Any moment he expected to hear a huge explosion as a shell landed among the ammunition they were carrying. But the guardship was not Rawlinson's only worry. At the last minute it had transpired that the vessel's captain and crew were strongly opposed to sailing and to the prospect of being blown to pieces. As they were about to sail, a representative of the Dictators arrived at the dockside and forbade them to leave. Less scrupulous than Dunsterville, Rawlinson solved this problem by locking the man in a cabin under armed guard. But as a result of the delay, the *Armenian* did not sail until half an hour after the *Kruger*, and only then with Rawlinson's service revolver pressed to the captain's head. As they raced for the open sea, they were challenged and then fired on by the guardship. Miraculously, though, none of the shells landed among the high explosives and ammunition, or below the water-line.

The following day the *Kruger* sailed into Enzeli to find the *Kurst* and the *Abo* already there. Of the *Armenian* there was no sign. Nor had anything been seen of her from the bridge of the *Kruger* as she sailed south from Baku. Fears for her safety now deepened. 'As the hours slipped by,' wrote Dunsterville, 'I despaired of her ever being seen again.' Then suddenly, just twelve hours after the *Kruger*'s arrival, smoke was spotted on the horizon. To everyone's relief, it was the missing ammunition ship. She had taken six direct hits from shells, yet had remained afloat. Rawlinson was greatly moved by the reception they received from Dunsterville's troops. 'As they saw the ship which they had all given up for lost coming in, and saw her battered condition and the little Union Jack flying proudly over all, they rose up with one accord and gave us a truly British reception,' he wrote. Dunsterville, still in his pyjamas, greeted Rawlinson at the top of the *Kruger*'s gangway like someone returned from the dead. Seizing him by both hands, he kept repeating: 'You have done very well!' Then he led Rawlinson down to his cabin where, despite the early hour, he poured out a large whisky and soda and thrust it into the colonel's hand.

Although the sacrifices made by Dunsterville's men had achieved little beyond delaying Baku's fall, the evacuation had been accomplished without the loss of a single British life.

During the actual fighting, however, casualties had amounted to 180 killed, missing or wounded – nearly 20 per cent of the original force. After the war, during a brief reoccupation of Baku by the British, a small war cemetery was built on the heights near Wolf's Gap for those who had been buried by their comrades during the fighting. When the city subsequently fell into the hands of the Bolsheviks, not surprisingly this disappeared, and today no traces of it remain – or not that I was able to discover. The names of Dunsterville's dead, though, are commemorated on a plaque in the British war cemetery overlooking the Bosphorus in Istanbul.

Soviet historians, even as recently as 1987, were to accuse the British of deliberately leaving Baku's defenders in the lurch for their own post-war ends. By allowing the Turks to do their own dirty work in destroying the troublesome local forces, and knowing that the war had not long to run, the British thus paved the way for their proposed seizure of the region, and particularly its oil. The British themselves certainly did not see it that way, for at that moment the war seemed anything but over. In London and Delhi much recrimination followed the evacuation, and the resulting loss of face for the British in the region. A scapegoat was found in Dunsterville, who was removed from his command at Enzeli and replaced by another general.

Dunsterville's men, as it happened, were not the only ones who managed to get away from Baku before it fell to the Turks. Over 8,000 local troops and others also fled the town in an armada of little ships, mostly to Astrakhan or Krasnovodsk, depending on their politics. For while the former was firmly in Bolshevik hands, the latter was still controlled by their rivals for power, the Ashkhabad Committee. Among the escapees, who included the five Dictators and their entourages, was another small but significant group. This consisted of Baku's former Bolshevik rulers – Stepan Shaumian and other leading members of the Baku Soviet. Ever since their arrest at sea by the Dictators' gunboats, they had been languishing in Baku's main gaol awaiting trial. They knew very well, however, that were they to fall into Turkish hands they would suffer a far worse fate than any meted out to them by the Dictators. For the Turks and their local Tartar allies held them personally responsible for unleashing the wrath of the Armenians against the city's Muslims during the massacres.

At the very last moment, just as the British were leaving, influential friends in Baku managed to secure their release to save them from the coming bloodbath. They were hurriedly found passages aboard a crowded refugee boat, the *Turkman*, bound for Astrakhan, where they knew they would be safe. At least that is where the twenty-six Baku commissars believed themselves to be bound when their vessel left the doomed city on that fateful night.

23

'Streets Running with Blood'

Considerable mystery will always surround the last days of the Baku commissars. All the witnesses to these events are long dead – many of them through violence of one kind or another – and no two accounts are the same. It will never be known, for example, why the *Turkman* suddenly altered course after leaving Baku on the night of September 14 and made for Krasnovodsk. According to one version the crew got cold feet about visiting Astrakhan and prevailed upon the captain to sail to Krasnovodsk instead. Another maintains that the vessel was found to have insufficient fuel to reach the Bolshevik stronghold, but enough to get to Krasnovodsk, which was considerably closer. According to Teague-Jones it was the ship's captain himself who decided to make for Krasnovodsk when he learned that the Bolsheviks were on board, and that he deliberately betrayed them to their foes. Again some accounts say that the commissars were armed, while others deny this.

Soviet historians have always insisted that it was British agents who secretly arranged for the *Turkman* to be diverted to Krasnovodsk, knowing very well what would befall Shaumian and his fellow commissars there. Inadvertently, in their subsequent accounts of the British evacuation, both MacDonell and Dunsterville were to provide the Soviets with fuel for their allegations, although this falls far short of any real evidence. MacDonell's disclosure that shortly before he left for Enzeli he went aboard the *Turkman* and 'split a bottle of sweet champagne with Shaumian and his companions' is seen as highly suspicious. In fact, MacDonell tells us, he was sternly reprimanded for this by Dunsterville, who pointed out to him that he might have been seized by the Bolsheviks and carried off to Astrakhan as a hostage. This, needless to say, was ignored by the Soviet researchers, as was MacDonell's assertion that he was present when Dunsterville gave orders that the commissars were to be delivered to Astrakhan 'as he wanted no truck with their political intrigues'.

What they seized upon most eagerly, though, was the general's disclosure that two of his men – a major and a sergeant – were among the mass of refugees aboard the *Turkman* when it left Baku. According to Dunsterville they had been accidentally left behind in the turmoil of the evacuation, but had managed to scramble aboard the *Turkman* at the very last minute, and so escape. To the Soviets, however, it was quite obvious that the two men had deliberately been infiltrated on board the vessel where they had conspired with the captain to deliver the commissars to Krasnovodsk. In view of the extreme risks involved for the two soldiers were the venture to go wrong, and they wound up in Bolshevik hands in Astrakhan, it seems highly unlikely that Dunsterville would have countenanced such a scheme. There were, after all, easier ways of removing the commissars from circulation, if only by ensuring that they remained behind in Baku, to be dealt with by the Turks and their Tartar allies.

Whatever the reason for the *Turkman*'s change of course, Shaumian and his colleagues awoke the following morning to find that they had jumped from the frying pan into the fire. For men who had just escaped from one set of enemies, not to mention from the wrath of the Turks, it must have been chilling to discover that they were now anchored off the town of Krasnovodsk, where the Bolsheviks had earned themselves an evil reputation during their brief rule there. At first their presence attracted little attention, for ships arriving from Baku crowded with refugees were a daily occurrence. It was only when the captain began to sound his siren in an agitated manner that the authorities realised that something unusual was afoot. The guardship was immediately sent out to investigate, and word that the commissars were on board quickly communicated to the town commandant, a tough Cossack officer named Kuhn. The *Turkman* was directed to a wharf where armed troops awaited her. Shaumian and his colleagues were arrested and marched into the town. There they were unceremoniously thrown into a makeshift prison – the town gaol being already overflowing – behind the small courthouse.

Commandant Kuhn now telegraphed his superiors in Ashkhabad to ask what should be done with the prisoners. For, although they were unarmed, they were obviously dangerous individuals to have around in an isolated town where no one could be trusted. There was a serious risk, he pointed out, of these experienced revolutionaries rallying support for a counter-coup in Krasnovodsk, the effects of which might spread rapidly eastwards along the railway to Ashkhabad, the anti-Bolshevik capital. News of Shaumian's arrival, together with his colleagues, on Transcaspian territory was to cause considerable alarm in Ashkhabad. Feeling anything but secure themselves, the authorities there, now grandly styling themselves the Transcaspian Government, were no keener than Kuhn to have these dangerous men in their midst. Telegrams concerning their future, and ultimately their fate, began to fly back and forth between Ashkhabad and Krasnovodsk. Very soon General Malleson at Meshed and his superiors in India found themselves drawn into the anguished affair of the twenty-six Baku commissars. But for one of Malleson's officers their arrest by Commandant Kuhn was to have the most bizarre and far-reaching consequences. This was Captain Reginald Teague-Jones, who had left Baku shortly before its fall on September 15 because Malleson needed his services at Ashkhabad. Malleson had just signed an agreement with Transcaspia's new rulers recognising 'the common danger from Bolshevism and a Turco-German invasion' and promising British military support against the Bolshevik force advancing from Tashkent. In return, the British were to be allowed to send a small force to Krasnovodsk to defend the railhead against a Turkish landing.

It was on disembarking from the ferry at Krasnovodsk that Teague-Jones had first learned that fighting had broken out between British Indian troops and the Tashkent Bolsheviks at Kaahka, eighty miles east of Ashkhabad. He decided to proceed there at once, feeling that Malleson's need for his presence in Ashkhabad had been overtaken by events, and also being most anxious this time not to miss out on the action, as he had at Baku. 'If the situation at the front was as serious as it appeared to be, then there would be urgent need of every man and certainly every officer we could get,' he wrote. He caught the next train, hoping that he would be able to pick up the latest news of the fighting at stations along the way. When eventually he reached Kaahka, which consisted of a railway station and a village, he found 500 men of the 16th Punjabis sent by Malleson and commanded by Colonel Denis Knollys. They formed part of a polyglot army of anti-Bolshevik troops from Ashkhabad comprising 100 Russians, 800 Armenians and a large number of Turcoman horsemen. The latter, for all their colourful appearance, were in the words of Colonel Knollys, 'utterly undependable . . . and of no use in attack or defence', coming and going as they pleased, and taking orders from no one.

For their part, the enemy consisted largely of Russian Bolshevik troops, but with a stiffening of ex-POWs, mainly Austro-Hungarians, from the camps around Tashkent. Although they had little or no ideological interest in Bolshevism, the latter had been promised that they would be free to go home once they had driven out the British and crushed the counter-revolutionaries. As the only alternative appeared to be to starve to death in Central Asia, they had agreed to fight. Being trained soldiers, they were to prove a formidable foe in the struggle which was to follow for control of Transcaspia. Indeed, without them the Bolshevik army, like the Ashkhabad contingent, would have been little more than a revolutionary rabble.

When the Bolsheviks launched a surprise attack against the Ashkhabad forces, the Turcomans were the first to flee the stronghold they were supposed to be defending, leaving the other positions highly exposed. Seeing this, other units of the Ashkhabad force also withdrew, leaving the Punjabis to defend Kaahka more or less single-handed. In the face of heavy rifle and machine-gun fire from the Indian positions, the enemy pressed on towards the railway station and the village. By now the situation was looking pretty desperate, for the defenders were without barbed wire to slow the

Bolsheviks' advance. But the day was saved at the last minute
by a company of Punjabi infantry, which Knollys had been
holding in reserve. As the Bolshevik troops approached the
station, the Punjabis suddenly charged them with fixed bayonets. 'Completely taken aback by this unprecedented form of
warfare,' wrote Knollys, 'the enemy immediately started to
retire.' This proved to be the turning point of the battle, for
the Bolsheviks were unwilling to face the Punjabis' bloodstained bayonets again. Although the fighting continued
throughout the day, Kaahka was saved. The enemy, who had
suffered many casualties, could now see that they were not
strong enough to take the town from its determined and well-
trained defenders. Knollys and his Punjabis knew, moreover,
that a company of the Hampshires, a battery of artillery and
an Indian cavalry unit were due to arrive very shortly from
Meshed.

The battle for Kaahka had not been without its bizarre
moments, however. At one point it was thought that the Bolsheviks had had enough and wished to surrender. 'Adopting a
common form of Bolshevik tactics, they put down their arms
and made a show of wanting to come to terms,' wrote Teague-
Jones. But when two emissaries were sent across it transpired
that they were, in fact, calling upon the Ashkhabad troops to
surrender. They declared that the Russians should not fight
against their brothers, and insisted that they had no quarrel
with the Indians, whom they would treat generously if they
agreed to lay down their arms and give themselves up. The
offer was contemptuously turned down, and the fighting
quickly erupted again when someone accidentally discharged
his rifle, sending everybody scurrying for cover.

It was during this action that Teague-Jones had the misfortune to be hit by a stray machine-gun bullet. The wound was
in the groin, making it impossible for him to walk. After he
had been treated by the British medical officer he was put on a
train with forty other casualties and evacuated to Ashkhabad,
where there was a small hospital originally intended for sick
and injured railway workers. It was now run along revolutionary (albeit not Bolshevik) lines, no distinction being made
between officers and men, Europeans and Indians, Muslims
and Hindus. Nonetheless, Teague-Jones's bed was placed

next to that of a badly wounded young British subaltern who spoke no Russian so that he could interpret for him. This officer had been shot in the back – deliberately, Teague-Jones was convinced, by a secret Bolshevik sympathiser among the Ashkhabad troops – and two days later he died. 'He went out of this world', Teague-Jones recalled sadly, 'in as brave a manner as anyone could wish'.

Teague-Jones himself was more fortunate, and was nursed back to health by the devoted Russian medical staff. Within ten days he was back on his feet, hobbling around on crutches. It was while he was here that word came through of the fall of Baku and the slaughter which had followed. When the Turks learned from their spies in the city that the British had suddenly evacuated the town, they deliberately held back before entering. This was to allow the local Tartar irregulars to avenge themselves on the Armenian population for their earlier massacre of Baku's Muslims. For two terrible nights they were allowed to rape, loot and kill. 'The horrors of St Bartholomew's night', wrote one Armenian who survived, 'were nothing in comparison with the murders at Baku on September 15 and 16. In some spots there were mountains of dead. One whole street was littered with the bodies of children no older than nine or ten. Many had been killed with swords or bayonets, or had their throats cut.' Even the hardened Turks, he added, were sickened by what they found when they finally entered the town, putting an immediate stop to the slaughter and shooting or hanging some of the perpetrators.

While Armenian estimates put the number of victims at nearly 9,000, the Soviet newspaper *Izvestia*, and Wilhelm Litten, a German intelligence officer, both suggest a considerably higher figure, the latter claiming it to be somewhere between 20,000 and 30,000. However, such wildly differing figures may be partly explained by the last-minute exodus of large numbers of Armenians and others by sea, many of whom never returned. Whatever the truth, the slaughter was to add to the city's long history of intercommunal bloodletting. 'When one speaks of the streets of a town running with blood,' a British political officer observed, 'one is generally employing a figure of speech. But if one is referring to Baku between 1917 and 1919, one is being starkly literal.'

As we are already aware, Shaumian and the other Baku commissars, most of whom were either Armenians or Christians of some other kind, were among those more fortunate ones who had escaped the fury of the Muslims. Although now crammed into a fetid communal cell at Krasnovodsk, without proper sanitation or bedding, they were at least still alive. However, to try to discover what next befell them is to enter a labyrinth of lies, evasion, missing telegrams, buck-passing and propaganda which has effectively obscured the truth ever since. For reasons which will become clear, all those who found themselves caught up in the affair were extremely keen to wash their hands of any responsibility or involvement.

By now their Cossack captor, Commandant Kuhn, was becoming more and more anxious to get rid of these revolutionary firebrands as soon as possible, preferably to the authorities in Ashkhabad. Already his two small gaols were overflowing with Bolsheviks and other prisoners, and he feared that the commissars might escape, or even be rescued, with most unpleasant consequences for himself. However, for similar reasons, his superiors in Ashkhabad were no more keen than he was to hold these dangerous individuals. There appeared to be only two possible solutions. One was to try to persuade the British – namely General Malleson at Meshed – to take them over, and arrange their dispatch, under armed escort, to India, where they would be no trouble to anyone. The other solution was to shoot them. Certainly few people in Transcaspia would shed any tears, for during the Bolsheviks' brief reign there they had earned an evil name for brutality. On the other hand, if by mischance they were somehow to come out on top again, the retribution would indeed be terrible for those who had martyred their heroes. It might therefore be wiser to try in the first place to get the British to take them off their hands.

Ashkhabad's newly appointed representative in Meshed was accordingly instructed by telegraph to arrange an immediate meeting with General Malleson to discuss the matter. From the British archives of the time it appears that Malleson agreed to accept responsibility for the twenty-six commissars. He had already learned of their presence in Krasnovodsk from Teague-Jones, who was by now sufficiently mobile to be back at work. On September 18, Malleson telegraphed as follows to the Chief of the General Staff in India: 'Ashkhabad government is being asked to hand over the above-mentioned leaders to me for dispatch to India as their presence in Transcaspia is most dangerous at present time when probably fully half Russians are preparing to turn their coats once more at the slightest sign of enemy success.' For this reason – according to Colonel C. H. Ellis, an Australian officer on his staff at Meshed – Malleson had made one stipulation with the Ashkhabad representative. In no circumstances must the commissars be allowed to travel from Krasnovodsk by the Transcaspian railway, since this had frequently been the scene of revolts and counter-revolts, both pro- and anti-Bolshevik. Some other means, or route, would have to be found for transferring the prisoners into Malleson's custody, the most obvious one being by sea to Enzeli and thence overland to Meshed for eventual removal to India.

Apart from wanting to extricate the Bolshevik firebrands from this highly volatile region before they could cause any mischief there, Malleson had another pressing reason for wishing to get his hands on Shaumian and his companions. Not long before, it may be recalled, a small British mission led by Colonel F. M. Bailey had been sent to Tashkent, the Bolshevik headquarters in Central Asia, via Kashgar. Their task was to ascertain Lenin's intentions towards British India, and also to endeavour to frustrate rumoured German schemes to mobilize a makeshift army of ex-POWs against northern India. However, following the mission's arrival there in August, relations between London and Moscow had sharply deteriorated. Since then nothing had been heard from Bailey, giving rise to fears that he and his party were being held by the local Bolsheviks. If this proved to be so, then Shaumian and his fellow revolutionaries would make valuable hostages who could be exchanged for the mission members and any other Britons unfortunate enough to fall into Bolshevik hands.

It is at this point that the waters begin to get muddier and muddier, as the several different accounts of what happened at Meshed, Ashkhabad and Krasnovodsk over the next forty-eight hours increasingly diverge. But even though the truth may never be known, in view of what was about to happen, and the long-lasting damage this would cause to Anglo-Soviet relations, these divergences need to be examined. Both Malleson and Ellis, in their subsequent accounts of their meeting with the Ashkhabad representative, suggest that far from having to be pressured by him into taking over the Baku commissars, they had in fact made most of the going. Indeed, according to them, after agreeing to telegraph Malleson's proposal to his superiors in Ashkhabad, their visitor had added ominously: 'If it is not already too late . . . ' Asked what he meant by this, he said he feared that Ashkhabad might already have decided what to do with the prisoners. Malleson immediately signalled Teague-Jones to alert him and urge him to discover precisely what was going on. That same day – it was still September 18 – Teague-Jones telegraphed to report that an emergency meeting of the Ashkhabad government was to be held that evening to consider the commissars' fate, adding that it was not clear what they proposed doing with them.

All this, of course, shows the British – not to mention Malleson and Ellis – in a favourable light. However, there exists another, quite different, version of what happened at Malleson's headquarters. Nearly half a century later, when the mysterious affair briefly resurfaced, another witness came forward with his recollections of what took place on that fateful day. On March 4, 1956, Colonel William Nash, who had served as a captain on Malleson's staff, wrote to *The Observer* declaring that 'to the best of my recollection' the Ashkhabad authorities had approached the general seeking his advice as to what should be done with the commissars. Their request, Nash said, came in the form of a telegram which he personally took to Malleson – 'at that time in bed with a severe attack of malaria' – to ask him what reply he should send. 'He told me', wrote Nash, 'that it was essentially a matter for the Russian authorities, and that he did not see his way to interfere. I therefore had a telegram put into Russian to the effect that they must dispose of the commissars as they thought fit.'

Nash's recollection of events is partially corroborated by Captain Teague-Jones in his posthumously published journal, which only came to light on his death in 1988. According to this, the Ashkhabad authorities sent a telegram to their representative in Meshed 'with instructions to try to persuade

General Malleson to take over the prisoners and deport them to India'. In his reply, Teague-Jones recounts, the general explained that 'it was very difficult to find the necessary guards to send them down to India, and suggested that the Transcaspian authorities should find some other way of disposing of them.' It is not clear from Teague-Jones's journal whether he actually saw these telegrams, or was merely told of their contents, truthfully or otherwise, by the Ashkhabad authorities, as he was subsequently to claim. But although the journal was never intended for publication, it was nonetheless written at around the time of these events, and presumably represented what he himself then believed. Later, however, after comparing notes with Malleson and Ellis over what happened at their end, he was to fall in line with their version. Indeed, were it not for Nash's very different account of what took place at Meshed, one might simply think that Teague-Jones had genuinely changed his view, but had not bothered to amend his journal. As it is, one is forced to conclude that someone somewhere is being economical with the truth, for Malleson and Nash cannot both have been right. Even so, this was nothing compared to the liberties which the Bolsheviks were to take with the facts, as we shall see.

*   *   *

Meanwhile, in their hot and overcrowded prison cell, Shaumian and his companions appear not to have realised the grave peril they were in as, 300 miles away to the east at Ashkhabad, their fate was about to be decided by their rivals for power. They were confident that eventually they would be exchanged for hostages held by their Bolshevik colleagues in Astrakhan, Moscow and elsewhere. But they appear to have been naïvely unaware of the violent hatred which their fellow Bolsheviks in Transcaspia had engendered in people there, or of the sanguinary turn that the worsening civil war was beginning to take throughout the country. Had they read the Ashkhabad newspaper, the *Voice of Central Asia*, on the morning after their capture, they might have been rather less optimistic about their prospects. 'Yesterday,' it reported, 'the Baku Bolshevik commissars, among them Stepan Shaumian, were arrested.' It then warned: 'We shall not stop at execution and torture. We shall thus be avenged for the thousands of our comrades languishing in Bolshevik torture chambers.' Quite what they were threatening is not clear, but what was now certain was that the Baku commissars were about to be held to account – *in absentia*, in a smoke-filled room in Ashkhabad – for the misdeeds of their comrades elsewhere.

Among the leaders of the Transcaspian government present at that fateful meeting were President Funtikov, who headed the proceedings, his deputy Kurilov, and the fledgling state's foreign minister Ziman. Funtikov, a former engine-driver, was a coarse individual with a weakness for the vodka bottle. Kurilov, also a railwayman, was rarely seen without a large, cocked revolver, while Ziman, the odd man out, was a rather decent but nervous schoolmaster. Also invited to attend the kangaroo court, as Malleson's representative, was Teague-Jones himself. Funtikov, already partly inebriated, was the first to speak. 'The President', wrote Teague-Jones in his subsequent report to the Foreign Office, 'made a statement to the effect that they had been informed from Meshed that General Malleson had declined to take over the prisoners, and had told the Ashkhabad representative that the government must make its own arrangements.' This, in fact, tallies with what Colonel Nash recalled years later. 'It was then argued', Teague-Jones continues, 'that the local prison was full, that Krasnovodsk had refused to keep the prisoners for the same reason, and that therefore there was no alternative but to shoot them.' In his journal Teague-Jones adds that Ziman and another speaker were opposed to shooting the commissars, but failed to come up with any alternative.

Teague-Jones has been criticised for not springing to his feet and contradicting Funtikov's statement that Malleson had washed his hands of the commissars, and was in fact demanding that they be handed over to the British as soon as arrangements for their transportation could be made. But, as he points out, he did not know that such a demand had been made by Malleson via the Ashkhabad representative, only learning of it afterwards. At the time he had to rely on Funtikov's version of what Malleson had told the Ashkhabad government's representative, a Russian named Dokhov. 'Either Dokhov lied to Funtikov,' he wrote, 'or else the latter lied to me.' And yet, if Nash is to be believed, neither lied. But why then, one may ask, had Malleson telegraphed his chiefs in India earlier that day to say that he had asked the Ashkhabad authorities to transfer the commissars into his custody? It is doubtful whether we will ever know the answer to this, or to the innumerable other questions surrounding the men's fate.

The meeting, which had begun in the early evening of September 18, was to continue until late into the night. 'The arguments', wrote Teague-Jones, 'continued endlessly, and finally I left the meeting before anything had really been definitely decided.' He has been censured, in the light of subsequent events, for not seeing the meeting through and doing more to save the commissars from what was clearly little more than lynch law. In fairness, however, it should be remembered that he was still hobbling painfully around on crutches, having discharged himself from hospital while far from well and against the advice of the doctors. More than likely, therefore, he lacked the stamina which would have been required to do battle with an inebriated Russian railway worker and other highly excited individuals over an issue which was really none of his business. When he left, after several hours of exhausting debate, the commissars' fate seemed no nearer to being decided than when the meeting had begun. He had, moreover, little reason to feel much sympathy for Shaumian and his fellow Bolsheviks. They had, after all, done all in their power to obstruct the British war effort by preventing the British from reaching Baku while there was still some hope of keeping it out of Turkish hands. Indeed, to Teague-Jones, the Bolsheviks were now as much Britain's enemies as the Germans and Turks. The machine-gun bullet in his groin had been evidence enough of that.

Not until the following evening did Teague-Jones discover the truth, and then only after pressing Funtikov hard for an answer. 'He informed me in confidence that it had been finally decided to shoot the prisoners, and that he, Funtikov, had dispatched Kurilov to Krasnovodsk the previous night to make the arrangements.' Teague-Jones immediately signalled Malleson to warn him of this, although he was unable to discover anything further from the Ashkhabad end. As it happened, however, at Malleson's urging, Major MacDonell was

at that moment on his way to Krasnovodsk from Enzeli to try
to discover precisely what was going on there. Unfortunately,
he did not get there until September 22, by which time it was
too late to do anything.

*   *   *

In Krasnovodsk, meanwhile, the drama was beginning to
unfold swiftly. The only first-hand account we have of what
happened there on the night of September 19 is that of one of
the commissars. He was a 23-year-old Armenian Bolshevik
named Anastas Mikoyan, who was destined to rise to the
highest rank in the Communist Party of the Soviet Union,
eventually becoming Chairman of the Presidium of the
Supreme Soviet. Not only did he somehow manage to avoid
the fate of the other Baku commissars that night, earning himself the nickname 'the twenty-seventh commissar', but he was
also one of the few old-guard Bolsheviks to survive the
Stalinist purges of the 1930s and 1940s. His survival led to
much uncharitable speculation, and it is said that whenever
Stalin wished to torment Mikoyan he would ask him how he
managed to escape the fate of the other twenty-six Baku commissars. The most probable explanation, however, is that his
name was not on a list of the Baku commissars found in the
pocket of one of them by Commandant Kuhn. For this only
included those who had been in prison in Baku, and Mikoyan
had not. Indeed, it was he who had arranged their last-minute
release there before joining them himself on their ill-fated
voyage into captivity.

Describing their last, unhappy night in their Krasnovodsk
cell, Mikoyan recalled: 'Some of us lay on benches, some on
the floor. Some were sitting, some were drowsing.' Then, at
about two o'clock on the morning of the 20th, they were suddenly awoken by the sound of a key grating in the lock. Armed
guards burst in and ordered them out of the cell and into the
corridor. When they inquired where they were being taken,
they were told: 'There is not room for you all here, so you are
going to Ashkhabad, to the regional prison.' When the young
Mikoyan, who was not on the guards' list for transfer, asked if
he might accompany them, he was refused. But before they
were parted, Shaumian told him: 'They will soon free you.

Try to get through to Astrakhan, and from there to Moscow. Go and see Lenin. Tell him everything that has happened to us here. Suggest that he seizes some leading Social Revolutionaries and Mensheviks and exchanges us for them.' Then Shaumian and the others were marched through the sleeping town to the railway station. There, beneath what Mikoyan calls 'a treacherous moon', they were herded silently into an empty goods wagon and locked in with their guards before the train set off eastwards into the desert in the direction of Ashkhabad. Later, as Shaumian had predicted, Mikoyan was released, together with Shaumian's two young sons, but by then the commissars were beyond any earthly help.

24

The Death Train

Shortly before dawn on that same morning, a maintenance worker walking home along the track of the
Transcaspian railway was startled to hear a train
approaching from the direction of Krasnovodsk. For he knew
that no trains were due at this remote spot on the single-track
line at such an hour. As it got closer he could see that it carried
no lights, something unheard of even in those disordered
times. Mystified, he scrambled up the embankment and hid
behind a clump of camel-thorn to watch this ghost train pass.
Instead it glided silently to a halt close to where he crouched
in the darkness.

Immediately, the doors of one of the wagons were flung
open and several armed guards leaped down on to the track.
They were closely followed by a group of prisoners whose
hands were tied behind their backs. Whatever they had
believed when they left Krasnovodsk three hours earlier, the
twenty-six Baku commissars could have had no illusions now
about what was in store for them. An order was shouted in
Russian, and the men were driven at gunpoint up the loose
sand of the embankment. From there they were marched
protesting a short distance into the desert. Here they were
offered blindfolds. Some accepted, others refused. All this was
witnessed by the hidden railwayman.

Next the doomed men were lined up along the crest of a
dune, where they stood out clearly against the dawn sky. The
guards took up position facing the commissars, some of whom
began to shout words of defiance. The firing squad raised their

rifles. An order was given, followed by a fusillade of shots. Most of the victims died instantly, but some were merely wounded and tried to run, only to be shot down or clubbed to death by the guards. An eerie silence now fell over the scene as the executioners dragged the dead men one by one over to a hollow in the dunes, out of sight of passing trains. There sand was heaped over them, using shovels brought specially for the purpose from Krasnovodsk. After a final look around to ensure that all evidence of the crime had been covered up, the guards made their way back towards the train, evidently well pleased with their night's work.

It was at that moment that one of them suddenly spotted the railwayman. Emerging badly shaken from his hiding place, he explained who he was – a Russian named Alexei Dirdikin – and how he came to be there. When he asked what had happened, he was told to mind his own business and warned never to tell a soul about what he had just witnessed. Why he was not eliminated by the executioners there and then is not clear, though perhaps their orders did not cover the possibility of being seen by anyone at so isolated a spot. The guards now climbed back on board the train, which continued towards Ashkhabad, 200 miles away across the desert. The frightened Dirdikin hurried home, but on the way ran into the track foreman and a party of maintenance men like himself. Breathlessly, he told them what he had just seen. He then led them to the spot where the commissars had been slaughtered. Horrified at what they found, they dug a communal grave for the murdered men so that the wild animals which roamed the desert would not attack their corpses. They said prayers over the spot and then hurriedly left.

Because these were hazardous times, they agreed among themselves to tell no one about what they had seen. It seems, though, that the executioners must have had second thoughts about Dirdikin. The following day his lifeless body was found in the nearby mountains. He had been murdered, but not before he had confided all to his family. In turn, they told the priest who conducted his funeral. The priest carefully noted it down. More than half a century later, long after the latter's death, his account was discovered. It is on this that the above description is largely based.

Such then was the appalling fate of Stepan Shaumian and his fellow Baku commissars. Their cold-blooded murder was to give birth to one of the great Russian revolutionary epics, one on which every Soviet schoolchild would be nurtured for the next seventy years. Their deaths, moreover, would plunge Britain and the new Soviet state into a bitter quarrel, involving Lenin, Trotsky and Stalin personally, which would last on and off until the collapse of Communism in Russia. However, due to the turmoil of the civil war and the breakdown of all communication between Transcaspia and Moscow, it was not for some time that news of the commissars' fate reached a shocked and angry Lenin. The British, though, were quick to learn of it, alerted by Captain Teague-Jones. Malleson was instructed to telegraph the Ashkhabad authorities expressing the British government's revulsion at this act of barbarism. Clearly they were upset too at losing the commissars as potential hostages who could be traded for Colonel Bailey and other missing Britons. In his correspondence with India, however, Malleson pointed out with unashamed cynicism that the executions were 'politically advantageous' to Britain, for it meant that the Ashkhabad government had 'burnt their boats' so far as the Bolsheviks were concerned. They would have been wiser, he added, to have hung on to Shaumian and his companions 'wherewith to save their own skins' were the Bolsheviks eventually to triumph.

By this time Major MacDonell had reached Krasnovodsk where he at once set to work trying to establish who had been responsible for the men's murder. Teague-Jones, as we know, had already pinned the blame on Funtikov and Kurilov. On his own admission the Transcaspian President had dispatched Kurilov to Krasnovodsk to arrange the commissars' execution. But MacDonell now found another culprit – Commandant Kuhn – who boasted openly of having personally organised it. He even told MacDonell that he had entered the doomed men on the railway manifest as 'goods', and told the escort commander to destroy this once the job was done. So that there could be no misunderstanding his instructions, he had provided the men assigned to carry out the executions with three shovels. Indeed, they had subsequently complained to him that they could have done with more to cover up the evidence of their grisly task. Later on, Kuhn told MacDonell, he had received a message from the men declaring: 'Your orders have been carried out.' Kuhn then boasted: 'You see, when I make up my mind I do it properly. They can never say of me, as they do of the British, that I talk of armies and arrive with two batmen, a Ford van and a general' – a sarcastic reference to Dunsterforce.

So far as the British were concerned, that was the end of it. 'For a long time,' wrote Teague-Jones in his journal, 'nothing more was heard about the episode, and in the course of a few weeks we had forgotten all about it.' General Malleson and his staff had far more pressing matters on their hands, for the Turks in Baku were reported to be trying to purchase the former Russian Caspian fleet in order to ship their troops across to Krasnovodsk. At all costs the Transcaspian railway, that dagger pointing towards Afghanistan and India, had to be kept out of their hands. It had also to be denied to the Bolsheviks, who were threatening it from the other end, lest they form an unholy alliance with the Turks against British India. To the British, at least, the treaty of Brest-Litovsk had shown that the Bolsheviks were capable of such treachery. If they wanted to retain control of this crucial section of the railway they had no choice but to ally themselves to the Ashkhabad government, however bloodstained its hands.

To make matters worse, Funtikov and his colleagues were becoming increasingly repressive and unpopular. 'The shortage of food was acute, and the railway workers who were responsible in the first place for the revolt against Tashkent were once more showing signs of restlessness,' wrote Colonel Ellis, an officer on Malleson's staff. This, in turn, provoked a witch-hunt against anyone suspected of harbouring Bolshevik sympathies. Nor was Funtikov beyond blaming the British for the worst of his excesses, spreading word behind their backs that it was they who had insisted on these, including the commissars' execution, which he maintained he had been strongly opposed to all along. Yet it was the British, admittedly out of self-interest, who were now preparing to save his skin.

The key to Funtikov's immediate survival lay in the desert 200 miles to the east of Ashkhabad. Here was to be found the great oasis of Merv, traditional supplier of most of

Ashkhabad's food. Right then, however, it was firmly in the hands of the Bolsheviks. By holding on to it they knew that they could eventually force Ashkhabad into submission, or force its increasingly hungry and restive population to rise against their rulers. And once Ashkhabad had fallen, resistance would quickly collapse throughout Transcaspia, enabling them to gain control of the entire railway, from Tashkent to Krasnovodsk. Malleson was painfully aware of this too. There was only one thing to do, and that was to try to wrest Merv, together with its desperately needed stocks of food, from the Bolsheviks. When Malleson had sought approval for this from his superiors in India, he had been told to use his own judgement and initiative. The truth was that there was no overall Allied policy or strategy towards the Bolsheviks, whom no power recognised and who were not at that time expected to survive for very much longer. Indeed, even within the British Cabinet there was little uniformity of view. Decisions had to be left to those on the spot. This, wrote Malleson afterwards, was like 'a gift from the Greeks'. If things went well, 'then some gentlemen in easy chairs 2,000 miles away would claim the credit'. But if they went badly, and there was criticism in press or Parliament, then one would be 'thrown remorselessly to the wolves'.

*   *   *

The single-track railway across the desert was the 'open sesame' to almost everything in Transcaspia, including the capture of the Merv oasis. The absence of roads and the enormous distances made the railway the only means of getting there. As it was, the troops of either side lived almost entirely in trains. These moved about in long processions, with an armoured train at the front and at the rear to protect them from surprise. Men, guns, horses and provisions were all carried on these trains. Water was transported in huge butts, while the cooking was done in field-kitchens mounted on open wagons. In addition there were hospital trains, the Transcaspian ones being staffed by Russian nurses. 'Had the Transcaspian troops possessed one quarter of the pluck of these nurses,' observed one British officer sourly, 'then it would have been a fine army.'

Because everything was thus centred on the railway, the advance on Merv presented Colonel Knollys, commander of the British Indian contingent, and his Transcaspian opposite numbers with unusual difficulties. Of the two sides, the Bolsheviks had the better armoured trains and artillery. 'The enemy's force', Knollys recalled, 'was to all intents and purposes contained in a movable fortress, armed with guns which far out-ranged anything that could be brought against it. If you marched against it in force, it moved away. If you posted your guns within range at night, it merely moved out of range and shelled you at leisure, for there was absolutely no cover for you. If you marched round to the rear, it would move forward, and as you could get neither water nor supplies you had to return whence you came, if you could.' There was only one other possibility, and that was somehow to bypass this movable fortress altogether, and try to seize the small Bolshevik-held town of Dushak, which lay half-way between Ashkhabad and Merv. It was this strategy which was adopted.

The plan of attack agreed on by Knollys and the Transcaspian commanders involved a surprise enveloping movement against the town's unsuspecting defenders. This necessitated secret night marches, to the north and south of the railway line, by infantry, cavalry and artillery. The infantry and artillery would skirt the railway well to the north, resting up during daylight in a ruined village in the desert where it was hoped they would not be spotted. At the same time Indian cavalrymen would proceed through the foothills to the south, well out of sight of the railway. The armoured train, meanwhile, would advance slowly eastwards, endeavouring to occupy the enemy's attention. Finally, the Turcoman horsemen would make a detour through the desert to the rear of the defenders' positions. There they would destroy the railway track, thus cutting off the Bolsheviks' line of retreat and at the same time preventing them from bringing up reinforcements by train from Tashkent.

The final assault on Dushak would be launched at dawn by all the Transcaspian forces simultaneously. The aim was not merely to seize Dushak, but also to destroy as much of the Bolshevik force as possible, putting the rest to flight, pursued by the Indian and Turcoman cavalry. Secrecy, of course, was vital, for everything depended upon surprise. But in a force known to harbour Bolshevik spies and sympathisers this was a real worry. Rumours were therefore deliberately spread of the impending arrival of large-scale reinforcements from India, including aircraft and heavy artillery, in preparation for a concerted attack much later. It was hoped that these would be picked up by the enemy's agents and passed to the Bolsheviks, who would therefore be caught off their guard. It was also hoped that the news would further undermine their morale, which had already been badly bruised following their earlier encounter with Punjabi bayonets at Kaahka.

By the night of October 12 all was ready. Two companies of the 19th Punjabis, 400 Transcaspian infantrymen and about the same number of Turcoman irregulars struck out north of the railway towards the abandoned village where they were to lie up during the hours of daylight before advancing on Dushak under cover of darkness. Accompanying them was a battery of British light artillery and two Russian-manned field-guns. At the same time, two squadrons of the 28th Indian Light Cavalry rode southwards into the foothills through which they would approach Dushak, while the Turcoman horsemen, well used to the desert, took a wider sweep aimed at placing them in the enemy's rear. Throughout that night all went according to plan, and long before dawn the next morning the British, Transcaspian and Turcoman units began to move silently into position in the darkness. So far there were no indications that the enemy were expecting them. Either the Bolsheviks had swallowed the rumours of a massive offensive planned for later, or Funtikov's secret police had successfully eliminated their spies in the Transcaspian ranks. Then suddenly, just when it seemed that the defenders would be taken totally by surprise, things began to go badly wrong.

Versions differ, but it appears that two Punjabi patrols opened fire on one another in the darkness, instantly alerting the Bolsheviks to their danger. However, there could be no going back now, although the troops were still well short of their positions for the assault on the town. Orders were immediately given for the advance. Dawn was now breaking, and the attackers could clearly be seen as they set out across the mile of open ground between them and the nearest Bolshevik positions. Completely flat, this offered little or no cover except for a few small nullahs, or dry watercourses, running in the wrong direction. The attackers soon found themselves under heavy fire from thirty machine-guns sited on commanding ground ahead of them, as well as from light artillery. British and Indian casualties were heavy in the fierce fighting which followed, the Punjabis quickly losing all their British officers, either killed or wounded, as well as nearly 200 other rank casualties. The 28th Indian Light Cavalry, by now bloodily engaged with the Bolsheviks on the far side of the town, were faring less badly, losing only 6 dead and 11 wounded. Transcaspian casualties, considering the size of their forces, were lighter still, totalling 7 dead and 30 wounded. However, this was because most of them immediately went to ground in the nullahs when the machine-guns opened up while the Turcoman irregulars simply melted away into the desert.

Despite their heavy losses, and led now by their Indian officers and NCOs, the gallant Punjabis continued to advance alone through the murderous hail of machine-gun and artillery fire. At last they reached the Bolshevik positions around Dushak station, where they were able to use their long, gleaming bayonets to deadly effect. The enemy now broke, fleeing in panic into the station, which provided the only cover. Then suddenly, from inside the station, came an enormous explosion. A British or Russian shell, it seems, had landed in a wagon filled with ammunition, killing large numbers of those sheltering there. This proved too much for the rest, many of whom fled towards the hills, only to be cut down by the sabres of the Indian cavalrymen. Others scrambled aboard three armoured trains which were then in the station. One of these tried to escape eastwards, only to be intercepted by the Turcoman horsemen, who slaughtered its crew and most of the troops it was carrying. The two other trains, however, managed to escape in all the turmoil by heading westwards, the Transcaspian troops who were supposed to prevent this being nowhere to be seen.

They were, in fact, engaged elsewhere. On seeing the Bolsheviks fleeing, they had suddenly regained their courage and emerged from the nullahs where they had been hiding.

Together with the Turcomans, they were now busy looting the Bolsheviks' abandoned stores. With little thought for what the enemy might be planning, they were feverishly loading their booty, which included everything from food to machineguns, on to the backs of captured horses, prior to heading back towards Kaahka. The Bolsheviks, meanwhile, had far from given up. Taking advantage of all the confusion among the Transcaspian ranks, they had started to bring up fresh troops from the direction of Tejend, the next town on the way to Merv. This was made possible by the failure of the Turcoman horsemen to cut the railway line, as they had been ordered to. At the same time those enemy troops who had succeeded in escaping by train westwards had re-formed and begun to make their way back towards Dushak, which the small British Indian contingent was preparing to defend with the sole support of eighty stalwart Russian regulars who had not fled or joined in the orgy of looting.

Shortly before midday on that same day the Bolsheviks launched a somewhat half-hearted counter-attack from east and west simultaneously. The defenders consisted of 150 Punjabis, 130 Indian cavalrymen, a battery of artillery and the Russians. Everyone else had vanished, carrying their booty with them. Although the enemy did not press the attack very determinedly, it was quickly realised that Dushak could not be held indefinitely by so small a force. Any moment now the Bolsheviks might bring up overwhelming numbers of troops by train from Tashkent or other garrisons along the line to the east, not to mention heavy artillery. An orderly withdrawal was decided upon before it was too late and the defenders found themselves trapped. The Punjabis, bearing their wounded with them and covered by the cavalry and the gunners, withdrew first. For some curious reason, perhaps because they suspected trickery, the Bolsheviks held back, and the last of the defenders were able to get away without any further loss of life. Nonetheless, to the British, the venture had proved a huge disappointment. What should have been a decisive victory, leading eventually to the capture of Merv, had been turned into a costly failure by the craven and rapacious Transcaspians and Turcomans. Even so, for the Bolsheviks it had proved considerably more costly, for they were estimated to have lost at least 1,000 troops, and large quantities of weapons and ammunition, in those five or six hours of fighting.

Greatly to their credit, and to everybody's surprise, the official Ashkhabad newspapers blamed the débâcle on the 'disgraceful conduct' of their own troops, while heaping praise on 'the heroic sepoys and Indian cavalrymen'. Also castigating the Transcaspian troops, the official Ashkhabad communiqué accused them of throwing away 'this golden opportunity to annihilate the Bolsheviks'. For their part the Bolsheviks sought to explain away the poor showing of their own forces and the large number of casualties they had suffered by introducing to the battle a wholly mythical Scottish regiment, and by raising the number of British Indian troops involved from 500 to 4,000. At the same time they hailed the action as a resounding victory for themselves.

News of the British losses and withdrawal from Dushak was received with gloom and profound disappointment by Malleson at Meshed. He immediately pressed his superiors in India to dispatch more troops to the spot. Given three cavalry regiments, three batteries of artillery, a brigade of infantry, and a few armoured cars and aircraft, he argued, he could clear the whole of Central Asia of Bolsheviks. Shortly after this a more cheering piece of intelligence reached his headquarters. The Bolsheviks had suddenly and unexpectedly withdrawn from Dushak in mid-October, leaving it undefended, and also from Tejend, the next town up the line towards Merv. Moreover, it appeared that they did not intend to return, for they had destroyed the railway line behind them to prevent pursuit. Their morale, it seemed, was even worse than had been thought. No longer were they prepared to face the fierce Punjabis or the sabre-wielding Indian cavalry merely to hold on to remote bits of the desert.

There was even better news to follow. Word next reached Malleson that the Bolsheviks had withdrawn from Merv too, and were pulling their forces back across the Oxus river towards Bokhara. Just why they were doing this was not clear, though it is conceivable that the carefully spread rumours of a coming British push towards Tashkent had worked beyond anyone's wildest expectations. Whatever the reason, on

November 1 the great Merv oasis was occupied by the British and Transcaspian troops, who thus attained their original objective without having to fire another shot. This immediately freed large quantities of meat, grain and other foodstuffs grown or stored there for the bazaars of Ashkhabad, greatly easing the plight, not to mention the tempers, of the people. There was widespread rejoicing, and as a result Funtikov and his fellow anti-Bolsheviks were able to cling on to power for a further few months.

Now that the Bolshevik forces appeared to be on the run, General Malleson was eager to pursue them eastwards, if necessary all the way to Bokhara, Samarkand and Tashkent, where they were reported to be increasingly unpopular. Malleson and his officers had little or no sympathy for revolutionaries of any kind, but their dislike of the Bolsheviks was particularly intense. Not only had they murdered their own royal family, and struck a treacherous deal with the enemy, but their revolutionary notions wrought havoc with military discipline, as had been shown at Baku and now at Dushak. Indeed, one of Malleson's greatest fears was that the Bolshevik bacillus would infect his own Indian troops. He was bitterly disappointed therefore when a high-level order arrived from India forbidding him to advance beyond Merv, and to avoid at all costs becoming caught up in an anti-Bolshevik crusade. As a result, Transcaspian forces tried to go it alone, only to find themselves chased all the way back to Merv.

By now winter had begun to set in, and the troops of either side retreated into their trains to escape the bitter winds and snow. With the Bolsheviks unwilling to confront the British Indian troops, and Malleson forbidden to advance beyond Merv, fighting virtually ceased in Transcaspia. Elsewhere, however, momentous events were taking shape as the war entered its final weeks, though nobody foresaw quite how quickly the end would come. Even the Chief of the Imperial General Staff was advising the War Cabinet that victory in Europe might not be won for another year. Nonetheless, from the two main theatres of war, France and Palestine, the news was extremely heartening. On the Western Front, following Ludendorff's failure to break the three-year stalemate with his massive hammer blow, the Germans were now in full retreat towards the celebrated Hindenburg Line, their remaining line of defence. In Palestine, too, the enemy was on the run as Allenby's armies, spearheaded by 15,000 cavalry and flanked by Arab irregulars, raced northwards towards Damascus, a prize second only to Constantinople.

In Constantinople itself, Enver Pasha had for some time been assuring his war-weary Cabinet colleagues that the German retreat in France was really a brilliant strategic ruse by Ludendorff to lure the Allies into a trap where their forces would be totally destroyed. At first they had swallowed this, but as the news from the Western Front and from Palestine grew rapidly worse they realised that both Turkey and Germany were doomed. Ordinary Turks, close to starvation, could see it too, and their resentment towards those who had dragged them into the war grew more intense by the day. British POWs, by now allowed to wander freely through the streets of the capital, delighted the Turks with their mocking imitations of the German goose-step, and there was a growing fear for the personal safety of German nationals, both military and civilian. As this hostility deepened, the German ambassador secretly transferred gold from Constantinople's German-owned banks to the embassy's vaults. Not only did he fear the mob, but also the Turkish government itself, which had been making inquiries about the banks' current holdings.

By this late stage in the war, only Enver himself still believed that something could be retrieved from the ruins of the Ottoman Empire. He alone wished to keep the war going, with or without Germany, for he had not yet abandoned his cherished dream of carving out a great new Turkic empire in Central Asia, using his forces in eastern Turkey and the Caucasus to achieve this. Again, from a stronghold in the Caucasus, Turkey itself could be wrested back from the Allies, were that to prove necessary. Ever a dreamer, he seemed deliberately to turn his eyes away from the painful reality surrounding him, perhaps even persuading himself that Ludendorff really was steering the Allies into an elaborate trap. But as the end drew closer, he found himself increasingly isolated from his less sanguine Cabinet colleagues. For everywhere except on the Caucasian front the situation appeared more and more desperate as the once mighty Ottoman Empire broke up before their eyes. Already large parts of it – including Mecca and Medina, Islam's two holiest cities, the Hejaz, Egypt, Sinai, Palestine, Trans-Jordan, and much of Mesopotamia (today's Iraq) – were in Allied or Arab hands, to be shared out between the victors after the war. All that was really left was the Turkish heartland, Syria and northern Mesopotamia, and even their days appeared numbered. Their capital, the Turks had learned from the Bolsheviks, had been promised to Russia, and although Lenin had repudiated any claim to it, this did not mean that it would remain in Turkish hands if they were defeated.

Much of the blame for the collapse of the Turkish forces in Palestine could be laid at the feet of Enver, for he had switched many of his best units from there to the Caucasus. This was to cause considerable resentment and bitterness among the German troops left with the hopeless task of trying to halt Allenby's onslaught. Greatly outnumbered, and with the Turks in flight around them, they nonetheless continued to fight with great courage. 'When attacked they halted, took position, fired to order,' wrote Lawrence in *Seven Pillars of Wisdom*. 'There was no haste, no crying, no hesitation. They were glorious.' But there was nothing they could do now to save Damascus, and on October 1, 1918, it fell to the combined Allied and Arab forces, to be followed soon afterwards by Beirut and Aleppo. In the meantime, the Turks had suffered another blow with the surrender to the Allies of Bulgaria, effectively severing all overland links between Constantinople and Berlin, and exposing Austria-Hungary's south-eastern flank to Allied attack. Even worse, from the Turks' point of view, this left Constantinople wide open to attack by the 500,000-strong French and British force in Salonica.

On October 5, the Allies received the first clear signal that some members of Turkey's ruling clique were anxious to discuss peace terms. Talaat, one of the triumvirate, put out a discreet feeler through President Wilson, hoping perhaps that his widely proclaimed Fourteen Points, which advocated a renunciation of all secret agreements, might somehow save the Ottoman Empire from being broken up and shared between the triumphant Allies. On October 8, the triumvirate resigned with the rest of the Cabinet, and for several days Turkey was without a government. Then, on October 14, a new Cabinet was appointed by the Sultan, who had just succeeded his father. It did not include Enver, Talaat or Djemal. Realising that their days were numbered, the three men hastily fled the country, escaping across the Black Sea on board a German warship. They were only just in time to save their own necks. For the Sultan, who detested Enver for bringing shame upon his country, was hoping to appease the Allies by putting him and the others on trial for treason, and then hanging them. He knew, moreover, that this would be a popular move among his subjects, upon whom they had brought such suffering and misery.

The end for Turkey was now very close – too close for some members of the British War Cabinet who feared that the war might end before Britain could occupy those crucial Middle Eastern regions which it hoped to dominate. One of these was the Mosul oilfields, which were still in Turkish hands. General Marshall, the British commander in Mesopotamia, was ordered 'to occupy as large a portion of the oil-bearing regions as possible'. Indeed, some Turkish historians have accused the British of deliberately delaying the signing of the armistice to give the general time to wrest this prize from their grasp, which he just succeeded in doing, his troops being greeted by a Turkish army band playing 'God Save the King'.

Whatever the truth of this claim, the first Turkish proposals were rejected by the British, acting for the Allies, as unacceptable. The Turks insisted that unless the terms they were offering were accepted, they would continue fighting. This was seen in London as an empty threat, however, for their armies were on the run everywhere except in the Caucasus. In the meantime, realising that its own position and that of its allies was now hopeless, Austria-Hungary had thrown in the towel. Finally, their bluff called by the British, the Turks signed an armistice aboard the battleship *Agamemnon* on October 30, under which all fighting would cease at noon the following day. It was a total and unconditional surrender, allowing the Allies to occupy key strategic regions within the Ottoman Empire, including Constantinople.

Only Germany now still held out, clinging desperately to a last-ditch defensive line stretching across eastern France and

Belgium. By now, with their allies caving in around them, the morale of the troops had all but collapsed, giving rise to mutinies and other disorders. Revolution was in the air, and on November 4 the Red Flag was run up by mutineers over the battleship *Kaiser*. Other warships refused to leave harbour, while in dockyards and barracks sailors and soldiers organised themselves into revolutionary councils along Bolshevik lines. Nonetheless, at the front, many of the troops remained loyal, making heroic but hopeless attempts to halt the Allied onrush.

On November 6, when it was clear that all further resistance was futile, a group of delegates left Berlin to begin negotiations with the Allies. They were received by Marshal Foch, the supreme Allied commander in France, who set the tone by announcing at the outset: 'You have come to *beg* for an armistice.' He then presented them with the harsh Allied terms, which he insisted had to be accepted, or refused, within seventy-two hours. These terms were immediately telephoned to Berlin, where they were to cause profound dismay. However, the Germans were in no position to argue, for things were rapidly deteriorating both on the battlefield and within the country itself. Many of the troops at the front were now starving, while in Berlin, Cologne and Hanover revolutionaries took over the streets. Ordinary Germans prayed for peace on almost any terms, and there were growing demands for the Emperor's abdication. Instead, he ordered the army to prepare for civil war, only to be told by his generals that the troops were no longer behind him. From the steps of the Reichstag a republic was unofficially declared. Amid all this chaos, it was far from clear at that moment whether Germany had a government at all.

Field-Marshal von Hindenburg, Chief of the German General Staff, now took control of his country's destiny. It was on his advice that Kaiser Wilhelm abdicated, his messianic visions of world leadership finally shattered. The next day, fearing that his own troops might seize him and bring him before a revolutionary court, he fled to neutral Holland where he was granted asylum. At the same time Hindenburg ordered the German armistice delegates to accept the Allied ultimatum, however humiliating its terms, for he knew that his broken armies were no longer capable of resisting the overwhelming might of the enemy, which every day was growing. It was Hindenburg, ironically, who had been responsible for the harsh terms imposed on the Russians by the Treaty of Brest-Litovsk, which now became invalid.

At 5 a.m. the following day – November 11, 1918 – the armistice was signed in a railway carriage which was serving as Foch's headquarters. Exactly six hours later, on the stroke of 11 o'clock, the guns stopped firing all along the line. An eerie silence fell over the battlefield. It lasted for several minutes, the longest anyone could remember, as the troops of either side, hardly daring to breathe, waited to see whether it would hold. Then suddenly there arose a strange sound, like a great sigh, which could be heard from far behind the lines. Those who were there likened it to the sound of a powerful wind. But it was men's voices. 'It was the sound', wrote John Buchan memorably, 'of men cheering from the Vosges to the sea.'

After four terrible years, which had cost nearly thirteen million human lives, it was suddenly all over. The Allies had paid dearly for their victory, however, for the grim arithmetic shows that they had lost at least a million more men in the fighting than the enemy. Indeed, it has been calculated that if all the dead of the British Empire alone were to march four abreast down Whitehall, it would take this ghostly army three and a half days to pass the Cenotaph. But although the shooting was over, the suffering was not. A further twenty million people, many already debilitated by hunger and privation, were to die in the 'flu epidemic which ravaged the world in the wake of the war.

In addition to the horrifying human toll, four empires – those of Germany, Austria-Hungary, Turkey and Russia – had perished amidst the wreckage of the *Drang nach Osten*. With the defeat of the world's most powerful army, the myth of Prussian invincibility had finally been exploded, while the Holy War, on which Kaiser Wilhelm had staked so much, had proved to be little more than wishful thinking by his advisers and their Indian and Persian collaborators. To add to his humiliation, Wilhelm was to see the Ottoman Empire, which he had once so coveted, broken up and divided between his foes, with the lion's share going to his detested British cousins.

Even the Berlin-to-Baghdad Railway, the linchpin of his expansionist schemes, had never been completed. All in all, the destruction of his reckless dreams, and those of his Turkish partner in crime Enver Pasha, could hardly have been more crushing.

But even now, for some of those who had found themselves caught up in these events, the story was not yet over. Indeed, perhaps the strangest tale of all has still to be told.

25

Teague-Jones Disappears

Despite angry Allied demands that Kaiser Wilhelm be extradited and hanged as a war criminal, the Dutch government refused to hand him over. He was thus to go unpunished for all the carnage and suffering which he had brought upon the world and upon his own people. Indeed, beyond losing his throne, he was to get off extraordinarily lightly. For the next twenty-two years, until his death at the age of 82 in 1941, he lived in regal comfort off the revenues from his vast estates in Germany, writing two self-justifying volumes of memoirs and directing forestry work at the magnificent Dutch castle he had acquired. Ancestral portraits, furniture and an entire marble staircase were transported to this home-from-home from his palace at Potsdam. Nonetheless, for fear of assassination or kidnap, he could never venture very far from his closely guarded estate. Nor was he ever again to set foot in his beloved Germany.

When, in 1940, Hitler's panzers invaded Holland, he was offered asylum by the British government, but this he politely declined. Likewise he refused a suggestion by Hitler that, for his own safety, he should return from exile to one of his former estates in Germany. However, when Paris fell to German troops, he sent the Führer an effusive telegram. A state funeral was offered him by Hitler when he died from a blood clot the following year, but he had already left instructions that he was to be buried in the grounds of his Dutch castle. His widow, whom he had married in 1922, lived to see Germany defeated in another war, dying in a Russian detention camp in 1947.

Turkey's wartime leaders – Enver, Talaat and Djemal – were considerably less fortunate than Wilhelm. Following their flight together from Constantinople to escape the hangman's noose, Talaat proceeded secretly to Berlin, where he had old friends whom he knew would give him sanctuary. For the next three years, under an assumed name and identity, he lived in a modest pension in the German capital. Then suddenly, on a spring morning in 1921, he was gunned down in the street by an assassin. His killer, a member of a vengeance-seeking Armenian murder squad code-named Nemesis, had spent months trailing him to his refuge. The assassin was arrested and charged with Talaat's murder. But after General Liman von Sanders had spoken on the man's behalf, and the court had been told that his family had all perished in the Armenian massacres – for which Talaat, as Minister of the Interior, bore considerable responsibility – he was set free. Two more Turks associated with the massacres were slain by an assassin in Berlin that same year, and a third in Rome.

The following summer, Djemal Pasha was killed by two Nemesis gunmen while standing outside the Bolshevik secret police headquarters in Tiflis, where he was now living. Shortly before, he had published his own version of events, *Memoirs of a Turkish Statesman*, in which he sought to wash his hands of all responsibility for the Armenian massacres. At the same time, however, he claimed that the Armenians had brought their fate upon themselves by going over to the enemy, the invading Russians, and by killing Turkish and Kurdish villagers. It could not be denied that many Armenians had been recruited into special units by the Russians, as is borne out by Philips Price, the *Manchester Guardian* correspondent, though this was hardly justification for the genocide unleashed against them by Constantinople.

The last of the triumvirate to get his come-uppance for his wartime sins was Enver Pasha himself, though not at the hands of the Armenians. After fleeing first to Berlin and then to Moscow, he had promised Lenin that in exchange for Bolshevik help in restoring him to power in Turkey he would deliver British India to Russia's new masters. Taken in by this offer, in November 1921 Lenin allowed him to travel to Central Asia where he was to begin his crusade by rallying the

Muslim masses to the banner of the Holy War. But Enver, who had not abandoned his dream of building a great new Ottoman Empire in Central Asia, double-crossed the Bolsheviks and turned, not against the British, but against them. At first he enjoyed considerable success at the head of the *basmachi*, the local Muslim freedom-fighters, in their struggle for independence from Moscow, even capturing Dushanbe in February 1922. As word of his victories over the Bolsheviks spread through Central Asia, more and more recruits flocked to his banner, even if the concept of Pan-Turkism which he preached was beyond the comprehension of most of them. But gradually, as the Bolsheviks got themselves organised, the tide began to turn, and finally Enver found himself trapped by Lenin's troops in what is now Tajikistan. The story of his dramatic and defiant end, while leading a suicidal cavalry charge against Bolshevik machine-gunners in August 1922, I have already told in *Setting the East Ablaze*, which picks up the tale of those turbulent times where this one ends.

But there were others, too, besides Kaiser Wilhelm, Enver, Talaat and Djemal, who found themselves on the run from Allied or other justice following the defeat of Germany and Turkey. These included the Indian revolutionaries who had twice sought to overthrow the British in India from the safety of Berlin by fomenting armed uprisings. They knew that if they were to escape the British hangman they must find a new safe haven from where they could continue their revolutionary activities against British rule in India. Once, America would have been the obvious choice, for it was in California that their movement had had its beginnings among the immigrant Indian population. But that was now ruled out, for following America's entry into the war there had been a witch-hunt there of German agents and Indian revolutionaries, resulting in a wave of arrests and what was then one of the longest-running trials in American history.

Known as the Hindu-German Conspiracy trial, it had lasted for five months. In all, seventeen Indians, nine Germans and four German Americans were charged with conspiring together on American soil to foment an armed insurrection against British rule in India. It was one of the most bizarre trials ever seen in the United States. 'In the dock,' wrote one reporter, 'aggressive blond German officers sat beside anaemic, swarthy turbaned Hindus.' To enable the jury to grasp the complexities of this far-flung conspiracy, with its secret shipments of arms across the Pacific, a map of half the world was spread across one wall of the court. Beside it, in large capital letters, were listed the names of the thirty accused, so strange were they to American ears. The most sensational moment of the trial came when one of the Indians suddenly pulled out a hidden revolver and shot dead a fellow conspirator, mistakenly believing that he had been in the pay of the British all along. He himself was then immediately shot dead by a court guard. In the end, all but one of the accused were found guilty. The judge, who put most of the blame for the conspiracy on the German High Command, sentenced all the leading defendants to various terms of imprisonment, though these were considerably less than those imposed by British Indian courts on revolutionaries tried there, many of whom were hanged.

The Indians in Berlin, meanwhile, seeing that all other avenues of escape were closed to them, had in 1919 turned to revolutionary Russia for both sanctuary and sympathy. In Moscow they were received enthusiastically by the Bolsheviks, who saw them as valuable allies in the coming struggle for British India. They were joined there by Raja Mahendra Pratap and Mohammed Barakatullah, who could see that they were getting nowhere in Kabul, and who had also decided to try their luck with the Bolsheviks. Again, what became of them and their dreams of liberating their homeland I have chronicled in *Setting the East Ablaze*.

However, there remains once strange consequence of this narrative which has still to be told. That is the singular misfortune which befell Captain Teague-Jones, and which was to haunt him for the rest of his life. In February 1919, General Malleson received orders from London to evacuate his small British Indian force from Transcaspia forthwith, now that the Turco-German threat to India was over, even if this meant abandoning the unfortunate Transcaspian government to face the Bolsheviks alone. When he pointed out that such a hurried evacuation would leave his own troops highly exposed to a Bolshevik attack, not to mention the understandable rage of the Transcaspian forces, he was given a further eight weeks in which to make discreet arrangements for the withdrawal. Only a handful of his officers were allowed to know what was afoot, lest word should leak out. Instead, a rumour was circulated that Malleson was planning to lure the Bolsheviks into a trap by appearing to evacuate Merv while actually, with the help of (non-existent) reinforcements, cutting them off from behind. The Bolsheviks swallowed the bait, and on April 1, only one day behind schedule, the last Indian contingent left for the Persian frontier, while the British troops entrained for the port of Krasnovodsk, where a vessel was awaiting them. The British evacuation, like the earlier one from Baku, was kept secret until the very last moment, whereupon it caused near panic among the Transcaspian leadership, who vainly begged Malleson to stay on.

With the British troops now gone, the Bolsheviks began to fight their way along the railway line towards Ashkhabad, this time greatly reinforced and led by General Frunze, an able soldier and strategist. Before long, the Transcaspian capital was back in Bolshevik hands, the Transcaspian government fleeing to Krasnovodsk. This finally fell to Frunze's troops in February 1920, leaving Moscow in control of the whole of Transcaspia. It was to remain that way until the collapse of the Soviet Empire seventy years later. Over the following twelve months a similar fate was shortly to befall the three Caucasian territories of Georgia, Armenia and Azerbaijan, after they too had enjoyed a brief period of independence. Such developments, however, like the post-war division of the Ottoman Empire and the former German colonies, are beyond the scope of this narrative, and anyway have no bearing on the curious affair of Captain Teague-Jones and the twenty-six Baku commissars.

It was only after the British withdrawal from Transcaspia that the Bolsheviks finally learned of the fate of the commissars. Until then it had been assumed that they were being held prisoner somewhere, for the Transcaspian government had gone to considerable lengths to suppress news of their execution. Moscow's reaction to the shocking discovery was one of absolute fury, and an immediate hunt was unleashed for those who had carried it out. It did not take the Bolsheviks very long to decide that it was the British, whose intervention in the civil war they bitterly resented, who were to blame. The charge, of course, was strenuously denied by the British government, whose relations with Moscow now plummeted to a new low. Meanwhile, the Baku commissars were being elevated by the Bolsheviks to the status of revolutionary martyrs, with every Soviet schoolchild being taught that it was the British who had murdered them in cold blood. At first, no attempt was made by the Bolsheviks to name any individuals in connection with their allegations.

Until then, Teague-Jones himself had given the matter little further thought, having been more than 200 miles away from the scene of the execution on the morning it took place, and never having set eyes on any of the victims. Moreover, he knew very well who had given the order – Funtikov – because he himself had told him so. He also knew, from MacDonell's inquiries at Krasnovodsk, that it was Commandant Kuhn who had organised the death train and the subsequent murders. Furthermore, such brutal killings were commonplace among the revolutionary rivals for power. Thousands, if not hundreds of thousands, were to perish thus during the course of the civil war, including numerous other commissars and officials.

The nightmare for Teague-Jones began when an article appeared in a Baku newspaper accusing him of being personally responsible for the deaths of the twenty-six Bolshevik heroes. It was written by a Social Revolutionary lawyer named Vadim Chaikin, who claimed to have conducted a painstaking investigation of the events leading to the massacre. His principal witness was ex-President Funtikov, by that time in gaol in Ashkhabad following his own downfall. According to a sworn statement which Chaikin claimed to have obtained from Funtikov, Teague-Jones had demanded that the prisoners be shot, and afterwards had expressed his satisfaction that this had been carried out 'in accordance with the wishes of the British mission'. Chaikin demanded that the British government conduct a full inquiry into the murders, saying that he would be willing to give evidence against Teague-Jones. He also challenged the British officer to sue him for libel in a British court if his charges were untrue, offering to come to

London for the hearings. Not long afterwards, Chaikin produced a 190-page book in which he repeated his allegations against Teague-Jones in greater detail. In this he demanded that the officer be brought before an international tribunal to face war crime charges.

Because Chaikin was a Social Revolutionary and not a Bolshevik, he was particularly valuable to Moscow's propaganda machine, then locked in a bitter wrangle with the interventionist powers, since he appeared to have no particular axe to grind in championing the Baku commissars, beyond wishing to see justice done. A less charitable observer, however, might have wondered whether Chaikin was not seeking to curry favour with the Bolsheviks, while trying at the same time to exonerate his Social Revolutionary friends from blame by pinning the entire responsibility on Teague-Jones, who could not deny his presence in Ashkhabad on the night it was decided to kill the commissars. If this was indeed Chaikin's purpose, then it was to prove in vain. For while blaming the British for the murders, the Bolsheviks also gave vent to their fury on anyone they could find, Social Revolutionary or otherwise, who had been even remotely or indirectly connected with the affair. In all, they managed to round up forty-two such individuals, of whom all but one were shot following a trial held at Krasnovodsk in 1921. Even Chaikin himself, having outlived his usefulness, was before long to find himself in a Bolshevik prison, where – perhaps because he knew too much – he was to spend the rest of his life.

But this was of little comfort to Captain Teague-Jones who, at the age of 29, now found himself facing the wrath of the entire Bolshevik leadership. Without a shred of evidence, first Stalin and then Trotsky joined in the witch-hunt. The former, himself of Caucasian birth, denounced the British as 'cannibals' for what he claimed to be their cold-blooded murder of the Bolshevik heroes. Trotsky, in a small book dealing with events in the Caucasus and Transcaspia at that time, declared that the commissars had been 'shot without investigation or trial . . . by Teague-Jones, chief of the military mission at Ashkhabad'. He based this charge on what he described as Chaikin's 'exact and irrefutable evidence'. He further accused the British military authorities in Transcaspia of 'aiding and abetting the crime' and of helping others involved in the massacre 'to escape trial and justice'.

In the meantime, with Transcaspia and the Caucasus now back in their hands, the Bolsheviks had located the commissars' decaying remains in their makeshift graves beside the railway and disinterred them, moving them first to Ashkhabad, where they were temporarily reburied, and finally back to their home town of Baku. There, in the summer of 1920, they were laid to rest in the main square, which was named after them. An impressive monument was erected over their communal grave, in the heart of which burned an eternal flame cupped in the hands of a worker, his head bowed in mourning. Individual sculptures of each of the twenty-six victims were placed at intervals around the square. At the same time, work was begun – it would take twenty-five years to complete – on a huge red granite relief graphically depicting the execution scene, the defiant figures before the firing squad symbolising Courage, Moral Conviction, Undaunted Spirit and other Bolshevik virtues. Elsewhere in Baku, streets, districts, various institutions and a railway station were named after the revolutionary martyrs, while some of their former homes – including that of Shaumian, where Major MacDonell had once played with his son's toy train set – were turned into memorial museums or shrines.

Above all, however, the Bolsheviks were determined to cast the British interventionists – and especially Captain Teague-Jones – as the villains in what was to become one of Russia's great revolutionary epics. A flood of official paintings, sculptures, films, books, poems, requiems and other propaganda was now unleashed, all of it hammering home the supposed role of the British. Whether or not the Bolshevik hierarchy believed a word of it will probably never be known, but this was clearly too good an opportunity to let slip for blackening those who had supported their rivals during the civil war in Transcaspia and elsewhere. Carried away by their revolutionary fervour – or more likely to please the party chiefs on whom their livelihoods depended – artists and writers vied with each other in vilifying the British, often going far beyond what even Chaikin alleged. One celebrated painting of the execution scene, by the Russian artist Isaac Brodsky, shows present no fewer than five uniformed British officers, some of whom are clearly urging on the executioners. One of the officers in the foreground bears more than a passing resemblance to Teague-Jones, moreover, while some written accounts of the scene describe him as ordering the commissars out of the train and personally commanding the firing squad.

To be denounced thus as the cold-blooded murderer of another country's heroes must have been a chilling experience, even for a hardened professional like Teague-Jones. Knowing at first hand what the Bolsheviks were capable of, he had good reason to fear some sort of vengeance, whether assassination, or kidnap followed by a show trial in Baku or Moscow. Was not the British government still trying to obtain redress and compensation for the execution by firing squad of a British citizen, Mr Charles Davison, erroneously convicted by a revolutionary court of spying? And had not an armed Bolshevik mob, accompanied by Cheka agents, burst into the British Embassy in Petrograd and shot dead Captain Cromie, the naval attaché, when he tried to resist them? These were just two of a number of such cases where violence or other mistreatment had been directed against foreign nationals by the Bolsheviks. It was no secret, moreover, that Moscow's death squads had both a long arm and a long memory – as Trotsky himself was later to discover. In view of the campaign of vilification orchestrated against him by the Bolshevik leadership, Teague-Jones knew that he could expect little mercy were he to fall, by whatever means, into the hands of his accusers. Furthermore, having no diplomatic relations with Britain at this time, the Bolsheviks did not have to concern themselves too much with the niceties observed by the Foreign Office, or with the constraints of international law.

By now – it was the spring of 1922 – Teague-Jones was on leave in London preparatory to resuming his pre-war career in the Indian political service. With him was his new wife, Valya Alexeeva, the attractive young Russian girl he had first met when in Baku four years earlier, and whose escape from Bolshevik Russia he had managed to organise. It was around this time that Teague-Jones decided, perhaps on the advice of his superiors, to vanish from public view. On May 23 he changed his name by deed poll to Ronald Sinclair, although no announcement of this was made in the newspapers. His two sisters are also believed to have changed their name, for fear of this inadvertently leading a determined Bolshevik agent to their brother.

The Foreign Office, however, was not prepared to let the matter rest there, for Moscow's charges of British complicity in the executions also impugned Britain's good name. In June, Teague-Jones was asked by the Foreign Office to prepare a detailed refutation of all the charges levelled against him in Chaikin's book – a copy of which they had managed to obtain – since these formed the only basis for the allegations of Trotsky, Stalin and others. His answers would then be used by the Foreign Office to draft a formal reply to Moscow's accusations. Disappearing while still in the throes of unfinished official business is clearly no easy matter. Nearly three months after Teague-Jones had changed his name to Sinclair, the Foreign Office was still addressing him as Captain Teague-Jones and writing to him in connection with the affair at his old address – 29, Castletown Road, Hammersmith. Later, the files fall silent on the question of his whereabouts, all correspondence being sent to him care of his bank, albeit still under the name Teague-Jones. Perhaps, however, this was merely an agreed part of the disappearing trick. Merely to have substituted Ronald Sinclair's name for that of Teague-Jones in the correspondence would not only have risked giving the game away, but would also have caused bureaucratic confusion in London and Delhi. For although he had been granted extended leave while the problem was resolved, and his own future decided, Teague-Jones/Sinclair was now back on the payroll of the Indian government. For the time being, therefore, he seems to have maintained both identities simultaneously, his new name and address being known only to a few colleagues who needed to know.

In November, after consulting General Malleson and other officers who had been in Meshed at the time, Teague-Jones produced his rebuttal of Chaikin's charges and his own account of the events leading to the commissars' deaths, as seen by him in Ashkhabad. Dismissing Chaikin's allegations, he wrote: 'I wish to state most emphatically that the charges are utterly false, and that they are without any foundation whatsoever.' As for Chaikin himself, he described him as 'a thoroughly unscrupulous political adventurer', a 'jackal' and a seeker after 'cheap notoriety'. Had Chaikin's claims been properly investigated by the Soviet authorities, he added, then 'Chaikin . . . would have doubtless suffered the fate of many hundreds of thousands of his fellow-countrymen.' Although Teague-Jones did not then know it, his tormentor was seemingly under an official cloud by this time, his days of liberty being numbered (he was finally executed in 1941).

In Teague-Jones's own version of what happened in Ashkhabad at that time he stuck firmly to what he had written in his journal – that it was President Funtikov who had ordered the commissars' execution, and who had sent Kurilov down to Krasnovodsk to arrange this with Commandant Kuhn. However, there still remained the awkward discrepancy between General Malleson's claim that he had ordered the commissars to be handed over to him for transfer to India as possible hostages, and Teague-Jones's belief at the time, repeated in his journal, that Malleson had washed his hands of them. In his report to the Foreign Office, which ran to 1,500 words, he accepted Malleson's version, declaring that Funtikov had either lied to him, or had himself been deliberately misled by his own representative in Meshed. Whether this was simply a closing of the ranks or the real truth will almost certainly never be known. But there is one further twist to the mystery of what happened that night in Ashkhabad. In a typescript found among Teague-Jones's papers after his death, which he had entitled 'Adventures with Turkmen, Tartars and Bolsheviks', he even suggests that he was not actually present at the fatal meeting when the commissars' fate was decided. That possibility I must leave to others to explore, but had it emerged before the collapse of Communism, and the subsequent thaw in Anglo-Russian relations, hard-line historians in Moscow might have had a field-day resurrecting the whole contentious affair.

Finally, following his rebuttal of all Chaikin's charges against him and his colleagues, Teague-Jones demanded that Moscow repudiate these, that they withdraw all copies of Chaikin's book, and that they publish their unqualified disavowal of both the book and its allegations in the official newspaper *Izvestia*. He added: 'I reserve the right to institute proceedings for libel against Vadim Chaikin, and against any or all of the newspapers which have published any of the charges against me, at such time as there shall be a civilised and responsible government in Russia.' His statement, which was passed straight to the Foreign Office, was signed and dated November 12, 1922.

On December 20, in a formal letter to Maxim Litvinov, the Deputy Soviet Commissar for Foreign Affairs, the British government informed him that it had made a thorough investigation of all the available evidence concerning the Baku commissars' deaths, but had failed to discover any grounds on which Chaikin's allegations could be maintained. 'Apart from showing that the accusations are baseless,' the letter went on, 'the evidence in possession of His Majesty's Government points to the fact that they are founded on mis-statements.' It concluded by requesting that all the allegations be withdrawn immediately, and that a statement to this effect be published in the official Soviet press.

But Moscow clearly had no intention of letting go of its propaganda advantage as easily as that, aware that it might well prove valuable later on as a bargaining counter. Because the two powers still had no diplomatic relations, and therefore no ambassadors or embassies, the Soviet reply was sent via the British trade agent. Although phrased in moderate language, it nonetheless totally rejected the British protest. 'The fact alone that the execution of the commissars took place during the military occupation of Transcaspia by British troops', the note declared, 'is sufficient to place the responsibility for such action on the British High Command.' It was 'beyond dispute', it went on, 'that the fate of the imprisoned commissars was in the hands of the British military authorities in the occupied territory.' Once again identifying Teague-Jones as the principal villain, it added that Moscow would welcome any 'conclusive evidence' showing that the British authorities in Transcaspia were not implicated in the massacre. 'But in the absence of such evidence,' the note concluded, 'it regrets its inability to consider the request of the British Government regarding the withdrawal of these charges.'

The Bolsheviks' outright rejection of the British note

clearly dashed any remaining hopes that Teague-Jones might have had of their dropping their vendetta against him, thereby allowing him to revert to a normal life. It can be no coincidence, therefore, that it was at this precise time that his disappearance became complete. Indeed, so successfully did he cover his tracks that anyone endeavouring to trace his movements or discover his whereabouts from this moment onwards could be excused for wondering whether the Bolsheviks had not got there first and discreetly eliminated him. In the Foreign Office files, which until then had concealed nothing, there is no further trace of him after the end of 1922. Because of the political sensitivity of the affair, and the fact that Teague-Jones was until recently still alive, the files dealing with his subsequent career and movements appear – at the time of writing, anyway – to have been withheld. However, as will be seen, there is one other possible reason for this official reticence besides fears of Bolshevik vengeance.

All this raises the intriguing question of what Teague-Jones was doing during the next thirty or so active years of his life, when normally he might have expected to be enjoying a promising career in the Indian political service. Even if the authorities had felt obliged, because of the circumstances, to pension him off early, a young and energetic man like Teague-Jones, with a relish for adventure, was unlikely to sit around for the rest of his life doing nothing. And how, one wonders, did he cope when, as Ronald Sinclair, he ran into old friends who had known him as Teague-Jones. Did he simply look blank and say: 'I'm sorry, you must be mistaken. My name is Ronald Sinclair. Perhaps I have a look-alike'? Or was word privately circulated among his former colleagues and friends that for good reason Teague-Jones had ceased to exist, and that to recognise or talk about him would be to put his life at serious risk? Certainly his former colleagues in wartime intelligence would have known all about his need to disappear, and no doubt some of them may have helped him to cover his tracks. His secret would also have been known to certain mandarins at the Foreign Office and India Office, and no doubt to someone in the Inland Revenue, lest Teague-Jones be pursued as a tax-defaulter.

But it was not for another seventy years, until his death at

the age of 99, that the truth about Teague-Jones's missing
years began to emerge, piece by piece, although even now it is
still far from complete. I had been trying for some time, while
researching this book, to discover what had become of the former British intelligence officer. Virtually all that I had been
able to find out was the name he had adopted, Ronald Sinclair.
I assumed, moreover, that by now he was almost certainly
dead. Then, on November 22, 1988, I spotted an obituary in
The Times headed RONALD SINCLAIR. It was evident that the
writer had no idea who he really was, the obituary concentrat-
ing on a book he had written about a motor journey through
Persia between the wars. As a result, I wrote a second obituary
for *The Times*, this time under his real name, for there was no
longer any need to protect the identity he had so successfully
kept secret for all those years.

I hoped, as a result of my disclosure, that someone might
now come forward who had known him during those missing
years, and who would be able to explain everything. No one
did. Then a year later Teague-Jones's wartime journal was
published under the title *The Spy Who Disappeared: Diary of
a Secret Mission to Russian Central Asia in 1918*. I contributed
to it an introduction and epilogue detailing all that I had then
been able to discover about him and his role in the affair of the
Baku commissars, and raising the question of the missing
years. This time one or two people who had known him in the
1930s, as Ronald Sinclair, did contact me. However, none of
them had realised who he really was, or what he did for a living. They claimed to be as astonished as anyone to learn the
truth.

In the meantime, however, one important clue had come to
light which suggested that there might be more to his disappearance than fear of Bolshevik fury. For among Ronald
Sinclair's many papers – none of which contained any mention of the name Teague-Jones – his publisher came upon a
large brown Manila envelope of the type used in Whitehall.
Written on it in pencil were the words 'Major Sinclair, M.I.5'.
Disappointingly, the envelope was empty, and there was no
way of dating what appeared to be a piece of internal office
mail. But here, perhaps, lay the answer to the riddle of where
he had been all this time. After ceasing to exist as Captain

Teague-Jones, wartime intelligence officer, he had now reappeared as Major Ronald Sinclair, peacetime intelligence officer. This would certainly make a lot of sense. His exceptional linguistic and other professional skills, his pre-war experience as an Indian police officer investigating seditious organisations, and his recently acquired familiarity with Bolshevik strategies in Transcaspia and Baku, made him far too valuable an individual for the intelligence services to lose – especially as this would have been due entirely to Bolshevik skulduggery. This was at a time, it should be remembered, when the heady new gospel of Marxism was viewed in London as a serious challenge to democracy, and in India as a menace to British rule.

Lending weight to the possibility that Teague-Jones continued to work in intelligence under his new name is the discovery that he remained a lifelong friend of Colonel C. H. Ellis, his wartime colleague from Meshed days, who by that time was in M.I.6 and who later was to become number three in its hierarchy. The two men, I learned from Ellis's son Peter, saw a great deal of one another over many years, suggesting, in that world anyway, a professional bond as well as a social one. But even Ellis's own son, who was himself to become an intelligence officer, never realised who Ronald Sinclair, whom he regarded almost as an uncle, really was. He told me that he was as astonished as anyone when he picked up a copy of *The Spy Who Disappeared* and learned the truth.

What sort of peacetime intelligence work, one may ask, was Teague-Jones, now Ronald Sinclair, engaged in at M.I.5 between the wars? The most likely answer is that he was working out of M.I.5's London headquarters for the Delhi Intelligence Bureau, as the Indian government's secret service was then called. This was headed by Sir David Petrie, who was later to become chief of M.I.5. Like Teague-Jones, Petrie was a former Punjabi police officer. He would have known all about Teague-Jones's special qualifications and experience in political work, and would no doubt have been keen to use these in the struggle against Bolshevism, then seen as the principal threat to India, indeed to the entire British Empire. The Delhi Intelligence Bureau, moreover, was known to have very close links with M.I.5, which shared its preoccupation with Bolshevism. If Teague-Jones was working as Petrie's London representative, then M.I.5 – with its 25,000 individual files on political activists, its worldwide network of contacts and its top-secret communications system – would have served as the ideal base from which to watch those plotting trouble for India from outside. Equally, he could have been Petrie's liaison man with the British intelligence services. In either case this would help to explain the mysterious envelope addressed to 'Major Sinclair, M.I.5'.

Other papers which came to light after his death suggest that he made a number of unexplained visits to the Middle and Far East during this period. One such journey, in 1926, was made alone by car across Persia. Ostensibly this was to investigate, on behalf of a group of British companies, the opportunities for trade with Persia. However, as his knowledge of commerce was virtually nil, it seems far more likely that he was sent to investigate the extent of Soviet penetration there. Given his fluency in Persian and Russian, not to mention his knowledge of Bolshevik strategies, his credentials for such a task could hardly have been better. Because of Persia's proximity to India and Afghanistan, Delhi was particularly anxious to know what the Bolsheviks were up to there. Teague-Jones's commercial cover gave him a plausible excuse for asking innumerable questions and establishing contacts in a region where such behaviour has always invited suspicion. His journey, in a Model A Ford, was to take him through a large number of Persian towns and villages. These stretched right across the country, from Tabriz near the Russian frontier in the north-west, to Zahidan on the border with India in the south-east. This was the journey which he describes in his book *Adventures in Persia*, published in his hundredth year shortly before his death. Written under the name Ronald Sinclair, it offers not the slightest hint that the mission was anything other than a purely commercial one. Men of his generation took the Official Secrets Act rather more seriously than some of their successors have.

Although his inter-war activities are still shrouded in secrecy, a little more is known of his movements in the Second World War, when his accusers in Moscow suddenly found themselves Britain's temporary allies. In 1941, at the age of 52,

Teague-Jones was posted to the British consulate-general in New York, officially as a vice-consul, but in fact as an intelligence officer. It was at this time that Peter Ellis recalled being startled to see him emerging from the New York headquarters of the British intelligence services, where he himself was then working. However, this was a world in which people came and went, and one learned not to ask too many questions.

After the war, his long career in intelligence finally at an end, Teague-Jones/Ronald Sinclair and his second wife – for he and Valya had long been divorced – retired to Florida, subsequently moving to Spain. His wife's failing health – she had Parkinson's Disease – forced their return to Britain, where shortly afterwards she died. On hearing of his loss, Valya, now in her eighties, made contact with him. Discovering that she was living in extremely straitened circumstances in London, he immediately invited her down to live, in her own room and at his expense, in his Plymouth retirement home, so that he could be with her until the very end, which was clearly not far off.

It was Valya who unwittingly provided a clue to their extraordinary past, although no one realised its significance at the time. Every morning Teague-Jones would make his way over to the block where she lived and sit for hours holding her hand and gently talking to her. Always she addressed him as 'Reggie' – not 'Ronnie', like everyone else. This was something which puzzled Anne Randal, the staff nurse who looked after him devotedly until his death, some months after Valya succumbed to pneumonia. It was only then, when she discovered his real name and learned of his remarkable career from the obituary in *The Times*, that she grasped its significance.

As far as Teague-Jones himself was concerned, he took his secret to the grave, his cover being finally blown only when he was beyond the reach of any mortal hand. And so there passed into history the last of that generation of men who once played the Great Game for King, Kaiser, Sultan and Tsar east of Constantinople.

EPILOGUE

'The blood of the twenty-six
shall never cool – never!'

Vladimir Mayakovsky,
revolutionary poet,
Eastern Dawn, 1924

Epilogue

As I write, momentous events are still taking place in the Caucasus and Transcaspia, following the collapse of Soviet rule there, and by the time this book appears much more may have happened in this highly volatile region. Already, several new countries have sprung up among the ruins of Moscow's former domains. Ancient quarrels and conflicts, so long suppressed, are being bloodily refought, while outside powers jockey for political, economic or religious influence in this oil- and mineral-rich region. History is back in the melting pot, and almost anything could happen.

When, in the autumn of 1984, I first visited Baku it was still firmly in the Soviet grip. The twenty-six commissar heroes were remembered in all aspects of the city's life, and a tour of the many monuments to their memory formed part of every visitor's itinerary. It was hard to escape the men's haunting presence, and foreigners were not allowed to forget for a moment the part the British, and Teague-Jones especially, were alleged to have played in their martyrdom. When I was insensitive enough to question this, politely asking for the evidence, I found myself officially cold-shouldered. Books on the affair, clearly intended for local consumption only, were discreetly removed from my hotel room before my departure.

But when, in the spring of 1991, I returned, just as the Caucasian peoples were beginning to prise off their Soviet shackles, I found that attitudes towards the revolutionary heroes had changed dramatically. Not long before, following the killing by Russian troops of 170 Muslim demonstrators, the pent-up wrath of the Azerbaijanis towards their Moscow masters had exploded in violence. Denouncing Shaumian and his fellow commissars as lackeys of Russian imperialism who had brought more than seventy years of oppression upon the city, an angry mob had descended on the square where the twenty-six are buried and attacked the monuments there. The crowd's passions were further fuelled by the knowledge that Shaumian and a number of the others were Armenians, a people for whom they have no love, as the world is only too well aware.

Of the twenty-six commemorative busts ranged around the square when I first visited Baku, there was now no sign, while the red granite relief depicting the execution scene lay in pieces. The authorities had taken the hint, in the hope of staving off further trouble. Already a street and a metro station bearing Shaumian's name had been renamed, while his and other memorial apartments had been closed. All this, and more, had clearly been ordered to appease anti-Armenian feelings. The violent nature of these, once unleashed, could be seen in the burned-out shell of the former Armenian cathedral in the centre of the city. In the wake of this, over 300,000 Armenians – that is virtually the entire community – had fled the city. And despite the ominous presence of Russian tanks around the parliament building and troops in the streets, Russian families, too, had begun to leave for fear of retribution. Baku, as we have seen, has been the scene of many massacres.

From Baku I flew across the Caspian Sea to Krasnovodsk, where in September 1918 the hapless commissars fell into the hands of their rivals for power. There the mood was less tense, the people less angry. Relations between the Muslims and the Armenian community were better. The Baku commissars, moreover, not being local men, arouse less passion there than in Baku. There was no sign of Russian troops in the streets. Officially Krasnovodsk had just been opened to foreigners for the first time since British troops left Transcaspia in the spring of 1919, but there was nothing in this sad little town likely to attract anyone there.

I found that the small courthouse in which the Baku commissars had been held by Commandant Kuhn while

Ashkhabad decided their fate had been turned into a simple museum, or shrine, to their memory. In the courtyard by the entrance burned an eternal flame. The grim communal cell into which they had been herded, and from where they were marched in the darkness to the railway station and to their fate, had been preserved exactly as it was on that sombre morning. Hung prominently in one of the galleries was Brodsky's dramatic painting of the execution scene, with uniformed British officers clearly present and the commissars striking defiant poses. In a glass case was a copy of *The Spy Who Disappeared*, containing Teague-Jones's version of the events leading to the commissars' deaths, together with my introduction and epilogue. I had sent a copy of this to the museum's director some time earlier. As a sign of changes already in the air, my account of the affair had been translated into Russian and serialised, without comment, in the local daily newspaper, the *Krasnovodsk Worker*. It was as a result of this that my wife and I had been officially invited to Krasnovodsk to visit the museum and to see, at my request, the remote spot in the Karakum desert where the commissars were dragged from the train and shot.

We were told that we were almost certainly the first Westerners ever to be allowed to go there. Accompanied by the museum director, a local Communist Party official and representatives of the Krasnovodsk press and television, we set out in a small convoy of vehicles on the three-hour desert drive to the execution scene. There, beside the single-track railway line, we came upon a small concrete monument bearing a red star. This marked the precise spot where the executions took place. Half a mile down the line was an unmanned railway halt named after the commissars, and here stood a larger, more impressive monument to them. In addition to listing all their names, it bore an inscription clearly blaming 'the British imperialists' for their murder.

Our small party clambered up the embankment in the footsteps of the condemned men and made its way across the dunes to the spot where they had faced the firing squad. No one – British, Russian or Turcoman – said very much, for we were all lost in our own private thoughts. Although the twenty-six victims had at the time been Britain's sworn enemies, standing at this once bloodstained place trying to visualise the terrible scene was both haunting and moving. I thought of Shaumian, the family man and intellectual in search of what he thought to be a better world, whose son had played trains with the imperialist agent MacDonell, while he himself got on with the Revolution. That same son was later to visit this spot and find empty cartridge cases left by his father's executioners. I picked up a handful of sand and a pebble as keepsakes of my own visit to this sombre place.

I have not been back to Baku or Krasnovodsk since, but I understand that the obliteration of the past and the de-mythologising of these former heroes is now virtually complete. In Baku, their home town, almost all traces of them, except for their remains beneath the square, have been destroyed. The huge and impressive monument which once stood over their mass grave, and which survived the angry mob's attack on the square, has had its inscription removed, and the eternal flame to their memory has been extinguished. The once-hallowed square itself, across which every hour the strains of a requiem to the Bolshevik martyrs used to ring, now lies eerily silent. Across the Caspian, the little courthouse museum at Krasnovodsk has been shut down, its relics absorbed into the nearby history museum. Before long, these too will no doubt disappear, or at least their labels will carry a very different story.

Bibliography

This narrative has been pieced together from a host of different sources, both published and unpublished. The following list of books and articles, while far from exhaustive, includes all those which I found particularly valuable. Unless stated otherwise, all were published in London. I have also drawn extensively on the British secret archives of the time, today to be found in the India Office Library and the Public Record Office.

Aaronsohn, Alexander, *With the Turks in Palestine*, 1916.
Adamec, Ludwig, *Afghanistan, 1900–1923. A Diplomatic History*, 1967.
—— *Afghanistan's Foreign Affairs to the Mid-Twentieth Century*, 1974.
Agayev, Emil, *Baku. A Guide*, Moscow, 1987.
Allen, W.E.D., & Muratoff, P., *Caucasian Battlefields. A History of the Wars on the Turco-Caucasian Border, 1828–1921*, 1953.
Anderson, M.S., *The Eastern Question*, 1966.
Andler, Charles, *Le Pangermanisme. Ses Plans d'Expansion Allemande dans le Monde*, Paris, 1915.
Anon., *Germany's Claim to Colonies*, Royal Institute of International Affairs, Paper No. 23, 1938.
Antonius, George, *The Arab Awakening. The Story of the Arab National Movement*, 1938.
Armstrong, H.C., *Unending Battle*, 1934.
Arslanian, A.H., *The British Military Involvement in Transcaucasia, 1917–1919*, USA, 1974.

Aydemir, S.S., *Enver Paşa*, 3 vols., Istanbul, 1971–8.

Baha, Lal, 'The North-West Frontier in the First World War', *Asian Affairs*, February 1970.

Barker, Brig. A.J., *The Neglected War. Mesopotamia, 1914–1918*, 1967.

Barrier, N.G., *Banned. Controversial Literature and Political Control in British India, 1907–1945*, USA, 1974.

Beesly, Patrick, *Room 40. British Naval Intelligence, 1914–1918*, 1982.

Benson, E.F., *Crescent & Iron Cross*, 1918.

Berghahn, V.R., *Germany and the Approach of War in 1914*, 1973.

Bernhardi, Gen. Friedrich von, *Germany and the Next War*, 1912.

―― *Britain as Germany's Vassal*, 1914.

Blacker, Capt. L.V.S., 'Travels in Turkestan, 1918–20', *Geographical Journal*, September 1921.

―― *On Secret Patrol in High Asia*, 1922.

Blood-Ryan, H.W., *Franz von Papen*, 1940.

Bose, A.C., 'Efforts of the Indian Revolutionaries at Securing German Arms during W.W.I.', *Calcutta Review*, January 1962.

―― *Indian Revolutionaries Abroad*, Patna, 1971.

Brailsford, H.N., *Turkey and the Roads to the East*, 1916.

Brandenburg, Prof. Erich, *From Bismarck to the World War. German Foreign Policy, 1870–1914*, 1927.

Bray, Major N.N.E., *Shifting Sands*, 1934.

Brown, Emily, *Har Dayal. Hindu Revolutionary and Rationalist*, 1975.

Buchan, John, *Greenmantle*, 1916.

―― *Nelson's History of the War*, 24 vols., 1915–19.

Busch, Briton, *Britain and the Persian Gulf, 1894–1914*, USA, 1967.

―― *Britain, India and the Arabs, 1914–21*, USA, 1971.

Candler, Edmund, *The Long Road to Baghdad*, 2 vols., 1919.

Cecil, Lamar, *The German Diplomatic Service, 1871–1914*, USA, 1976.

Central Asian Review. Various issues of this journal containing translations of articles from the Soviet Press: 1959/60/61.

Cheradame, Andre, *The Baghdad Railway*, Central Asian Society, 1911.

Childs, W.J., 'Germany in Asia Minor', *Blackwood's Magazine*, February 1916.

Chirol, Valentine, *The Middle Eastern Question. Or some Political Problems of Indian Defence*, 1903.

—— *Indian Unrest*, 1910.

Coan, Frederick, *Yesterdays in Persia and Kurdistan*, USA, 1939.

Cohen, Stuart, *British Policy in Mesopotamia, 1903–1914*, 1976.

Coole, W.W., & Potter, M.F. (eds.), *Thus Spake Germany*, 1941.

Crampton, R.J., *The Hollow Détente. Anglo-German Relations in the Balkans, 1911–1914*, n.d. [1979].

Crutwell, C.R., *A History of the Great War*, 1934.

Curzon, Hon. George, *Persia and the Persian Question*, 2 vols., 1892.

Datta, V.N., *Madan Lal Dhingra and the Revolutionary Movement*, Delhi, 1978.

Dayal, Har, *Forty-Four Months in Germany and Turkey, February 1915 to October 1918*, 1920.

Derogy, Jacques, *Resistance & Revenge*, USA, 1990.

Dickson, Brig.-Gen. W.E., *East Persia. A Backwater of the Great War*, 1924.

Dillon, Dr E.J., *A Scrap of Paper. The Inner History of German Diplomacy, and her Scheme of World-wide Conquest*, 1914.

Djemal Pasha, *Memoirs of a Turkish Statesman, 1913–1919*, n.d. [1920].

Donohoe, Maj. M.H., *With the Persian Expedition*, 1919.

Dunsterville, Maj.-Gen. L.C., *The Adventures of Dunsterforce*, 1920.

—— 'From Baghdad to the Caspian in 1918', *Geographical Journal*, March 1921.

Dyer, Brig.-Gen. R., *The Raiders of the Sarhad*, 1921.

Earle, Meade, *Turkey, the Great Powers and the Baghdad Railway*, USA, 1923.

Edmonds, C.J., 'The Persian Gulf Prelude to the Zimmermann Telegram', *Royal Central Asian Journal*, January 1960.

Einstein, Lewis, *Inside Constantinople. A Diplomatic Diary*, 1917.

Ellis, Col. C.H., 'The Transcaspian Episode. Operations in Central Asia, 1918–1919', *Royal Central Asian Society Journal*, 1959.

—— 'Operations in Transcaspia 1918–19 & the 26 Commissars Case', *Soviet Affairs*, No. 2, 1959.

—— *The Transcaspian Episode, 1918–19*, 1963.

Emin, Ahmet, *Turkey in the World War*, USA, 1930.

Essad-Bey, Mohammed, *Blood and Oil in the Orient*, 1930.

Fatema, Nasrollah, *Diplomatic History of Persia, 1917–1923*, USA, 1952.

Fischer, Fritz, *Germany's Aims in the First World War*, 1967.

—— *War of Illusions*, 1975.

Fischer, Louis, *Oil Imperialism. The International Struggle for Petroleum*, USA, 1926.

—— *The Soviets in World Affairs*, 2 vols., 1930.

Foreign Office Handbook, *German Colonisation*, 1919.

—— *The Pan-Islamic Movement*, 1919.

—— *The Pan-Turanian Movement*, 1919.

—— *The Rise of the Turks*, 1919.

—— *The Rise of Islam and the Caliphate*, 1919.

Fraser, David, *The Short Cut to India. A Journey along the Route of the Baghdad Railway*, 1909.

Fraser, T.G., *The Intrigues of the German Government and the Ghadr Party against British Rule in India, 1914–18*, London Ph.D. thesis, 1974–5.

—— 'Germany and Indian Revolution, 1914–1918', *Journal of Contemporary History*, Vol. 12.

—— 'India in Anglo-Japanese Relations during the First World War', *History*, October 1978.

French, Lt.-Col. F.J., *From Whitehall to the Caspian*, n.d. [1920s].

Friedman, Isaiah, *Germany, Turkey and Zionism, 1897–1918*, 1977.

Frobenius, Col. H., *The German Empire's Hour of Destiny*, 1914.

Fromkin, David, *A Peace to End all Peace. Creating the Modern Middle East, 1914–1922*, 1989.

Gehrke, Ulrich, *Persien in der Deutschen Orientpolitik wahrend des ersten Weltkrieges*, 2 vols., Stuttgart, 1960.

Geiss, Prof. Imanuel, *German Foreign Policy, 1871–1914*, 1976.

Gillard, David, *The Struggle for Asia, 1828–1914*, 1977.

Goltz, Kolmar von der, *Anatolische Ausfluge*, Berlin, 1896.

Gottlieb, W.W., *Studies in Secret Diplomacy during the First World War*, 1957.

Gould, Sir Basil, *The Jewel in the Lotus. Recollections of an Indian Political*, 1957.

Graves, Philip, *Briton and Turk*, 1941.

—— *The Life of Sir Percy Cox*, 1941.

Griesinger, Walter, *German Intrigues in Persia. The Diary of a German Agent. The Niedermayer Expedition through Persia to Afghanistan and India* (from Griesinger's captured diary), 1918.

Grumbach, S., *Germany's Annexationist Aims*, 1917.

Guha, A.C., *First Spark of Revolution. The Early Phase of India's Struggle for Independence, 1900–1920*, Bombay, 1971.

Hale, F., *From Persian Uplands*, 1920.

Hamilton, Angus, *Problems of the Middle East*, 1909.

Hanssen, Hans, *Diary of a Dying Empire*, USA, 1955.

Hardinge, Lord, *My Indian Years*, 1948.

Harper, R., & Miller, H., *Singapore Mutiny* [of 1915], Singapore, 1984.

Hartill, Leonard, *Men Are Like That*, 1928.

Haslip, Joan, *The Sultan. The Life of Abdul Hamid II*, 1958.

Helfferich, Karl, *Die Deutsche Turkenpolitik*, Berlin, 1921.

Heller, Joseph, *British Policy towards the Ottoman Empire, 1908–1914*, 1983.

Hentig, Otto von, *Meine Diplomatenfahrt ins Verschlossene Land*, Berlin, 1918.

—— *Mein Leben – Eine Dienstreise*, Gottingen, 1962.

Hopkirk, Peter, *Setting the East Ablaze. Lenin's Dream of an Empire in Asia*, 1984.

—— *The Great Game. On Secret Service in High Asia*, 1990.

Hopkirk, Peter, Prologue & Epilogue to *The Spy Who Disappeared. Diary of a Secret Mission to Russian Central Asia in 1918. See under* Teague-Jones.

Hostler, Charles, *Turkism and the Soviets*, 1957.

Hovannisian, Richard, *Armenia on the Road to Independence, 1918*, USA, 1967.

Hurgronje, C. Snouck, *The Holy War Made in Germany*, USA, 1915.

—— *The Revolt in Arabia*, USA, 1917.

Isemonger, F.C., and Slatterly, J., *An Account of the Ghadar Conspiracy, 1913–1915*, Lahore, 1919 (official police intelligence report).

Jackh, Ernest, *The Rising Crescent*, 1944.

James, Capt. Frank, *Faraway Campaign*, 1934.

Jastrow, Morris, *The War and the Baghdad Railway*, USA, 1917.

Kayaloff, Jacques, *The Fall of Baku*, USA, 1976.

Kazemzadeh, Firuz, *The Struggle for Transcaucasia, 1917–1921*, 1951.

—— *Russia and Britain in Persia, 1864–1914. A Study in Imperialism*, USA, 1968.

Kedouri, Elie, *England and the Middle East. The Vital Years, 1914–1921*, 1956.

Keer, Dhananjay, *Veer Savarkar*, Bombay, 1950.

Kenez, Peter, *Civil War in South Russia, 1919–1920*, USA, 1977.

Kennedy, Paul, *The Rise of the Anglo-German Antagonism, 1860–1914*, 1980.

Ker, James, *Political Trouble in India – Confidential Report*, Calcutta, 1917.

Khairallah, Shereen, *Railways in the Middle East, 1856–1948. Political & Economic Background*, Beirut, 1991.

Knollys, Lt.-Col. D.E., 'Military Operations in Transcaspia, 1918–1919', *Journal of the Central Asian Society*, April 1926.

Kocabas, Suleyman, *Tarihte Turkler ve Almanlar. Pancermanizm'in 'Sark'a Dogru' Politikasi*, Istanbul, 1988.

Koeppen, F. von, *Moltke in Kleinasien*, 1883.

Kreyer, Maj. J.A., & Uloth, Capt. G., *The 28th Light Cavalry in Persia and Russian Turkistan, 1915–1920*, 1926.

Kruger, Horst, 'Germany and Early Indian Revolutionaries', *Mainstream*, Delhi, January 1964.

Kumar, Ravinder, 'Records of the Government of India on the Berlin-Baghdad Railway Question', *Historical Journal*, 1962, No. 1.

Landau, Jacob, *Pan-Turkism in Turkey. A Study in Irredentism*, 1981.

Langer, William, *The Diplomacy of Imperialism, 1890–1902*, 2 vols., USA, 1935.

Laushey, David, *Bengal Terrorism & the Marxist Left, 1905–1942*, Calcutta, 1975.

Lawrence, T.E., *Seven Pillars of Wisdom. A Triumph*, 1935.

Le Rire. *The All Highest Goes to Jerusalem. Being the Diary of the German Emperor's Journey to the Holy Land* (a satire from the Paris humorist magazine). English translation, 1918.

Lenczowski, George, *The Middle East in World Affairs*, USA, 1952.

Lewin, Evans, *The German Road to the East. An Account of the 'Drang Nach Osten' and of Teutonic Aims in the Near and Middle East*, 1916.

MacDonell, Ranald, *'And Nothing Long'*, 1938.

MacMunn, Lt.-Gen. Sir George, *Turmoil and Tragedy in India – 1914 and After*, 1935.

Malleson, Maj.-Gen. Sir Wilfrid, 'The British Military Mission to Turkestan, 1918–1920', *Journal of Central Asian Society*, Vol. 9, 1922.

—— 'The Twenty-Six Commissars', *Fortnightly Review*, March 1933.

Malraux, André, *The Walnut Trees of Altenburg*, trans. (fiction: Turco-German Holy War), 1952.

Marlowe, John, *The Persian Gulf in the Twentieth Century*, 1962.

—— *Late Victorian. The Life of Sir Arnold Wilson*, 1967.

Marriott, Sir John, *The Eastern Question. An Historical Study in European Diplomacy*, Oxford, 1917.

Martin, Bradford, *German and Persian Diplomatic Relations, 1873–1912*, The Hague, 1959.

Marvey, S.M., *A Thousand Years of German Aggression*, 1943.

Massie, Robert, *Dreadnought. Britain, Germany, and the Coming of the Great War*, 1992.

Mathur, L.P., *Indian Revolutionary Movement in the United States of America*, Delhi, 1970.

Mejcher, Helmut, *Imperial Quest for Oil: Iraq, 1910–1928*, 1976.

Melka, R.L., 'Max Freiherr von Oppenheim: Sixty Years of Scholarship and Political Intrigue in the Middle East', *Middle Eastern Studies*, January 1973.

Mitrokhin, Leonid, *Failure of Three Missions. British Efforts to Overthrow Soviet Government in Central Asia*, Moscow, 1987.

Moberly, Brig.-Gen. Frederick, *Operations in Persia, 1914–1919*, 1929.

Moltke, Helmuth von, *Briefe über Zustände und Begebenheiten in der Türkei aus den Jahren 1835 bis 1839*, Berlin, 1911.

Morgenthau, Henry, *Secrets of the Bosphorus*, 1918.

Morris, Prof. A.J.A., *The Scaremongers. The Advocacy of War and Rearmament, 1896–1914*, 1984.

Morris, James, *The Hashemite Kings*, 1959.

Mundy, Talbot, *Hira Singh's Tale* (fiction: set against Turco-German Holy War), n.d. [*c.* 1918].

Murphy, Lt.-Col. C.C.R., *Soldiers of the Prophet*, 1921.

—— *A Mixed Bag*, 1936.

Nassibian, Akaby, *Britain and the Armenian Question, 1915–1923*, 1984.

Nazem, Hossein, *Russia and Great Britain in Iran, 1900–1914*, Teheran, 1975.

Newcombe, Capt. S.F., 'The Baghdad Railway', *Geographical Journal*, December 1914.

Niedermayer, Oskar von, *Afghanistan*, Leipzig, 1924.

—— *Unter der Glutsonne Irans*, Hamburg, 1925.

Noel, Lt.-Col. Edward, 'A Prisoner among the Jungali Bolsheviks', *On the Run: Escaping Tales*, 1934.

Nogales, Rafael de, *Four Years Beneath the Crescent*, USA, 1926.

Oberling, Pierre, *The Qashqa'i Nomads of Fars*, The Hague, 1974.

O'Connor, Sir Frederick, *On the Frontier and Beyond*, 1931.

O'Dwyer, Sir Michael, *India As I Knew It, 1885–1925*, 1925.

Olson, William, *Anglo-Iranian Relations during World War I*, 1984.

Ozyuksel, Murat, *Anadolu ve Bagdat Demiryollari*, Istanbul, 1988.

Palmer, Alan, *The Kaiser. Warlord of the Second Reich*, 1978.

Papen, Franz von, *Memoirs*, English trans., 1952.

Parfit, Canon J.T., *Twenty Years in Baghdad and Syria. Germany's Bid for the Mastery of the East*, n.d. [*c*.1915].
—— *The Romance of the Baghdad Railway*, 1933.
Parmanand, Bhai, *The Story of My Life*, Delhi, 1982.
Pearce, Brian: important articles on Captain Reginald Teague-Jones and the fate of the 26 Commissars in the Soviet affairs journal *Sbornik*.
Pears, Sir Edwin, *Forty Years in Constantinople*, 1916.
Persits, M.A., *Revolutionaries of India in Soviet Russia*, Moscow, 1983.
Pipes, Richard, *The Formation of the Soviet Union. Communism and Nationalism, 1917–1923*, USA, 1954.
Polovtsov, Gen. P.A., *Glory and Downfall. Reminiscences of a Russian General Staff Officer*, 1935.
Popplewell, Richard, 'The Surveillance of Indian Seditionists in North America, 1905–1915', *Intelligence and International Relations, 1900–1945*, 1987.
Pratap, Raja Mahendra, 'My German Mission to High Asia. How I joined forces with the Kaiser to enlist Afghanistan against Great Britain', *Asia*, USA, May 1925.
—— *My Life Story of Fifty-Five Years*, Dehra Dun, 1947.
Price, M. Philips, *War and Revolution in Asiatic Russia*, 1918.
Puri, Harish, *Ghadar Movement. Ideology, Organization & Strategy*, Amritsar, 1983.
Ramazani, Rouhollah, *The Foreign Policy of Iran, 1500–1941*, USA, 1966.
Ramsay, Sir William, *The Revolution in Constantinople and Turkey*, 1916.
Rawlinson, Lt.-Col. A., *Adventures in the Near East, 1918–22*, 1923.
Ribin, Valentin, *Zakaspii*. A 'revolutionary historical novel' (in Russian) accusing Captain Teague-Jones of murdering the Baku Commissars, Ashkhabad, 1987.
Ritter, Gerhard, *The Sword and the Sceptre*, 4 vols., USA, 1971–3.
[Ross, Sir Denison], *A Manual on the Turanians and Pan-Turanians*, Naval Staff Intelligence, 1918.
Rothwell, V.H., 'Mesopotamia in British War Aims, 1914–1918', *Historical Journal*, June 1970.

—— 'The British Government and Japanese Military Assistance, 1914–1918', *History*, February 1971.

Rowlatt, Mr Justice, et al., *Sedition Committee Report*, Calcutta, 1918.

Roy, M.N., *Memoirs*, Bombay, 1964.

Ryan, Sir Andrew, *The Last of the Dragomans*, 1951.

Saleh, Dr Zaki, *Mesopotamia, 1600–1914. A Study in British Foreign Affairs*, Baghdad, 1957.

Sanders, Gen. Liman von, *Five Years in Turkey*, USA, 1927.

Sareen, Dr T.J., *Indian Revolutionary Movement Abroad, 1905–1920*, Delhi, 1979.

Sarkisyanz, Manuel, *A Modern History of Transcaucasian Armenia*, Leiden, 1975.

Sarolea, Charles, *The Baghdad Railway and German Expansion*, 1907.

Savarkar, V.D., *The Indian War of Independence, 1857*, 1909.

—— *The Story of My Transportation for Life*, Bombay, 1950.

Schaefer, C.A., *Deutsch-Türkische Freundschaft*, Stuttgart, 1914.

Schmitt, Bernadotte, *England and Germany, 1740–1914*, USA, 1916.

Schmitz-Kairo, Paul, *Die Arabische Revolution*, Leipzig, 1942.

Searight, Sarah, *Steaming East*, 1991.

Seton-Watson, R.W., *German, Slav and Magyar*, 1916.

Seymour, Dr Charles, *The Diplomatic Background of the War, 1870–1914*, USA, 1916.

Singh, Randhir, *The Ghadar Heroes. Forgotten Story of the Punjab Revolutionaries of 1914–15*, Bombay, 1945.

Singha, P.B., *Indian National Liberation Movement and Russia, 1905–17*, Delhi, 1975.

Skrine, Sir Clarmont, *World War in Iran*, 1962.

Sokol, E.D., *The Revolt of 1916 in Russian Central Asia*, USA, 1953.

Srivastava, Harindra, *Five Stormy Years. Savarkar in London*, Delhi, 1983.

Stanwood, Frederick, *War, Revolution & British Imperialism in Central Asia*, 1983.

Stewart, Rhea, *Fire in Afghanistan, 1914–1929*, USA, 1973.

Strother, French, *Fighting Germany's Spies*, USA, 1919 (chapter on German-Hindu conspiracy).

Stuermer, Dr Harry, *Two War Years in Constantinople*, 1917.
Suny, Ronald, *The Baku Commune, 1917–1918*, USA, 1972.
Swietochowski, Tadeusz, *Russian Azerbaijan, 1905–1920*, 1985.
Sykes, Christopher, *Wassmuss. 'The German Lawrence'*, 1936.
Sykes, Brig.-Gen. Sir Percy, 'South Persia and the Great War', *Geographical Journal*, August 1921.
—— *A History of Persia*, 2 vols., 3rd edn. (including First World War), 1930.
—— *A History of Afghanistan*, 2 vols., 1940.
Taylor, A.J.P., *Germany's First Bid for Colonies*, 1938.
—— *The Struggle for the Mastery of Europe, 1848–1918*, 1954.
Teague-Jones, Reginald, *The Spy who Disappeared. Diary of a Secret Mission to Russian Central Asia in 1918* (Prologue & Epilogue by Peter Hopkirk), 1990.
Temple, Bernard, *The Place of Persia in World Politics*, Central Asian Society, 1910.
Thomson, Sir Basil, *The Allied Secret Service in Greece*, 1931.
Tod, Col. J., 'The Malleson Mission to Transcaspia in 1918', *Journal of the Royal Central Asian Society*, Vol. 27, 1940.
Townshend, Maj.-Gen. Sir Charles, *My Campaign in Mesopotamia*, 1920.
Toynbee, Arnold, *Nationality and the War*, 1915.
Treitsche, Heinrich von, *Origins of Prussianism*, English trans. 1942.
Treloar, Sir William, *With the Kaiser in the East*, 1915.
Trevor, Charles, *Drums of Asia*, 1934 (novel set against Turco-German Holy War).
Trotsky, Leon, *Between Red and White*, 1922.
Trumpener, Ulrich, *Germany and the Ottoman Empire, 1914–1918*, USA, 1968.
Tuchman, Barbara, *The Zimmermann Telegram*, 1959.
Tuohy, Capt. Ferdinand, *The Secret Corps*, 1920.
—— *The Crater of Mars*, 1929.
Ullman, Richard, *Anglo-Soviet Relations, 1917–1921*, 3 vols., 1961/68/73.
Ussher, Dr Clarence, *An American Physician in Turkey*, USA, 1917.
Vogel, Renate, *Die Persien und Afghanexpedition Oskar Ritter von Niedermayers 1915/16*, Osnabruck, 1976.

Walker, C.J., *Armenia. The Survival of a Nation*, 1980.

Weber, Frank, *Eagles on the Crescent*, USA, 1970.

Westrate, Bruce, *The Arab Bureau. British Policy in the Middle East, 1916–1920*, USA, 1992.

Wheeler, Col. Geoffrey (ed.), 'The Red Army in Turkestan', *Central Asian Review*, No. 1, 1965.

—— 'Russia's Relations with Indian Emigrés', *Central Asian Review*, No. 4, 1967.

Wilson, Sir Arnold, *Loyalties. Mesopotamia, 1914–1917*, Oxford, 1930.

—— *Mesopotamia, 1918–1920. A Clash of Loyalties*, Oxford, 1931.

Wilson, Jeremy, *Lawrence of Arabia*, 1989.

Winstone, H.V.F., *The Illicit Adventure*, 1982.

Wolff, J.B., *The Diplomatic History of the Baghdad Railway*, 1936.

Woods, Charles, *The Cradle of the War. The Near East and Pan-Germanism*, 1918.

Wright, Sir Denis, *The English Amongst the Persians, 1787–1921*, 1977.

Wyman Bury, G., *Pan-Islam*, 1919.

Ybert-Chabrier, Edith, 'Gilan, 1917–1920: The Jengelist Movement', *Central Asian Survey*, November 1983.

Yesenin, Sergei, 'Ballad of the Twenty-Six' (poem commemorating the Baku Commissars), *The Baku Worker*, September 22, 1925.

Yovanovitch, V., *The Near Eastern Problem and the Pan-German Peril*, 1915.

Zahm, J.A., *From Berlin to Bagdad and Babylon*, 1922.

Zenkovsky, Serge, *Pan-Turkism and Islam in Russia*, 1960.

Zugmayer, Dr Erich, *Eine Reise Durch Vorder-Asien im Jahre 1904*, Berlin, 1905.

—— *Eine Reise Durch Zentral-Asien im Jahre 1906*, Berlin, 1908.

Index

KODANSHA GLOBE

International in scope, this series offers distinguished books that explore the lives, customs, and mindsets of peoples and cultures around the world.

In addition to *Like Hidden Fire*, Vol. II in the *Great Game* trilogy, Kodansha Globe also publishes by Peter Hopkirk:

Vol. I: **THE GREAT GAME:**
The Struggle for Empire in Central Asia
Hopkirk's immensely readable account of the history at the core of today's geopolitics. "History buffs with a taste for reliving the swashbuckling exploits of the Victorian Age will be delighted that Hopkirk has set down such a readable record of the Great Game."
—Ron Grossman, *Chicago Tribune*
($15, 1-56836-022-3)

Vol. III: **SETTING THE EAST ABLAZE:**
Lenin's Dream of an Empire in Asia
A riveting tale of espionage, starring Frederick Bailey, a real-life Indiana Jones. "There is the stuff of about a dozen adventure movies in this rousing tale. [It has] everything a ripping yarn should have: suspense, comedy, even messages in invisible ink."
—Sarah Ferrell, *The New York Times Book Review*
($14, 1-56836-102-5)
and

TRESPASSERS ON THE ROOF OF THE WORLD:
The Secret Exploration of Tibet
"Hopkirk's wonderfully vivid book describes the . . . always thrilling efforts of explorers, spies . . . to plumb Tibet's secrets."
—*Philadelphia Inquirer*
($14, 1-56836-050-9)

Please contact your local bookseller for these and other Kodansha titles, or mail your order with payment to:

KODANSHA
Mail Order Department
c/o The Putnam Publishing Group
P.O. Box 12289
Newark, NJ 07101-5289

All orders must be accompanied by payment in full *(check or money order payable to KODANSHA, in U.S. funds only, no cash or C.O.D.s)*, including shipping & handling charges ($3.50 for the first book, $.75 for each additional book). New York State residents please include applicable sales tax. Allow 3–6 weeks for delivery. Prices are subject to change without notice.

When ordering by credit card call **1-800-788-6262.**